The Film Music of
JOHN WILLIAMS

WISCONSIN FILM STUDIES

Patrick McGilligan, *series editor*

The Film Music of
JOHN WILLIAMS

*Reviving Hollywood's
Classical Style*

SECOND EDITION

Emilio Audissino

THE UNIVERSITY OF WISCONSIN PRESS

The University of Wisconsin Press
728 State Street, Suite 443
Madison, Wisconsin 53706
uwpress.wisc.edu

Gray's Inn House, 127 Clerkenwell Road
London ECIR 5DB, United Kingdom
eurospanbookstore.com

Printed in the United States of America
This book may be available in a digital edition.

Library of Congress Cataloging-in-Publication Data

Names: Audissino, Emilio, author.
Title: The film music of John Williams : reviving Hollywood's classical style /
Emilio Audissino.
Other titles: John Williams's film music | Wisconsin film studies.
Description: Second edition. | Madison, Wisconsin : The University of
Wisconsin Press, [2021] | Series: Wisconsin film studies | Originally published
under the title John Williams's Film Music : Jaws, Star Wars, Raiders of the Lost Ark,
and the return of the classical Hollywood music style, copyright ©2014. |
Includes bibliographical references and index.
Identifiers: LCCN 2020044532 | ISBN 9780299332341 (paperback)
Subjects: LCSH: Williams, John, 1932—Criticism and interpretation. |
Motion picture music—History and criticism.
Classification: LCC ML410.W71335 A83 2021 | DDC 781.5/4213092—dc23
LC record available at https://lccn.loc.gov/2020044532

To the many friends who have put up with me
in the past forty years, especially my marvelous and
marvelously patience-endowed family.
Grazie, vi voglio bene.

There is nobody in my experience who made the kind of impact on my career and my films than this man. This man has absolutely transformed everything that I have done into something that I could not imagine ever having done. And he does it because he communicates so well with all of you. He has rediscovered something that was very popular and important in the 1930s and 1940s. . . . And I know of no one who knows how to write film music that goes straight to your heart and straight to your soul than my good friend John Williams. . . . And John is actually one of the greatest storytellers of all time.

—STEVEN SPIELBERG, "Hollywood Bowl Hall of Fame Ceremony," 23 June 2000

The great thing about John is this: Composer equals maestro. Maestro equals ego. John never writes his score. He writes the movie's score. He's not doing the work to aggrandize himself. He's doing it to make the movie as good as it possibly can. You don't find that very often.

—GEORGE LUCAS, "USC John Williams Scoring Stage" dedication ceremony, 26 April 2011

He's such a generous person and he's such a humble person too. He respects his musicians so that they give 150% to him all the time. And honesty. That is what we have in his music. That is why we have connected to all of these melodies from all of his great films.

—GUSTAVO DUDAMEL, "American Film Institute Life Achievement Award to John Williams," 9 June 2016

Contents

Illustrations

Acknowledgments

There are many people who have accompanied me throughout the preparation of the first edition of this book. I seize the occasion of this second edition
to reiterate my appreciation to those whose support has proven unabated and
to add mentions of those friends and colleagues I have met between the first
and this second edition. The majority of the research for the preparation of
this book was conducted in the (now defunct) Dipartimento di Storia delle
Arti at the University of Pisa, Italy, where I completed my first PhD. Special
mentions go to Alessandra Lischi and Cinzia Maria Sicca Bursill-Hall.

Part of this book is based on fieldwork carried out in Boston, Massachusetts.
On the one hand, it consisted of my regular presence at all John Williams
concerts with the Boston Pops from 2007 to 2013. On the other hand, it consisted of archival research at the Boston Symphony Orchestra Archives and at
the WGBH Educational Foundation Media Library and Archives. Many thanks
for their advice and assistance go to Bridget P. Carr and Barbara Perkel (BSO
Archives) and to Keith Luf, Nancy Dillon, and Leah Weisse (WGBH Archives).
My warmest thanks go to my dear friends in Boston and at Boston's Symphony
Hall, Doreen M. Reis, Vincenzo Peppino Natale, and Adam Castiglioni, for
their constant friendship and support. A special tip of the hat goes to radio
legend Ron Della Chiesa, not only for his friendship and in fond memory of
our conversations about the history of the Boston Symphony Orchestra and
the Boston Pops but also for being the host and presenter at the book launch
in June 2014 at Boston's Prudential Center. A special acknowledgment also
goes to my Bostonian friend Victor Brogna, who lent a very helpful hand both
with legal issues and with the proofreading of the first edition.

My friend John Norris deserves my warmest gratitude and a central niche
of his own. He is a thorough connoisseur of film music and John Williams's

works and was an invaluable assistant in my archival research in Boston. He was also my eyes and ears at those concerts that I was not able to attend. At the concerts I was able to attend, he and his wife, Christine Dehil, have been my delightful companions—and the photographers of my meetings with the Maestro. More friends have more recently shared with me some "Williams experiences," and we regularly entertain exchanges about the latest news from the Williams universe. To them and their partners goes my friendliest "ciao": Simone Pedroni and Elisa Petrarulo, and Maurizio Caschetto and Ilaria Ruffoni.

The updates and revisions of the book have matured during my stay at the University of Southampton, UK, where I had the opportunity to present lectures and classes on Williams's music during the years. My sincerest appreciation goes to my mentor Kevin J. Donnelly and to the other colleagues I worked with there: Tim Bergfelder, Beth Carroll, Mike Hammond, Sally Keenan, Lucy Mazdon, Paola Visconti, and Michael Williams.

I would also like to mention Cynthia Wilson and Emile Wennekes (Utrecht University, the Netherlands), who have always shown a true appreciation of my book: we got acquainted as colleagues, to soon become collaborators on many projects and, most importantly, friends. *Dank je wel, Cynthia en Emile!*

As to the form and appearance of the book, I wish to express my appreciation to the many people who gave their contributions at the various stages of the process, from the first version of the manuscript back in 2013 to the 2021 second edition. First, I'm grateful to the University of Wisconsin Press for giving me the opportunity to bring this book to fruition. For the first edition, I reiterate my sincere gratitude to Executive Editor Raphael Kadushin, to his assistant Matthew Cosby, and to all the nice persons I worked with at UW Press: Andrea Christofferson, Sheila Leary, Carla Marolt, Sheila McMahon, Adam Mehring, and Elena Spagnolie. For this new edition, I am grateful to UW Press director Dennis Lloyd for asking me to return to the drawing board to update and expand the book for a new release, to Jacqulyn Gaik-Ing Teoh for her assistance, and to Sheila McMahon for outstanding copyediting work. Acknowledgments for the cover design of this new edition go to Jennifer Conn and the marketing and art-direction staff at UW Press. My thanks also go to the late George Burt, and to Vincent LoBrutto, Jeff Smith, and Larry Timm, who read the manuscript in its first version, and to Kevin Donnelly and Emile Wennekes, who read new parts of this current version—the "Closing Remarks" and chapter 11, respectively. All offered insightful and enhancing comments and pieces of advice, which I hope I have been able to implement successfully.

For their competent legal advice on US copyright law and on the fair use doctrine, my deepest appreciation goes to attorneys-at-law Redenta Enne and Bill Lee. As for the visual part, my appreciation goes to Mrs. Samantha Winslow Williams for generously giving her permission to feature her exquisite John Williams portraits, of which the one that closes the book perfectly captures the Maestro at work and his piano-and-pencil modus operandi.

I wish to restate my deepest gratitude to Jamie Richardson for his patience and kindness in replying to my (many, many) requests as well as for his indispensable advice throughout these years. Last but not least, my most sincere and affectionate thanks go to Maestro John Williams for the friendliness, graciousness, and appreciation he has always shown in each of our meetings. Having known him personally, I can say that he is not only an exceptional artist but also an exceptional human being.

The Film Music of
JOHN WILLIAMS

Introduction to the
Second Edition

It can be said that John Williams has now achieved a legendary status as one of the most successful composers in film *and* music history. His name is associated with many of the major Hollywood box office blockbusters of the past fifty years. In a career spanning more than sixty years, Williams has won four Golden Globes, three Emmys, twenty-five Grammys, seven BAFTA Awards, a number of Gold and Platinum Records, honorary degrees from twenty-one American universities, the American Film Institute's Lifetime Achievement Award (the first time in history for a composer), five Academy Awards, and he is the recipient of the Kennedy Center Honors and of the President of the United States' National Medal of Arts. Even more staggering, with fifty-two Oscar nominations, he is the second-most-nominated person in history, ranking just behind Walt Disney.[1] His film scores have sold millions of copies, with *Star Wars* breaking the record at the time of its release as the best-selling all-symphonic album.

Williams's success and fame are not confined to the film industry. For fourteen years, he served as conductor-in-residence and artistic director of one of the most famous American symphony orchestras, the Boston Pops. As Boston Pops conductor, he performed not only in the United States but also in three tours to Japan. As a "Boston Pops Laureate Conductor" since 1994, he has maintained a busy concert schedule, both with his annual appearances in Boston and as a guest conductor with other famed orchestras. Williams also pursued a career as a concert composer, receiving commissions from such important institutions as the New York Philharmonic, the Chicago Symphony, the Boston Symphony, and the Los Angeles Philharmonic. Plácido Domingo even tried to lure him into composing an opera for the Los Angeles Opera House.[2]

Over the years, Williams has also become America's "Composer Laureate." In particular, the number of celebratory pieces commissioned for many important events of American history and life have made him a modern-day American version of Georg Friedrich Händel. His fanfares, marches, miniature pieces, and overtures have been performed on worldwide TV broadcasts; they accompanied the Los Angeles Olympics in 1984, the centennial celebrations of the Statue of Liberty in 1986, the Atlanta Centennial Olympics in 1996, the Salt Lake City Winter Olympics in 2002, and President Barack Obama's first inauguration in 2009. In 2012 Williams wrote the "Fanfare for Fenway" to celebrate the first centennial of the Red Sox and his beloved Boston's Fenway Park. As the London *Times* reported, "Williams' work is often described as quintessentially American. He writes big music for big studio movies. He has been called 'the king of grandiosity.'"[3]

In contrast to this huge success, Williams has received little attention in the past from essayists and critics, and often a sort of ill-concealed animosity. In my twenty-plus years studying Williams's work, the one thing that has kept striking me as extremely odd was the paucity of academic literature. One might expect a lack of interest from the European intellectuals because Williams may be judged as a symbol of the "imperialistic" America and its cinema: "If, as some argue, American cinema has conquered the world, then Williams can lay claim to have written the victory march."[4] The surprising, and much less comprehensible, fact is the neglect of Williams in his own country. Before this monograph, the US produced no book-length study of its most successful film composer; the previous books were published outside the US and written by non-Americans and in languages other than English.[5]

In Williams's own country, such indifference may have derived from suspicion about a film composer who enjoyed enormous success also *outside* the films, "daring" to trespass upon the territories of "serious" concert music. After the release of *Star Wars* (George Lucas, 1977), the music Williams wrote for the film not only sold spectacularly as an LP album but also gradually entered the symphonic repertoire. Williams has thus attracted as many admirers (who think his music has been fundamental to a film's success) as detractors (who prefer to think that a *film*'s success has been fundamental to his music). Composers in classical Hollywood too were typical targets of highbrow critics. For example, Miklós Rózsa saw his credibility as an art composer questioned as a consequence of his ties with Hollywood.[6] This attitude is a consequence of the nineteenth-century distinction between "absolute music" (music that is *ab soluta* (untied), composed for a stand-alone listening experience freed from any external influences and extramusical references), and "applied music" (a musical rendition of a literary text, like a symphonic poem, or a musical accompaniment to an extramusical event, such as a ballet, an opera, or a film). The idea that the former is intrinsically and necessarily better music than the latter and that the two types must be kept distinct and neatly separated harks back to a nineteenth-century dictum.[7] Among the US intelligentsia, prejudices against applied music written for film were disseminated by art composers who had experiences (or had tried to have experiences) in the film industry—for example, Virgil Thomson, Aaron Copland, Igor Stravinsky, and George Antheil—but more importantly by Theodor W. Adorno and Hanns Eisler in their 1947 film-music book.[8] Adorno and Eisler's general idea was that those who worked in the film industry were lesser composers unable to have a "proper" career in "absolute" art music and had to compromise and accept jobs in a merely commercial arena—or venal composers selling out in exchange for Hollywood's money. Other composers have worked in both film and concert music; yet probably no other has been so equally and prominently successful in both at the same time, while expressing satisfaction for both, as Williams has: "I consider movie music as a legitimate art form like a symphony or an opera," he explains.[9] With a career in film and concert music and, above all, extensively engaged in conducting film music in concert halls, Williams has always been a composer fully committed to both compositional arenas, taking both seriously and aiming at being taken seriously in both.

Being a *film* composer who also wanted to have a say in concert halls is arguably the root of why Williams has been a particularly prominent target for music critics. In the 1980s—when he took the baton of the Boston Pops Orchestra and also started to guest-conduct the major American orchestras—the attacks on Williams became, significantly, vitriolic to the extreme. The *Los Angeles Times* music critic wrote in 1983, when Williams was invited to conduct the Los Angeles Philharmonic: "Why? Why . . . entrust a presumably serious winter-season program to John Williams, an amiable musician whose claim to fame and fortune are predicated on movie-score bombast and Boston Pops bagatelles? . . . Why would our cultural guardians want to devote an entire evening's diet to such junk food?"[10] In 1988 we have a different reviewer but the same mindset: "John Williams brought his lackluster music and conducting to Orange County. . . . As a composer, Williams knows how to manipulate cliches. . . . But away from the glamorous images, his music sounds threadbare, endlessly repetitive, overblown and heavily indebted to serious composers."[11] The latter raises a criticism that has been for years the warhorse of the Williams naysayers: the accusation of merely copying his music from "serious" composers. When not accused of plagiarism, Williams has been accused of not being the *real* author of his music: his orchestrators supposedly are. The misconception has often circulated—among those who ignore the Hollywood practice and its labor division but also the difference between an *arranger* and an *orchestrator*—that using an orchestrator equals being lesser composers (see chapter 2). Williams, like most Hollywood composers and as per the Hollywood workflow, needs the help of orchestrators to meet deadlines (see chapter 8). Where he does *not* need the help of orchestrators is in shaping his own music, as anyone who has taken a look at his sketches can confirm; borrowing the words of the orchestrator Arthur Morton, Angela Morley has said that with Williams, what orchestrators do is "score preparation" rather than "orchestration."[12]

Williams has sometimes also been disfavored over film composers considered more modern, revolutionary, and perceived as more politically committed. Williams's restoration of Hollywood's musical past and his association with big box office hits have made some critical circles look at him as a composer complacent of and complicit in the dominant cultural discourse. For example, Neil Lerner, in an analysis of *Star Wars* and *Close Encounters of the Third Kind*, while praising the effectiveness of Williams's music also sees it as a key enabler of the films' authoritarianism: "What is so remarkable about Williams' scores . . . is the way that they so effectively limit any oppositional readings of the films they accompany. . . . Williams' sweepingly nostalgic music reassures, persuades, and above all else, lulls us into being uncritical."[13] As the composer who brought back the musical style of old Hollywood, Williams may automatically be seen as an ideologically reactionary composer. Being past-oriented, he may be judged as regressive and conservative. Inversely, other composers who challenged traditional rules instead of restoring them—such as Ennio Morricone, to name one—may be seen as progressive and revolutionary, hence necessarily better, if ideology is conflated with style. For this same prejudice, arguably, the Spielberg/Williams duo—despite the almost forty-plus years and the outstanding output of this artistic collaboration—has often been underrepresented. For example, in his 1994 book *Overtones and Undertones: Reading Film Music*, Royal S. Brown does not even passingly mention the duo but defines the collaboration between Claude Chabrol and Pierre Jansen as "the most fruitful director/composer collaboration in the history of cinema."[14]

In the years after the release of this book's first edition, the number of rigorous academic studies on Williams—in the form of journal articles, PhD
dissertations, and conference papers—has significantly increased.[15] In particular, the old accusation of plagiarism has been contested and confuted by the
musicologist Jeremy Orosz.

> All music is intertextual; virtually any piece includes moments that remind us of
> another musical work. . . . Not only can Williams's methods be deemed respect-
> able within a progressive attitude toward creative production, he can hardly be
> accused of plagiarism or aesthetic impropriety even in a Romantic sense. . . .
> Examining the analytical evidence in detail, it is clear that Williams is not a thief.
> Even when Williams paraphrases music from other sources, this can hardly
> be considered a flaw of his working method. . . . The fact that so many accuse
> Williams of having an aesthetically dubious method of composition is presum-
> ably a consequence of his fame. . . . Yet Williams's creative process places him
> not only in the company of other film composers but also in that of countless
> composers of concert music who use pre-existing material as their starting
> point for crafting a new piece.[16]

As the musicologist Emile Wennekes writes, "musical borrowing has been
a non-negligible compositional feature since the early stages of music history."[17] Consequently, the feeling is that the accusations against Williams are
merely perfunctory ad hominem attacks. The majority of music critics have
now acknowledged Williams's importance and are taking him seriously. *New
Yorker*'s Alex Ross states that "Williams's wider influence on musical culture
can't be quantified, but it's surely vast," and "the conductor David Robertson,
a disciple of Pierre Boulez and an unabashed Williams fan, . . . observed that
professional musicians enjoy playing the scores because they are full of the
kinds of intricacies and motivic connections that enliven the classic reper-
tory."[18] *Washington Post*'s music critic Anne Midget even offered a sort of mea
culpa for the entire category in an article titled "As a Classical Music Critic, I
Used to Think the *Star Wars* Score Was beneath Me. I Was Wrong."[19] "Serious"
composers, conductors, and performers—the "cultural guardians"—have also
largely recognized Williams's merits.[20] The conductor Seiji Ozawa admitted
that he had been wrong: "Many people—I was one of them—misjudged
him as a composer. . . . But I found out when I studied his pieces. His knowledge and background and training, how he does his music [demonstrates] a
very high standard and deep musicianship."[21] The (very) "serious" composer

Milton Babbitt—"leader of the diehard modernist camp in American composition," in Alex Ross's words—used to entertain a sustained mail correspondence with Williams.[22] The revered Wiener Philharmoniker—the one institution most would probably select to represent tradition and "cultural guardianship" at the highest levels in "classical" music—invited Williams to conduct its first all-film-music concert in January 2020. In the first edition of this book, an entire chapter was devoted to the confutation of such criticisms against Williams. The first step in the revision for this second edition was the deletion of that chapter: there is no longer a need to defend John Williams—provided there had ever been the need.

The Book's Aim and Focus

Williams's output, particularly if one goes beyond the most famous blockbuster scores, is so varied and conspicuous that it can be explored from many angles. One, for instance, could be a study of his equilibrium between versatility and recognizable personal touch. Versatility is central to Williams.

> When I do a film . . . I'm not thinking about stylistic purity; I'm not thinking about anything but, "Okay, here's a film and my musical job is to construct something that will live within it and seem to be part of it and will sound like the picture looks." If I have to write a scene from *Jane Eyre* for instance, I write something that sounds like Yorkshire in the eighteen-sixties. Why? Not because I'm trying to write original music, but because I'm trying to get something behind the picture that smells like Yorkshire. . . . If you have only one style of music and do only one thing . . . you're in trouble in the film business. If you want to have a career in films, and do a hundred films, you need to be very versatile.[23]

Yet this versatility—often sidelined by the fame of his most famous space/adventure scores—coexists in Williams with a strong musical personality and a recognizable general style. Such a study would require musicological skills and interests to an extent that I do not have; I am a film scholar, primarily, and interested in film history and film analysis more than musical analysis.[24]

Another area that would call for further examination is Williams's collaboration with Steven Spielberg. The director/producer once remarked, "Without question, John Williams has been the single most significant contributor to my success as a filmmaker."[25] And Williams, in turn, admits: "I've been lucky to work with Steven because he loves music. Some directors feel as though they've failed if they need lots of music. It's cosmetic, even unwanted.

Spielberg's aesthetic is a very fanciful one and is comfortable in the pres
ence of music, so his pictures always offer the opportunity for lots of music."[26]
The study of the Spielberg/Williams relationship, though important, would
not be the right angle to capture the uniqueness of Williams. Also, in recent
years, studies have already made up for the *damnatio memoriae* to which the
Spielberg/Williams duo was subjected in the past.[27] Williams's versatility, and
specifically the variety of outputs he produced for Spielberg, is succinctly surveyed in appendix I, but versatility and the Spielberg collaboration are not at
the core of this book.

My original aim for this study was to concentrate on what I think is
Williams's unique and most specific contribution: the revival of the classical
Hollywood music style. This is the core of this book. Besides his single scores,
commercial success, and artistic achievements—other film composers, if not
this successful, have been successful—Williams is a pivotal figure in Hollywood history because he has been single-handedly responsible for bringing
back the classical Hollywood musical style and, more important, leading
people to rediscover and appreciate the music of Hollywood's Golden Age. In
the 1970s, Williams revived some then-disused features of the classical style and
consequently launched a film-music trend that I call "neoclassical"—because
it is the recuperation of Hollywood's classical music style. The restoration
of the Hollywood film-music tradition was not limited to the screens: as conductor of the Boston Pops Orchestra, Williams acted as the leading promoter
of film music by presenting its best achievements in concert, which contributed highly to its acceptance. While others have signaled Williams's importance in bringing back the symphonic style, this book focuses more closely on
how Williams brought back the classical Hollywood music style, and to what
extent, and analyzes the historical landmarks of the process.[28]

Part I focuses on the classical Hollywood music style. This style is given
an articulate definition and its history charted for its temporal borders, its
main authors, its language, its compositional techniques, and the musical
means typically used. This section constitutes a Williams-oriented account of
classical Hollywood music that is different from others: in its highlighting of
the thin red line of influences, historical events, and stylistic traits that connect Williams to the classical period, it is a preparatory reassessment of what
happened before Williams. Williams's role as the composer who revived the
classical style and founded the film-music neoclassical trend is fully covered in
part II, which centers on the 1975–83 period, the peak of the neoclassical trend.
The survey is not done chronologically. I first examine the case of *Star Wars*

(George Lucas, 1977) and its impact and legacy, it being the most famous of Williams's contributions. Then I go back to Williams's early years to individuate the already present neoclassical traits. Next comes a chapter on *Jaws* (Steven Spielberg, 1975), which I see as the inaugural film of that neoclassicism that would be expressed to the maximum in *Star Wars*. This is followed by a chapter that analyzes Williams's neoclassical style—I call it "neoclassical" because it is an updated revival of the classical Hollywood music style—and two entire chapters are devoted to an in-depth analysis of *Raiders of the Lost Ark* (Steven Spielberg, 1981) as a neoclassical film with a neoclassical score. There are many more films that can be listed in the neoclassical Williams canon, such as *Superman: The Movie* (Richard Donner, 1978), *1941* (Steven Spielberg, 1979), *E.T. the Extra-Terrestrial* (Steven Spielberg, 1982), the other chapters of the *Star Wars* saga, and a few others. They all would deserve a similarly in-depth analysis. Given the possibility of adding an entire brand-new chapter to this second edition, I resolved to devote it to one of the lesser known of Williams's neoclassical scores—which I consider a hidden gem and also Williams's one and only entry into the territories of the horror genre sensu stricto: *Dracula* (John Badham, 1979). There is then a chapter that offers an overview of Williams's conductorship of the Boston Pops Orchestra, a highly influential period in which Williams brought the classical film-music repertoire into the limelight.

The book closes with a few considerations on present-day Hollywood music. The conclusion has been expanded for this new edition. In the first edition, I may have sounded too curt and dismissive in regard to contemporary Hollywood music, and Hans Zimmer in particular: according to the Zimmer-school composer Tod Haberman, I "hold specific, and perhaps archaic, notions of what a score could and should be."[29] While I have no qualms in admitting that I may have a bias in favor of more traditional scoring approaches—and this book is about Hollywood's neoclassicism, after all—my "archaic" stance may also act as a healthy and pluralistic counterbalance to some of today's practitioners and academics, who can be accused of being uncritically laudatory of whatever is new in the same way as I can be accused of defending what is old. I seize the opportunity to elaborate on this in the "Closing Remarks" chapter.

I have previously mentioned the characteristic balance between a chameleonlike versatility and a recognizable personal mark in Williams's film music. While the investigation of this is not the focus of the book, I nevertheless felt that an ampler overview of his film production would be a welcome way to "complete the picture" and provide the reader with some, though cursory, information about other film works that have not been included among the case studies. The first appendix includes such overview, while the second appendix is a filmography that lists Williams's film and television outputs.

This book is not a composer's biography but a historiographic and stylistic survey. It is not written from a musicological perspective but from that of film studies: although a few themes and motifs are analyzed musically, extensive music analysis is not at the core of this book. Nor does it give an exhaustive account of Williams's music output, covering all his scores and each period of his career: its aim is to present a micro-history within the larger Hollywood history, centering not so much on Williams the composer as on Williams the "restorer" of a part of Hollywood's classicism. There are many film composers who can be studied and appreciated for their fine musical achievements, and perhaps such studies can be undertaken more efficiently by musicologists. However, Williams is a unique figure for his knowledgeable retrieval and ingenious updating of a piece of Hollywood's history, and here the film historian can perhaps say more than the musicologist.

Preliminary Explanation of Methodology

I call my approach "film/music analysis": "If I say that I perform a 'film–music analysis' the general understanding is that I am going to dissect musicologically a piece of music written for the screen. The slash sign in film/music analysis is to be interpreted as a relational sign: this is an instance of film analysis in which particular attention is placed on the music as to its interaction with the other components of the film. And the order is also important: in 'Film/Music Analysis' film analysis is the first concern, as it stems from a film scholar's perspective."[30] This approach is based on Kristin Thompson's neoformalism.[31] The film is seen as an artwork created according to specific norms in a specific historical context in order to produce specific aesthetic effects. Unlike semiotics, neoformalism sees the film not so much as a text conveying a message to be studied in terms of its communicational strategies but as an artifact to be studied in terms of its perceptual strategies.

Each film is a formal system consisting of an interplay of a series of devices. Devices are all those elements of a stylistic, narrative, or thematic nature that combine to shape the film's overall form: three-point lighting, tracking shots, fades, costumes, settings and scenery, flashbacks, montages, crosscutting, characters, extratextual allusions, philosophical/political ideas, and so on. These devices fulfill a specific *function* within the film and their presence must justify itself by some *motivation*. There are four types of motivation for the presence of a device in a film: (1) *compositional motivation*—a device is in the film because it is essential to build either the causal, temporal, or spatial system of the narrative; (2) *realistic motivation*—a device is in the film because its presence is plausible according to our experience of how things are in the real world; (3) *transtextual motivation*—a device is in the film because it follows the conventions of a given genre; and (4) *artistic motivation*—a device is in the film for no other motivation than an aesthetic one.

Music is one of the many devices used in films and its presence in a given scene is explained by one or more of the defined motivations. The opening scene of *The Abominable Dr. Phibes* (Robert Fuest, 1971) is a good example. The film tells the story of a disfigured theologian who retaliates against the doctors he holds responsible for his wife's death. The plot consists of a series of Grand-Guignolesque deeds of deathly revenge inspired by biblical episodes. The film opens with a black-hooded figure seen from the back—Dr. Phibes, we will soon find out—playing some music on a reddish neon-lighted plexiglass pipe organ. The presence of the opening title organ music is motivated *realistically*, since there is someone onscreen playing an organ. The choice of organ music is also motivated *transtextually*, since the pipe organ has not only had a long association with horror films but is also an overt quotation of *The Phantom of the Opera* (Rupert Jullian, 1925), in which the similarly disfigured and vengeful Lon Chaney character is used to playing such instrument. Moreover, the musical piece being played is Felix Mendelssohn's "War March of the Priests" ("Kriegsmarsch der Priester" from *Athalie*, incidental music, op. 74, 1845) and the *compositional* motivation of such a choice is to anticipate what the film is about: the war of a priestlike theologian against his wife's murderers. Finally, in the scene, Dr. Phibes's hands swipe the air in histrionic gestures mostly unsynchronized with the music he is supposed to be playing, and such flamboyant and unrealistic moves can be motivated *artistically* so as to introduce compellingly this larger-than-life villain.

It goes without saying that music operates powerfully in films. Music can contribute to the clarification of the narrative events, not only for the narrative logic (suggesting the thoughts of a character and thereby motivating the reasons for his actions) but also for time construction (providing the fragments of a montage sequence with some linking and temporal continuity) and space construction (hinting at the nationality of a place through the use of a representative tune or anthem). Music can also reinforce some stylistic traits of the film: through the use of dark timbres, music can enhance the dark shadows of low-key lighting, as Bernard Herrmann's score for *Citizen Kane* (Orson Welles, 1941) does. Music can also help in the creation of meaning: the grotesque version of "La Marseillaise" in *Metropolis* (Fritz Lang, 1927) accompanying the workers' wild rebellion may suggest a negative interpretation of revolutions in general. I see music as operating three classes of functions, named after the three levels of engagement of the viewer: emotion, perception, and cognition.[32]

The *macro-emotive function* is what unifies the aesthetic experience of the film for the viewer. It performs the function of the frame in a painting. By presenting the theme in the opening titles, then reprising it in variations throughout the film, and finally presenting it again at the end of the film, music helps the shaping of the perception of the film's formal unity. It acts as a conventional indicator of the boundaries of the narrative, marking the initial and final limit.[33] Emotionally, the feeling of an overall cohesion is given by the pleasure of recognizing recurrent musical themes throughout the film, with which we come to be progressively familiar. An example is provided by the famous "Tara's Theme" by Max Steiner, which opens, closes, and runs throughout *Gone with the Wind* (Victor Fleming, 1939), reinforcing its formal cohesion.

The *micro-emotive function* is the solicitation of a particular emotional response from the viewer in a particular moment of the film. Music transfers to the images its emotional component. The most common—and banal— examples are love scenes accompanied by sentimental violin music. However, there are many more instances in which the micro-emotive function can significantly affect the success of a scene. A famous example is the opening scene of *The Lost Weekend* (Billy Wilder, 1945), where Ray Milland is "fishing" a bottle of whiskey out of the window. Before Miklós Rózsa's stern music was put on the scene, that incipit had induced many viewers to expect an urban comedy instead of a drama on alcoholism.[34]

Music guides or modifies the perception of the viewer, pointing his attention to a particular element inside the framed space (*spatial* perceptive function) or by altering or enhancing the perception of the visual rhythm and speed of the cutting (*temporal* perceptive function). An example of *temporal* perceptive function is the car chase in *North by Northwest* (Alfred Hitchcock, 1959), in which Cary Grant's drunken character is trying to keep his car on the road and avoid crashing into the precipice. Bernard Herrmann's frenetic *fandango* punctuates the rapidity of the editing pace, making the action appear more frantic. An example of *spatial* perceptive function appears in *The Sea Hawk* (Michael Curtiz, 1940). In one scene, a harp chord resounds in the silence to direct our attention to an event occurring in the film space: Erich Wolfgang Korngold's score uses the chord to punctuate the change of facial expression of one of the Spaniards when he sees in his chalice the reflection of Captain Thorpe and his men, freed from their chains and eager to retaliate.

Since it acts on time, space, and narrative logic, music also contributes to the understanding of denotations and in the interpretation of connotations—*cognitive* function. Music may unite the fragments of a montage sequence and aid the understanding of the progression of time; it may denote a place or a historical period by referring to some repertoire pieces; it may link fairly disconnected shots, thus making the film's space look as a consistent whole; it may reveal the thoughts of a character presenting a musical theme previously associated with another narrative element, thus clarifying the reason for his action; it can link two distant narrative elements and suggest an implicit meaning. For example, in *Taxi Driver* (Martin Scorsese, 1976), Herrmann's music closes the film with the same three-note "madness motif" that closed *Psycho* (Alfred Hitchcock, 1960), suggesting that despite the circumstances, Travis is not a hero but a psychopath no less dangerous than *Psycho*'s Norman Bates. *The Adventures of Robin Hood* (Michael Curtiz and William Keighley, 1938) opens with a royal herald saying: "News has come from Vienna." Korngold used as the main theme his own waltz "Miss Austria," which colors Robin Hood's story with a Viennese flavor and thus contributes to give contemporary political connotations—the Anschluss had just been proclaimed and Hitler's invasion of Austria just begun—to a film that is otherwise about a medieval legend.[35]

Preliminary Explanation of Terminology

In film-music studies, there is a traditional distinction between music at *diegetic* level (music comes from a source within the narrative world and can be heard by the film's characters) and at *nondiegetic* level (music comes from some sort of narrator outside the narrative world and only the viewers can hear it, not the characters).[36] These terms originated from literary studies, leading to much debate about the legitimacy of their application to music in film.[37] For clarity's sake, though, the traditional "diegetic/nondiegetic" couple is employed hereafter.

The use of *leitmotiv*, drawn from Richard Wagner's works, in cinema has been similarly criticized, both for being an inadequate practice for this medium and for being an imprecise term to refer to the technique as it is used in films;

the alternative term "leitmotivic function" has been proposed.[38] The issue, however, is still being debated [39] Nonetheless, I use the term "leitmotiv" here because it is more convenient than other periphrases although I am perfectly aware of its difference from Wagner's idea.

In general parlance, *soundtrack* is used to define all the music composed for/featured in a given film, but this is incorrect. The soundtrack is the part of the filmstrip on which the sound mix comprising all the acoustic components is impressed: the dialogue track, the sound-effect track, and the music track. When referring to the musical component of a film, the correct term will be used: *music track*.

The terms "theme" and "motif" will indicate respectively an eight-bar melody and shorter melodic lines, both having their own musical "personality." *Cells* are one- or two-bar fragments deriving from a theme or motif already presented. Further classifications will be avoided, which are more accurate from a musicological point of view but which also risk being confusing.

I use *wallpaper music* to define a nondiegetic musical background, which is neutral to the action and dialogue, that is, music that fills an otherwise silent background. For example, it may be some kind of light waltz underscoring a dialogue—think of Ernst Lubitsch's early sound operettas. I contrast "wallpaper music" with "functional accompaniment," where nondiegetic music fulfills other functions than simply filling the silence, and it is composed so as to follow the developments of the actions and dialogue closely and meaningfully.[40]

The first section of this book provides a chronicle and definition of the classical Hollywood music style. Here, it is necessary to clarify the meaning of the terms "style" and "classical" as they are used. When talking about music, there is a tendency to think of style in a narrow sense, that is, as the language used to compose a certain type of music: *Baroque* style, *Classical* style, *Romantic* style, *atonal* style, and the like. In this work, I use a broader meaning of style. Indeed, classical Hollywood music is both a musical piece of work, one that employs a certain "musical style" in the narrowest sense, and an industrial product, one that responds to precise standards, is realized according to specific techniques and procedures, and uses the musical means provided by the "industry." Therefore, when I refer to the classical Hollywood music style, I refer not only to its musical language but also to the techniques, musical means, and typical formal functions that the classical Hollywood music style is expected to perform in films.[41]

When referring to *style in the narrower sense*—that is, the musical language employed—I adopt, after Leonard B. Meyer, a three-term subdivision: *dialect,* a shared musical language employed within a school; *idiom*, the idiosyncratic musical language of a given composer; and *intra-opus style*, the particular musical language that characterizes a single film score.[42] For instance, consider Max Steiner and Erich Wolfgang Korngold, two key composers of Hollywood's Golden Age. Both worked at Warner Bros. within the overarching classical Hollywood music *style*, following those institutional practices required by the industry. For example, both used the leitmotiv technique. They wrote in the same *dialect* largely favored within the Hollywood music departments, that of late Mitteleuropean Romanticism. Even if they used the same style and the same dialect, their *idioms* were different, one characterized by fragmentation and higher adherence to the visuals (Steiner) and the other by extended melodies and stronger motivic-thematic linking of operatic nature (Korngold).[43] Moreover, within their own production, the *intra-opus* style could change significantly from one work to others—from flowing tonal melodies as in Steiner's *Gone with the Wind* and Korngold's *The Adventures of Robin Hood* to darker and more dissonant writing, as in Steiner's *King Kong* (Merian C. Cooper and Ernest B. Schoedsack, 1933) and Korngold's *The Sea Wolf* (Michael Curtiz, 1941).

The adjective "classical" that I use to identify the music style of the Golden Age is a loan from David Bordwell, Janet Staiger, and Kristin Thompson's famous study, *The Classical Hollywood Cinema*. Music is one of the many devices used by narration in order to construct a film within the norms of the classical Hollywood paradigm.[44] Consequently, the term "classical" as used here must not be confused with the linguistic category of "classical" used in music historiography, meaning the music of the second half of the eighteenth century, of Joseph Haydn and Wolfgang Amadeus Mozart. Hollywood music style was not "classical" in that sense. Hereafter, "classical" is meant as a historical film category and refers to an idea of music molded according to the needs of the classical film style of the studio system. Some of Meyer's remarks on classicism in music can be of help to better understand the difference between "classical" as a linguistic classification and "classical" as an approach to music making. As he writes, "Classicism has been characterized by a valuing of shared conventions and rational restraint, the playful exploitation of established constraints and the satisfaction of actuality (Being), the coherence of closed forms and the clarity of explicit meanings; while romanticism has been characterized by a valuing of the peculiarities of the individual innovation and the yearning arising from potentiality (Becoming), the informality of open structures and the suggestiveness of implicit significance."[45] He further explains, "In the eighteenth century . . . unity of expression is significantly dependent upon kinds of dance steps, rhetorical figures, syntactic processes, and other conventional means. . . . Classic composers use such means to represent sentiment shared by humankind. Romantic composers, on the other hand, reject convention in order to express—to present, not *represent*—their own personal and individual feelings."[46]

A *classical* conception of music-making based on "shared conventions" and seeking to communicate "sentiment[s] shared by humankind" was fundamental in the classical Hollywood system that aimed at reaching the largest audience possible. The term "classical" is thus helpful in underlying not only the universality sought by that musical style but also its exemplariness: classical Hollywood music, like all classical works, has come to be a model and a reference point, either to be followed or to be rejected.

PART ONE

The Rise and Demise of the Classical Hollywood Music Style

Fine symphonic scores for motion pictures cannot help but influence mass acceptance of finer music. The cinema is a direct avenue to the ears and hearts of the great public and all musicians should see the screen as a musical opportunity.

—ERICH WOLFGANG KORNGOLD

Portrait of John Williams, ca. 1977. Photograph by Samantha Winslow Williams. Courtesy of BSO Archives/John Williams.

CHAPTER I

A Chronicle of Classical Hollywood Music

The regular presence of music as an accompaniment to film projections during cinema's infancy—between 1895 and 1905—is not certain.[1] At that stage, cinema was seen as a kind of carnival amusement, a lowbrow draw based on "attractions" presented in simple single-shot tableaux running a few minutes.[2] Music, however, became an essential part of the film experience in the 1910s. The attention and care for music in terms of thematic consistency and coherent integration with the film's narrative rose significantly when cinema turned from showing attractions to telling stories. Improvised, unwillingly comical, and incongruous forms of accompaniment such as those typical of the "cinema of attractions" were no longer tolerated. Practitioners now realized that a botched-up performance or an unsuitable musical accompaniment could be harmful to the film's reception and could radically modify the intended effects that the film was designed to have on the viewers.[3]

In the 1910s, there was a flourishing of articles that theorized and prescribed the manner in which music should be written and performed in order to serve the film in a proper way.[4] Yet there was still a major problem: the arbitrariness of the live performance. The struggle of many critics and theorists for music that should be congruent with the film's narrative clashed with a technical issue: music could not be stably placed on the filmstrip as happened with the visuals, following the best possible standards and the exact producers' intent. The live performance was under the control of the individual exhibitors. Even if they had closely followed the list of music pieces—the so-called cue sheet—provided by distributors along with the exhibition prints, the actual performance would have varied significantly, depending on the musical means available in each venue. Attending the screening of a film at the Roxy Theatre in New York with an orchestra of 110 players was quite different from attending the screening of the same film in a small-town third-rate movie house. Here the same music would be played from a piano reduction on a perhaps out-of-tune upright piano by a perhaps drunk pianist.[5] From a musical point of view, a silent film was never the same from one venue to another.

Sound technology was introduced with the principal aim of fixing the film's *musical* dimension more than of having characters talk. Alfred Hitchcock claimed that "the accompanying music came at last entirely under the control of the people who made the picture."[6] Now it was possible to bring the impeccable performance of a large orchestra, which one might have heard only in a luxurious picture palace, even to small provincial-circuit theaters. Therefore, in 1926 Warner Bros. could present its *Don Juan* (Alan Crosland, music by William Axt and David Mendoza) in every equipped theater with the flawless rendition of the New York Philharmonic Orchestra.[7]

In the early years of sound films, the use of nondiegetic music was not a widely accepted convention, although recent studies have shown evidence of a number of exceptions.[8] For instance, a viewing of *The Singing Fool* (Lloyd Bacon, 1928) reveals that the film has wallpaper music accompaniment under most dialogue scenes, and some early thirties Ernst Lubitsch productions at Paramount, like *Montecarlo* (1930), have episodes of dialogue underscoring. However, in most films, nondiegetic music was rare, limited to the opening titles, to a couple of chords emphasizing the title "The End," to bridging passages between two scenes, and to montage sequences. In the drama *Dishonored* (Josef von Sternberg, 1931), Marlene Dietrich plays an amateur pianist spy, X27, who manages to smuggle strategic information from the enemy by encoding it into musical notes. Her diegetic piano playing provides most of the musical parts of the film; there are even some unusually atonal pieces, which is what the codes would sound like if played. The only episode of nondiegetic music is a brief montage sequence summarizing some war actions. The final, dramatic scene of X27 facing the firing squad after being sentenced to death has no music at all, which sounds rather strange to the ears of a present-day viewer. The same can be said of *Madam Satan* (Cecil B. DeMille, 1930), a comedy with only diegetic music, and *Anna Christie* (Clarence Brown, 1930), a drama that has virtually no music at all. The presence of music was mostly at the diegetic level: music had to seem to come from the narrative world and was synchronized with some kind of on-screen performance—a singer, an orchestra, a pianist—or had to be motivated realistically by showing or implying the presence of some kind of sound source such as a phonograph or a radio: hence the term "source music."

Most directors thought that nondiegetic music could be harmful to drama and realism. The composer Max Steiner provides an example of this "musical realism."

> But they [producers and directors] felt it was necessary to explain the music pictorially. For example, if they wanted music for a street scene, an organ grinder was shown. It was easy to use music in [a] nightclub, ballroom or theater scene, as here the orchestras played a necessary part in the picture. Many strange devices were used to introduce the music. For instance, a love scene might take place in the woods and in order to justify the music thought necessary to accompany it, a wandering violinist would be brought in for no reason at all. Or, again, a shepherd would be seen herding his sheep and playing his flute, to the accompaniment of a fifty-piece orchestra.[9]

How can this obsession with musical realism be explained? One clarification is of an aesthetic nature and connected with the new idea of cinema that derived from synchronized dialogue. In the silent era, the lack of words implied a more stylized conception of cinema as a kind of spiritual, paintlike art, a sort of visual symphony. Since reality in sound films could be reproduced with greater fidelity, the aesthetics of the medium slipped toward a greater realism, which obviously favored the dialogue over the artificial nondiegetic music.

Another motivation is of an economic nature. At first—in the years 1927–28—sound films were produced following the 1926 model of *Don Juan*. These films were basically silent (no dialogue) with synchronized music tracks. Another famous example is *Sunrise* (Friedrich Wilhelm Murnau, 1927, music by Hugo Riesenfeld). After the huge box office success of *The Singing Fool* (1928, music by Louis Silvers et al.) and the first "all-talking" *Lights of New York* (Bryan Foy, 1928), it was clear that the novelty of synchronized sound was quite successful in attracting the audience, thus bringing in big profits. In such films as *Sunrise*, this innovation was less evident. Although music was indeed synchronized with the images from a technical point of view, from the audience perspective, the innovation could hardly be noticed. The sound of the orchestra that once came out live from the orchestra pit now simply emerged through loudspeakers from a recorded support. At this point, the innovation could be better exploited if the synchronization process were explicitly displayed. This meant favoring dialogue, on-screen music numbers, and the diegetic use of music, visibly synchronized with an identifiable on-screen source. Consequently, Hollywood produced talkies having a realistic narrative and setting, like that in *Scarface* (Howard Hawks, 1932), a film with no music at all besides the diegetic whistling by Paul Muni / Tony Camonte. Another much-exploited genre was the musical, where diegetic music prevailed, especially in the revue subgenre, which was made up of a string of musical numbers: famous examples are *The Hollywood Revue of 1929* (Charles Reisner, 1929, music by Nacio Herb Brown et al.) and *Paramount on Parade* (Dorothy Arzner et al., 1930, music by Howard Jackson).

The third factor that discouraged the use of nondiegetic music was a technical one: before 1932, sound editing and mixing were very difficult operations, and this could prevent the simultaneous presence of multiple audio tracks.[10] The result of this was the inability to blend music and dialogue in terms of acceptable sound quality. The technical limitations made feasible neither *postrecording* (later used to stage diegetic numbers in musicals) nor *dubbing* (later used to add nondiegetic music to the soundtrack).[11] In the earliest years of sound cinema, music was recorded during the filming at the same time as the dialogue. Music numbers had to be staged by shooting the action and simultaneously recording the orchestra and singers playing live on set. Having the orchestra and singers on set with actors, and having to handle the filming and recording of all the sound elements, meant an increase in production costs and shooting time.[12] Because this process was so cumbersome, music was obviously used only when absolutely necessary and profitable, in other words, only in diegetic numbers, in which the innovation of synchronized sound could be patently shown off to attract the audience and offset the high costs.

The technical issues were solved in 1932, when sound editing and multitrack mixing became feasible. Nondiegetic music, called *background music*, could now find its place in the sound cinema. The economic reason disappeared in 1930, after the unexpected flop of musical films at the box office. The audience had had enough of all those songs and musical numbers that were partly a kind of revival of the primitive "cinema of attractions" rather than a narrative cinema.[13] As a consequence, many producers decided to dismiss musicians and to reduce the production of musicals, with the intent of focusing on talkies without music.[14]

Max Steiner (1888–1971) had moved to Hollywood during the early years of sound films and was one of those composers in danger of being laid off. Eventually, though, he managed to invert the trend in Hollywood.[15] The last obstacle to the emergence of the classical style—the poetics of musical realism—was removed by Steiner with his work at RKO Pictures. *The Most Dangerous Game*

(Ernest B. Schoedsack and Irving Pichel, 1932) and *Bird of Paradise* (King Vidor, 1932) strengthened Steiner's reputation and increased the producers' confidence in background music.[16] *King Kong* (Merian C. Cooper and Ernest B. Schoedsack, 1933) completed the dismantling of the musical realism poetics, for which Steiner, despite the slim musical budget, insisted on composing an original score instead of using preexisting music pieces.[17] *King Kong* is definitely *not* a realistic film, and the most important function of Steiner's music is to give credibility to Kong, a fairly rudimentary stop-motion animated puppet. Without Steiner's score, the audience could have derided the monster instead of being scared at the beginning of the film and feeling pity for him at the end: "Here the music is required, perhaps for the first time in an American film, to explain to the audience what is actually happening on the screen, since the camera is unable to articulate Kong's instinctive feelings of tenderness towards his helpless victim."[18]

Hollywood Music's First Generation

For its historical and stylistic importance, *King Kong* can be identified as the inaugural film of the classical Hollywood music style. *King Kong* was also the first case to reveal a general trend in the use of film music: genres that are best at ease with music are the least realistic ones. Music is more easily placed in films about the past, distant places, fancy romances, and exotic adventures, where the narrative is more in need of music to suspend the disbelief of the audience and to ensure the formal cohesion of the film, all of which confirms what Jack Warner used to say: "Films are fantasy—and fantasy needs music."[19] In the 1930s, the genres where music is most present and often takes a leading role are adventure films, period dramas, melodramas, and horror movies, while comedies are almost musically deprived: they tell contemporary stories and the screenplays are arguably strong enough to provide a formal cohesion: when music is present, it has a minor role—mostly diegetic—and in many cases it is not present at all.

To grasp the difference between the previous realistic trend and the new trend, compare *Frankenstein* (James Whale, 1931) with its sequel, *The Bride of Frankenstein* (James Whale, 1935). In the former—like in other horror films such as *Dracula* (Tod Browning, 1931), *Murders in the Rue Morgue* (Robert Florey, 1932), and *Island of Lost Souls* (Erle C. Kenton, 1932)—music is present only in the opening and closing titles, while the monster's appearances or the suspenseful scenes have no music. But in *The Bride of Frankenstein*, Franz Waxman's score is fundamental in supporting the narration for the entire running time, with color effects, timbre inventions, and a network of musical motifs associated with the various characters. Only four years separate these two films, both directed by the same person. The difference, however, could not be more radical.

If 1933 can be seen as the year of the beginning of classical Hollywood music, it is in 1935 that this musical style reached its maturity and a pervasive spread. Three films—all veritable milestones in film-music history—attest to the strength of the classical style. The first one is *The Informer* (John Ford, 1935, music by Max Steiner), a drama about betrayal and remorse, and often singled out as the most extreme example of the classical close adhesion of music to visuals.[20] Another influential score is Waxman's already mentioned *The Bride of Frankenstein*, which set the basis for horror-film music. The third is *Captain Blood* (Michael Curtiz, 1935), with which Erich Wolfgang Korngold made his official debut as a Hollywood composer. Korngold did not only institutionalize the way a score for an adventure film should sound—late-Romantic dialect, lush orchestration, prominent brass flourishes—but brought to the task the sensitivity and mastery of an opera composer and the formal strength that lacked in Steiner's fragmentary idiom and "hyperexplicit moment-by-moment musical illustration."[21]

Classical Hollywood music style was now well grounded. Film studios opened music departments, according to the assembly-line logic that characterized the studio system. A musical director was in charge of the entire operations, facilities, and branches of the department, which included a musical archive, a legal department for contracts and copyright clearance, and a casting office to recruit singers and musicians. Their staff also included singing coaches and instrument instructors, and a technical team in charge of recording, editing, mixing, and dubbing. The artistic workforce included composers, orchestrators, arrangers, conductors, piano accompanists, copyists, proofreaders, and an in-house symphony orchestra.[22] The composers were payrolled; they were given a fixed weekly salary rather than being paid for each individual work. They had to do office hours, often supplemented by overtime to meet the short deadlines. In 1939 Steiner worked on eight films, including the mammoth score for *Gone with the Wind*, which alone contains about three hours of music. Some of Hollywood's first generation of composers in the years from 1933 to 1945 were Franz Waxman (1906–67), Victor Young (1899–1956), Dimitri Tiomkin (1894–1979), Hugo Friedhofer (1901–81), and Alfred Newman (1901–70), the powerful and influential music director of 20th Century Fox (rebranded as "20th Century Studios" in 2020 after Disney's acquisition).[23]

The young craft of film music attracted the suspicion and disdain of many art composers, but it also aroused the interest of others. Among the preeminent art composers who worked in Hollywood, we should mention Aaron Copland (1900–1990), although he was only sporadically involved.[24] However, it is the Mitteleuropean art composer Erich Wolfgang Korngold (1897–1957) who gave the most fundamental and lasting contribution to the classical style and deserves more space.[25]

> Hailed as a second Mozart, he had astounded the music world with his concert works and his operas. As a teenage composer, pianist and conductor he had the most prominent composers of the day shaking their heads in disbelief. Richard Strauss said: "This firmness of style, this sovereignty of form, this individual expression, this harmonic structure—one shudders with awe to realise these compositions were written by a boy." When Korngold was ten, his father took him to Gustav Mahler for a critical judgment. The boy played from memory a dramatic cantata as Mahler walked up and down reading the score, his pace quickening with growing excitement. At the end he looked at the father and said, "A genius," and made suggestions for education. A few years later, with a pair of one-act Korngold operas playing all over Europe, Puccini remarked, "The boy has so much talent he could easily give us some and still have enough left for himself." . . . An analysis of Korngold reveals a Straussian orchestral colour, a Mahlerian feeling, and the melodic concepts of Puccini, all of them somehow melded and dominated by a strong Viennese character—plus Korngold's own personality.[26]

The highly talented Korngold penned some of the best film scores in history, examples of how film music can be good *music for films* while also being good music per se: *Captain Blood, Anthony Adverse* (Mervyn Le Roy, 1936); *The Prince and the Pauper* (William Keighley, 1937); *The Adventures of Robin Hood* (Michael Curtiz and William Keighley, 1938), *The Sea Hawk* (Michael Curtiz, 1940); and *Kings Row* (Sam Wood, 1942). Korngold's touch consisted in treating the film score as an opera score. Korngold would see a film as a libretto to be scored and applied to the film work with the same energy, creativity, and expertise that he would devote to his art music. *The Sea Hawk* score has a true operatic presence, especially in the sequence where Captain Thorpe and his men unchain themselves from the oars, defeat the Spanish enemies, take possession of the galley, and finally sing exultantly "Strike for the Shores of Dover" as they steer the ship back to their beloved England. The ambush sequence in

Sherwood Forest in *The Adventures of Robin Hood* is very much like a ballet.[27] Korngold was able to compose highly functional music without necessarily following every turn of the action too closely, which would have given the music a fragmentary form—typical of Steiner's music, for example. He showed, more than anyone else, how to compose scores that successfully served the film while maintaining full-bodied phrasing and a proper overall musical solidity of form and development.

In the 1930s, Hollywood music took form and institutionalized its practices, soon becoming part of the classical Hollywood cinema paradigm and giving a seminal contribution to the formation of Hollywood's conventional image: glamour, first-rate polished film-making, upbeat feelings, and happy endings: "Most 1930s films do not even start out in the direction of a problem. They disavow it for a trip to a fantasy place where the 'magic of cinema' simply transcends the urgent realities confronting offscreen America in the 1930s."[28]

Hollywood Music's Second Generation

In the 1940s, the world situation changed, and a series of events affected the film industry as well. First, there had been World War II and its horrors, but there was also the rapidly changing sociocultural context: the Cold War instilling suspicion and fear in American society; the baby boomer generation reshaping demography and urbanization; the growing success of television creating a new competitive entertainment medium. Films increasingly began to feature more controversial, negative, and even unpleasant stories and characters. The rising genre of those years, which would become the symbol of the decade, was the film noir, characterized by existential malaise, moral ambiguity, and a creeping sense of disorientation.

> Much of the appeal of film noir involves its masochistic erotics of doom, its ability to draw viewers into nightmare-like, paranoid narratives of degeneration and failure. Where many genres, such as the Western, romantic comedy, or coming-of-age films, explore the prospect of a successful future for sympathetic characters, film noir tends to present flawed characters without a future and show how their past went wrong. It bucks the cliché that Hollywood films must end happily; film noir cued its audiences in multiple ways to expect these films to end badly, very badly. . . . For their initial audiences, films noirs resembled nightmares in contemporary life. They were set in and about "today." Although they evoked the audience's deepest fears about all going wrong, they did not engage the supernatural as did horror films. Film noir invoked dark

forces, from within individuals or from criminal conspiracies or social injus-
tices, but rooted there throw in the everyday contemporary world of domestic
or business antagonisms, psychic disturbances, criminal schemes, and political
machinations.[29]

The low-key cinematography and menacing shadows inherited from German Expressionism—used in the previous decade for horror films—now
spilled over into contemporary urban space; its high-contrast chiaroscuro,
dark spots, and slashes of violent light replaced the well-balanced middle
tones of the soft-focus, high-key style previously used. Découpage and selec-
tive focus—signs of a narration that guided the viewer's attention and understanding around the pro-filmic space and the narrative's causal chain—were
replaced with *plan-séquence* and deep-focus cinematography, which made the
viewer's experience freer and more self-directed but also the orphan of a reliable narrational guide.[30]

This social uneasiness influenced film music too. The symptoms were a
shift from the late nineteenth-century Romantic dialect to twentieth-century
modernism, with a decrease of consonance, soothing melodies, and heroic
fanfares giving way to a rise of angular melodies, unstable harmonies, and
more grating dissonance. The main authors emerging during this period—
the second generation—introduced into film music some dialectal traits of
the twentieth century and updated the style of the previous decade in outstanding films such as *Citizen Kane* (Orson Welles, 1941), *Double Indemnity*
(Billy Wilder, 1944), *Laura* (Otto Preminger, 1944), and *The Lost Weekend* (Billy
Wilder, 1945).

The most influential composer of this second generation was perhaps
Bernard Herrmann (1911–75). He made his film debut at the age of twenty-
nine with his groundbreaking score for *Citizen Kane*. In Welles's film, musical
ideas are linked to concepts or characters—Xanadu, Death, the Chronicle—
but they can hardly be defined as themes; instead they are shorter fragments
or motifs and they lack the typical "hummable quality" of Romantic melodies. The motivic and modular writing can be said to be Herrmann's most
prominent trademark.[31] Think of the scores for *North by Northwest* (Alfred
Hitchcock, 1959) and *Psycho* (Alfred Hitchcock, 1960) to notice how they are
based on brief and incisive motifs that are varied and repeated in a modular fashion. The famous *Psycho* prelude highlights the Herrmann trademark
major-seventh chord (which Royal S. Brown calls the "Hitchcock chord").[32]
This is alternated with a two-bar hysteria-depicting module for violins and

then a longer melodic line that does not resolve to anything and has no final destination.[33] Everything sounds almost juxtaposed, without melodic or harmonic development, often floating in a tonal uncertainty. In *North by Northwest*, the main motif of the film is not even a melodic fragment but just a rhythmic fandango figure, reprised in different orchestral thicknesses and colors. Another characteristic of Herrmann's idiom is indeed his mastery in the use of expressive and evocative orchestral palette. The rapid pace of film editing and the fast shifts from one atmosphere and tone to another can make it difficult to use the traditional harmonic and melodic development techniques, because they require a longer time to unfold properly. Herrmann then opted for "coloristic development": he responded to these fast cinematic transitions by modifying the orchestration in order to obtain faster music reactions. Because of this approach, Herrmann's music comes with an innovative orchestral color range. *Citizen Kane* opens with unusually turbid bass writing—bassoons, contrabassoons, bass clarinets, alto flute, vibes—with no clearly distinguishable melody but a slowly creeping movement. Another recurring Herrmann trait is the use of classical forms and dances, more as rhythmic patterns than full-bodied forms. Besides the already mentioned fandango, we can find a habanera—actually, the rhythmic pattern of a habanera—as Carlotta's motif in *Vertigo* (Alfred Hitchcock, 1958). The *Citizen Kane* score is almost a suite of dances and traditional forms: "Hornpipe Polka," "Scherzo," "Waltz," "Gallop," a kind of *Grand Opéra* aria specifically composed for the scene of Mrs. Kane's debut—"Salaambo's Aria"—and a "Theme and Variations" as a sarcastic accompaniment to the montage where we see the gradual deterioration of the relationship between Kane and his first wife. Another example of a suite-like score is *The Three Worlds of Gulliver* (Jack Sher, 1960), which contains an overture, a minuet, and several marches in the eighteenth-century dialect as well as a love theme that uses the modal dialect of old English folksongs.

Miklós Rózsa (1907–95) was an art composer with parallel careers in film and concert music.[34] Born in Hungary, Rózsa was influenced by the popular forms of his land, Gypsy and Magyar songs, much like his countryman Béla Bartók. His idiom is chromatic and characterized by a rhythmic incisiveness, metrical irregularities, and dissonant harmonies. In Hollywood, Rózsa's name became associated with two large trends. In the 1940s, after *Double Indemnity*, he worked mostly for films dealing with crime, self-destruction, and madness: the already mentioned *The Lost Weekend*, *Spellbound* (Alfred Hitchcock, 1945),

The Strange Love of Martha Ivers (Lewis Milestone, 1946), *The Red House* (Dalmar Daves, 1947), *Secret beyond the Door* (Fritz Lang, 1948), and *The Asphalt Jungle* (John Huston, 1950). Rózsa's dissonant, harsh music was ideal for the new problematic topics of postwar cinema. He pioneered the use of the theremin in Hollywood; this electro-acoustic instrument was the ancestor, along with the Ondes martenot and the Novachord, of modern synthesizers.[35] Its ethereal, trembling, and eerie sound was extremely effective in conveying the characters' moral disorder or mental disorientation, starting with *Spellbound*, in which the theremin is introduced to "suggest moments of psychological instability" and "plays a distorted version of the love theme."[36] In the following decade, Rózsa changed hats and became the undisputed master of biblical-historical epics like *Quo Vadis* (Mervyn Le Roy, 1950), *Ivanhoe* (Richard Thorpe, 1952), *Plymouth Adventure* (Clarence Brown, 1952), *Julius Caesar* (Joseph L. Mankiewicz, 1952), *Knights of the Round Table* (Richard Thorpe, 1953), *Ben-Hur* (William Wyler, 1959), *King of Kings* (Nicholas Ray, 1961), *El Cid* (Anthony Mann, 1961), and *Sodom and Gomorrah* (Robert Aldrich, 1962). In preparation for these films, Rózsa would research the music of the period in order to reach a sort of philological accurateness, employing touches of archaic modal writing and ancient-sounding instrumentation.

David Raksin (1912–2004), after years of hard work at 20th Century Fox, won visibility in 1944 with his score for *Laura*, whose unforgettable theme soon turned into a successful popular song. This melody is interesting not just for the harmonic complexity when compared with coeval songs but also because it is the only theme present in the film. Indeed, this is one of the earliest examples of a "monothematic" score. In Preminger's film, everybody is obsessed or in love with Laura, a "ghost-woman" whose haunting presence is aptly represented by this obsessive melody. "Laura's Theme" is everywhere and appears throughout the film, alternately shifting from the diegetic level to the nondiegetic, floating through the "walls" of the various narrative levels, just like a ghost would do. The theme becomes Laura's musical substitute. The dead woman cannot be seen, but her presence hovers constantly in the air as her musical theme does. Raksin's idiom is refined and harmonically sophisticated; his writing is more complex than the Hollywood standards, with a penchant for the variation and development of the musical material. Moreover, the *Laura* music track contains an occurrence of electronically distorted piano—a rare instance in the classical period—to depict the male protagonist disturbingly falling in love with the late Laura.[37]

Stylistic Changes and the End of an Era

In the 1950s, Hollywood entered a period of crisis. In order to differentiate their products from those of television, film companies resorted insistently to technological innovations with arresting spectacular impact. The idea was to lure moviegoers into theaters with the promise of big shows that could not be seen, or properly appreciated, on the small screen of the TV sets. Such gimmicks consisted of various types of wide-screen format (Cinerama, Cinemascope, Todd-AO, Vistavision), color cinematography (the swan song of the tripack Technicolor process before being overpowered by Eastmancolor in the following decade), stereophonic sound (with the introduction of the magnetic sound recording), and short-lived technical curiosities: 3D, as in *Dial M for Murder* (Alfred Hitchcock, 1954) or the bizarre "Percepto."[38] This particular gadget—a sign of how Hollywood producers were badly in need of bringing people back to theaters—consisted of electrical buzzers attached to the underside of the seats that would vibrate to increase the startle of the audience during a sudden horror shot.[39] Percepto was used, for example, in *The Tingler* (William Castle, 1959). In this kind of production, music would not deviate significantly from the dialect of the previous decade.

A genre that took on great importance in this period was the musical, consistent with Hollywood's concentration on spectacular films. For its rich music, charming songs, lush set design, and spectacular pieces of choreography, the musical became one of the decade's most popular genres, especially in the "Arthur Freed Unit" output at MGM, including *An American in Paris* (Vincente Minnelli, 1951), *Singin' in the Rain* (Stanley Donen and Gene Kelly, 1952), *Seven Brides for Seven Brothers* (Stanley Donen, 1956), and *Gigi* (Vincente Minnelli, 1958). In musicals, songs were foregrounded and presented in musical numbers at diegetic level, while film music sensu stricto—background nondiegetic music—had a secondary role. Nonetheless, we should mention some arrangers and orchestrators working in musical films whose contributions have left an indelible mark: Conrad Salinger, Saul Chaplin, Adolph Deutsch, Alexander "Sandy" Courage, and Johnny Green, music director at MGM in that decade.

The main musical innovations of the 1950s can be found in the least spectacular films, that is, in realistic dramas dealing with contemporary life. Such innovations, which were not just incorporations of other dialects but had started to affect the overall style and were thus the first signs of the forthcoming "modern style" of the 1960s, were the introduction of jazz, atonality, and even twelve-tone music.

Jazz, in its various forms and varieties, had been used up to this time or diegetic music to give a negative connotation to criminal characters or disreputable clubs: for example, to characterize the vice and immorality of the slimy jazz drummer played by Elisha Cook Jr. in *Phantom Lady* (Robert Siodmak, 1944). Jazz was also associated with African Americans as a race connotation, as in *King of Jazz* (John Murray Anderson, 1930), *Hellzapoppin'* (Henry C. Potter, 1941); *Cabin in the Sky* (Vincente Minnelli, 1943), and *High Society* (Charles Walters, 1956). In some 1950s films, jazz was used for the first time even at the nondiegetic level, losing the racial connotation but sometimes keeping the criminal one.[40] Alex North (1910–91) applied the jazz dialect to a symphonic score in *A Streetcar Named Desire* (Elia Kazan, 1951). North's carnal music is the perfect aural complement of New Orleans's torrid setting where the sordid story of Blanche, Stella, and Stanley takes place.[41]

Leonard Rosenman (1924–2008) ushered in the twelve-tone dialect in Hollywood in *The Cobweb* (Vincente Minnelli, 1955). This choice, however, can hardly be seen as the advent of the "new music" in cinema—replacing the old late-Romantic music—as advocated by Adorno and Eisler in *Composing for the Films*.[42] Rather, the twelve-tone dialect entered the classical style because it was appropriate for narrative reasons. *The Cobweb* is set in a psychiatric hospital, and twelve-tone music was the musical equivalent of madness, as opposed to tonal music, which in turn corresponded to normality, in the Hollywood categorization. Similarly, Rózsa wrote the only twelve-tone piece of music of his entire career for Satan's appearance in *King of Kings*. It was "perverse" music for a perverse creature; this seemed to be the equation in Hollywood.[43] The use of jazz in *A Streetcar Named Desire* and twelve-tone music in *The Cobweb* was not a straight revolution but merely the acquisition of new dialectal tools and their integration into the paradigm, in order to better respond to new expressive needs.

Elmer Bernstein (1922–2004) brought in a more substantial innovation. With the music for *The Man with the Golden Arm* (Otto Preminger, 1955), he did not just adopt the jazz dialect as North had done but also recorded the score with the drummer Shelly Manne and a jazz combo, instead of the traditional symphony orchestra. This choice prefigured the modern style of the next decade and placed the score outside the classical style.

As to negative connotations, the usual association of jazz with the criminal underworld, for example in *The Man with the Golden Arm*, a story about drug addiction, is abandoned in *Anatomy of a Murder* (Otto Preminger, 1959), whose music was composed by Duke Ellington, also appearing in a cameo role. Here, jazz music is finally no longer associated necessarily with outlaws but with a lawyer—Paul Biegler, played by James Stewart—who is also an amateur pianist and jazz enthusiast.

As for other genres, the change of dialect in the music for Westerns must be mentioned. This type of music used to be based on folk inflections and quotes contained in the otherwise classical Hollywood late-Romantic symphonic dialect. At most, the dialect was colored with some threatening modal topics conventionally used as "Indian music"—as in Max Steiner's score for *The Searchers* (John Ford, 1956).[44] Examples of folk influences are the ballad "Do Not Forsake Me, Oh My Darling," written by Dimitri Tiomkin and Ned Washington for *High Noon* (Fred Zinnemann, 1952), or the *degüello*, a slow Mexican figuration for trumpet announcing the imminent battle, which is heard before the arrival of Burdette's gang in *Rio Bravo* (Howard Hawks, 1959) and is also used in *The Alamo* (John Wayne, 1960), both scored again by Tiomkin. A Russian native influenced by Rachmaninov, Tiomkin became the most important composer of Western genre music in classical Hollywood. Between this "Russian" period and Ennio Morricone's revolutionary approach—which overthrew all the Western stereotypes by bringing in elements of rock, archaic-sounding modalism, and onomatopoeic sounds, before becoming itself a stereotype—a dialectal innovation took place in Hollywood. Jerome Moross (1913–83), an art composer of ballets, symphonic music, and chamber music, and Aaron Copland's collaborator, brought Copland's twentieth-century idiom—a kind of pandiatonic neoclassicism that retrieved the oldest American musical heritage and its modal harmony—into the Western genre. This way, Moross proposed a tonal dialect that was authentically American and far from both the turgid old late-Romanticism and the "perverse" twelve-tone music. With Moross's *The Big Country* (William Wyler, 1958), the American genre par excellence found a congenial, truly American music. The modal harmonization, pentatonic melodies, syncopated rhythms, and bright orchestral sound of *The Big Country* were and still are a model, distinguishing the tradition-oriented Westerns—*The Magnificent Seven* (John Sturges, 1960, music by Elmer Bernstein), *The Cowboys* (Mark Rydell, 1972, music by John Williams), and *Silverado* (Lawrence Kasdan, 1985, music by Bruce Broughton)—from revisionist or postclassical Westerns such as *The Wild Bunch* (Sam Peckinpah, 1969, music by Jerry Fielding), whose model is instead Morricone.

The classical studio system, which had been suffering an income crisis since the 1950s, fell apart in the 1960s. Film companies were being acquired by big corporations for which film production was just one of the many interests and business lines. Hollywood studios had to reduce in size; RKO no longer existed, having already been wound up in 1956, and many studios turned to what can be called survival strategies, if compared to the exuberant expansion strategies of the Golden Age. The last efforts to bring the masses back into film theaters, in particular the technological gimmickry and spectacular epics and musicals of the 1950s, had not produced the desired effects. Hollywood was no longer the "dream factory" because of a number of factors, the most notable of which was the spread of television.[45]

The crisis also affected the music departments, which were severely reduced or closed down altogether. In 1958 a strike by the American Federation of Musicians (AFM), aiming at renegotiating the contracts between the musicians and the film industry, paralyzed Hollywood's music making. A notable consequence was that the score for *Vertigo* had to be recorded in London, not conducted by Herrmann (AFM) but by the local specialist and non-union musician Muir Mathieson.[46] Eventually, the new contract was not signed with AFM but with a new union, the Musicians Guild of America (MGA). According to James Wierzbicki, "Under the old pact with the AFM, the major studios had no choice but to hire 'contract orchestras.' . . . The new agreement with the MGA provided musicians with higher pay, but the pay was now determined by 'variable wage rates according to the number of musicians called for every three-hour recording session. . . . Certain musicians indeed stood to gain considerably from the MGA agreement. But the studios gained as well, for they no longer had to engage—or at least, pay for, whether they used it or not—a full orchestra for every recording session.'"[47]

As Hugo Friedhofer recalls, "All of the big studios had big orchestras under contract. And they had to utilize them. So the composer was forced to write more expansively and extensively than he might have liked."[48] From a stylistic point of view, this contractual renegotiation caused the progressive discarding of the symphony orchestra as the preferred musical means for film music. Smaller, less costly instrumental ensembles, which were closer to the musical tastes of the moment and indeed more trendy, won favor with film producers, a tendency anticipated by Bernstein with *The Man with the Golden Arm*.

The composer who guided Hollywood music from the classical to the modern style was Henry Mancini, who can be considered one of the leading representatives of the new style. Having grown up professionally in the music department of Universal Pictures, Mancini was perhaps the first person to perceive the new tide and to contribute to this change with his own work. He was very clever in integrating in his scores commercially successful songs such as "Moon River" (lyrics by Johnny Mercer) in *Breakfast at Tiffany's* (Blake Edward, 1961), balancing the formal functions of the classical style with the trendy commercial appeal that music was supposed to have now.

As the classical style began to emerge before 1933 and reached its maturity later in 1935, similarly classical-style film music can still be heard after 1958, in films such as *How the West Was Won* (John Ford et al., 1962, music by Alfred Newman), *Lawrence of Arabia* (David Lean, 1962, music by Maurice Jarre), and the previously mentioned Rózsa-scored *Ben-Hur*. Classical-style film music became definitively obsolete only in the mid-1960s. However, 1958 was the year that marked the official suppression of the standard studio orchestras, and this date seems to be the most appropriate to mark the end of film music's classical style, which for the past twenty-five years had been strongly associated with those very orchestras.

CHAPTER 2

The Style of Classical Hollywood Music

W hat exactly is the classical Hollywood music style? How can we distinguish a classical Hollywood score from, say, a coeval Italian score? To answer the first question, we have to detect the typical characteristics that define classical Hollywood music. In short, we have to define its style. To give a definition as articulate as possible, I subdivide film-music style into four areas: *language, techniques, musical means*, and typical *formal functions*.

Language

In chapter 1, I surveyed the linguistic changes of classical Hollywood music throughout its history. Besides influences, updates, and the composers' idiomatic differences, Hollywood music language is basically *tonal* and *Romantic*. In particular, the model is the late-Romantic art music bridging the nineteenth and twentieth centuries, the most prominent names being Richard Wagner, Richard Strauss, Gustav Mahler, Giacomo Puccini, Pyotr Tchaikovsky, and Sergei Rachmaninov. Linguistically, in the 1930s, Hollywood music was already old—drawing from a dialect that was already considered outdated and "conservative." The avant-garde twentieth-century music—atonality, polytonality, twelve-tone music, and the like—was at first completely ignored and then integrated only partially and mostly for specific narrative reasons.

Why did Hollywood choose an old-fashioned dialect, rather than a contemporary one, as advocated, for example, by Adorno and Eisler? The use of a twentieth-century modernist dialect, they explained, would make music more flexible and better responsive to the speed and fragmentation of film editing, compared to the long melodies of the Romantic tonal dialect.[1] There were several reasons for opting for an outmoded dialect, some of which can be easily guessed. For example, the producers, those who paid for the music, were notoriously uncultured musically—and not only musically. Anecdotal testimonies on this point abound: "A motion picture producer is a man who knows everything there is to know about everything—except music."[2] Consequently, they preferred the musical dialect with which they were most familiar, namely the accessible Romantic tonal dialect as popularized by musical theater and popular songs. For the same reason, it is easy to see how products like Hollywood films—aiming at reaching as wide an audience as possible—obviously tended to use well-known "easy" formulas, familiar to the vast majority of viewers. Instinctively, those who were in charge of film production used themselves and their own tastes as a model of the average viewer.

Even more, the conservatism of the Hollywood music departments relied on the very musical education of the founding fathers of the craft, as Christopher Palmer explains.

> The main conservatory-bred composers like Miklós Rózsa, Erich Wolfgang Korngold and Bernard Herrmann were the exception rather than the rule: musical theatre was the cradle of Hollywood music, and the musical idiom of the theatre has always been conservative. Hence the fact that in Hollywood's formative years there grew up a deeply-entrenched conservatism which jealously guarded its prerogatives and was quick to suppress any "progressive" or "modernistic" tendencies among juniors or novices. . . . This musical isolationism was wholly typical: the "real" world would have decried the music of Korngold, Newman and Steiner as anachronistic and refused it a place, whereas the "fantasy-world" of Hollywood not only wanted it but encouraged its procreation in vast quantities. "Romantic" music, music of romance, of fantasy, dream, illusion: what more logical than that it should find a final refuge in the real world's dream-factory?[3]

Palmer's comments suggest two additional explanations for the choice of Romantic dialect: (1) the adoption of well-tested tools of nineteenth-century music theater—the leitmotiv being the most prominent—and (2) the "illusionistic" complicity that music was expected to have in the Hollywood "dream-factory." This illusionistic complicity is what I call "macro-emotive function" (see the introduction). Music consolidates the overall coherence of the film, helps viewers enter the film's "possible world," and facilitates the "suspension of disbelief" necessary to accept the narrative conventions.

Another explanation of the choice of the Romantic dialect has been given in terms of ideology and psychoanalysis. Caryl Flinn explains how this "outdated" music has a soothing effect on listeners since it evokes a "romantic" past, happier times in which people (supposedly) lived a simpler life in more cohesive communities, as opposed to the fragmentation, individualism, and complexity of contemporary society.[4] This nostalgia effect produced by the hummable nature of Romantic music makes it possible for film viewers to recover the "lost maternal object" in a sort of pleasant regression. Romantic music nostalgically reenacts the fusion with the mother's womb where the fetus lives in a sort of sound envelope: before seeing, the fetus can already hear his mother's voice, a hearing that is not yet semantic but musical.[5] Timothy E. Scheurer—from a semio-anthropological perspective—sees in Hollywood music, in its formulaic Romanticism and its many clichés, a musical equivalent of those recurring elements that make Hollywood genres—also based on formulas and clichés—a form of popular myth.[6]

The orchestra conductor John Mauceri reflects on how Hollywood and its musical community has been a sort of protected oasis in which Romantic dialect and its performance practices were preserved, as in a sort of time capsule.

> There is a real dynasty, a tradition that continues, and the tradition is based on a European tradition untouched by the horrors of the bombings of World War II. In fact, it [Hollywood] was the beneficiary of the people who escaped the war. The great European tradition came to Hollywood like that—suddenly. . . . I love working in Los Angeles. . . . There is a tremendous cultural tradition. . . . [Hollywood musicians] sound more like the Vienna Philharmonic before the war than the Vienna Philharmonic today. . . . In Europe, it became very wrong to play long notes, to play with vibrato, to play portamento, because this was considered emotional and maybe without taste. European orchestras are much colder now. Boulez and Stockhausen were just symptomatic of a change toward music. They played more schematic performances of Brahms; it is really inexcusable to take the emotion out of the music and to play a post–World War II twentieth-century style. Whereas in Hollywood one continues the great instrumental traditions of Europe because their homes were not bombed, they did not have to go into air-raid shelters, their children were not screaming in the night.[7]

More concretely, a formal/functional explanation of Hollywood's tendency to use the Romantic dialect lies in the narrative form of Hollywood films themselves. In classical Hollywood cinema, the primary purpose was to tell a story. Consequently, filmmakers had to make sure that viewers were able to easily reach an empathetic connection with the characters and to follow and understand the narrative in the simplest way possible. "Invisible editing," "transparent storytelling," and "unobtrusive style" are some terms recurrently associated with classical Hollywood cinema, where a well-constructed narrative is more important than the display of originality and personal style. Indeed, the narrative form is based on strong and proven formulas and norms: the "stairstep construction" that alternates propulsive and delaying narrative events; "dialogue hooks" that anticipate and help connect one scene to the next scene (antecedent/consequent); the "canonic story" that replicates the outline of the hero's journey typical of fairy tales; well-shaped characters who undertake well-motivated actions to achieve their well-defined goals; clearly specified deadlines; "closure effect" given by the closing of all the story lines and their channeling to the happy ending; and neoclassical criteria of unity of time, space, and action linked by a strong causality.[8] The storytelling is foregrounded, while the stylistic level tends to become invisible because it works in the background. Devices should not draw attention to themselves as technical processes: for example, a camera movement or an editing match must not be gratuitous but should respond to a narrative function and have a proper motivation. Likewise, music should cooperate to the narrative without drawing attention to itself.

The criterion of "inaudibility" is somewhat valid for all film-music styles, meaning that film music is generally subordinated to the visuals. This is particularly true with regard to the classical Hollywood style. For instance, it is evident how Ennio Morricone's music in a Sergio Leone Western is decidedly more obtrusive than Dimitri Tiomkin's in a Howard Hawks Western. Both composers and scholars have widely commented on the paradox of a kind of music that is supposed to be composed in such a way that it be almost inaudible and have rejected the idea that not being audible means not being useful or valuable.[9]

In Claudia Gorbman's *Unheard Melodies: Narrative Film Music*, "inaudibility" is the starting point to explain the role of film music, again from a psychoanalytic perspective. Gorbman equates film music with "Muzak," the background music aired in elevators and supermarkets. The function of Muzak (rebranded since 2013 as "Mood") is to soothe the consumers—in our case, the viewers—and to make them less problematic social elements: if they think less, they are supposed to buy more, either the goods in a supermarket or the story events in a film. Like Muzak/Mood in supermarkets and airports, film music is not intended to be listened to but is intended to make viewers less critical and to lubricate the cogs of the fictional machine. Music hides the technical "cinematic apparatus," makes it easier to accept the fictional world, and unites all viewers in a homogeneous listening community.[10] Anahid Kassabian has

more recently called this luring of the viewers into the film enacted by classi
cal Hollywood music "assimilating identification." [11]

Cognitive psychology, unlike psychoanalysis, presupposes an active viewer
who constructs the meaning of the film rather than passively receiving it;
then, the inaudibility phenomenon is explained within the "Congruence-
Associationist" framework, on the grounds of music's two components: the
acoustical and the affective. [12] In Annabel J. Cohen's words:

> While music in the film serves as a vehicle used to transport emotional mean-
> ing, it is a vehicle that is often "inaudible" . . . , much as the font of this page is
> transparent until I draw attention to it. We can discriminate between Courier
> and Galliard, but when reading, we don't really much care whether it is one
> or the other, as long as it is legible. Similarly, the viewer-listener accepts the
> musical meaning, but acoustical properties of the music itself seem to function
> transparently as a kind of "acoustical font." . . . In this analogy, we can consider
> music to have two components: an affective component and an acoustical,
> structural component. When these two components of music are presented
> simultaneously with a visual image, the conjunction of the affective element
> and the visual image makes a new meaningful whole, a whole much closer to
> our sense of reality than the visual image alone, or than the visual image con-
> joined with both the affective and acoustical components. Through the illusory
> conjunction process, the affect, originally carried via the acoustic properties of
> music, attaches to the visual stimulus. . . . Music is a vehicle transporting a vari-
> ety of information, only some of which is relevant to a particular cinematic
> goal. The brain seems to be able to select what is useful for the goal at hand. . . .
> This framework explains the puzzling and paradoxical role of background music
> in film. Music adds information that is both consistent and inconsistent with the
> narrative. The affective quality is consistent; the acoustical aspects of the music
> are not. Although the affective associations produced by the music seem to
> belong to the corresponding images, the sounds that produced those associa-
> tions do not. Somehow, the brain attends to this affective meaning, while ignor-
> ing or attenuating its acoustical source. [13]

This is why film music is inaudible: the acoustical/structural component—
the one on which we generally focus our attention during a concert—becomes
secondary in the audiovisual film experience, because our attention is focused
on something else. The viewer is concentrated on the unfolding of the narrative, and all the stylistic devices, including music, become unnoticeable. The

average viewer does not notice the nature or even the presence of music as he or she does not notice either the number of cuts and kinds of editing matches in a scene or the lighting pattern in a shot.

Hollywood's vocation for storytelling also explains why the tonal system is preferred to atonality. The tonal system, besides being based on universally shared intervals as the fifth and the octave, has a strong narrative nature.[14] In its moving to and from the tonic, it tells the story of a back-to-home journey across obstacles (dissonances), the clearing of such obstacles (resolution of the dissonances), and the final return to the starting point (the return to the tonic, often with a IV–V–I authentic cadence, a sort of musical happy ending). This journey looks very much like the archetypal journey narrated by Hollywood films.[15] Because of the widespread familiarity of its dialect, Romantic music could better act as a neutral vehicle of the affective component and thus was the best choice to fit the functional transparency that cinematic devices were required to have. On the contrary, avant-garde music, with its esoteric dialect, can hardly be perceived as neutral and would draw the listener's attention to its structural component. That is why—*pace* Adorno and Eisler—modernist music had almost no use in classical Hollywood cinema.

According to the musicologist Leonard B. Meyer, the universal appeal of Romantic music is due to the importance given more to secondary parameters (such as dynamics, agogics, and expression) than to primary parameters (overall form, harmony rules, syntactic relations between tones, and so forth).[16] Primary and secondary parameters are similar to the structural/affective distinction previously made. In Romantic music, the affective component has a greater importance than the structural one. The dialect of the Classical period, as in the music of Mozart and Haydn, is also based on melody and tonality, but the primary parameters are more important than the secondary ones and such music is then less suited to convey the affective/emotional component. On the other hand, according to Meyer, the modernist dialects inflate the secondary parameters to an extreme, to the detriment of the primary parameters that tend to lose any importance.[17] For instance, aleatoric music such as that of John Cage tends to have only secondary parameters. In Romantic music, despite the emphasis on secondary parameters, the primary parameters are still present to orientate the musical understanding. In modernist music, on the contrary, the common listener has no guide to follow; the piece of music may sound simply meaningless and emotionally neutral to the listener, when not causing anxiety because of the frustration of expectations and the total lack of some kind of conventional orientation signs.[18] For this

reason, unresolved dissonances and atonal writing can be accepted in Holly
wood when they are devices that perform an emotive function, as when they
can give their disorienting and distressing contribution to disturbing stories,
creepy characters, and ominous places.

Another characteristic of classical Hollywood music and of film music in
general, unlike the music compilations of silent cinema and apart from some
modern instances such as Stanley Kubrick's films, is the almost exclusive use of
original material instead of repertoire pieces. The reasons are both economic
and narrative. The economic reason can be easily explained: it was more afford-
able using original music—whose copyrights were owned by the studio—
than undertaking the costly and often intricate legal paperwork required to
secure the clearance for a copyrighted piece of music.[19] From a narrative
viewpoint, a famous repertoire piece such as Beethoven's Symphony no. 6 in
F Major (the *Pastoral* Symphony) or any easily recognizable piece is likely to
distract from the storytelling. If the viewer recognizes the piece, his attention
can be drawn away from the visuals and the accompanying affective component of the music. In this case, the listener already knows the piece; its
general structure is present to his memory and can be retrieved, inducing
the listener to follow the musical flow, to anticipate its development, to focus
on its structure. When hearing this music in a scene, the viewer would probably disconnect from the narrative and be led to metatextual considerations
such as "Ah! They are using the *Pastoral*. I wonder why they have chosen
it," not to mention the connotations and extratextual associations that each
famous repertoire piece carries along with it. In a hypothetical film where the
Pastoral were used as a background for an amiable party conversation in a
trendy Manhattan flat, the viewer might project the piece's traditional associations with shepherds and rural scenes on the visuals and judge the music to
be out of place.[20]

According to Hollywood conventions, the use of repertoire music should
have some kind of clear motivation. For example, in *People Will Talk* (Joseph L.
Mankiewicz, 1951, musical direction by Alfred Newman), Cary Grant plays
a professor who is also the conductor of the faculty's amateur orchestra.
They are shown rehearsing, quite appropriately, Brahms's *Academic Festival
Overture* (*Akademische Festouvertüre*, 1880, op. 80.) The film score presents
Brahms's theme even at a nondiegetic level, which is motivated both by the
congruence of the piece with the academic locale and because this piece is
also present within the narrative world. One of the most common uses of
repertoire music, and a Max Steiner trademark, is that of using it to clarify in

which geographical place or historical period the film is set. Think of Steiner's use of the southern folk tune "Dixie" in *Gone with the Wind* (Victor Fleming, 1939), or "London Bridge Is Falling Down" in the opening sequence of *Top Hat* (Mark Sandrich, 1935), to denote the British austerity of the "London Thackeray Club, Founded 1864" as the narration shows us the plaque at the club's entrance.

Techniques

In general, film music does not use the classical art-music forms of sonata, rondo, fugue, and the like. They are structurally too rigid, and their development requires too long a time and too foregrounded a position for the film's standards. Apparently with no form, film music actually has its own form in the film itself.[21] If film music cannot be said to have forms sensu stricto, it surely can be said to use structural techniques and formal strategies, the most widely used being *theme and variations*, *leitmotiv*, so-called *Mickey-Mousing*, and *dialogue underscoring*.

The *theme and variations* technique is borrowed from art music—it consists in presenting a theme, which will later be reprised and transformed in terms of rhythm, harmony, melodic shape, instrumentation, and so forth.[22] While theme and variations can be found in many styles of film music, two other techniques are more characteristic of the classical Hollywood style: leitmotiv and Mickey-Mousing.

Leitmotiv—coined for Richard Wagner's *Wort-Ton-Dramas*—is the association and identification of each character, situation, or idea with a musical motif, which is reprised and developed narratively throughout the work.[23] After Wagner, the leitmotiv has, borrowing Matthew Bribitzer-Stull's words, "provided a paradigm adopted by countless later composers across a wide variety of genres" and can be characterized as "bifurcated in nature, comprising both a musical physiognomy and an emotional association; . . . developmental in nature, evolving to reflect and create new musico-dramatic contexts. . . . Leitmotifs contribute to and function within a larger musical structure."[24] Probably also because of the Founding Fathers' familiarity with Wagnerian music, the leitmotiv was largely adopted in Hollywood, in a more concise version that could better fit the shorter developmental space available in films, what Royal Brown has called a "condensed leitmotiv."[25] The leitmotiv technique is an excellent fit for film narration because it is an efficient aid to memorize and recognize characters and situations; it reinforces the film narrative through a parallel musical storytelling and gives the overall score a coat of cohesion and formal coherence.

The other typical technique is *Mickey-Mousing*. In American cinema, it seems to have been inherited from the musical accompaniment used in vaudeville, where the actors' antics and tumbles used to be stressed and punctuated by snare-drum rolls and cymbal clashes.[26] Musically, Mickey-Mousing is largely informal and designed to adhere tightly to the visuals, and it can be defined as a tight series of "explicit sync points." An explicit sync point is that moment where a musical gesture and a visual action undoubtedly match, the composer having deliberately composed with that precise sync point in mind.[27] A typical example is a descending movement in the visuals mirrored by a descending gesture in the music, like someone falling down a flight of stairs accompanied by a rapidly descending violins scale. As the term itself suggests, Mickey-Mousing derives from cartoons, where this technique is strongly present: think of Scott Bradley's scores for MGM's *Tom and Jerry* short films, in which the mouse's furtive footsteps are individually mirrored by plucks of *pizzicato* strings.[28] Herein, the term "Mickey-Mousing" is used each time the music closely duplicates the visual action, not just as a technique for cartoons or slapstick comedies. The term is used this way by practitioners too, and in classical Hollywood music, Mickey-Mousing is employed, in a more or less marked way, for dramatic effect as well, not merely for comic episodes.[29] Steiner was the undisputed champion of dramatic Mickey-Mousing. For him, film music had to "fit like a glove," and his point is clearly demonstrated in the score he composed for *The Informer* (John Ford, 1935).[30] Even Korngold's music, which is less adherent to visuals, presents episodes of Mickey-Mousing: in *The Sea Hawk* (Michael Curtiz, 1940), Alan Hale's character stuns the prison guard with a bang on the head, which is stressed by music. In *The Adventures of Robin Hood* (Michael Curtiz and William Keighley, 1938), the villain Sir Guy / Basil Rathbone is stabbed to death by Robin and falls down the stairs accompanied by a descending musical gesture. Part of the Mickey-Mousing technique is the *stinger*, that is, a *sforzando* chord that dramatically underlines a crucial event, often a narrative twist as seen in *Casablanca* (Michael Curtiz, 1942), when Ilsa / Ingrid Bergman suddenly points a gun at Rick / Humphrey Bogart.[31]

The preference of the classical Hollywood style for the leitmotiv and Mickey-Mousing techniques can be explained by the strong penchant for storytelling, which tends to have all formal devices invisible/inaudible and motivated compositionally so that they do not distract from the narrative.

Consider the poetics of musical realism of the early years of sound cinema: it reveals a concern that the presence of music, not motivated realistically by showing a diegetic on-screen source, could indeed draw the viewer's attention to the music rather than to the narrative. Similarly, the tight adherence of nondiegetic music to the visuals can be explained by the attempt to motivate its source. These days, the Mickey-Mousing technique is obsolete and attracts the viewer's attention to the structural aspects of music rather than making the music transparent. Yet, following the aforementioned "Congruence-Associationist" theory, it can be argued that in the early days when nondiegetic music was suspected of not being transparent and motivated enough, Steiner had this idea: if music seemed to emanate from the actors' movements, maybe viewers would not be distracted by asking themselves where that music came from.[32] The same can be said of leitmotivs. A leitmotiv is so tied to the character that the music appearance is simply motivated by the character's arrival.

Another technique that sometimes showed a similarly tight correspondence between the music and what happened on-screen was *dialogue underscoring*, that is, music accompanying a dialogue scene. Virtually all dialogue—especially sentimental exchanges—had a musical backing in classical Hollywood. However, one needs to distinguish the case in which some music was merely placed in the background to fill the silence—what has been derogatorily called "wallpaper" music—from that in which dialogue underscoring was modeled around the actor's lines, as an opera composer would work taking the libretto into account.[33] In the first instance, music acted as a sound-coloring layer for the actors' lines; for an extreme example that resorts to stock music just as a silence filler, see *Glen or Glenda* (Edward D. Wood Jr., 1953). In the second instance, the composer would take into consideration the pitch of the actors' voices, their timbre, the meaning of the single lines, and the pace and flow and the pauses in the dialogue, and he would write the music accordingly. The composer would write above or below the actors' pitches so that music would not interfere with the frequencies of their voices; he would make sure that the orchestral timbres blended harmoniously with those of the actors; he would meaningfully introduce a musical cell of an already presented leitmotiv to reinforce one particular line; and he would calculate when the dialogue paused, so that music could soar in those moments and retreat in the background as the dialogue resumed. For an example by the master of such technique, Korngold, listen to Robin and Marian's dialogue scenes in *The Adventures of Robin Hood*.

Musical Means

The score composed with all such aforementioned techniques had to be brought to life, performed through some *musical means*. The classical Hollywood standard was the richly orchestrated sound of the late nineteenth-century symphony orchestra. However, while Wagner's, Strauss's, and Mahler's orchestras had one hundred or more players, studio orchestras were assembled for recording, not for live performance, and consisted of a maximum of sixty players.[34] The symphony orchestra was the characteristic musical means for the entire period of the classical Hollywood music style. The first reason is historical. In the nickelodeons of the silent period, projections were accompanied by a pianist or a couple of instrumentalists. Larger theaters had a chamber orchestra made up of a dozen players. Only the luxurious picture palaces had a full symphony orchestra, and the most ambitious and important film productions, such as *The Birth of a Nation* (D. W. Griffith, 1915), used to tour along with a large symphony orchestra.[35] Thus the sound of the symphony orchestra began to be identified with quality screenings and first-class motion pictures. When introducing synchronized sound, Hollywood kept up with this association and enlarged the string section. As a matter of fact, these instruments, mostly for timbre reasons, are those that better blend with dialogue without masking effects—despite their being the most difficult to record and yielding an inferior sound fidelity in the new "microphone orchestras," according to early commentators.[36] Yet the predominance of the string section can again be seen as an aftermath of the silent period; a large string section was typical of the symphony orchestras of first-class theaters and distinguished them from the smaller "salon orchestras."[37] And so this was the reasoning: the symphony orchestra meant prestige; a large string section meant a symphony orchestra; hence, a large presence of strings meant prestige.

The preference for the symphony orchestra as the musical means for film music can also be explained in narrative terms: it is the richest ensemble as to instrumental timbres and is capable of so many color combinations and hues as to make it completely versatile in meeting a wide array of narrative demands.[38] Finally, the use of such musical means until the end of the 1950s was also due to union agreements stating that each studio had to maintain an in-house orchestra. As things were, the studios, following a criterion of efficiency, obviously tended to use the tools already at their disposal.

Speaking of musical means, a few words must be said about orchestration and orchestrators, those collaborators of the composer who we regularly find in the Hollywood film-scoring routines. In general, "to orchestrate" means expanding a piece of music—for example, one written in a condensed form on four staves—to a multiple-stave full score so that it is suitable for being played by a symphony orchestra. An "arrangement," on the other hand, means heavier interventions on the original composition, involving harmonic and contrapuntal additions or reshaping too, for example.[39] Orchestration is a crucial step in creating the overall color and sound of the piece by carefully balancing the various timbres of the orchestra. It affects greatly how a piece of music will finally sound and is not a mechanical operation but an essential part of the art of composition—an art itself, as Maurice Ravel's *Bolero* shows. That of the orchestrator has long been a controversial and often misunderstood role.[40] If you read through the end credits of the 1977 *Star Wars* film, you will spot "Music by John Williams" but then "Orchestrations: Herbert W. Spencer." The same happened with the 1930s Korngold scores: one would see Korngold's name accompanied by those of the orchestrators Hugo Friedhofer and Milan Roder. In a film scored by Morricone, on the contrary, one would read "Music composed, orchestrated and conducted by Ennio Morricone." This difference might produce (and it has indeed produced) the impression that there are, on the one hand, composers who are less musically literate and cannot really and fully "compose" and thus need to resort to the help of an orchestrator, and, on the other hand, fully trained composers capable of taking care of every aspect of the job.

The controversy is a long-standing one, as can be spotted in the reprinted tit-for-tat exchanges that followed the 1950 International Music Conference in Florence, where "the conference's European delegates [expressed] a general disdain for Hollywood film music."[41] Of particular interest was the duel between the American Lawrence Morton (who tried to explain the different work routines to the European colleagues) and the Austrian/British Hans Keller (who proudly and defiantly asserted the inferiority of Hollywood's music and Hollywood composers).[42] Unlike most European cinemas, Hollywood is a veritable industry and has traditionally had a strong hierarchical structure following a Fordist division of work. In the Hollywood music departments, it was not only customary but even stated by union rules that the composer had to sketch the music and then hand it to someone else to orchestrate it.[43] A biased view soon spread in less factorylike film industries such as those in Europe, where the composer was in charge of the entire process. Discussions about this controversy seem to be endless, as attested, for example, by the recurrence of themed contributions across the years in the *Film Score Monthly* magazine too—for example, in the article "What Orchestrators Do."[44]

Ben Winters reminds us of the traditional reluctance of accepting some share in paternity of the music: "Contextualizing composers within a community of creative personae certainly downplays the authorial power traditionally accorded them; and although Western musicology is now far more willing to recognize the complexities of authorship discourse, the figure of the 'genius' composer continues to cast a long shadow."[45] The artist/genius, as depicted since the Romantic era, is the one who creates in inspired solitude and is solely responsible for his creation, like God. This Romantic aesthetic bias, evidently, placed applied music and its collaborative nature—of which film music is perhaps the most salient twentieth-century manifestation—quite low in the rankings: "The very creation of a film score is often itself a collaborative process. Composers may work with other musicians to produce a score, and they might also frequently be required to co-operate with producers, directors, editors, recording engineers or other members of a film's creative team. In Hollywood, at least, this collaboration seems to have been most institutionalized during the studio system of the 1930s and 1940s."[46] At the aforementioned 1950 Florence conference, British composer Anthony Hopkins emphatically questioned the legitimacy of Hollywood composers with a language that clearly betrays the idealist "genius composer" viewpoint: "Who are these people, whose names never seem to appear on any concert programmes? What else have they written; what pages have they placed upon the altar of Art rather than on the lap of Mammon?"[47]

If in art-music circles not using an orchestrator is a matter of supposed artistic integrity, with Hollywood's time constraints and schedules, using an orchestration is a matter of absolute necessity. Pressing deadlines have been a general and international problem for film composers: in 1950 the Italian composer Enzo Masetti calculated that a thirty-minute film score could be delivered in the standard thirty days—orchestrated by the composer himself, as per the Italian custom—if the composer worked ten to eleven hours every day.[48] Concretely, writing music is also a matter of putting down on paper all the notes that an orchestra has to play. If the score is twenty minutes long with lento/andante melodies—long notes mean fewer notes—the composer may have time to orchestrate it himself in those thirty days. If, like in the Hollywood case, the score is sixty minutes long or more and with action-oriented cues—short notes mean more notes—there are just too many dots and lines to physically write them down on paper in the allotted time without any assistance. In Hollywood, to meet what Mervyn Cooke has called "punishing production schedules" and allow the already pressed composer to focus entirely on the key operation of creating the leitmotivs and composing the tight-timed single cues to accompany the scenes, all other technical and less-creative steps were assigned to the orchestrators.[49]

The orchestrator's task, then, was to transcribe and expand the composer's sketches, a basically condensed score, to a detailed full score without adding anything substantial. The sketches, typically written in haste and in a shorthand that could be idiosyncratic, would have been unintelligible for a conductor to lead the orchestra from or for a copyist to extract the individual parts.[50] The orchestrator would transform the shorthand into longhand, also proofreading and amending the possible errors that could have occurred in the hurry, such as a note not sharpened or flattened. Each composer had his trusted collaborators, who were familiar with his idiom and knew how to interpret the composer's shorthand. Even composers such as Copland, Korngold, and Rózsa, who skillfully orchestrated their own art-music compositions, used orchestrators when working in Hollywood. As admitted by Rózsa, "with the Hollywood tempo, it is not possible to write out the full score."[51] In these instances, the Hollywood orchestrator is not an arranger/orchestrator but an *expander/orchestrator*, an "intelligent copyist."[52] Thus Steiner describes his work on *Gone with the Wind* and his use of orchestrators: "But it's all from me. Nobody arranges anything from me. They just orchestrate what I write down. . . . Why sure, you got to have orchestrators. How are you going to write all that? [*laughs*] You couldn't do it. It's done from score. You see, I write six lines, or eight lines. The original. They take it off and put it in score. It's no great trick."[53]

There are film composers who have worked for/in Hollywood and have resisted the use of orchestrators: for example, Ennio Morricone, Georges Delerue, more recently Howard Shore, and more notoriously Bernard Herrmann. These composers have preferred to do all the work themselves, a choice that can be the result of an unconventional temperament, a lack of trust in collaborators, the desire to stand out, being granted sufficient time to take care of the entire process themselves, or an influence from the aforementioned art-music prejudices. Herrmann explains: "This whole rubbish of other people orchestrating your music is so wrong. . . . To orchestrate is like a thumbprint. I can't understand having someone else do it. It would be like someone putting color to your paintings."[54] In reply to this negative myth of orchestrators, Prendergast writes:

The myth is simply that Bernard Herrmann is the only major film composer in Hollywood who does his own orchestrations. . . . This assertion has found its way into the film-music aficionado's lore and seems to owe its existence to two things: (1) An ignorance of the real relationship between the composer and the orchestrator in Hollywood, and (2) a blind faith in the word of Bernard Herrmann on this subject who is in no small part responsible for the propagation of the myth. There are numerous composers in Hollywood whose sketches are so complete and so detailed that the orchestrator really becomes, in effect, an intelligent copyist.[55]

Prendergast also nuances the film-music versus art-music contraposition, noting that having an orchestrator helping with the expansion of a composer's sketches is a practice that predates film scoring and has not been limited to it: "Prokofiev, with the ironic exception of his score to the film *Alexander Nevsky*, had all of his scores orchestrated from detailed sketches."[56]

However, for the sake of nuancing, the other side of the spectrum should also be acknowledged: there are indeed cases where the orchestrator can be said to be a coauthor of the final result—an *arranger/orchestrator* in this case—in scoring projects in which teamwork has decidedly more weight. Charlie Chaplin was credited as the music composer for his films. Actually, he mostly whistled the tunes, which were then arranged for orchestra by a number of collaborators, among them David Raksin, who took care of Chaplin's melodies for *Modern Times* (1936).[57] In the Danny Elfman / Steve Bartek duo, the self-taught Elfman writes the overall musical structure and then hands it to his longtime collaborator to arrange it for orchestra: tellingly, unlike other composers who do their own orchestrations when not pressed by the Hollywood deadlines, Elfman's concert work *Serenata Schizophrana* also credits Bartek as "orchestrator" (and Edgardo Simone).[58] In *Pirates of the Caribbean: On Stranger Tides* (Rob Marshall, 2011), Hans Zimmer is credited as the film's composer, but as many as four orchestrators and seven "additional music" composers are credited. For his Oscar-winning score to *The Artist* (Michel Hazanavicius, 2011), Ludovic Bource—trained in piano, jazz, and pop music—was assisted by a team of eleven orchestrators, additional composers, and arrangers, according to IMDb.

Given the problematic ambiguity of the term "orchestrator," the divergence in film-scoring practices from one cinematic culture to another, the diverse personal idioms that come with diverse quantity of concrete note-input work, and the different deadlines and work organization of film music and art music, any assessment of what using an orchestrator means should be carefully gauged vis-à-vis the situation and context under examination. The orchestrator was not and is not necessarily the "ghost writer" of Hollywood composers. The fact of using or not using an orchestrator should not per se be seen as a stigma or a merit but as a manifestation of a different modus operandi based on different production contexts.

Functions

What is the typical formal function fulfilled by the classical Hollywood style? Claudia Gorbman sees Max Steiner as the epitome of the classical style and illustrates his style in these terms: "So while illustration to the minutest detail was a hallmark of Steiner's style in particular, our overall model of classical-era film music also must include the general tendency toward musical illustration."[59] Peter Larsen writes that "the continuous accompaniment in *King Kong* . . . points forwards towards what was going to be one of the characteristics of Steiner and the other composers of the Golden Age: the exact synchronization of music and images."[60] Similarly, Mervyn Cooke adds, "One of two principal types of nondiegetic scoring in the Golden Age [was] the graphically illustrative music popularly known as mickey-mousing, or 'catching the action.'"[61] Fred Karlin and Rayburn Wright explain: "If you provide a musical accent for a specific moment in the drama, you are hitting the action. . . . Almost all film music from the thirties, forties, and fifties was conceived this way."[62] For Kathryn Kalinak, the fundamental characteristic of classical Hollywood music is the "musical illustration of narrative content, especially the direct synchronization between music and narrative action."[63] There is a general agreement, as can be seen, that the most peculiar characteristic of the classical style was the tight synchronization of music and image achieved through Mickey-Mousing. Yet Mickey-Mousing is a *technique* (an approach to composition that results in music being closely adherent to the visuals); it is *not* a function (the purpose of a given technique, in this case). In other words, Mickey-Mousing was employed to achieve some effect or implement some strategy, not for its own aesthetic value. It is not sufficient here to notice that the classical Hollywood scoring employed Mickey-Mousing, musical illustration, direct synchronization, etcetera. We need to take a further step and determine why composers used this technique so extensively and universally, which begs the question: What is the function that Mickey-Mousing fulfilled?

The classical Hollywood style has been called "excessively obvious" since narrative information tended to be overstated in case viewers might fail to notice something important.[64] Classical narration used music, among other devices, to help viewers understand and interpret correctly and as effortlessly as possible the *plot* presented in the film so that they could mentally construct from it the chronologically and causally ordered *story*.[65] In order to have a correct mental *construction* of a certain world, a necessary prerequisite is to gain a correct and as complete as possible *perception* of that world. Music helped this perception: it pinpointed the important information and guided the viewers' attention, not only through Mickey-Mousing but also through leitmotiv. What Michel Chion says about sound in general can be applied to music as well.

> If the sound cinema often has complex and fleeting movements issuing from the heart of a frame and teeming with characters and the other visual details, this is because the sound superimposed on the image is capable of directing our attention to a particular visual trajectory. . . . [Mickey-Mousing] . . . has been criticized for being redundant, but it has an obvious function nonetheless. Try watching a Tex Avery cartoon without the sound, especially without the musical part. Silent, the visual figures tend to telescope, they do not impress themselves well in the mind, they go by too fast. Owing to the eye's relative inertia and laziness compared to the ear's agility in identifying moving figures, sound helps to imprint rapid visual sensations into memory. Indeed, it plays a more important role in its capacity of aiding the apprehension of visual movements than in focusing on its own substance and aural density.[66]

The Mickey-Mousing technique thus primarily fulfills what I call a *spatial perceptive function*.[67] It makes viewers notice what narration wants them to notice by pointing their attention to a given action or visual detail within the framed space. For example, in *Casablanca*, when French captain Renault finally sides with the anti-Nazi cause and throws a bottle of Vichy water in the trash can, Steiner marks the dumping of the bottle with a synchronized low chord to point our attention to the highly symbolic meaning of this action. Mickey-Mousing might appear the least interesting of writing techniques to analysts and critics who search a film score for some "message" or implicit meaning: Mickey-Mousing just does not "communicate" anything; it "merely" replicates (parrots, some would perhaps say) what we are already seeing.[68] Yet, even if it may not communicate anything, the Mickey-Mousing technique can fulfill an important function: that of guiding the viewers' eyes within the filmic space.

To summarize the four-point stylistic definition that has been articulated so far, the classical Hollywood style is characterized by the adoption of the late-Romantic dialect (*language*); the use of leitmotiv and Mickey-Mousing (*techniques*); the use of the symphony orchestra (*musical means*); and although it also performed other *formal functions* typical of film music—such as the macro-emotive function, the micro-emotive function, the temporal perceptive function, and the cognitive function—its identifying one was the spatial perceptive function. In the next chapter, we shall see how these stylistic parameters changed in the passage from the "classical" to the "modern" style.

CHAPTER 3

The Modern Hollywood
Music Style

The change in contractual arrangements between musicians and studios in 1958 can be seen as the end boundary of the classical style. Film music underwent such changes in terms of language, techniques, musical means, and functions that the new style blossoming in the 1960s can be called "modern style."[1]

Cinema and Film Music in the 1960s

In the 1960s, European cinema regained positions over Hollywood on the international scene, and Indian, Japanese, South American, and other cinemas also gained an increased visibility. A more personal, experimental, or socially engaged cinema made by "auteurs" challenged the studio- and producer-based escapist cinema of Hollywood. In modern art cinema, style and themes became more important than narrative. Consider Federico Fellini's "excessive" and conspicuously idiosyncratic style, or Alain Resnais's narrative ambiguity, or Ingmar Bergman's "important topics," or Michelangelo Antonioni's idle moments and *temps mort*, in which the action slackens and narrative causality is weakened. "Specific sorts of realism motivate a loosening of cause and effect, an episodic construction . . . , and an enhancement of the film's symbolic dimension through an emphasis on the fluctuations of character psychology. . . . In the name of verisimilitude, the tight causality of classical Hollywood construction is replaced by a more tenuous linking of events," David Bordwell explains.[2]

Now cinema was not much interested in the exterior development of actions linked one to another in a straight line, oriented toward a final resolution, and following tight cause/effect relationships. Cinema was instead concerned with the visual representation of the characters' inner life. As the use of film style, so the use of music became freer and even defiant of traditional norms. Russell Lack explains:

> Music becomes especially important since characters come increasingly to resemble feelings rather than having fully sketched-out biographies. Feelings rather than characters are transformed depending on what type of cinematic time they inhabit. This is something like a psychology of pure feelings as opposed to one rooted in characters or individuals. Accordingly, music acts crucially as a navigator of feeling dispossessed from bodies, from biographies. . . . Music in the modern cinema freely moves between the diegetic source that is revealed in the image and the non-diegetic music whose source is never revealed and vice versa.[3]

Many emerging European authors of the period were wary of using music, such as Michelangelo Antonioni or Robert Bresson: "How many films are patched up by music! Films are flooded with music. This prevents us from seeing that there is nothing in those images."[4] Some were even openly hostile. For instance, Eric Rohmer said, "With few exceptions, I reject the so-called film music, that is music that is not actually located in the space and time of the film. . . . Music is cinema's falsest friend, as it deprives film time of its peculiar exclusivity and objectivity."[5] When employed, music was not to sustain the narrative step by step because now cinema deliberately sought non-linear and ambiguous forms. Discussing one of the central films of the 1960s auteur cinema, Ermanno Comuzio reveals that "when Alain Resnais hired Fusco to work for *Hiroshima, mon amour* (1959), the composer immediately decided that he would not work out fixed themes for the characters, would not systematically emphasize the images, and would elude synchronism and carefully avoid any references to the Japanese locale."[6] As can be seen, here we have multiple departures from Hollywood's musical style: no leitmotiv ("fixed themes"); no Mickey-Mousing or music/image parallelism ("emphasize the images"; "synchronism"); no musical quotes to add ethnic color or denote places, as Steiner typically used to ("references to the Japanese locale"). Commenting on Georges Delerue's music for the film *Love on the Run* (*L'Amour en fuite*, François Truffaut, 1979), Lack explains, "The most notable difference from the Hollywood tradition of romanticism is that orchestral flourishes are not generally used to track movement but rather to set a scene."[7]

The Style of Modern Film Music

If we examine the works of Ennio Morricone (1928–2020), John Barry (1933–2011), and Henry Mancini (1924–94), three of the most successful representatives of this new style, it is patent that the classical-style "spatial perceptive function" (the case in which music directs the viewer's attention to a particular element inside the framing) holds a minority position in the new style. Consequently, the Mickey-Mousing and leitmotiv techniques became obsolete. Modern style favored the emotive function (adding or reinforcing the emotional tone of a scene) or the cognitive function (clarifying or implying connotations and implicit meanings). The only kind of perceptive function retained is the temporal one: changing the perception of the visual rhythm, or temporally linking through a musical *continuum* events that might otherwise seem disconnected.

In the 1960s, the classical studio system was weakened by a severe crisis: "Hollywood seemed besieged from a variety of fronts."[8] The crisis was triggered or fueled by a number of factors, including new demographics, changes in urbanization, competing entertainment and spare-time activities, and the rising popularity and technical advancement of television, which had entered, at the end of the previous decade, its own "Golden Age."[9] Obviously, the crisis of what used to be the principal medium of mass entertainment manifested itself as a contraction of the production and consumption: "In the ten-year period from 1960 to 1970, the number of feature films released by the seven major film companies . . . dropped from 184 to 151. In the same period, the number of movie theaters in the country dropped from almost 17,000 to just under 13,500."[10] Yet American cinema, like the phoenix, was about to rise again from its own ashes: "the years between 1967 and 1975 became the Golden Age of the 'New Hollywood.'"[11] The new generation of American filmmakers who started their careers in these years was strongly influenced by the Nouvelle Vague (the "New Wave") and the European auteur cinema.[12]

The use and style of music, similarly, was also influenced by the European music style. Compared to the classical Hollywood tradition, European style had always been characterized by a lower adherence between music and visuals and a less insisted use of leitmotiv.[13] Also, the European style distinctly favored the technique of the *closed musical number*. Instead of a continuous stream of music based on interwoven leitmotivs, the score was structured through a series of isolated set pieces closed in themselves. This is more similar to the Italian and French operas, constituted by musically self-sufficient arias clearly separated by *recitativi*, rather than to the continuous musical stream of Wagner's *Wort-Ton-Dramas*, which had such a seminal influence on Hollywood music.[14] This modern stylistic feature can be found in the works of Nino Rota, for instance, as elaborated by Jerrold Levinson: "Another function of non-diegetic film music is to bind the incidents of a film together into a common ambiance. The thematic, instrumental, and stylistic continuities typical of film scores help create a consistency of tone or feeling across the span of a film, especially where the events presented are not tightly connected in a dramatic sense. Thus, rather than any narrative task, this seems to be the main function of Rota's score for Fellini's *Amarcord*."[15] Rota's score for *The Godfather* (Francis Ford Coppola, 1972), an American production by a less eccentric author than Fellini, nevertheless still shows that his technique is not akin to the Hollywood style but based on closed musical numbers and little adherence to the visual action. In the 1960s, this style spread internationally because of the worldwide success of European films; Rota's music, for instance, had a large diffusion and visibility thanks to his collaboration with Fellini.

The technique of the closed musical number was also used by Ennio Morricone and disseminated through the enormous success of his scores for Sergio Leone's "Spaghetti Westerns."[16] Morricone was certainly one of the leading representatives of the new style, and he was equally far from both Hollywood's as well as Italy's classical film music, exemplified by Alessandro Cicognini's scores for the films of Alessandro Blasetti, or Vittorio De Sica's Neorealism, or the *Don Camillo* series: *cantabile* music in a basically Romantic dialect that incorporates gestures and inflections from the Italian opera as well as from regional and vernacular musical heritages. Morricone—not only rigorously conservatory-trained but also an active promoter of avant-garde music—openly rejected the classical style: "In composing the music for Leone's movies I deliberately ignored the American precedents. In general the Americans use symphonic music even for Westerns, something I never do. I find symphonic language excessive, too rich for films. For the main theme of *A Fistful of Dollars* I played an old Gypsy piece for Sergio which I had arranged years before for a television program, accompanying it with whip lashes, whistles, and anvils."[17] Besides musical language, Morricone also contested classical Hollywood's wall-to-wall music: "The screen reflects a flat image that, perhaps, without music would remain flat. Music gives it a sense of vertical depth and horizontal dynamism, which can only be possible if music is surrounded by silence. This is necessary because our hearing, and therefore our brain, cannot listen and understand more sounds of a different nature simultaneously. We will never understand four people speaking at the same time. It is absolutely necessary, if the director wants to consider music *in the right way*, to isolate music and give the audience the time to listen to it in the best way."[18] Morricone argues against not only the dialogue-underscoring technique but also other classical techniques, such as Mickey-Mousing and leitmotiv, that do not give music a central perceptual position. In Leone's films, music emerges in closed musical numbers when there is no dialogue, similar to Italian opera: "I think that music should be present when the action stops and crystallizes; as in musical theater we can find the *recitativo* and the aria, music in cinema should be placed in correspondence with the aria, when the action stops and there are thoughts and introspection, not when the action has its own narrative dynamics."[19] As to the adherence to visuals, Morricone categorically rejects synchronism: "Music must follow its own discourse and have its own unity; encouraging synchronism means giving up all this."[20] In general, what Morricone rejects is the inaudibility of film music, which we have seen as being one of the cornerstones of the classical Hollywood style, and the consequent *background music*. "In fact, Morricone's music can best be described as foreground music," Charles Leinberger argues.[21]

Unlike the classical Hollywood style that undoubtedly influenced the practice of composition for film in general but was applied in its full form only in Hollywood, modern style was an international style, its features being present in films from different nations. Low adherence to action and closed musical numbers can be found in the scores by the French composers Francis Lai and Michel Legrand, the Argentinian Lalo Schifrin, the British John Barry, and the American Henry Mancini. Consider the action sequences in many James Bond films. John Barry's music gives pace and suspense, but compared to the classic adventure films, it follows a freer musical development, one not tightly synchronized with the visuals. The difference is remarkable if we compare Monty Norman's score for the first James Bond film, *Dr. No* (Terence Young, 1962), with those composed by Barry for the following films of the series. In the *Dr. No* scene where Bond squashes the tarantula that the villains had hidden in his bed, Norman uses many punctuational stingers and a kind of Mickey-Mousing to accentuate each time Bond hits the spider. Norman seems to still be following more traditional techniques. Other occurrences of such explicit synchronism are not found in the following Barry scores, when the modern style was already well established.

As to the *musical means*, the symphony orchestra was no longer the standard in modern style. However, it was still used in some blockbusters or prestige films such as *The Lion in Winter* (Anthony Harvey, 1968, music by John Barry), *Ryan's Daughter* (David Lean, 1970, music by Maurice Jarre), *Tom Jones* (Tony Richardson, 1963, music by John Addison), and *The Godfather*. The choice now ranged from jazz combos to big bands to small chamber ensembles

(*To Kill a Mockingbird*, Robert Mulligan, 1962, music by Elmer Bernstein) or even solo improvisation on the visuals (Miles Davis's music for *Ascenseur pour l'échafaud*, Louis Malle, 1957).[22]

As to the *language*, modern style included a wide variety, ranging from jazz to funk-soul, rhythm 'n' blues, rock, and "easy-listening" pop. It was open to any other languages that were either trendy or experimental, including dialects of twentieth-century art music such as atonality, modalism, and dodecaphonism—for example, Leonard Rosenman's atonal score for *Fantastic Voyage* (Richard Fleischer, 1966) or David Shire's twelve-tone score for *The Taking of Pelham 123* (Joseph Sargent, 1974). These linguistic innovations were due not only to aesthetic or realistic reasons but also to an unprecedented phenomenon: the increasing commercial importance of film-music albums in the 1960s. The adoption of contemporary and popular dialects in film music was an effective way to attract young audiences, which were now the basis of cinema attendance. Film music had to update according to the tastes of the new audience, which were certainly not in line with the symphonic late-Romanticism of the classical style.[23] One of the reasons for this linguistic renewal, then—and certainly not the least important—was market orientation. The most obvious consequence was the growing importance of pop songs as core elements of the music track.

Modern Style and the Economic Motivation

The relation between cinema and songs is as old as cinema itself.[24] The main reason has always been that of achieving the maximum economic benefit by having the film and the music industries supporting each other. As early as the nickelodeon period, the fad of *illustrated songs*, a kind of "pre-karaoke," had been launched and was directly financed by music publishing houses.[25] Music composed to accompany such silent films as *The Birth of a Nation* (D. W. Griffith, 1915, music by Joseph Carl Breil) and *What Price Glory* (Raoul Walsh, 1926, music by Erno Rapée) was immediately adapted into songs and sold successfully.[26] In the early sound films, the presence of music was either sparse and diegetic in the talkies or assembled in a string of musical numbers in the all-singing musical revues. In either case, popular songs had the lion's share, and film studios either merged with music publishing companies or started their own subsidiaries in order to gain fully from the profitable song craze.[27] With the end of this trend and the emergence of the classical music style, songs continued to be featured in films, since their economic potential was still very important. All-symphonic film-music albums were rare and the market for film-music records was almost exclusively concerned with songs, which were consequently included in the films' soundtrack to promote the sale of the records.[28]

In classical Hollywood cinema, the "economic motivation" for the presence of a song in a film was masked with a realistic motivation: the song appeared at diegetic level as a live performance or as a broadcast coming from some on-screen visible radio. The proper locus to showcase a saleable song was the diegetic musical number by the female lead—a striking example of Laura Mulvey's "female spectacle"—often accompanied by some bankable musician.[29] Such instances can be found both in comedies such as *Ball of Fire* (Howard Hawks, 1941), featuring Barbara Stanwyck singing "Drum Boogie" accompanied by drummer Gene Krupa; and in dramas such as *To Have and Have Not* (Howard Hawks, 1944), where Lauren Bacall sings a couple of songs by Hoagy Carmichael, with the composer himself playing the piano. In the classical-style invisible narration, songs used at nondiegetic level were problematic because they were too noticeable. First, lyrics could distract from the storytelling and interfere with dialogue. Famous songs could evoke associations and connotations that were likely to disconnect the viewer from the film's narrative world. Lyrics are sung words that can overlap with and mask the spoken words of dialogue, while instrumental music is a background of a different sonic quality: a wordless background that leaves better room for the words of the dialogue. Also, a song is in itself less "inaudible" and less concealable than instrumental music: the structure of a song is more rigid and cannot be bent and adapted to visuals, as is the case with orchestral music.[30] The use of a song at diegetic level—through the presentation of a musical number—put the narrative to a temporary stop, but it did not disrupt the narration's invisibility because it was motivated realistically. In this way, it was possible to elegantly mask the actual economic motivation, which was to prompt viewers to go and buy tie-in records or sheet music when leaving the theater.

The balance between realistically motivated diegetic songs and compositionally motivated nondiegetic orchestral music broke down in the 1960s, when an extrinsic economic motivation became mostly evident and prevailed over intrinsic aesthetic and formal motivations. The first reason was technological. The introduction and rapid diffusion of the 33⅓ rpm long-playing disc caused the blossoming of a massive record industry.[31] Whereas previous 78 rpm discs could reach a maximum of four to five minutes of music per side, accommodating the standard length of one song, the new format could store up to forty minutes, meaning that just a couple of songs were not enough to make a disc. Another reason was a change in the audience demographics. In the 1950s, film producers had discovered the potential of the teen audience and the importance of complying with its musical tastes, especially after the huge success of such films as *Blackboard Jungle* (Richard Brooks, 1955), which featured rock 'n' roll music by Bill Haley and His Comets, and whose LP album sold spectacularly.[32] Most important, the demise of the classical studio system in the 1960s caused a radical change in production practice. Whereas in the old days the decisive profits were the total net revenue of the studio (the sum of all the film projects), now the decisive profits were those of the single films: "as the studios concentrated more on distribution than production . . . , independent producers assembled their own production 'packages,' including personnel."[33] In the new highly competitive market, the consequence was that each film had to be an economic success. To secure such a success, a good solution was to team up with the burgeoning record industry, balancing a weak box office performance with potentially better sales of the film's LP album. Controlling both the film and record industries and applying a carefully devised, synergistic cross-promotion not only advertised the film via the presence of the song on the radio and in record stores but also promoted the song by having it showcased in the film. In the 1960s, every major studio became a shareholder in some existing record company, created its own subsidiary in order to collect profits from both markets, or became part of a merger with some music publishing company—for example, Universal Pictures was acquired by MCA, Music Corporation of America, in 1962, together with Decca Records.[34] All these factors led to a new pop song craze that fueled the rise of the modern style, of which the use of economically motivated pop songs is a central feature.

If we compare the classical style with the modern style as to the way songs were inserted in films, the difference can be seen in the move from the diegetic to the nondiegetic level, that is, the "interpolated songs" phenomenon.[35] From the 1960s, pop songs were placed at the nondiegetic level and took over some of the formal functions previously performed by orchestral music, such as linking together the segments of a montage sequence or clarifying the emotional mood of a scene. The film credited with having established this trend—thanks to its resounding success both in theaters and in record stores—is *A Man and a Woman* (*Un homme et une femme*, Claude Lelouch, 1966, music by Francis Lai).[36] Again, the problem is that songs used at nondiegetic level are less flexible than orchestral music and risk appearing as being arbitrarily inserted into the film for an overtly economic motivation. Sometimes songs are indeed thematically congruent, narratively functional, cleverly placed, and can function as effectively as an orchestral score. The music track of *American Graffiti* (George Lucas, 1973), for example, is made up of early 1960s songs, with each scene supported by a different song—having a formally consistent compositional motivation and being functional to the nostalgic mood of the film. The music is also motivated realistically, not just because of the time setting of the story but also because of the constant presence of car radios in the pro-filmic space. This results in a subtly ambiguous play between diegetic and nondiegetic levels: Are the songs broadcast by the radio sets or are they nondiegetic? Can the characters actually hear the songs or, because the songs are outside the narrative world, can they be heard only by the viewers?[37] Other examples of songs included in a film for economic reasons and yet well integrated into the narrative can be found in John Barry's works for the James Bond series, starting with *Goldfinger* (Guy Hamilton, 1964). The theme song ("Goldfinger") is showcased in a dedicated spot outside the narrative, in a title sequence constructed like a "proto-video clip."[38] The lyrics tie in with the film's narrative and themes, and its musical theme is recurrently presented in instrumental versions within the narrative, thus fulfilling formal functions similar to those once fulfilled by leitmotivs in the classical style.[39]

Nonetheless, a poorly motivated orchestral intervention is still less incongruous and obtrusive than a poorly motivated song, because the latter tends to be more noticeable. The minor flexibility of songs resulted in debatable cases of incongruity and misplacement. One example is *The Graduate* (Mike Nichols, 1967), in which Paul Simon and Art Garfunkel's songs have little or nothing to do with what happens in the visuals. Even the lyrics of the only song expressly written for the film ("Mrs. Robinson") have nothing to do with the Mrs. Robinson portrayed on-screen, as if the singer/songwriter duo was involved simply for a mutual commercial benefit and without even knowing what the film was about.[40] A textbook example is the bicycle-ride sequence in *Butch Cassidy* (George Roy Hill, 1969).[41] In this case, not only have the lyrics nothing to do with the film sequence, but the music idiom is also inconsistent with that of the rest of the score. "Raindrops Keep Fallin' on My Head" seems to have been forcefully inserted with the sole purpose of promoting Burt Bacharach's song.[42] The ultimate result of this market-oriented approach was the phenomenon of the *compilation score*, a film-music track built out of repertoire pop songs instead of original instrumental music in symphonic, jazz, pop, or rock dialect.[43] This technique was largely adopted by the industry after the success of *The Graduate* and applied with successful results in such films as *Easy Rider* (Dennis Hopper, 1969), *Mean Streets* (Martin Scorsese, 1973), and *The Last Picture Show* (Peter Bogdanovich, 1971). In these cases, the risk that more attention was paid to the commercial allure of a song rather than to its actual functionality and consistency with the film was at its highest.

Henry Mancini, the most influential modern-style Hollywood composer, was perhaps the deftest "tunesmith" of the period—"practically a brand name in pop culture"—balancing the old-school sense of drama with a knack for staying in tune with or even shaping himself the current musical trends.[44] John Caps explains:

> In a sense, Mancini was reinventing the language of film scoring. His personal sound was more than mere pop music while something less than pure jazz: a combination of pop melody and jazz inflections of the so-called West Coast Cool school. Mancini's first reinvention, then, was to popularize that sound in Hollywood and adapt it to the dramatic, narrative needs of movie soundtrack scoring. . . . He was the first multimedia music superstar precisely because he was reinventing the relationship between the soundtrack and those boomer ticket buyers, speaking in their vernacular. . . . Mancini's second reinvention . . . was to repackage soundtrack music as widely marketable discs for home listening. Best-seller charts, recording industry Grammy Awards, and even *DownBeat* magazine jazz polls all praised and promoted his early television music for the detective series *Peter Gunn* and, soon, a whole sequence of jazz-pop albums by Mancini.[45]

Typically, in Jeff Smith's words, "Mancini's scores emerge as collections of themes . . . [that] retain the shape and formal character of individual musical numbers, and they typically function with a comparable measure of musical autonomy. Like the songs of a musical, Mancini's themes display a mastery of song structures, a plethora of musical hooks, and a surfeit of memorable melodies. In their orientation toward tunes, Mancini's multitheme scores proved eminently suited to the format of pop album."[46]

The closed musical number technique is clearly more functional than the continuous leitmotivic flow of the classical style if the aim is to have the film score also exploited in a marketable easy-listening album. Many Mancini scores, while working efficiently in the films, seem to be also composed with the very album in mind, as they are typically made up of a string of independent and well-defined musical numbers. Think of the party sequences in

The Party (Blake Edwards, 1968), a slapstick comedy that once would have widely featured the Mickey-Mousing technique. On the contrary, the music track is a collection of cocktail and dance pieces, mainly diegetic. *Variety's* Eddie Kalish thus commented in 1961: "Most film scorers don't write with commercial values for the music in mind. They compose strictly for the film's requirements. Mancini says he does both. He, of course, composes to do the best job for the particular pic on which he's working, but he also considers the commercial value of the music as well."[47] *Bachelor in Paradise* (Jack Arnold, 1961) is another example of Mancini's ingenuity in displaying and promoting the title song throughout the film. The title song is introduced in the opening titles and then reprised in instrumental form, not only in the nondiegetic score but also as a Muzak-like diegetic wallpaper in the supermarket sequence. It is even evoked through the sound of the protagonist's doorbell, whose three tones are the very opening notes of the title song. Mancini perfectly incarnated and served the film industry / music industry synergy that was vital to 1960s Hollywood.

The Demise of the Classical Music Style

The landmark event of the end of the classical music style was perhaps the infamous sacking of Bernard Herrmann by Alfred Hitchcock, after Universal pressed the director to include an easy-listening song in *Torn Curtain* (1966).[48] Herrmann, who had composed the scores for eight of Hitchcock's films, including some of his biggest hits, was notoriously against the use of songs in films.[49] However, he had accepted the practice in a previous Hitchcock film, *The Man Who Knew Too Much* (1956), the song being "Que Sera, Sera" by Ray Evans and Jay Livingston. Ten years later, Herrmann refused to follow Hitchcock along the pop path. Herrmann recounts the breakup as follows: "[Hitchcock] said he was entitled to a great pop tune, I said, 'Look, Hitch, you can't outjump your own shadow. And you don't make pop pictures. What do you want with me? I don't write pop music.'"[50] The comparison of these two episodes clearly shows how the modern-style placement of songs in films radically differed from the classical style. The 1956 film had an orchestral score that served the film in the classical way. The marketable diegetic song featured in the film was motivated not only realistically—Doris Day's character is a singer and therefore it is highly plausible that she should sing—but also compositionally because the song is the narrative device that allows the kidnapped boy to be rescued. The presence of the song was not arbitrary, and its economic motivation was cleverly hidden. Using Herrmann's words, it was not "a pre-meditated attempt at song plugging."[51] On the contrary, in *Torn Curtain*, a tense and often crude portrayal of East Germany under the Stasi's yoke, there was no motivation at all to include a song, except that of selling tie-in LPs. Hitchcock replaced the uncooperative Herrmann with John Addison, who agreed to compose a singable love theme, which was adapted into the song "Green Years" (by Addison, Ray Evans, and Jay Livingston). Eventually, Hitchcock himself realized how the song would have been nonsensical in the film and decided not to use it, relegating it to the LP album.[52]

Mancini, Barry, and Morricone's growing reputation and the outstanding success in theater box offices and record stores of films such as *A Hard Day's Night* (Richard Lester, 1964, music by the Beatles), *A Man and a Woman*, and *The Graduate* led to the prevalence of the modern style, pop idioms, and songs throughout 1965–77. The young classically trained symphonic composers active in those years, such as Jerry Goldsmith, for one, were a discomforted minority: "Well, many of us composers are upset about this, because we get requests from producers that we've got to write a hit song. It's a real pain, because they forget what we're really supposed to be doing. It's a completely commercial device to try to promote the film. . . . It has nothing to do with anything dramatic in the picture, and this is a great annoyance to us all, but it's one of the syndromes of the business, and there isn't very much we can do about it."[53] Veteran film composer and University of Southern California teacher David Raksin lamented in 1974:

> I feel absurdly virtuous when I ask [my students] whether they can imagine pictures like *Easy Rider* or *The Last Picture Show* or *American Graffiti* with any other kind of music. The fact is that the music in those films was just what it should have been. But I do not find this to be equally true of all films in which such music is used. For unless we are willing to concede that what is essentially the music of the young is appropriate to all of the aspects of human experience with which films are concerned, we must ask what it is doing on the soundtracks of pictures that deal with other times and generations, other lives. It is one thing to appreciate the freshness and naivete of Pop music and quite another to accept it as inevitable no matter what the subject at hand.[54]

Even Mancini was well aware of the excessively commercial importance given to songs, to the detriment of narration: "The minute you put a song over the titles or in any part of the picture, you're unconsciously trying to play on the viewer's pocketbook—you're trying to get him to listen, to go out and buy. Often these songs don't really make the action progress or make any kind of comment."[55]

The modern style and its innovations did not oust the classical style overnight. After 1958 and through the first half of the 1960s, the last traces of the classical style can still be heard in films such as *The Magnificent Seven* (John Sturges, 1960, music by Elmer Bernstein), *Spartacus* (Stanley Kubrick, 1960, music by Alex North), *The Alamo* (John Wayne, 1960, music by Dimitri Tiomkin), *King of Kings* (Nicholas Ray, 1961, music by Miklós Rózsa), *El Cid* (Anthony Mann, 1961, music by Miklós Rózsa), *The Guns of Navarone* (J. Lee Thompson, 1961, music by Dimitri Tiomkin), *Taras Bulba* (J. Lee Thompson, 1962, music by Franz Waxman), and *How the West Was Won* (John Ford, Henry Hathaway, and George Marshall, 1962, music by Alfred Newman).[56] The stylistic change became well established and strongly evident only in the second half of the 1960s. The symphony orchestra as a musical means did not disappear entirely but became a definitely less common option, appearing in such films as *The Lion in Winter* (Anthony Harvey, 1968, music by John Barry), *Planet of the Apes* (Franklin J. Schaffner, 1968, music by Jerry Goldsmith), *The Reivers* (Mark Rydell, 1969, music by John Williams), *Patton* (Franklin J. Schaffner, 1970, music by Jerry Goldsmith), *Ryan's Daughter* (David Lean, 1970, music by Maurice Jarre), *The Wind and the Lion* (John Milius, 1975, music by Jerry Goldsmith), *The Omen* (Richard Donner, 1976, music by Jerry Goldsmith), and Bernard Herrmann's final contributions for *Sisters* (Brian De Palma, 1973) and *Obsession* (Brian De Palma, 1976). What became marginal if not defunct were the techniques and functions of the classical Hollywood music style. In particular, the old-style spatial perceptive function survived mostly in an exaggerated farcical form in such comedies as *That Touch of Mink* (Delbert Mann, 1962, music by George Duning), *Send Me No Flowers* (Norman Jewison, 1964, music by Frank De Vol), and *The Glass Bottom Boat* (Frank Tashlin, 1966, music by Frank De Vol) or in the mannerist thunderous stingers of some horror/ thriller B-movies such as *The Terror* (Roger Corman, 1963, music by Ronald Stein), *Strait-Jacket* (William Castle, 1964, music by Van Alexander), and *The Oblong Box* (Gordon Hessler, 1969, music by Harry Robertson).

Not until *Star Wars* (George Lucas, 1977) did there appear patent signs that the old style could still have something to say to contemporary audiences, both in film theaters and in music-record stores. Large orchestras, symphonic writing, and the leitmotiv technique were about to make a comeback: "While its lapse may be open to interpretation, the revival of leitmotivic film scoring in the 1970s is not; . . . the sea change came with the score to *Star Wars*."[57] The classical musical style of Hollywood was about to be resurrected. According to Jack Sullivan: "When Bernard Herrmann died in 1975, many declared that with him had perished symphonic movie music, a victim of pop and synthesizer sounds through the 60s and early 70s. Then *Star Wars* blazed into theaters, powered by the London Symphony Orchestra, and the talk stopped."[58]

PART TWO

John Williams and the Classical Hollywood Music Style

"Steven, you really need a better composer than I am for this film."
"I know, John. But they're all dead."

—John Williams and Steven Spielberg discussing the music for
Schindler's List

Top: John Williams conducting, ca. 1980. Photographer unknown. Courtesy BSO Archives. *Bottom*: John Williams composing, ca. 1990. Photographer unknown. Courtesy BSO Archives.

CHAPTER 4

Star Wars

An Oppositional Score

After his not very convincing debut with the Orwellian sci-fi film *THX 1138* (1971), the emerging film director George Lucas hit the box office with *American Graffiti* (1973) and became powerful enough to carry on with a big project that he had been contemplating for several years: *The Star Wars*.[1] The idea was to make a film that blended sci-fi with mythology, technology with fairy-tale magic, comics with epics, future with past: "A long time ago, in a galaxy far, far away . . ." These are the words that open the film, clearly establishing that what we are about to watch is, for Lucas, a "classic fairy tale."[2] The main models were the *Flash Gordon* and *Buck Rogers* serials, the adventure films and B-movies produced by Monogram, Republic, and other minor production companies—the so-called poverty-row studios. Other models were *The Hidden Fortress* (*Kakushi-toride no san-akunin*, Akira Kurosawa, 1958) and *The Searchers* (John Ford, 1956).[3] Besides films, the influence of Carlos Castaneda's anthropological and philosophical theories and of Joseph Campbell's studies on the mythological archetypes was also reported as a seminal one.[4]

Lucas's project was abandoned by United Artists and then rejected by Universal, to finally be picked up by 20th Century Fox, which, although skeptically, agreed to finance the preproduction.[5] The executives experienced some difficulty in understanding and envisioning Lucas's idea because of the confusing nature and constantly changing structure of the screenplay.[6] Most important, the main doubt about the commercial result of the project was that the sci-fi genre was out of fashion in 1970s cinema. Recent exceptions had been *2001: A Space Odyssey* (Stanley Kubrick, 1968) and *Planet of the Apes* (Franklin J. Schaffner, 1968). As Lucas's publicist Charles Lippincott recalls: "Kubrick's *2001* didn't break even until late 1975—and that was the most successful science-fiction film of all time. . . . You had to be crazy to make a science-fiction film when we wanted to."[7] Moreover, *2001* and *Planet of the*

Apes were very different films from Lucas's project. They were adult sci-fi, dystopian tales with philosophical subtexts, while *The Star Wars* seemed to be a kind of expensive B-movie for kids. In 1975, in the midst of laborious pre-production first steps, screenplay rewriting, and budget discussions, the time came to decide what kind of music the film would require.

The Sci-Fi Genre and Music

Traditionally, music for the sci-fi genre would use a language inspired by twentieth-century musical modernism—atonalism, twelve-tone technique, aleatoric music, and so forth—or would use electronic instruments, timbres, or even *musique concrète* to provide the musical equivalent of futuristic or hypertechnological worlds.[8] Bernard Herrmann employed a modernist dialect for *The Day the Earth Stood Still* (Robert Wise, 1951) and also used the theremin, thus producing a shift in identification for that instrument's tremulous timbre from the psychosis-centered 1940s thrillers to the sci-fi genre. In *Planet of the Apes*, Jerry Goldsmith used a traditional orchestra but adopted the atonal dialect, avant-garde instrumental techniques (key taps on clarinets or horns played without mouthpieces, for example), and experimental timbres (a ram's horn and metal mixing bowls of different sizes used as percussion) to produce the musical complement of the hallucinatory topsy-turvy world presented in the film.[9] In *Forbidden Planet* (Fred M. Wilcox, 1956), there is no music but we hear "electronic tonalities" by Bebe and Louis Barron.[10] Stanley Kubrick in 2001 chose to combine images of deep space and unseen worlds with a compilation of repertoire orchestral pieces—after having discourteously discarded Alex North's original score.[11] The selection spanned from classic pieces such as Richard Strauss's *Thus Spoke Zarathustra* (*Also Sprach Zarathustra*, op. 30, 1896) and Johann Strauss Jr.'s *The Blue Danube* (*An der Schönen Blauen Donau*, op. 314, 1866) to contemporary art music such as György Ligeti's *Lux Aeterna* (1966), *Atmospheres* (1961), *Requiem* (1963–65), and *Adventures* (1962). Stanley Kubrick chose to create a special "asynchronism" with the visuals. Music had to serve as an intellectual stimulus by pointing to extrafilmic references and creating an intertextual dimension, which would actively involve the viewer in deciphering this enigmatic film. Yet Kubrick's choice was seemingly also the consequence of a lack of trust in film composers. He stated, "However good our best film composers may be, they are not a Beethoven, a Mozart or a Brahms. Why use music which is less good when there is such a multitude of great orchestral music from the past and from our own time?"[12]

Lucas rejected the modernist and electronic options and chose Kubrick's approach. He wrote the script while listening to the symphonic repertoire of

William Walton, Richard Wagner, Gustav Holst, Richard Strauss, Antonín Dvořák, and Maurice Ravel along with the film music of Erich Wolfgang Korngold and Miklós Rózsa.[13] He resolved that the film should have an extensive musical coverage and, although information on the point is contradictory, he seemed to be planning to have the music track made of preexisting symphonic selections, or at least to use preexisting themes arranged as leitmotivs for the film.[14] While pondering such musical decisions, Lucas happened to have a very fruitful conversation: "I had known Steven Spielberg for a long time up to this point and, you know, we were talking about the film . . . and I said, 'I want a classical score, I want the Korngold kind of feel about this thing, it's an old fashion kinda movie and I want that kind of grand soundtrack they used to have on movies.' And he said, 'The guy you gotta talk to is John Williams. He made *Jaws*, I love him, he is the greatest composer who ever lived. You gotta talk to him!'"[15] Lucas had some qualms about hiring Williams: "I only knew him primarily as a jazz guy; I wasn't that aware of his film work. . . . I thought, 'Really? He can really do [Erich Wolfgang] Korngold and [Alfred] Newman and all the classic guys?' And Steven said, 'Oh yeah, he's perfect.' When you get into this kind of score, it's a much more complex and difficult undertaking, and if you don't have somebody who really knows what they're doing, it can get out of hand and go crazy very fast."[16]

In April 1975 Lucas had his first meeting with Williams.[17] "I told him 'I'm basically doing a silent movie,'" recalls Lucas.[18] Williams remarked, "I looked at the movie and I liked it—I had no idea at the time it was going to be a trilogy—and I thought the film would give me the opportunity to write an old-fashioned swashbuckling symphonic score, so that's what I did."[19] Reportedly, Williams—contrary to his own habit—agreed to read the script.[20] If the compilation-score story is the true one, he was responsible for convincing Lucas not to use repertoire music but an original score instead: "*2001* and several other films have utilized this technique very well. But what I think this technique doesn't do is take a piece of melodic material, develop it and relate it to a character all the way through the film. For instance if you took a theme from one of the selections of Holst's *The Planets* and played it at the beginning of the film, it wouldn't necessarily fit in the middle or at the end. On the other hand, I did not want to hear a piece of Dvořák here, a piece of Tchaikovsky there, and a piece of Holst in another place. For formal reasons, I felt that the film wanted thematic unity."[21] He employed Lucas's temp track as a stylistic blueprint on which to build his own musical retelling of the film. "Williams . . . acknowledged the director's favorites while demonstrating the power of a freshly composed score. He seems to be saying: I can mimic anything you want, but you need a living voice," as pointed out by Alex Ross.[22]

Finding the Musical Solution

Which music language could be suitable for a film like that? The modernist hypothesis had clearly been rejected, and Lucas, through his own temp track, showed Williams that his preference was for the late-Romantic dialect, that of classical Hollywood.[23] *Star Wars* is in fact more a "supergenre" than a sci-fi film. Only a few elements of the sci-fi genre, such as robots, laser weapons, and spaceships, are present. *Star Wars* is often referred to as a "nostalgia film" within the framework of postmodernism. Nostalgia films allude to the past and revisit old-time formulas with "complex and interesting new formal inventiveness; it being understood that the nostalgia film was never a matter of some old-fashioned 'representation' of historical content, but instead approached the 'past' through stylistic connotation, conveying 'pastness' by the glossy qualities of the image," in the words of Fredric Jameson, one of postmodernism's key thinkers.[24] One way to this postmodern approach to the past is through pastiche, that is, an imitation of past styles and genres.[25] *Star Wars* is precisely a recuperation and reworking of past styles and genres. More than plain sci-fi, then, the film is a mixture of generic and stylistic elements from Western, fantasy, and swashbuckler films; instead of being similar to the sci-fi films of its day, it was closer to the Warner Bros. adventure films of the 1930s, directed by Michael Curtiz, featuring Errol Flynn's prowess and Erich Wolfgang Korngold's opulent music. Korngold himself was Williams's main model, as he remarked: "A warm theatrical operatic almost kind of package. The kind of thing that Korngold in fact did so beautifully. He brought the Vienna Opera House to the American West. And in an odd way, in a similar way, it worked, I think."[26] Music adopted a similar past-oriented and stylistic-imitation approach, responding accordingly to the general design of the film. "From the beginning the heroic note is struck, and it is struck in a very nostalgic fashion as well; this is music which does indeed recall the great swashbuckling films and epics of decades past, and it does so unabashedly," notes Timothy Scheurer.[27] Williams explains the choice of having very traditional music combined with a futuristic setting.

The music for the film is very non-futuristic. The films themselves showed us characters we hadn't seen before and planets unimagined and so on, but the music was—this is actually George Lucas's conception and a very good one — emotionally familiar. It was not music that might describe *terra incognita* but the opposite of that, music that would put us in touch with very familiar and remembered emotions, which for me as a musician translated into the use of a 19th century operatic idiom, if you like, Wagner and this sort of thing. These sorts of influences would put us in touch with remembered theatrical experiences as well—all western experiences to be sure.[28]

This choice was unexpected to most. Mark Hamill confessed, "I thought, 'Well, you know, science fiction, maybe they'll do some kind of cold electronic score? It had sort of a western feel—maybe they'll do that sort of [*laughs*] *Man with No Name*, Sergio Leone, spare guitar . . . ' I don't know what. I certainly didn't see it in my head as much as a swashbuckler."[29] Many in the film-critic circles also failed to understand the nature of the film and its music: some critics would label the score as "corny Romanticism" and wonder why, since the film was set in the future, avant-garde music had not been used instead.[30] This is a simplistically superficial complaint, actually: it cannot be simply said that since it features spaceships and robots, *Star Wars* is therefore sci-fi. The film begins with "A long time ago, in a galaxy far far away . . ." That is, it begins as a traditional fairy tale set in a distant past. Other critics grasped the sense of the musical choice: "If one is writing music for a movie that is supposed to take place in the future, then futuristic music should theoretically suit the 'set' better than a score based on music from the late nineteenth and early twentieth centuries. But Williams hits closer to the mark when he points out that such films tend to cater to the audience's desire for escapism, 'and in that escapist thing is the whole romantic idea of getting away, of being transported into another kind of atmosphere.'"[31]

Williams provided a symphonic tonal score based on a dozen leitmotivs covering almost the entire film: Luke's theme, Leia's theme, the Jawas' theme, Ben Kenobi / the Force's theme, the Empire's motif, and many more. They are elaborated and combined into extensive and refined Korngold-like dialogue underscoring (think of the dialogue between Kenobi and Luke after they have watched Princess Leia's video message through R2-D2); into old-fashioned heroic fanfares, as when Luke rescues Leia and, with her in his arms, crosses the chasm à la Robin Hood under the stormtroopers' fire; and into episodes of detailed Mickey-Mousing, for example, in the detention block ambush scene. Williams designed such clear-cut recognizable motifs and themes so as to support the film narration in a straightforward way:

I think in my mind, and possibly also George Lucas', when I was writing the score, I thought it was a children's film. I thought that it was something that kids would go to on a Saturday afternoon, and that it had a kind of cartoon-like character, and the orchestra and the music should somehow be in that genre, whatever that is. But I thought, I have to grab the attention of the ten-year-olds with this. The emotion would have to be large, a sense of good versus evil made palpable. Simple tunes would be the key, though that was easier said than done. To say Darth Vader to a ten-year-old in clear, memorable and immediately affecting terms is a big challenge. And it's an opportunity probably is, maybe sadly, found only in the craft of film scoring any more. I mean, where else can you do that?[32]

In 1975–76 the choice of a full symphonic score was definitely against the tide and a very risky one: if the sci-fi genre was considered unfashionable, even more so was the classical music style. The studio feared that the film would have a disastrous performance at the box office and that, lacking an attractive pop score, such failure could not be offset by the sale of records. In fact, 20th Century Fox Records—believing that nobody would buy a symphonic film-music album—was planning not to release any tie-in disc.[33] Against the odds, Lucas and Williams not only carried on but even enlisted the services of a first-class musical institution. The production took place in England, and the world-famous London Symphony Orchestra was chosen. Two conflicting stories coexist as to how the LSO ended up being involved in the project. The most established has it that the LSO was selected by Williams and the music director of 20th Century Fox, Lionel Newman. Williams recounts:

We decided to record the music for the films in London. . . .

We were going to use a freelance orchestra, as I had done with *Fiddler* [*On the Roof* (Norman Jewison, 1971)] and other films. . . . [Newman] suggested to me, "Why don't we just use the London Symphony Orchestra for this recording? We won't have to be troubled with hiring freelance players, we'll just make one contractual arrangement with the London Symphony."

It also happened at that time that our friend from Hollywood, Andre Previn, was then the music director of the London Symphony. I rang him up and said, "How would it be if we borrowed your orchestra for this recording?" Andre was very positive and very excited.[34]

A different story claims that it was the other way around, with the LSO applying for a film job, as reported by an orchestra member.

The LSO had a large patch of no work; . . . so the chairman at the time, Anthony Camden, spoke to André Previn, the principal conductor, and asked if he was composing any film music. André said, "I'm not doing film music anymore, but why don't you give John Williams a ring?" . . . So Anthony called John and asked if he had any work for a symphony orchestra in the near future. Williams apparently said, "Well, you're the London Symphony Orchestra, you're not going to be interested in this. I've got a film called *Star Wars* coming up, but there's going to be 18 sessions. You're never going to be able to fit it in." Anthony replied, "Oh yes we are!"[35]

Whichever the truth, with *Star Wars* the LSO inaugurated a string of collaborations with Williams and became a fundamental part not only of the *Star Wars* sound (playing on the first six installments) but of Williams's 1977–83 period. One key ingredient of the Williams sound in this period was the virtuoso playing of LSO's principal trumpet Maurice Murphy. Williams recalls:

The first day we did *Star Wars* with the big high C that starts it was the first day that a trumpeter called Maurice Murphy had been admitted as a member to the London Symphony Orchestra. So the first service he did with the London orchestra was *Star Wars* recording number one and he came into the stage and blew that top C which sort of blew the world's head off. He's no longer with us, I'm sorry to say, but the story illustrates what energy and virtuosity this orchestra brings to films in general.[36]

Another key ingredient was the detailed miking and crisp and hot recording by the sound engineer Eric Tomlinson, who would also record the subsequent Williams/LSO projects: "Setting levels a few dB hotter than normal produced an appealing sound."[37] Famous for its skillful sight-reading, versatility, and powerful brass section, the LSO is, in Williams's words, "a very 'hot' orchestra, its decibel level is large, and the orchestra looms at the audience in a very vigorous, athletic way" and "contributed enormously to the energy and sound of what *Star Wars* has been."[38] In 1977, moreover, the orchestra had already accrued a series of consistent film-scoring experiences, boasting a prestigious track record of collaborations.[39] On 5 March 1977, all parties involved convened at the Anvil Studios in Denham (UK), where Williams conducted eighty-six musicians in the first recording session of the more-than-eight-hundred-page score.[40] After eight days on the recording stage, the resulting *Star Wars* music track covered 88 minutes of the film's total 120-minute running time. Such an extended musical coverage coupled with such strong leitmotivic variety and interconnection was unheard of since Steiner and Korngold's heydays.

The very beginning of the film is a kind of manifesto of the restoration of the classical Hollywood music tradition. For the 20th Century Fox opening logo, the full Cinemascope version of the "20th Century Fox Fanfare" by Alfred Newman was resuscitated after a decade of less than sporadic use.[41] After a brief silence, the "STAR WARS" title flashes on the screen in tight synchronism with a startling *fortissimo* B-flat-major chord—"*Maestoso sffz*" in the score—in the same B-flat-major key as Newman's fanfare. Williams comments:

> Looking at that thing, I thought, well, it has to be a grand fanfare and it has to start off with, put it this way, with a bang, with a full fortissimo explosion of energy and trumpets and the rest of it. And so I wrote the piece that I wrote. It starts with an unprepared, high C on the trumpet. . . . There's no preparation note for the trumpeters. It's very difficult. They have to grab it right out of the ether. It was a particularly great performance of brass playing. And so the spirit of, I think you could also say, militarism of the British brass tradition is apparent in the performance I think, in the writing also. Because it is a military piece after all, spaceships and an army of space, if you like to think of it that way. So it has that swagger and that sense of commitment and dedication to the journey.[42]

This explosive chord also affirms a continuity with the past: the deliberate tonal affinity with Newman's fanfare marks the recovery of the tradition and the score's affiliation with it. Moreover, the chord's precise synchronism with the appearance of the "STAR WARS" main title—the chord being like a stinger—and the fact that the chord is played by a full symphony orchestra mark the simultaneous retrieval of two other characteristic traits of the classical style: the tight adherence between music and images and the symphonic sound. Interestingly enough, the first "Main Title" version, rather than beginning with a bursting tonic chord, featured an upward *crescendo* leap from the dominant to the tonic. This was soon removed, probably because as the title appears suddenly from the black, so music should accordingly appear suddenly from the silence—a crescendo with a dominant-to-tonic leap would have better suited a fade-in.[43] The overwhelming chord is followed by a canon-structured fanfare and finally by the film's main theme—the "Luke Skywalker" leitmotiv—followed by a secondary theme played by strings. "Like many of the overtures to old Hollywood melodramas, the *Star Wars* overture is divided into two sections, based on a musical contrast between a 'hard' masculine and a 'soft' feminine theme," Peter Larsen notes.[44] Williams further describes the effect he sought

> The opening of the film was visually so stunning . . . that it was clear that that music had to kind of smack you right in the eye and do something very strong. It's in my mind a very simple, very direct tune that jumps an octave in a very dramatic way, and has a triplet placed in it that has a kind of grab. I tried to construct something that again would have this idealistic, uplifting but military flare to it . . . set in the most brilliant register of the trumpets, horns and trombones so that we'd have a blazingly brilliant fanfare at the opening of the piece. And contrast that with the second theme that was lyrical and romantic and adventurous also.[45]

If it might sound like a "very simple, very direct tune," it is certainly *not* simplistic. Behind the emotionally gripping and ear-catching theme is, on the contrary, a high-profile writing and a sophisticated texture that astutely translates the film's main story line into music. In Alex Ross's insightful analysis:

> There's a rhythmic quirk in the basic pattern of a triplet followed by two held notes: the first triplet falls on the fourth beat of the bar, while later ones fall on the first beat, with the second held note foreshortened. There are harmonic quirks, too. The opening fanfare is based on chains of fourths, adorning the initial B-flat-major triad with E-flats and A-flats. Those notes recur in the orchestral swirl around the trumpet theme. In the reprise, a bass line moves in contrary motion, further tweaking the chords above. All this interior activity creates dynamism. . . . Furthermore, the rhythms of the fanfares are tricky, setting patterns of four against three. There's a hint of chaos in this tangy sound, as if free-spirited individuals were scrambling to coalesce into a whole. Even when the march theme kicks in, it retains an uneven, lopsided feeling—the perfect image of the rag-tag rebel army that is defying Darth Vader.[46]

In such a film, the score should not only support the narration but also have a mythopoeic function by strengthening those archetypal structures and references to the collective unconscious and mythical heritage inspired by Joseph Campbell's works.[47] Accordingly, Williams injected into the music hints, allusions, and quotations that could evoke past musical experiences in the listeners and connect them with a sort of musical collective unconscious: "That's what in performance one tries to get with orchestras, and we talk about that at orchestral rehearsals: that it isn't only notes, it's this reaching back into the past. As creatures we don't know if we have a future, but we certainly share a great past. We remember it, in language and in pre-language, and that's where music lives—it's to this area in our souls that it can speak."[48] This vision explains Williams's fondness for brass instruments, like the trumpets and the horns: "When I've tried to analyze my lifelong love of the French horn, I've had to conclude that it's mainly because of the horn's capacity to stir memories of antiquity. The very sound of the French horn conjures images stored in the collective psyche. It's an instrument that invites us to 'dream backward to the ancient time.'"[49] The memories of antiquity are also evoked by tone intervals, namely the perfect fifth, an idiomatic trait of Williams's that can also be found, for example, in *Superman: The Movie* (Richard Donner, 1978) and *E.T. the Extra-Terrestrial* (Steven Spielberg, 1982). "The interval of the perfect fifth also rattles our memories of antiquity," and "the interval of the musical fifth we use to celebrate has been with us thousands of years," says Williams.[50]

Some critics have attacked Williams's music in general—and *Star Wars* in particular—for being allegedly too derivative and based on "stealing" from the great composers of the past.[51] The dissonant orchestral chords that can be heard right after the opening titles—during the attack by the Imperial ship— are similar to those of "Mars, the Bringer of War" from the suite *The Planets* (1916) by Gustav Holst (see figure 1).

Figure 1. *Above*: Gustav Holst, "Mars, the Bringer of War" (Movement 7, mm. 1–7), from *The Planets* (1921, public domain), originally published by Goodwin & Tabb Ltd., reprinted by Dover Publications Inc., 1996. *Below*: John Williams, "Main Title" (mm. 84–88), from *Star Wars: Suite for Orchestra* (© 1977 BMI), published by Bantha Music and Warner-Tamerlane Publishing Corp., administered by Warner-Tamerlane Publishing Corp., printed/distributed by Hal Leonard, "John Williams Signature Edition," 044900057. Used in compliance with the US Copyright Act, Section 107.

More blatantly, the "Main Title" is not only similar in spirit to many of Korn-gold's themes, such as those found in *Captain Blood* (Michael Curtiz, 1935), *The Adventures of Robin Hood* (Michael Curtiz and William Keighley, 1938), and *The Sea Hawk* (Michael Curtiz, 1940), but it is also almost a direct reference to the main theme of *Kings Row* (Sam Wood, 1942) (see figure 2).

Figure 2. *Above*: Erich Wolfgang Korngold, "Main Title," from the *Kings Row* film score (© 1942 ASCAP), published by Warner Olive Music LLC, administered by Universal Music (ear transcription from the film's soundtrack). Used in compliance with the US Copyright Act, Section 107. *Below*: John Williams, "Main Title" (mm. 3–10), from *Star Wars: Suite for Orchestra* (© 1977 BMI), published by Bantha Music and Warner-Tamerlane Publishing Corp., administered by Warner-Tamerlane Publishing Corp., printed/distributed by Hal Leonard, "John Williams Signature Edition," 044900057. Used in compliance with the US Copyright Act, Section 107.

To people who revel in pointing out these similarities with an accusatory and self-righteous tone, one could respond with Alex Ross's words: "[This] brings to mind the famous retort made by Brahms when it was pointed out that the big tune in the finale of his First Symphony resembled Beethoven's Ode to Joy: 'Any ass can hear that.' Williams takes material from Korngold and uses it to forge something new. . . . Although it's fun to play tune detective, what makes these ideas indelible is the way they're fleshed out, in harmony, rhythm, and orchestration."[52] Moving from the isolated musical level to *film* music (that is, music written to work within a film), Williams's choices have a precise rationale. The derivative nature and the musical quotations are another method that he uses to trigger in the viewer/listener's mind some musical memories of a shared past in order to prompt a precise emotional response (noble heroism, villainous treats, tragic sadness, jubilation, etc.). Williams admits:

A lot of these references are deliberate. They're an attempt to evoke a response in the audience where we want to elicit a certain kind of reaction. Another thing is that, whenever one is involved in writing incidental music—where you have specific backgrounds, specific periods, certain kinds of characters and so on—the work is bound to be derivative in a certain sense. The degree to which you can experiment, as you can in a concert work, is very limited. You're fulfilling more of a role of a designer, in the same way that a set designer would do a design for a period opera.[53]

More insightful—and less prejudiced—scholars and critics have, eventually, come to recognize this: "Williams seemed to be able to capture the emotional core of the film in his music. . . . What Williams has done in his scores is capture and articulate what the audience sees—or better, what the audience wants to see—as the emotional core of the film. He leaves aside his need to experiment, to push the artistic envelope, and constantly looks for the musical metaphor that will enable the audience to have that larger than life experience they expect the movies to give them."[54] As to the derivative halo of the *Star Wars* music, it is now acknowledged that "the originality, in the music as in the film, lay in the flair with which familiar formulas were used and transformed."[55]

Despite the concern of Lucas and many others involved that the film would be a box office failure, *Star Wars* opened on 25 May 1977 and met a rapidly growing audience. Thanks to word-of-mouth advertising, it soon won enormous success, totaling $127 million by the end of the year and even surpassing the highest-grossing film to date, *Jaws* (Steven Spielberg, 1975).[56] Unexpectedly, the music was a resounding hit too: in mid-July, the double LP featuring seventy-four minutes of straight symphonic music and no songs at all had already sold 650,000 copies and grossed $9 million.[57] Its sales were certified "Platinum" by the Recording Industry Association of America as early as 17 August 1977, and it would eventually sell more than 4 million copies, becoming the best-selling symphonic album at the time.[58] Lucas acknowledged the music's central contribution to the film's success to such an extent that he awarded the composer an extra bonus: a 1 percent share of the film's profits.[59] Meanwhile, Williams won his third Academy Award, one Golden Globe, and three Grammy Awards, and he also received a Grammy nomination for "Best Album of the Year," unprecedented for an album of symphonic film music.[60]

Williams reestablished the symphony orchestra as a musical means for film music and as a stylistic device for film narration. And Williams's orchestra was a grand symphony orchestra. According to Lionel Newman, "He has taught us to use full orchestra; in the old days, 50–60 men on a picture was considered a large orchestra—now, because of him, you can't think of a big movie without thinking of using a full symphony orchestra."[61] Williams's introduction

of the large, full symphony orchestra was also facilitated by technical inno
vations in sound recording, namely the Dolby Stereo process, which made
it feasible to have a level of sound fidelity and clarity previously impossible.[62]
A sign of the new favor regained by the symphonic sound after the film's
release was that the London Symphony Orchestra resumed a steady involvement in film projects: during the 1960s and 1970s, when the modern style had
ousted the symphonic sound, the LSO had basically exited the film market;
thanks to *Star Wars*, the LSO not only returned to work in films but also
became sought after. In the following years, Williams himself worked with
the LSO on various projects: *Superman: The Movie* (Richard Donner, 1978),
Dracula (John Badham, 1979), *Raiders of the Lost Ark* (Steven Spielberg, 1981),
and *Monsignor* (Frank Perry, 1982). The LSO also stayed on board for five additional *Star Wars* films.

What originally may have seemed like a one-off Saturday-afternoon kids
movie soon wound up to be the inaugural chapter of a multi-installment
saga, which Williams's music continued to provide with a seemingly endless
flow of musical imagination, compositional ingenuity, and dramaturgic acumen. The next chapter explores how the saga of the *Star Wars* music continued in the following installments, a musical universe whose Big Bang was that
high-C trumpet note blown on 5 March 1977.

CHAPTER 5

The Saga of the
Star Wars Music

John Williams's work within the *Star Wars* universe continued after the first film (now known as *Star Wars: Episode IV—A New Hope*). Williams's *Star Wars* series can be considered his magnum opus and eventually resulted in a ponderous and unprecedented corpus of symphonic film music, totaling nine installments over a period of forty-two years, more than twenty hours of music, and a cornucopia of themes and motifs.[1] For *The Empire Strikes Back* (Irvin Kershner, 1980, later rebranded as *Star Wars: Episode V—The Empire Strikes Back*), Williams enlarged the orchestral setting to include up to 129 musicians and synthesizer touches—notably for the magic tree scene.[2] Three new memorable leitmotivs are presented: a serene theme for the sage Jedi master Yoda, a passionate love theme for Han Solo and Princess Leia, and a threateningly imposing militaristic march for the villain Darth Vader that prominently features the Wagnerian "Tarnhelm progression" (two minor chords that are a major third apart) and its intimation of malevolence and dark magic.[3] Among the outstanding musical episodes are the "Battle of Hoth" sequence, whose orchestration called for five piccolos, five oboes, an eight-percussion battery, two grand pianos, and three harps; and the balletic accompaniment to the Millennium Falcon crossing the asteroid field.[4] *Return of the Jedi* (Richard Marquand, 1983, now *Star Wars: Episode VI—Return of the Jedi*) saw the introduction of a sinister motif for the evil Emperor, performed in dark timbre by a wordless male chorus; a brisk Prokofiev-like march for the teddy-bear-like inhabitants of planet Endor, the Ewoks; a warm and lyrical theme for the Luke and Leia sibling relationship, and a slimy tuba leitmotiv for the obese space mobster Jabba the Hutt: "When I first saw Jabba, I said, 'Oh, dear, a regular Tubby the Tuba.' So I guess I did the obvious; I wrote his theme as a concerto for tuba," recalls the composer.[5] Memorable musical sequences are

the majestic arrival of the Emperor on board (accompanied by his own sinister leitmotiv); the highly kinetic, and again ballet-like, battle of Endor; and
the climactic duel between the Emperor and Luke, with Darth Vader eventually siding with Luke, resulting in an unexpectedly poignant rendition of
Darth Vader's theme for harp and flute as the archvillain gives his life to save
Luke—a good example of what Bribitzer-Stull calls a "change of texture" of
a leitmotiv in order to "show a change in [a] character."[6] The first trilogy constitutes a corpus of scores unified by an idiomatic and thematic congruence,
firmly classifiable within Williams's best neoclassical works. Though continuing the composer's neoclassical trend, the following chapters saw—while consistently enriching the catalog by also reprising the old themes and motifs—a
slight modification of the music's idiom and the scoring techniques that make
them less directly neoclassical scores.

For starters, in the second trilogy, there are fewer new leitmotivs per episode.
Moreover, the first trilogy (1977–83) tells the story of a journey from tyranny
to freedom, but the second one (1999–2005) is a prequel trilogy and concerns
the events that had caused that tyranny, thus being a journey from freedom
to tyranny. Consequently, the music for the first trilogy is more buoyant,
optimistic, and hopeful in tone—"swashbucklingly" adventurous—while in
the second trilogy, the music becomes more somber, doom-laden, and desperate as the plot progresses and things get worse. Making a comparison with
Hollywood's history, it is as if the first trilogy looked back to a 1930s ethos,
while the second trilogy harkened to the more complex and darker musical
atmospheres of the 1940s. Reuniting with the London Symphony Orchestra,
for *Star Wars: Episode I—The Phantom Menace* (1999), Williams composed "Duel
of the Fates," a minor-mode Carmina Burana–like relentless piece for chorus
and orchestra, which alternates driving ostinato writing with arresting a cappella choral salvos. Williams explains:

> This choral piece . . . is a result of my thinking that something ritualistic and/
> or pagan and antique might be very effective. I thought that the introduction of
> a chorus at a certain point in the film might just be the right thing to use. And,
> to take that idea of simplicity a bit further, I thought that I needed some kind of
> a text in order to do this. . . . One of my favorite books is Robert Graves' *White
> Goddess*, which is basically a history of poetry, but also has a lot to do with Celtic
> folklore. . . . I remembered the great Celtic epic poem *The Battle of the Trees*. . . .
> There is a stanza in that poem . . . which is roughly, "Under the tongue root a
> fight most dread / While another rages behind the head." And for no conscious

sensible reason, the idea of a fight, something raging and imagined in the head
more than anywhere seemed to be a good mystical cryptic piece of business.
I collaborated with some friends at Harvard University, first asking them to
translate it into Celtic, then into Greek, and finally into Sanskrit, just looking
for good choral sounds and good vowels. The reason we like to sing in Italian
is because it does not have consonant word endings, like our English, which is
so hard to sing. Celtic does not work either for that same reason, nor does
Greek. But Sanskrit is less well-known and has beautiful sounds. . . . I have
reduced the stanza which was translated literally and used either single words
or syllables or combinations of these things, the words "dreaded fight" for
example, and repeated them.[7]

For the little boy Anakin Skywalker, who is doomed to become the archvillain Darth Vader, Williams penned a theme that already presents the "Darth
Vader" theme concealed within: "It's the kind of theme you would have for
a young boy, very innocent, lyrical and idealistic. But it's made up of intervals
from Darth Vader's 'Imperial March' . . . an archetypical evil expression. I
made Anakin's theme out of those intervals by inverting them or rearrang-
ing them rhythmically or accompanying them harmonically in a different
way. It sounds familiar, very sweet. But if you listen to it carefully, there's
a hint [of evil]."[8]

   Star Wars: Episode II—Attack of the Clones (2002) adds to the thematic catalog a passionate love theme for the illegitimate, ill-fated romance between
Anakin and Padme. The theme, "Across the Stars," reworks the intervals of
"Main Title" (Luke's leitmotiv) to remind us that Luke will be the offspring
of Anakin and Padme's love: "George [Lucas] wanted me to write a real old-
fashioned love theme, and that is one of the hardest things to do—to write
something that is melodic, accessible, and direct, able to take the lead but also
able to be heard as an accompaniment to dialogue. There has to be a kind of
space around it. In this case, there needed to be a tragic element in it, too."[9]

   Star Wars: Episode III—Revenge of the Sith (2005) further expands the musical
treatment of the tragic love story between Anakin and Padme, with episodes
of "thematic irony" in which Williams anticipates with music the hopeless
development of their romance, as Bribitzer-Stull explains: "The audience hears
the 'Doomed Love' theme, a clear case of romantic irony since the audience
knows what horrible fate lies in store for the two characters, though the characters themselves do not."[10] The central set piece of Star Wars: Episode III—
Revenge of the Sith is a furious theme for chorus and orchestra, "Battle of the

Heroes." It features violent wordless choral bursts and interweaves "The Force"
theme—associated throughout the saga with the Jedis and the good side of
the Force with an ominous horn motif based on the medieval sequence *Dies
Irae* (Day of Wrath), traditionally employed in the music for Requiem Masses.
Fittingly, the piece is showcased in the final duel between Obi Wan and his
pupil Anakin, who has just betrayed the Jedis and passed to the "Dark Side."
The duel results in the transformation of Anakin into Darth Vader and will
eventually mark the demise of the Jedis—apocalyptically enough.[11]

In 2012 Disney acquired LucasFilm and, consequently, the rights to the
entire *Star Wars* franchise. An intense exploitation of the new asset was soon
launched, with a new trilogy put in development to continue the "canonical"
series as well as a set of spin-off films and TV shows.[12] Williams, in his eight-
ies now, got on board again to expand his work: "This is a unique opportunity.
It has never happened, in the theater, in the film, whatever . . . where a composer can keep working on the same body of work and continue to add to
it. What a privilege is that! One of the challenges has been, 'Should it be
so new that it doesn't fit the body?' 'Can you play [the new] Rey's theme
alongside of [the old] Leia's theme and have them be same part of the family
even if I'm forty years older?'"[13] The new installment of the third trilogy was
released in December 2015, *Star Wars: Episode VII—The Force Awakens* (J. J.
Abrams). The film is a sequel per se because it tells the story of what happens
after *Episode VI*. But it is also a reboot because it almost restages the same
Episode IV plot—Rey in lieu of Luke; Kylo Ren in lieu of Vader; BB8 in lieu of
R2-D2, etcetera. Due to the production routine of the digital-era film-making
(see "Closing Remarks" in this book), the LSO could not join Williams in his
continuation of the *Star Wars* adventures: "The schedule has evolved to the
point that I'll need to be working with the orchestra continuously for several
months, and that's obviously easier for me to do here in Los Angeles, than it
would be in London," explained Williams.[14]

In the film, the score presents a balance between continuity and novelty. The
familiar themes from the first trilogy are quoted in appropriate key points
but preponderantly new music is added to enrich the saga's musical universe.
"I think, about 102 minutes of music in the film, and we've measured that
there's seven minutes of references to the earlier films. So the great preponderance of material is new—90 percent or more. And my task and my challenge was to make it feel friendly and related, interrelated, to the other scores,
so that it feels comfortably *Star-Wars*-ian, if you can use that word. And at the
same time be new and original to this particular piece," tells the composer.[15]

One of the new pieces is for Kylo Ren, the new archvillain and Vader's grandson: "I thought that it should be a relative of Darth Vader, but something entirely different also," says Williams.[16] Unlike Vader's mechanically resolute and seemingly unstoppable grand march, Kylo's music is characterized by a swinging mood. The "official" motif that we hear as he acts in public is an ostentatiously evil five-note motto played markedly by assertive horns "that seems to be the embodiment of evil."[17] Yet it is the music of someone who *wants* to play the villain more than of someone who *is* a villain. "Like his music, Kylo Ren is unbalanced and unfinished, still just a boy in a mask," notes Frank Lehman.[18] When Kylo is seen in private scenes, we hear a different motif, a brooding slithering line that oscillates between $\frac{3}{4}$ and $\frac{4}{4}$, followed by repeated seemingly obsessive notes. The configuration of the music communicates hesitation, emotional instability, psychic fixation, and at times even remorse, perhaps—its slithering movements are akin to the "Guilt Motif" from Giuseppe Verdi's *Traviata* (no. 11, "Finale Ultimo," bars 39–45).

The other principal novelty is "Rey's Theme," associated with the film's heroine and the major and more extended leitmotif in the score. In the composer's words: "It's an interesting challenge with her, because her theme doesn't suggest a love theme in any way. It suggests an adventurer, a *female* adventurer, but with great strength. She's a fighter, she's infused with the Force, and it needed to be something that was strong but thoughtful. She's a very young girl, but she's a woman of diverse parts, and so there's a maturity, I think, about the approach, melodically, to her that I hope will fit her."[19] The opening bars of Rey's theme, played by flutes, have a modal feeling that places it surprisingly far from the more operatic Western mood of the themes of the classic trilogy and closer to the Eastern atmospheres that Williams had explored in *Memoirs of a Geisha* (Rob Marshall, 2005). The delicate and exotic melody soon expands into a more epic development, with strings and horns joining for the rising arc. The result is a balance of feminine grace, determination, and resilience that fully captures the Rey character, "the right degree of strength and beauty for an adventuress," says Williams.[20] We also find new exemplars of Williams's trademark action scherzos ("Scherzo for X-Wings") propelled by his unmistakable brass writing, and his clever use of counterpoint, for example when Rey's theme is meaningfully intertwined with "The Force" theme to suggest her destiny as one of the leaders of the resistance, which also has its collective new theme. The "March of the Resistance," the anthem of the newly born rebel movement, is called a march but is not one of the exuberant "swashbuckling" major-mode marches that we find aplenty in the previous films; it is instead a powerful and rigorous fugato in minor mode, as if Williams here decided to focus not so much on the youthful adventurous side as on the serious determination of the fighters.

For the second Disney addendum, *Star Wars: Episode VIII—The Last Jedi* (Rian Johnson, 2017), Williams concentrates on the thematic development of the materials introduced in the previous film and those written for the first trilogy, in a score that has few self-contained musical numbers—one being "The Fathiers," a prominent, balletic action scherzo—and instead develops into a more continuous leitmotivic flow. The prominent new piece is "The Rebellion Is Reborn"—associated with the new character Rose, a young resistance fighter—which alternates an expanding lyrical melody that intimates hope for a brighter future with more tumultuous passages that indicate that the final victory is still far from reach. Williams also produces an amusing nod to his old "Cantina Band" source music from *Episode IV*: during the casino sequence on the planet Canto Bight, we can hear a similarly parodic pastiche of 1930s big-band music for an even more disreputable place—"a sort of Artie Shaw imitation," Williams calls it.[21] If for the seedy small-time-crooks tavern of "Cantina Band" the model was Benny Goodman's dance music, now for this luxurious lair of arms traffickers the model is Duke Ellington's "jungle style" and its associations with the Cotton Club, a notorious recreational destination for the top mobsters of the 1930s. A snippet of lounge-piano music within the Canto Bight sequence also provides Williams experts with an inside joke: a quotation of Williams's own score from the neo-noir film *The Long Goodbye* (Robert Altman, 1973), recorded on the piano by Williams himself.[22]

In the meantime, Williams also gave his contribution outside the Skywalker trilogies. He penned "The Adventures of Han," the spiritedly acrobatic main theme of *Solo: A Star Wars Story* (Ron Howard, 2018), a spin-off that chronicles the first exploits of the young Han Solo and whose score was written by John Powell. Williams also provided brand-new musical material for the *Star Wars*–themed area opened in Disney parks in 2019: a miniature concert suite titled "Galaxy's Edge," which brought the composer his twenty-fifth Grammy Award (Best Instrumental Composition).[23]

The last curtain call for the Skywalker saga—apparently—and the putting of "the bow on the package" for Williams came in 2019.[24] On 21 November 2019—forty-two years and eight months after the first-ever *Star Wars* recording session—Williams wrapped up his magnum opus with *Star Wars: Episode IX—The Rise of Skywalker* (J. J. Abrams). For his final contribution to the *Star Wars* franchise, Williams wrote a score that recapitulates his entire thematic production, bridging the first and the third trilogy with quotes, interpolations, and interminglings of the old and the new themes. The central theme is "The Rise of Skywalker," a bright soaring melody that indicates achievement and reunion, the ideal sequel to "The Rebellion Is Reborn": if that alternated hope and the uncertainty about the ongoing fight, this certifies that the unrelenting hope has finally resulted in a victory against the Dark Side. Rey's theme and Kylo's motif are elaborated with sensibility; Rey is now a woman and a trained Jedi, and music reflects this achieved maturity: "With Rey's theme I could treat it in the orchestra so that it is in a more grown-up way."[25] Kylo eventually repents and dies for the good cause, the hesitation of his musical motif finally turned into altruistic heroism by the shift of the music from the previous minor-mode harmonization to an uplifting major-mode setting. The Emperor's theme also resurfaces (as its character does), more malevolent and powerful than ever, with Williams augmenting "his 102-piece ensemble [with] the 100-voice Los Angeles Master Chorale."[26] The "Main Title" theme (or Luke's leitmotif) is employed during the final battle—bringing back some of the swashbuckling atmospheres of the first trilogy—and "The Force" theme is the protagonist of the film's final shot to infuse the saga's closure with a sense of nostalgic recapitulation and coming-full-circle fulfillment. The final chapter gave Williams the opportunity to be immortalized also *visually* within the *Star Wars* universe: he appears in a cameo role as the judgmental bartender on the planet Kijimi, under the name Oma Tres (an anagram for "Maestro").

Williams's music has always been an essential ingredient in the *Star Wars* universe. "The score is a very, very important element of the success of the [*Star Wars*] movies. Without somebody as brilliant as Johnny doing the scores, I don't think they would have been as successful as they were. The score is a major element," Lucas admitted recently.[27] The saga's reception history has seen highs and lows and mixed reviews. For all its uncertainties and drawbacks, the prequel trilogy nevertheless still had Lucas at the helm, the unifying supervisor who made sure that his vision maintained a general coherence and consistency, and a straightforward storytelling trajectory that connected the new films with the old ones. This straightforward trajectory and unified vision are arguably what the third trilogy lacked. With Lucas gone, the appointment of a showrunner-like figure would have been extremely helpful.[28] The Disney films, on the contrary, have oscillated between orthodox adherence to the classics, unprepared bouts of radical revisionism, and harsh U-turns back to more faithful and fan-appeasing paths. *Episode VII* was so concerned with recapturing the mood and look of the classic films that, as we mentioned, it is

more a reboot than a sequel. *Episode VIII* took a detour so divisive and controversial that it caused outraged reactions from hard-core fans, even resulting in
petitions.[29] *Episode IX* steered the (space)ship back to well-tested territories
again by undoing the setups and premises and sidelining characters (Rose, for
example) from the previous film. *Cinematically*, Williams's music has been the
binding agent that, throughout all the saga's vicissitudes, managed to make
each new episode consistent and recognizable as part of the familiar universe.

Musically, the *Star Wars* saga is a unique achievement because of the mag-
nitude of its corpus of scores. Williams commented:

> The *Star Wars* experience has been, I think, unique in music history, film music
> history. Not because of me, there's no waving my own flag, but because of this
> simple reason. . . . I thought that Star Wars was just over and completed when
> I put the baton down at the end of the first recording. And a year or so later,
> he [Lucas] rang up and said, "I have the next installment. And we need the old
> music from the first film, but we also need new music for new characters, new
> situations." So a process started . . . of adding bits and pieces of material to a
> musical tapestry that started . . . to pile up off the floors, quite an extensive
> library of music. Each film having over two hours of music. . . . And that, I
> think, is a unique opportunity for a composer, . . . to go back over and perhaps
> improve some of the things I'd done. And what's fascinating is, to me, that
> maybe some of the newer music isn't any better or as good as the earlier ones.
> That's one's own personal inner struggle, inner voice. When you write some-
> thing when you're 40 years old, you wouldn't write it the same way when one
> is 70 and vice versa. One may be better than the other or a different kind of
> energy or different kind of acuity, whatever will go with it.[30]

After completing the recording of the final chapter, Williams added: "Forty
years ago, if you said to me, 'Here's a project, John, and I want you to write
25 hours of music,' I would have dropped my pencil case and said, 'It's impossible. No one can do that.'"[31]

Apart from this unique set of scores written for the films, the music for
Lucas's space opera has enjoyed great success beyond the screen, and the
interest has remained high for each new musical chapter that Williams has
added since. In 1994 the scores for the first trilogy were reissued as a four-CD
box set containing some additional previously unreleased material, which sold
more than 150,000 copies, quite a staggering figure for a film-music re-release.[32]
In 1997, on the twentieth anniversary of the first film's screening, BMG issued

a series of double CDs featuring the complete score of each chapter of the trilogy. In 2004 the same double CDs were reissued by Sony Classical. Over the years, there have also been huge numbers of suites and anthologies recorded by various orchestras around the world. In 2005 the American Film Institute chose *Star Wars* (1977) as the best film score of all time.[33] In 1999 "Duel of the Fates," the Williams piece for chorus and orchestra from *Star Wars: Episode I—The Phantom Menace,* was reportedly the first symphonic video clip to be featured on the music channel MTV; excerpts from the film are alternated with shots of Williams conducting the London Symphony Orchestra and the London Voices choir.

The presence on MTV shows how widely Williams's music spread, reaching unexpected targets for symphonic music. As Williams pointed out, "That's not a rock band on the sound track, not a Fender bass or a rhythm section. Yet even the kids liked the sound of it, they felt the need for this kind of communication."[34] One of the merits of the *Star Wars* score is that it has introduced many people to symphonic music, and thus one of the motivations for Williams having been awarded an honorary degree by Boston University in 1985.

> In an age when, in both popular and serious music, melody and harmony have had their backs to the wall, you have led millions to enjoy and appreciate music that would have been recognized as such by Beethoven or Brahms. This is no small achievement. We have watched and listened with delighted astonishment as you have ennobled anew the art of background music. But your cinematic music is more than background: it takes on an existence outside the movie house, selling millions of albums. Your suite from *Star Wars* has become part of the concert repertoire. Through your music . . . you expose children who have studied music neither privately nor in school and who hear little but single-note rhythms in popular music to ambitious melodies and to complex harmonic and rhythmic structures on a symphonic scale. In the tradition of Rachmaninov, Prokofiev, and Korngold, you have made orchestral music accessible to and enjoyable by the millions.[35]

Williams's score has been successful in concert halls too. On 20 November 1977 Zubin Mehta conducted a thirty-minute-long suite with the Los Angeles Philharmonic in front of 17,500 people in a sold-out concert at the Hollywood Bowl in Los Angeles.[36] This was the first one of the many "Star Wars concerts" to follow.[37] Williams himself was later invited to conduct his music by such musical institutions as the London Symphony Orchestra (16 February 1978) and the National Philharmonic (18 October 1980), both at the Royal Albert Hall in London. On 1 April 1978 Mehta repeated the previous year's program, adding Williams's suite from *Close Encounters of the Third Kind* (Steven Spielberg, 1977), and in that same month Williams conducted his music in San Francisco. On 26 March 1978 Williams also appeared as a guest conductor on the TV show *Previn and the Pittsburgh* on PBS, in which André Previn invited him to conduct the Pittsburgh Symphony Orchestra in two extracts from the *Star Wars Suite*: "Princess Leia" and "Throne Room and Finale." David Wessel's 1983 *Boston Globe* quote gives a better idea of the success of the *Star Wars* music in concert halls.

> On "Star Wars," according to his business manager, Williams has made almost as much money from performances as he did from record sales. After the film was released, Williams reworked the score into a 36-minute piece for orchestras. Fourteen sets of sheet music for full orchestras were prepared and rented to orchestras. [Herb] Eiseman, then running 20th Century Fox's music publishing house, set a sliding scale rental fee that ran from $250 a performance for a 4500-seat auditorium to $1000 for one with more than 20,000 seats. "We had close to 1000 concerts—maybe more than 1000 concerts now," Eiseman said. Williams got half the money.[38]

Since Disney's acquisition of the *Star Wars* franchise, a series of "film concerts" of the classic trilogy and of *The Force Awakens* have successfully been held all over the world: audiences can enjoy an orchestra playing the entire score live as the film is screened.[39] This vast exposure and the success of his music favored Williams's appointment as conductor-in-residence of the Boston Pops Orchestra, a fundamental step toward the cracking of the "iron curtain" that isolated film music from art/absolute music and other types of applied music.

Above all, what *Star Wars* demonstrated, in the pop-oriented 1970s, was that the traditional practice and models of Hollywood symphonic film scoring were still feasible and could also be successful for the contemporaneous film industry; indeed, they could compete with the pop genre not only as a better way to help the narration but also in terms of revenue from "soundtrack" album sales. As Scheurer writes:

> Williams's influence has been felt in the industry—look at Jerry Goldsmith's score for *Star Trek* (1979) or Danny Elfman's score for *Batman* (1989). Both these

men and composers like James Newton Howard, James Homer, and Bruce Broughton seem to recall the heroic, to be unabashedly reaching out to the audience and attempting to stir them by hearkening back to the scores of the classical Hollywood film. . . . It is difficult to know and perhaps dangerous to speculate on whether these men would be as busy today writing for films, especially writing in this "old-fashioned" style, if it had not been for John Williams, but without him their type of "conservatism" might not be judged suitable anymore especially when a filmmaker/producer can hammer together a soundtrack based on current pop tunes.[40]

Film-Music Renaissance(?)

After *Star Wars*, the use of the symphonic score grew consistently in importance in the late 1970s and throughout the 1980s. Some post–*Star Wars* films that adopted symphonic scores are *The Black Hole* (Gary Nelson, 1979, music by John Barry), *Star Trek: The Motion Picture* (Robert Wise, 1979, music by Jerry Goldsmith), *Conan the Barbarian* (John Milius, 1982, music by Basil Poledouris), *The Right Stuff* (Philip Kaufman, 1983, music by Bill Conti), *Out of Africa* (Sidney Pollack, 1985, music by John Barry), *Silverado* (Lawrence Kasdan, 1985, music by Bruce Broughton), *Back to the Future* (Robert Zemeckis, 1985, music by Alan Silvestri), *Lionheart* (Franklin J. Schaffner, 1987, music by Jerry Goldsmith), *Willow* (Ron Howard, 1988, music by James Horner), *Who Framed Roger Rabbit* (Robert Zemeckis, 1988, music by Alan Silvestri), *Batman* (Tim Burton, 1989, music by Danny Elfman), in addition to Williams's own scores. One of the most amusing and, at the same time, touching homages to classical Hollywood music is Miklós Rózsa's final film score, for *Dead Men Don't Wear Plaid* (Carl Reiner, 1982), a parody of the classical film noir for which Rózsa composed an affectionate musical parody of his own idiom. Scholars, film-music historians, and experts are also more or less unanimous in giving Williams's score credit for launching a sort of "film music renaissance."[41] Williams is typically humble and rather cautious in giving his score the merit of having single-handedly created such a thing.

Well, I don't know if it's fair to say the *Star Wars* films brought back symphonic scores per se. We've been using symphony orchestras since even before sound. Anyone interested in film knows that music seems to be an indispensable ingredient for filmmakers. . . . I think if the use of symphony orchestras went out of fad in the '50s and '60s for some reason it was just that: it was out of fad. Someone would have brought it back. It's too useful and too successful not to have it back. I think that after the success of *Star Wars* the orchestras enjoyed a very successful period because of that. . . . I don't think we can claim that it was a renaissance really, more than just a change of fad if you'd like. . . . A little helping push.[42]

Williams perfectly understood what type of music was needed for a film like *Star Wars*; he possessed a deep understanding and a thorough knowledge of both the art-music and the Hollywood film-music repertoires, and he possessed such skills to be able to compose exactly the required type of music. He remarked, in 1983, "In the sixties and seventies directors were interested in super-realism and a kind of proletarian leanness, where the cosmetic effect of a large symphony orchestra was just exactly what was not wanted. But now fantasy films have come back into fashion, and as a musician I'm very happy about it."[43]

However, Williams's aforementioned caution is acute and historically accurate. To state that *Star Wars* restored the classical Hollywood music style altogether is not correct, as it is not true to say that since *Star Wars*, the symphony orchestra has become the dominant musical means in Hollywood cinema. Only six months after the release of *Star Wars*, the Bee Gees disco music used for the music track of *Saturday Night Fever* (John Badham, 1977) was not only a central factor of the box office success but also became one of the best-selling albums in history.[44] Similarly, Giorgio Moroder won an Oscar for his electronic pop music for *Midnight Express* (Alan Parker, 1978), defeating both Morricone's lyrical symphonic score for *Days of Heaven* (Terrence Malick, 1978) and Williams's rousing grand-orchestral score for *Superman: The Movie* (Richard Donner, 1978).

In the following years, new idioms emerged as highly successful in Hollywood, among them disco music, New Age impressionism, ethnic influences (World Music), minimalism, *musique concrète* or "noise music," and the like. In particular, the 1980s saw the wide spread of synthesizers and electronic music, preferred (also for economic reasons) by a number of emerging practitioners, such as Vangelis in *Blade Runner* (Ridley Scott, 1982) and *Chariots of Fire* (Hugh Hudson, 1981); Giorgio Moroder in *Midnight Express* and *Flashdance* (Adrian Lyne, 1983); Brad Fiedel in *The Terminator* (James Cameron, 1984); Harold Faltermeyer's "synth-pop" for *Beverly Hills Cop* (Martin Brest, 1984); the Angelo Badalamenti and David Lynch collaboration, starting with *Blue Velvet* (1986); and the director/musician John Carpenter in *Halloween* (1978). Even a composer from the previous generation like Maurice Jarre—formerly famous for embracing the lush symphonic Hollywood music in David Lean's *Lawrence of Arabia* (1962), *Dr. Zhivago* (1965), and *Ryan's Daughter* (1970)—discarded the symphony orchestra and opted for the synthesizer in *The Year of Living Dangerously* (Peter Weir, 1982), *Witness* (Peter Weir, 1985), and *Fatal Attraction* (Adrian Lyne, 1987). These examples show that the 1980s were as much the decade of Williams's new symphonism as the decade of synthesized pop music.

The style of film music after 1978 is perhaps best defined, after James Wierzbicki, as "eclecticism," which can be characterized by a freer, hybridized, and varied wide-range mingling of previous styles, languages, techniques, and musical means.[45] Cases of Mickey-Mousing, leitmotiv, electronic music, rock, pop, jazz, world music, and symphonic sound coexist not only in the general paradigm but sometimes also in the same film. For example, the *Flashdance* score is in a pop language and uses electronic means, but classical techniques such as Mickey-Mousing are also employed.[46] The contemporary style, which has also intensified the internationalism inherited from the modern style, can be said to be not only eclectic but also cosmopolitan. National film-music schools tend to disappear in favor of an international style that sounds similar almost everywhere.

The main contribution of *Star Wars* to the overall paradigm of the eclectic style is the large orchestra as the sound de rigueur for blockbuster films, regardless of the language, which can range from David Arnold's mimicry of Williams's idiom in *Independence Day* (Roland Emmerich, 1996) to Hans Zimmer's rock music arranged for orchestra in *The Rock* (Michael Bay, 1996). Moreover, *Star Wars* has promoted the revival of certain classical techniques, such as Mickey-Mousing, mostly used in adventure films and comedies, and leitmotiv used, for example, by Danny Elfman in *Batman* and *Batman Returns* (Tim Burton, 1992), and in the *Star Trek* series. As to the late-Romantic dialect, even Williams's intra-opus style became more eclectic in the following chapters of the saga, including atonal writing and electronic-music episodes.

Even if there were not really a symphonic film-music renaissance or a return of the classical style as such, how can Williams's work and idiom be defined within the post–*Star Wars* eclectic paradigm? Williams has founded a "neoclassical trend" that revived and renovated the style of the classical Hollywood music, a trend of which he has continued to be the greatest exponent. The peak of this neoclassical trend can be placed between 1975 and 1983. The year 1975 saw the release of *Jaws* (Steven Spielberg), a film that was a key contribution to the launch of the neoclassical style. The peak itself lasted a mere eight years and, already in 1980, Williams stated, "I don't expect what

I have been doing for the last two or three years will last—nothing does; already in some studios they are calling for more pop music, for more youth-oriental pop noise."[47] The year 1983 has been chosen as the end of the neo-classical trend for a couple of reasons. In that year the album from the score of *Return of the Jedi*, the closing chapter of the first *Star Wars* trilogy, was not released as a double LP but as a single LP, unlike the albums from the previous two films, even though more than 130 minutes of music had been composed for the film. And unlike the two previous albums, it had disappointing sales.[48] That same year also marked the last collaboration between Williams and the LSO, the "official" and most sought-after orchestra of the neoclassical trend. The second and third chapters of the Indiana Jones trilogy, *Indiana Jones and the Temple of Doom* (Steven Spielberg, 1984) and *Indiana Jones and the Last Crusade* (Steven Spielberg, 1989), were recorded in Los Angeles with a free-lance studio orchestra. Williams would not work again with the LSO on a film until 1999, when he returned to Abbey Road Studios to record *Star Wars: Episode I—The Phantom Menace*. In 1984, for the adventure film *Romancing the Stone* (Robert Zemeckis), the emerging composer Alan Silvestri used elec-tronic means and a modern pop dialect instead of following in Williams's neoclassical footsteps. In 1985 Silvestri's theme for *Back to the Future* (Robert Zemeckis) sounded more orchestral rock than symphonic neoclassical. More-over, the songs "The Power of Love" and "Back in Time" by Huey Lewis and the News were the highlights of both the film and the album. A further proof of the anything-but-hegemonic role of neoclassicism is the case of *Legend* (Ridley Scott, 1985). The rich symphonic score composed by Jerry Goldsmith was removed from the US version and replaced with Tangerine Dream's elec-tronic New Age music.[49]

The classical style did not actually rise again. With the first *Star Wars* film and his subsequent works, Williams composed neoclassical scores in which he recovered many features of the classical style. After years of mostly market-oriented music, his narrative-oriented scores brought back to general atten-tion the importance and power of music as a device of cinematic art, and the fundamental help that it can give to film narration. This also caused a stronger awareness and interest for the rediscovery of Hollywood's musical tradition. Yet if *Star Wars* can be seen as the first clamorous manifestation of the neoclassical trend, the first signs of Williams's penchant for neoclassicism are already visible in his first 1960s film works.

CHAPTER 6

Williams's Early Years

Spotting the First Traces of Neoclassicism

John Towner Williams was born in Flushing, Queens, New York, on 8 February 1932. His father, John Francis Williams—known as Johnny Williams—was a percussionist in the CBS Radio Orchestra and a member of the Raymond Scott Quintette.[1] Young Williams studied music and learned to play the trumpet, the trombone, the bassoon, the cello, and the clarinet, and used to follow his father into the recording studios and attend the sessions.[2] He soon decided to devote himself primarily to the piano, aiming to pursue a career as a classical concert pianist. As the family relocated to Los Angeles in 1948, John Jr. studied privately there with pianist Robert Van Eps, who was also an active Hollywood orchestrator, while John Sr. worked as a session percussionist with Hollywood orchestras, in particular with the Columbia Studio Orchestra, "for composers like Bernard Herrmann. . . . ('Bernard loved the way he played timpani,' said [John's brother] Don Williams.)."[3] These might be considered Williams's first contacts with the world of film music. Tim Grieving reports that his was a musical family: "The Williams house was a constant jam session. All of Johnny Sr.'s friends were musicians, people like film composer George Duning ('From Here to Eternity'), Perry Botkin Sr. (Bing Crosby's guitarist) and pianist Claude Thornhill, and they would drop by to talk music and make music, with Johnny Jr. often tickling the ivories."[4] Williams also showed uncommon skills for composition and arrangement. During his years at North Hollywood High School, he used to arrange music for the school band—"the hottest band in Hollywood," according to a 1949 *Time* magazine article—applying to popular melodies the techniques he had learned from orchestration manuals: "I always composed. As a child, I tried to write little pieces and, as a teenager, began to orchestrate some of them. And my father was a musician, and there were theory books sitting around the house that were there underfoot since age eight or ten or whatever. But piano was my serious study. I hadn't intended ever to become a professional composer. In fact I wouldn't imagine anyone could earn a living doing that."[5] Later, he moved to the Los Angeles City College and the University of California at Los Angeles. Meanwhile, he was privately tutored in composition and counterpoint by Mario Castelnuovo Tedesco.[6]

In 1952 Williams was drafted, and during his service in the US Air Force, he had the chance to work on his first film score. He reminisces:

I . . . spent two years with the Northeast Air Command Band in St. John's, Newfoundland. This was a wonderful experience, and it seemed I was the only one there who could write arrangements for that band. I conducted some of the rehearsals, and the band played summer concerts in a gazebo during which the base commander often requested his favorite songs. After the end of World War II, the Canadian government commissioned a German company, North Atlantic Films, to make a documentary about the Maritime Provinces of Canada. In 1953 the company was working in St. John's, and some of these people attended the summer concerts and heard my band arrangements. As a result they asked my commanding officer if I could write music for the film. He not only granted me permission but allowed me to use several band members. I discovered some folk songs of Newfoundland in the library and wove these into the score. This was my first attempt at film writing, and I used only winds.[7]

An article of the time was devoted to the young soldier/composer: "With discharge day coming his way in January 1955, Johnny plans to continue his studies at UCLA with a goal of writing and playing for motion pictures. If his advancement continues to be as rapid as it has been to this point, soon the words 'Music by Johnny Williams' will flash on the local screen and tell the realization of the goal of a former March airman."[8]

After military service, apparently not sure whether to opt for a career as a composer or as a pianist, Williams mused, "I guess I wanted to play Rachmaninoff with the New York Philharmonic."[9] Williams moved to New York and was admitted to the prestigious Juilliard School in the piano class of Rosina Lhévinne, where Van Cliburn was one of Williams's schoolmates.[10] To earn some money while studying, he worked as a pianist in jazz ensembles. However, his skills in composition proved, again, his strongest talent: "I started to hear some of her [Lhévinne's] other students who were even younger than

I was playing around the building . . . and I thought 'Well, if that's what the competition is, maybe I should be a composer.'"[11]

A Serendipitous Start in Hollywood

Back in Los Angeles in 1956, Williams became a father—after marrying singer/actress Barbara Ruick—and thus needed a stable job to sustain his new family. There happened to be a vacant pianist chair in the studio orchestra at Columbia Pictures, and Williams auditioned for the post. He was hired, thus entering the world of film music as an orchestra member: "The audition process was very simple. It was a sight-reading session. I was a pretty good sight reader as a youngster. And I played in the orchestras of studios in Hollywood for four or five years."[12] Williams's piano playing can be heard in *Funny Face* (Stanley Donen, 1957, music adapted by Adolph Deutsch), *South Pacific* (Joshua Logan, 1958, musical direction by Alfred Newman); *The Big Country* (William Wyler, 1958, music by Jerome Moross), *Some Like It Hot* (Billy Wilder, 1959, music by Adolph Deutsch), *City of Fear* (Irving Lerner, 1959, music by Jerry Goldsmith), *Breakfast at Tiffany's* (Blake Edwards, 1961, music by Henry Mancini), *West Side Story* (Jerome Robbins and Robert Wise, 1961, music by Leonard Bernstein); and *To Kill a Mockingbird* (Robert Mulligan, 1962, music by Elmer Bernstein). Perhaps his most famous contribution is the piano riff that opens the title music in the TV series *Peter Gunn* (Blake Edwards, 1958–61, music by Henry Mancini). During this stint as a pianist, in addition to working for Columbia Pictures, he also played for the 20th Century Fox studio from 1958 on.

Williams gradually left the piano bench to undertake the typical career path in Hollywood's music departments: he worked as an orchestrator on *The Apartment* (Billy Wilder, 1960, music by Adolph Deutsch) and *The Guns of Navarone* (J. Lee Thompson, 1961, music by Dimitri Tiomkin): "I still didn't have the notion that I might be a film composer or professional composer until some of these older colleagues began to say to me, 'Can you orchestrate X scene, this is Tuesday, we need it for Thursday morning, next Monday morning.' Of course, with the temerity of youth, when everything seems possible, we always say yes."[13] The work with the orchestra was the element of attraction, as Williams confesses: "I was never that into the movies. . . . Never. Even as a youngster. I became interested in movie music only because of the studio orchestras in Hollywood. I'd been studying orchestration books since I was about 14, because my parents had them in the house and they always fascinated me."[14] Outside the film studios, he was also working in the record industry as an arranger and conductor for Columbia Records, with such singers as Mahalia Jackson, Doris Day, and Vic Damone. As John Towner Williams / John T. Williams, he was also quite active as a recording artist with his own quartet, septet, octet, and orchestra—notably in the albums *The John Towner Touch* (Kapp Records KL-1055, 1957), *Modern Jazz Gallery* (Kapp Records KXL 5001, 1957), *World on a String* (Bethlehem Records BCP-6025, 1958), *Rhythm in Motion* (Columbia CS 8467, 1961), and the movie-themed easy-listening *Big Hits from Columbia Pictures* (Golden Tone 9632S, 1958). In 1964 he also arranged a jazz version of the musical *My Fair Lady* (Alan Jay Lerner and Frederick Loewe, 1956) for Shelly Manne. His jazz roots as a performer/arranger can be classified within the West Coast cool school of the 1950s: "My involvement in jazz was never very extensive, but it occurred during a rich period of jazz development and invention."[15] The next step was composition, and the gradual shift started in 1958, when he was offered a seven-year contract in the music department of the Revue Television Studios, later known as Universal Television Studios. He worked on such TV series as *M Squad* (1958–59), *Wagon Train* (1958–63), *Checkmate* (1960–62), *Bachelor Father* (1959–60), *Kraft Suspense Theater* (1960), *Alcoa Premiere* (1961–62), *The Crisis* (1963–65), *Gilligan's Island* (1964–65), and *Lost in Space* (1965). He also served as the piano-playing double for actor John Cassavetes in the TV show *Johnny Staccato* (1959–60), and in the first episode, "The Naked Truth," he can also be spotted in a cameo appearance.[16] Meanwhile, he also stepped up to the podium to conduct recordings of his own music, not so much for ambition as for "self-defense" from lesser conductors, and soon left piano gigs to concentrate fully on composition: "A very gradual process took place, from working primarily on the piano bench in the orchestras of the studios to the orchestrator's desk and eventually to the composing desk and [I] was invited then to conduct some scores of my own and of others."[17]

Television work in those years was good training for film composers. They had to deliver a steady output of music, always working under tight deadlines, and they had to learn to write fast and develop a quick, sure-fire instinct for what was suitable for the narrative needs of a given scene. As a staff composer, Williams had to work on thirty-nine one-hour TV shows per year, churning out scores of the most diverse kinds, from comedies to thrillers to Westerns: "The shows I was assigned to were the hardest shows, the hour shows, which meant I had to write about 20 to 25 minutes of music a week, score it and record it. It was a tremendous learning opportunity for me. What I wrote may not have been good—it probably wasn't good; but the

main idea was to get it done, and I got it done."[18] This work routine in television was very similar to that of the music departments in the old studios—
although smaller in proportion. In this formative period, dividing his time
between playing piano in studio orchestras and composing in the Revue Studio music department, Williams had the opportunity of mixing with, and learning the tricks of the trade from, some of the masters of Hollywood music:
Alfred Newman, Dimitri Tiomkin, Franz Waxman, and Bernard Herrmann—
with whom he became a close friend. Williams also acknowledges the important teachings of Conrad Salinger, one of the top arrangers and orchestrators
in Hollywood, whose influence can be heard in Williams's arrangement of
Cole Porter's "Anything Goes" that opens *Indiana Jones and the Temple of Doom*
(Steven Spielberg, 1984).

> "[I] spent a lot of time with Conrad Salinger. [I] learned a tremendous amount
> from him—mostly from looking at his scores. As you know, he principally did
> musicals; he was the architect of what you might call the "MGM sound"—that
> marvelous glow that the orchestra had. And it really came from his writing. His
> scores were highly idiosyncratic: he'd have the third trombone way up in tenor
> clef, and trumpets low down doing funny things . . . ! And then you'd go on the
> sound stage the next day and hear the result . . . it was like a wonder. No one
> quite had his touch. . . . Of all the orchestrators . . . I think I learned more from
> Conrad Salinger than anyone else, even though I don't write anything like him.[19]

Most of Williams's career would be spent as a freelance composer in the
post-studio-era "package-unit" system—each film project is a team-up of freelance artists and technicians assembled and contracted for that single project,
unlike the typical in-house staff of payrolled people that used to work on
each film of their studio in the old system.[20] Yet Williams moved his first steps
into the business during the last days of the studio system and in-house music
departments, and he acquired an extensive training in the high-pressure schedules of television production. The relevance of this early "imprinting" within
the old practice was of enormous importance in shaping Williams's neoclassical approach; it had a considerable influence on his work habits, which
retain a number of old-school characteristics, as we shall see.

Johnny Williams, Emerging Composer

After television, Williams moved on to cinema. His first significant collaborations in feature films were with Don Siegel for the thriller *The Killers* (1964),

with Frank Sinatra for the war film *None but the Brave* (1965)—the singer/actor's only directorial credit—and with Andrew V. McLaglen for the Western *The Rare Breed* (1966, starring James Stewart and Maureen O'Hara). After these multifaceted experiences, in the mid-1960s Williams was pigeonholed as a comedy composer.[21] Williams provided scores for such films as *John Goldfarb, Please Come Home!* (J. Lee Thompson, 1965), *Not with My Wife, You Don't!* (Norman Panama, 1966), *Penelope* (Arthur Hiller, 1966), *How to Steal a Million* (William Wyler, 1966), *A Guide for the Married Man* (Gene Kelly, 1967), and *Fitzwilly* (Delbert Mann, 1967). Most of them were somewhat spicy comedies in the typical post–Hays Code, liberated-mores style of the 1960s—"lots of brass chords on cuts to brassieres," Williams recalls.[22]

In the next decade, Williams moved to another genre, and thanks to his previous collaboration with producer Irwin Allen for *Lost in Space*, he became the composer of choice for "disaster movies" such as *The Poseidon Adventure* (Ronald Neame, 1972), *Earthquake* (Mark Robson, 1974), and *The Towering Inferno* (John Guillermin, 1974). He also worked in Europe on *Heidi* (Delbert Mann, 1968), coproduced by the Federal Republic of Germany and featuring a Richard Straussian *Eine Alpensinfonie*–like score performed by members of the Hamburg Opera; *Jane Eyre* (Delbert Mann, 1970) for British television, showcasing a sensitive score in the British idioms of Ralph Vaughan Williams and Frederick Delius; and *Story of a Woman* (Leonardo Bercovici, 1970), an Italian coproduction to which he also contributed the song "Uno di qua, l'altra di là," sung by Ornella Vanoni and recorded in Milan.[23]

Besides demonstrating his ability to produce functional and well-written scores, Williams was already distinguishing himself from the average composers with a number of outstanding scores. For *The Reivers* (Mark Rydell, 1969), he adopted Copland's Americana idiom to paint a lively score imbued with nostalgia, which is the perfect musical correlative of William Faulkner's eponymous novel set in 1905. For *The Long Goodbye* (Robert Altman, 1973), he composed a monothematic score à la *Laura* in which the melody of the theme song (lyrics by Johnny Mercer) is skillfully arranged for different sets of instrumentation and used at both nondiegetic and diegetic levels. And again, for *Jane Eyre*, Williams wrote a refined score that shows his thorough knowledge and love for British music. For *The Cowboys* (Mark Rydell, 1972), he provided a driving theme for full orchestra in line with the Copland-Moross-Bernstein Western tradition. The most notable and experimental work of the period is *Images* (Robert Altman, 1972), the story of the psychic double life of a schizophrenic woman, a children's book author, for which Williams composed a similarly schizophrenic score. A melancholic melody for piano and strings accompanies the woman's fantasies and the peaceful moments in which she works on her book. On the other hand, the psychotic episodes in which she sees her double self or talks with her dead lover are accompanied by disturbingly atonal and aleatoric music, performed by the percussionist Stomu Yamash'ta on metal and glass sculptures by the Parisian artists François and Bernard Baschet.[24]

In the first part of his career, Williams ranked among the most gifted and versatile composers of his generation. In addition to traditional symphonic scores for large orchestra—such as *The Rare Breed* or *The Cowboys*—he composed a modern-style restrained score for *The Missouri Breaks* (Arthur Penn, 1976), scored for guitars, banjos, bass guitars, and harmonicas. Besides Copland's idiom and jazz dialect used in detective stories like *Checkmate*, Williams could also handle up-to-date pop dialects: rhythms and inflections typical of the current dance music can be found either in light-hearted versions in comedies such as *A Guide for the Married Man*, or dramatically arranged for orchestra in thrillers such as *Towering Inferno* and *Earthquake*. Williams's versatility was such that he followed one of the most characteristic practices of modern style as well, namely the incorporation of at least one pop song in each film. He wrote songs both for comedies ("A Big Beautiful Ball" for *Not with My Wife, You Don't!* or "Two Lovers" for *How to Steal a Million*) and for dramas ("None but the Brave" for *None but the Brave*, "Dream Way" for *The Man Who Loved Cat Dancing* [Richard C. Sarafian, 1973], and "Daddy's Gone A-Hunting" for *Daddy's Gone A-Hunting* [Mark Robson, 1969]). In an early 1970s interview, however, Williams confessed feeling uncomfortable as a songwriter.

> Well, it has been overdone. God knows, it's a practice that I've been involved in on a few occasions myself. Not very happily, ever; some people seem to have a better touch at that than I do. Again, there I have mixed emotions. It's a practice that can be vile and obnoxious, and awful—very often. On the other hand, the commercial part of me says something has to do some business, and the music-selling business is not altogether a bad thing. . . . So on the positive side of it, this business of title song and popular success from film music is both a good thing and a bad thing. It isn't a great thing for the art of music vis-à-vis film scoring. But it does help the sort of general health of the music-publishing, revenue-creating areas of the music business—and the music "business" affects us all.[25]

Although versatility was a key feature of the young Williams, some neo-classical traits were already scattered within his 1960s works. As we have seen, the "spatial perceptive function" became obsolete after the classical period, surviving sporadically as mannerist bursts of Mickey-Mousing in some comedies. In the "modern style" of the 1960s, Henry Mancini was the leading composer in Hollywood and the major model. "Mancini was becoming a force of influence within each of those categories. Colleagues in Hollywood talked about their own music as having 'Mancini chords' and spoke of themselves as being freer to write, thanks to him," says John Caps.[26] At that time, instead of embracing the up-to-date comedy musical style à la Mancini, found for example in Burt Bacharach's and Quincy Jones's scores for *Casino Royale* (John Huston et al., 1967) and *Cactus Flower* (Gene Saks, 1969), respectively, Williams-the-emerging-composer opted for the illustrative and not-so-up-to-date musical approach featured in such comedies as *Gambit* (Ronald Neame, 1966, music by Maurice Jarre) and *The Glass Bottom Boat* (Frank Tashlin, 1966, music by Frank De Vol). Besides already showing a peculiar interest in explicit sync points and Mickey-Mousing, Williams also showed a penchant for the leitmotiv technique. A close look at his 1960s films shows that he applied these classical techniques more extensively and systematically than most colleagues. Moreover, he applied them not only to comedies but also to dramas.

A Mancini/Williams Comparison

Zooming in on Williams's early film scores, this section has the scope of substantiating the claim that his style already appeared more "neoclassical" compared to those of his coeval colleagues. To build such a comparative survey, the chosen approach has been that of tracing the higher number of recurrences of classical-style traits—leitmotiv technique, continuous musical flow rather than closed musical number, and, above all, the "spatial perceptive function" (Mickey-Mousing and explicit sync points)—and contrasting it with the lower number of occurrences in Hollywood's most influential composer at the time, Mancini. Without any pretense of statistical exhaustiveness, a sample of films has been chosen for each composer. The selection is based on a mix including both celebrated titles and lesser-known works, within the period 1962 to 1972, choosing five comedies and three dramas for each composer and favoring titles that are easily available. The Mancini sample contains:

- *Breakfast at Tiffany's* (Blake Edwards, 1961), a bittersweet comedy about nostalgia and loneliness concerning the serendipitous meeting between an eccentric and naive prostitute (Holly) and a discouraged writer (Paul) maintained as a boy toy by a rich woman

- *Man's Favorite Sport?* (Howard Hawks, 1964), a screwball comedy in the spirit of Hawks's own 1938 *Bringing Up Baby*, the story of Roger, a successful author of fishing manuals who is forced to join a fishing tournament and has to conceal the fact that he is merely a theorist, having never fished before, while also having to cope with a relentless courtship by a troublemaking woman (Abigail)
- *A Shot in the Dark* (Blake Edwards, 1964), a slapstick comedy and the second chapter of Inspector Clouseau's adventures, in which the inane detective falls in love with a blonde homicide suspect and strenuously tries to prove her innocence
- *The Great Race* (Blake Edwards, 1965), a cartoonlike epic about a car race set in the early twentieth century
- *The Party* (Blake Edwards, 1968), a slapstick humor-filled story of how a Hollywood extra is mistakenly invited to a big-shot party and ends up unintentionally destroying the host's mansion

The dramas are:

- *Arabesque* (Stanley Donen, 1966), the story of university professor Pollock getting involved, along with a charming female spy, in the hunt for a mysterious code, at the risk of his life
- *Wait until Dark* (Terence Young, 1967), a thriller in which a blind woman (Susy) is trapped alone in her apartment with three criminals who want to retrieve a drug-stuffed doll they believe she is hiding somewhere in the apartment
- *The Night Visitor* (Laslo Benedek, 1971), a thriller in which a psychopath (Salem) escapes from an asylum to take revenge on those who had him locked up[27]

As for the Williams sample, the comedies are:

- *How to Steal a Million* (William Wyler, 1966), a sophisticated comedy in which Nicole, the daughter of a forger, organizes the theft of a statue her father leased to a museum in order to prevent her father's forgeries from being discovered
- *Fitzwilly* (Delbert Mann, 1967), in which the austere butler Fitzwilliam coordinates thefts and cons to maintain the high standard of living of his oblivious old-lady employer in order to conceal from her the fact that she is now broke
- *Not with My Wife, You Don't!* (Norman Panama, 1966), about the jealousy of two ex-comrades (Tom and "Tank") who continue to contend for the same woman (Julie) even if she is now married to Tom
- *Penelope* (Arthur Hiller, 1966), in which the rich kleptomaniac Penelope resorts to psychoanalysis to discover the origin of her thieving drive but ends up robbing her own husband's bank

- *A Guide for the Married Man* (Gene Kelly, 1967), a farce concerning a clumsy would-be pursuer of extramarital affairs (Paul) who is instructed by an experienced friend on the supposedly successful techniques for cheating on one's wife

The dramas are:

- *The Killers* (Don Siegel, 1964), the story of a penniless race car driver (Johnny) hired by a gang of bank robbers and then implicated in the ruthless pursuit of the lost loot—a remake of Robert Siodmak's 1946 film
- *Daddy's Gone A-Hunting* (Mark Robson, 1969), a thriller about a married woman (Cathy) who is stalked by her psychopathic ex-boyfriend (Kenneth), who wants to kill her baby to retaliate for her past abortion of the child he had fathered
- *Images* (Robert Altman, 1972), a tale about the psychic double life of a schizophrenic woman

Comedies outnumber dramas because in the chosen time period, both Williams and Mancini worked more in that genre than in dramas. Each film has been analyzed by focusing on the presence of the spatial perspective function and of the leitmotiv and Mickey-Mousing techniques but also by taking into consideration other traits of the classical style vis-à-vis the modern style. (For brevity's sake, only the results of the comparison are given here, complemented with highlights from the films as evidence.)

First, the comparison confirms Mancini's preference for the closed musical numbers, typical of modern style. The comedies in the sample are for the most part directed by Blake Edwards, whose main model was the visual and physical comedy of silent-cinema slapstick. "Finding the proper modern idiom for an old mode of comedy is arguably the central challenge of Edwards' career" is how Sam Wasson summarizes Edwards's poetics.[28] Yet his gags were not highlighted by openly attention-catching devices such as rim shots or a trombone's derisive wha-wha as it would happen in silent cinema; Edwards typically let the visual gags speak for themselves, sometimes unfolding in the background. In this sense, one model of his comedic style was Jacques Tati: the viewer has to scan the frame herself to spot the gags, without being too closely guided by the film narration. Tati was, of course, less comically direct than Edwards, but both avoided emphasizing the comic actions with nondiegetic music.[29] Mickey-Mousing would be too intrusive and perceptually "coercive" in this type of comedy: for Mancini, says Caps, "intentionally 'funny' music behind a comedy scene is redundant and destructive. The 'Pink Panther Theme,' though witty in itself, is not a joke, not a novelty number. It is, besides its grin, a seriously swinging piece of jazz-pop with an invigorating sense of both fun and sophistication. So it does not overkill the comedy."[30] Consequently, the Edwards/Mancini duo chose to accompany the comic scenes mostly with diegetic music, which flows independently in the background, as can be seen in *The Party* when Bakshi is clumsily trying to retrieve his shoe from the water stream. Apart from the director's artistic choice, this is also due to the modern-style, market-oriented approach. All films, except *The Night Visitor*, contain one or more songs skillfully placed in the right spot by Mancini to advertise them. *The Party* is a hilarious comedy in itself, of course, and since the film is about a party, the many diegetic pieces have a solid realistic motivation; but the film is also a clever showcase to promote Mancini's *cocktail music* and to advertise the tie-in LP album.

The same can be said of *Breakfast at Tiffany's*. In one scene, Paul pays a visit to Holly and they start a conversation only after Holly has put on a disc and switched on the turntable, the mellow light dance-music acting as a diegetic background for their dialogue. Similarly, the many party scenes are accompanied by fashionable dance music. The main theme—"Moon River" (lyrics by Johnny Mercer)—is presented in an instrumental version during the opening credits, is sung by Holly at a diegetic level with guitar accompaniment, is reprised by the chorus at the end of the film, and also appears as a diegetic "Cha-cha-cha" during a party scene. The only substantial occurrence of spatial perceptive function can be found in a short chain of sync points in the shoplifting sequence. A stinger by the trombones emphasizes the shop assistant's suspicious look, followed by an answering vibraphone chord underlining Holly's look of feigned innocence. Then, an upward harp glissando culminates in Holly playing the toy trumpet that she was about to steal. Oddly, when the two shoplifters flee and almost collide with a policeman, the music does not mark the event, as we might have expected; it keeps up uninterrupted with its excited flow accompanying the couple's escape.

A Shot in the Dark opens with a long sequence in which we see the inhabitants of a luxurious mansion engaged in a network of nocturnal stealthy visits to their secret lovers. The sequence is accompanied by the song "Shadows of Paris" (lyrics by Robert Wells)—the instrumental version of which serves as the film's love theme—and the song flows independently as a closed musical number, without following the visual actions. During the following opening credits, the theme associated with Clouseau's investigation is introduced—it is a jazzy piece akin to the more famous "Pink Panther" theme—and is presented again arranged for big band as diegetic music during the nudist camp sequence. Clouseau's tumbles are rarely punctuated by music: when he falls into the fountain, when he inadvertently sets fire to his raincoat, or when he jumps out the window, music places little emphasis on the action. Even the overtly comic fights between Clouseau and Kato are left without music. The only explicit sync points are the strident bass chords that mark the appearance of the mysterious black-gloved murderer and the stingers that in the denouement scene introduce each close-up of the suspects' worried faces after Clouseau says, "One of you is a murderer."

The Great Race is a striking example, as Mancini rejects Mickey-Mousing in a couple of scenes that would have been a perfect place for this technique. In the sword fight between the Great Leslie and the Baron, everything harkens back to the classical duels starring Errol Flynn in Michael Curtiz's films: swashbuckling costumes, castle halls with chandeliers and stone walls, even the duelists' shadows cast on the walls—a typical Curtiz stylistic trait. Mancini, in spite of that, did not compose a Korngoldian score by treating the duel like a ballet but opted for a simple strings sound pad with slow modulations keeping the harmony unresolved. In line with modern style, he preferred the emotive function, that is, creating tension. Even the following custard-pie fight scene—a traditional slapstick comedy gag since the days of vaudeville, typically having each comic action accompanied by a musical gesture—has no Mickey-Mousing accompaniment, but instead a spirited polka develops independently as a closed musical number throughout the scene.[31]

Who was responsible for the musical choices of these three films? The director Blake Edwards or the composer Henry Mancini? It is clear that a composer has to meet the director's demands, but a director rarely ventures into detailed discussions on the nature of the music to be adopted in each scene; more often, a director will hire a trusted composer known for being in tune with his ideas on music. Therefore, the composer is mainly responsible for a particular musical solution, especially in the case of well-established collaborations like that between Mancini and Edwards.[32] Indeed, Mancini's stylistic choices were the same when he worked for Howard Hawks, whose comic style is quite different from Edwards's.[33]

In Hawk's *Man's Favorite Sport?* Roger's clumsy attempt to erect a tent is scored with nondiegetic dance music as well as the gag of a bear ending up riding Roger's motorcycle. Most of the dialogue—like that between Roger and the two girls during the dinner on the terrace, or the conversation between the two girls in their rooms—is accompanied by dance music or piano-bar-style Muzak, used at diegetic level. When nondiegetic music accompanies romantic dialogue, its style is modern, since the traditional strings are replaced by woodwinds—following the big-band influence—as in the final dialogue in the woods between Roger and Abigail. Only a few comic moments are highlighted by explicit sync points. When Roger catches his first fish, music builds an upward harmonic progression closed by a sharp chord marking the moment in which the man has to dive in to retrieve his fishing rod. Another case is the scene in which Roger's girlfriend unexpectedly arrives and finds him sharing the room with two women. When the bedroom door opens, revealing Abigail, the supposed lover, in pajamas, a snare-drum roll marks the surprise. Then, a cymbal clash, a plucked strings note, and a triangle tinkle respectively underline the consequent three close-ups on the astonished faces.

As for dramas, it can be noted that music, when not completely absent, performs, again, a purely emotive function. In *Wait until Dark*, for example, the scene in which Susy, the blind woman, enters her house unaware of the three criminals waiting inside, takes place without music. The first dialogue between Susy and Mike, one of the criminals, is accompanied by a diegetic pop song coming from the on-screen turntable. Finally, the end credits are accompanied by the theme song.[34] There is only one effective episode of spatial perceptive function, when Roat, the boss of the gang, threatens Susy, then teases and disorients her by brushing her face from different directions with a silk scarf. Mancini underlines each scarf touch with a tam-tam rub, a sound that aptly conveys Susy's shivers.[35]

In *Arabesque*, explicit sync points are more frequent, perhaps because of director Stanley Donen's background as a choreographer. Again, the tam-tam rub is used as a stinger to punctuate different events: the appearance of Beauchamp the "villain" in Professor Pollock's classroom; Pollock's image reflected on the coachwork of the prime minister's Rolls Royce; the threatening revelation of a gun holster under Beauchamp's jacket; Pollock being given an injection of Pentothal. During the chase sequence at the zoo, four shots of snakes are punctuated by four synchronized stingers. In one of the comic-relief moments of the film, Yasmin, the female spy, tries to seduce a Grenadier Guard: we hear a triangle tinkle when she winks and a flute trill when she blinks her eyes.

The Night Visitor score is interesting for the use of an unusual ensemble: twelve woodwinds, one organ, two pianos and two harpsichords, the two couples of pianos and harpsichords being tuned with a quarter-tone difference from one another, which creates a dizzy feeling.[36] The score does not have explicit sync points at all, and its main function is emotive.

As for Williams's scores, the surface shows modern-style traits and the influence of Mancini's practices (e.g., the use of a title song on the opening titles of *Penelope*, *Not with My Wife, You Don't!*, and *A Guide for the Married Man*, and the jazz dialect and big-band sound for crime stories such as *The Killers*). Yet, if we look closer, we can immediately see that Williams's idiom is far more classical. The use of explicit sync points and spatial perceptive function is definitely more frequent, and the orchestral writing has a stronger symphonic structure when compared to Mancini's light/pop music orchestral writing.

Williams's writing is decidedly more contrapuntal, as can be seen when comparing the main theme for *Breakfast at Tiffany's* with that for *Penelope*: unlike the former homophonic tune, the latter features a canon-like answer to the main melody by the horns, somewhat reminiscent of Rózsa's love themes. Williams also uses more insistently some classical techniques such as the leitmotiv or theme and variations. Mancini seems to be interested in variations mainly because they give musical variety to the tie-in album: think of the many multistyle versions of "Moon River" in *Breakfast at Tiffany's*. On the contrary, Williams seems to be interested in variations mainly in terms of functionality within the film. For example, the title song "A Guide for the Married Man" is sung in the opening titles of the film of the same name by the Turtles in a sunshine-pop style, accompanying images of voluptuous women and colorful graphics. Later in the film, when Paul finally has to move from fantasy (having an adulterous affair with a gorgeous woman) to action (fulfilling his desire by cheating on his wife), the music comically emphasizes the discrepancy between theory and practice: the theme of the title song is now presented in orchestral form, played clumsily and wearily by muted trombones.

In dialogue scenes, Williams also shows his preference for the classical underscoring technique. Music makes room for the dialogue not just by having its volume turned down in the sound mix, as is the case with Mancini's diegetic pieces. Williams makes room for the dialogue by thinning the musical texture and lightening the instrumentation. When the dialogue pauses, he inflates the writing and shifts the music to the foreground, presenting melodic cells; as soon as the dialogue resumes, he shifts the music to the background again. In using this composing-around-the-dialogue technique, the composer is required to precisely follow what is happening on-screen when writing the piece. Like Mickey-Mousing, this is another technique that requires great attention to the adherence of music to visuals. A good example of Williams's underscoring can be found in *The Reivers*. When Boon pays a visit to Corrie, his favorite mistress at the Memphis brothel, and kisses her, the love theme

accompanies the kiss. However, the melodic phrase stops and harmony remains suspended when Corrie moves away from him and tries to say a few
words. When Boon hushes the woman by kissing her again, the music resumes
and the melodic phrase is completed. In an early 1970s interview, Williams
talked about music and dialogue as Korngold would do.

> I think a composer should think of the dialogue as part of the score; he could
> write it as accompaniment for a violin concerto rather than compose a score
> to exist on its own. There are a few little tips, for example, low strings. . . . This
> isn't to say that one can't have high frequencies as well, but I think the choice
> of textures under the dialogue, the register of the speaking voices, and also the
> tempo of the dialogue—if a man says a line, and there's a pause, and the woman
> says the next line after another pregnant pause, it may be possible to color the
> music somewhat differently.[37]

The first sequence of *Fitzwilly* is an excellent example of extensive underscoring. After the main title sequence in which the main theme is introduced,
the music starts again at the fifth minute of the film and accompanies the protagonist on his shopping activities around New York. Music continues un-
interruptedly for the next five minutes: it accompanies the car journeys with
variations of the main theme in march form; it gets thinner in the presence
of dialogue, repeating cells of the main theme during the pauses between
lines; it even emphasizes the shifts of place and marks the closures of the sub-
episodes with harp glissandos.[38] During the romantic scenes, Williams uses
the classical strings and not Mancini's modern woodwind sound; similarly,
strings are preferred in *The Killers, How to Steal a Million,* and *Penelope.* As expected, explicit sync points and even extensive episodes of Mickey-Mousing
are considerably more present in the Williams sample. Some noteworthy examples follow.

In *Not with My Wife, You Don't!* the music replicates the movement of butter-
flies flying out of a chocolate box; it duplicates the scattering of some roses in
the wind during a funeral with a fast woodwinds run; it quotes Mendelssohn's
wedding march—as Max Steiner would have done—when we learn of the
marriage between Julie and Tom.

In *Penelope,* when the protagonist exits through the revolving doors of
Bergdorf Goodman, the music accompanies the door's rotation with a harp
glissando and introduces the main theme. When Penelope tells her psycho-
analyst that the trauma that caused her kleptomania was an attempt of sexual

assault by a teacher during her college years, we see a flashback of the event in an overtly comic tone. The scene opens in a classroom and is given an appropriately poised academic tone by the aloof sound of the harpsichord. Then, suddenly, the professor gets less poised and jumps on the girl. The harpsichord gives way to a wildly aggressive brass riff backed by relentless percussion and punctuated by "horny" horns rips. Mickey-Mousing underlines with a downward trombones glissando the fall of a book stand that reveals the girl in underwear—the teacher had already torn her outer clothes off. This moment is immediately followed by a flute and piccolo trill that comically exaggerates the teacher's wildly excited gaze. Penelope—in her underwear—finally flees the classroom and runs along the lawns of the campus accompanied by her leitmotiv. Later, we see Penelope steal different items: a rapid harpsichord scale duplicates the rapid movement of her hand stealing a pair of earrings; Penelope's underwater theft of a precious brooch used to fasten a bikini top is scored with an upward scale that tracks the emergence of the loosened bra on the surface of the water, followed by a triangle trill when Penelope surfaces holding the loot.

In *Fitzwilly*, the sequence of the Christmas theft at Gimbels department store closes with Fitzwilliam—the head of the gang—entering the bathroom to take off the wig used as a disguise. From one of the toilet cubicles, a puzzled drunkard witnesses the scene. The music underlines the baffled man's face with a trombones glissando, then a second glissando marks the bout of sickness that makes him rush back into the cubicle. The music continues in a march arrangement that follows Fitzwilliam breezing into the elevator and showing the loot to his partners—the dialogue starts and the music texture thins accordingly. When the dialogue ends, music soars to become a triumphal march when Fitzwilliam exits the elevator and drops the self-addressed parcel containing the loot in the store's outgoing mail—the music closes the sequence and the successful operation with a *forte* authentic cadence in Baroque dialect right on the cut-in on the address label.

In *How to Steal a Million*, during the heavily guarded transportation of the supposedly priceless (and actually fake) Venus statuette through the street of Paris, the music accompanies the action with a solemn march. When a group of gendarmes deferentially salutes the convoy, Williams humorously quotes "La Marseillaise," and when we see a group of priests looking on reverently, the solemn sound of a pipe organ comes in. Later Nicole's father—the forger—learns that his Venus will be examined by an insurance assessor, who will surely discover the fraud. The piece of bad news makes his heart skip a beat: a loud pedal-portamento hit by the timpani gives the idea, and it is followed by a downward scale that mimics Nicole and her father fainting into the chairs.[39] To spare her father the ignominy and imprisonment, Nicole comes up with the idea of stealing the Venus before the assessor can examine it and talks Simon into helping her, believing that he is a proficient art thief. In a later scene, a circular musical cell replicates the round test flights of a boomerang—which will be a key element in Simon's ingenious plan. A bright triangle trill is used three times in the score to draw attention to Nicole's diamond ring—for example, when Nicole is disguised as a humble cleaning lady, she suddenly realizes that she has forgotten to remove the conspicuously incongruous jewel. A tight Mickey-Mousing adheres to the visuals when the captain of the museum guards decides to set off the supposedly faulty alarm system: a pompous march accompanies his walk to the control panel; three dissonant piano chords emphasize the lowering of the switch and the turning off respectively of the upper and lower photocells around the Venus pedestal. Finally, a downward cellos and contrabasses scale marks the closure of the door of the closet where Simon and Nicole are hiding. After the theft, when Nicole walks away dressed as a cleaning lady, the music follows her closely. For example, music guides our view within a long shot of the main hall to focus our attention on a distant action: Nicole sneakily stretches her arm out a door to get back the brush that she has left behind on the ground—a high-pitched piccolo trill being synchronized with the arm's swift gesture and the closure of the door marked by a short cellos and contrabasses *pizzicato* downward scale. Williams comments, "There's a chase in the museum and I treated it in a very burlesque way—sort of slipping on banana skins followed by a crash from the orchestra, and running semiquavers all over the place. . . . I thought I'd gone too far but Wyler loved it."[40]

Equally rich in Mickey-Mousing episodes is *A Guide for the Married Man*, where music has a foregrounded position and an extensive presence, partly because of the film's farcical nature, and partly because of director Gene Kelly's dance background.[41] The pantomime-like nature of the score is evident from the outset. The title song starts on the shot of a buxom female neighbor wiggling her hips, the rhythm of the song synchronized with the woman's enticing walking. The film showcases many instances of Mickey-Mousing: the gestures of a worker who hooks up the phone and shrugs his shoulders—after lying to his wife—is ironically accompanied by the xylophone; a stereotypical gong hit points out the presence of a Chinese man on the tarmac of an airport; an upward violins and harp glissando replicates the night breeze coming through the window; the Romanoff's restaurant scene is practically a silent film piece accompanied by music, which at one point renders a woman's enraged cries with furious *sforzando* horns rips. The cartoonlike scene in which an unfaithful husband hastily flees, forgetting his shoes in his mistress's home, also has, again, neither dialogue nor sound but only foregrounded music: explicit sync points stress his jumping off the wall, the surprise when he realizes that he is barefoot, his pantomimic slapping his forehead in disappointment, and his taking off his hat to greet a shoe salesman when he enters his shop.

So far we have dealt with comedies, a genre in which the old practice of Mickey-Mousing may be more tolerated. However, the Williams sample features explicit sync points in the dramas as well. In *The Killers*, romantic music for trumpet and strings underscores the dialogue between the race driver Johnny and the beautiful Sheila during their first meeting. The full string orchestra that accompanies the two lovers driving away gives way to an ironic episode of *staccato* woodwinds when we see Johnny's friend left alone on the racing track. After a ride in Johnny's car, Sheila playfully kicks him, and the score punctuates the gesture with a contrabasses *pizzicato*. When Sheila hires Johnny as a driver for a private job, woodwinds music underscores the dialogue. When Johnny asks about the job and his race opponents, and Sheila answers, "The police," three *staccato* notes of the cellos and contrabasses emphasize the reaction shot of Johnny's astonishment. In the final act of the film, when the chased Johnny slips into a ditch, the score accompanies his fall with a downward scale.

In the thriller *Daddy's Gone A-Hunting*, the deranged Kenneth stalks Cathy, his former girlfriend, who left him after aborting his child. Cathy is now married and is pregnant again. Kenneth is obsessed with his lost son and wants to retaliate; to get even Kenneth demands that Cathy have a second abortion. She refuses and decides to give birth to her child. As a consequence, Kenneth schemes to force Cathy to kill her baby. The musical interventions are limited and mostly of an emotive function: music is used to increase the suspense. There are, however, two explicit sync points: the first consists of low-pitched male vocalized tones that mark the shot of Cathy's womb when Kenneth appears dressed in a Santa Claus disguise; the second one is a contrabasses *pizzicato* punctuating the switching on of the red light during the scene in which Cathy agrees to meet Kenneth in his photography darkroom.

We have already discussed *Images* and the experimental nature of its score. There is no Mickey-Mousing here, and the only explicit sync points can be found in the appearance of atonal-music bursts punctuating Cathryn's hallucinations. When comparing this film with a similar insanity-based thriller like

The Night Visitor where Mancini's score has no songs and features a similarly experimental intra-opus style, it is evident that Williams's score is closer to the film's narrative structure. Thematically, *The Night Visitor* is also about madness and uncertainty between reality and hallucination: the village doctor is the only one to have seen Salem the psychopath, but no one believes him since Salem is still locked and guarded in a high-security mental asylum. Unlike the Mancini score, Williams's *Images* score is closely shaped on this reality/hallucination ambivalence. The peaceful dimension of Cathryn's fantasies linked to unicorns when she works on her children's books have melodic piano music, while atonal or even aleatoric music accompanies the scary hallucinations that will increasingly take over reality. As the woman's mental state degenerates, the melodic side of the score disappears, and the atonal/aleatoric one takes the lead.

Another observation arises from the comparison of the two samples. In Mancini's scores, explicit sync points and episodes of Mickey-Mousing, besides being more rarely found, are usually placed as isolated elements; that is, they apply to the visuals as if they were sound effects instead of pieces of music. For example, think of the aforementioned appearance of the killer in the classroom in *Arabesque* or the girl coming out of the bedroom in *Man's Favorite Sport?* The various tam-tam rubs, triangle tinkles, and timpani hits punctuating these actions come in from the silence as individual sounds. On the contrary, in Williams's case, explicit sync points are musical elements embedded in the score texture, and they come in at the right moment as part of the musical phrases, emerging from a wider structure.

As for the musical means, Williams's orchestra during the period was not much different from Mancini's: it blended the traditional symphonic setting with big bands or jazz combos. Yet we have seen that Williams preferred classical strings to more modern-style woodwinds in dialogue underscoring.

In his use of music language, Mancini was more interested in exploring the rhythms and colors of contemporary pop music (cocktail music, cool jazz, blues, Latin American). Williams also employed the musical dialect of the time in many instances—for example, in title songs, diegetic Muzak, and in action scenes scored with the contemporary Bond big-band style à la John Barry. However, a significant number of cases show Williams's preference for the dialects of both the art-music canon and the Hollywood tradition. Consider the cartoon prologue of *A Guide for the Married Man.* It is divided into three episodes of marital infidelity through the ages. In the first segment—the Stone Age—music is percussive and "primitive" in the manner of Stravinsky's *Le Sacre du printemps.* In the second segment—Ancient Rome—Williams presents a modal organum-like parallel-motion march for brass mimicking Rózsa's *Ben-Hur.* In the final segment—Victorian England—there is an ironically dignified piece of *galante* music for harpsichord, celesta, harp, and flute. In the film, when Paul is asked to recollect the feelings he felt during his very first date with a girl, we are shown an overt parody: Paul runs with open arms, in an overly sentimental slow motion, toward a blonde girl in a bucolic meadow. Williams accompanies the ridiculous scene with an unabashedly kitsch Rachmaninov imitation—actually, a Rachmaninov-via-Tiomkin imitation. In another scene, when a shy man finally takes a chance and kisses the girl, we hear a heroic fanfare à la Korngold. The scene of the barefoot man fleeing his mistress's house is scored with a frenetic scherzo that recalls Scott Bradley's music for the MGM Tom and Jerry cartoons. In *How to Steal a Million*, the opening party at the museum is appropriately paired with a lofty Baroque Handel-like overture. In a scene of *Not with My Wife, You Don't!*, Julie is in a movie theater watching a parody of an Italian-cinema stereotypical "jealousy drama," scored with passionate music evoking Mascagni's *verismo* operas. Finally, for the upper-class setting of *Fitzwilly*, Williams wrote an overture in Baroque dialect—updated with comic dissonances and amusing polytonal episodes—played by trumpets, harpsichord, and tuba, the latter having an unusual number of prominent solos during the score.

The comparison has revealed that some elements of Williams's 1960s scores already placed the composer closer to the classical style than to the modern style. The undeniable evidence would appear in the 1970s with *Star Wars*. Yet a fundamental milestone in the development of the neoclassical trend was *Jaws* (Steven Spielberg, 1975). The film—one of the inaugurals of the so-called New Hollywood—bridged the two periods of Williams's work: the emerging composer's multifaceted modern-style first period and the following stardom as the *Star Wars* composer who revived the Hollywood music tradition.

CHAPTER 7

Jaws

Williams's Neoclassicism Floats Up
to the Surface

John Williams reached stardom in the mid-1970s, a period in which Hollywood cinema was recovering from the previous decade's debacles. In those
years, a new generation of filmmakers and screenwriters—among them George
Lucas and Steven Spielberg—was building its reputation, launching the so-
called New Hollywood. The term "New Hollywood" is somewhat equivocal.
It is sometimes applied to films that are very different from each other: on
the one hand, *Bonnie and Clyde* (Arthur Penn, 1967) and *Easy Rider* (Dennis
Hopper, 1969); on the other hand, *Star Wars* (George Lucas, 1977) and *Superman: The Movie* (Richard Donner, 1978).[1] The period between approximately
1967 and 1975, often called "Hollywood Renaissance" or "American New Wave"
and including the first two films, may get confused or at least fused with the
subsequent period, in which the Hollywood film industry regained its international predominance. Here, "New Hollywood" refers only to this second
period, to indicate Hollywood's reorganization around new distribution practices and horizontal integration. Film companies became merely a portion—
often of minor importance—of the network of business of larger corporations
operating in the multimedia market, and Hollywood studios were at this
point taken over by multinational entertainment companies. Although there
seems to be a general consensus on using the term "New Hollywood" in this
sense, when it comes to defining the period in terms of aesthetics and form,
things get more controversial.[2]

Some contrast the New Hollywood style with the classical one and equate
New Hollywood with "postclassical" cinema.[3] According to these positions,
contemporary Hollywood cinema, compared to the classical one, has a different form and style, characterized by fragmented and superficial narratives,
and an emphatic style that largely displays bombastic visual and sound effects

to induce visceral sensations and intense emotions. According to the post-classical theorists, this style is the direct consequence of New Hollywood's market fragmentation and the reduction of films to mere commodities to an unprecedented extent.[4] Other scholars argue against this sharp break between the classical period and the so-called postclassical period, claiming that regardless of market fragmentation and pervasive commercial practices, the general form and style are not that different from those of classical cinema.[5] These continuity theorists use two different approaches. David Bordwell calls "hyperclassical" those films that emphasize their affiliation with the classical form and their use of classical norms.[6] Other authors call these films "neo-classical," to mark the New Hollywood sense of continuity with and update of the classical models.[7]

One of the most resorted to of discontinuity theories applies the concept of "postmodern" to the New Hollywood cinema: style mirrors the very fragmented and superficial identity of contemporary men and women and the society they live in.[8] Postmodern films are said to be those with anticlassical, nonlinear, less causally tight narrative forms, and these characteristics may derive from the postmodern idea that the old all-embracing "grand narratives" no longer exist.[9] The style of postmodern films is flamboyant and showy, and based on pastiche, parody, and stylistic patchwork—a reflection of the life of postmodern humans, characterized by a tourist-like superficiality, a ludic attitude, and a decontextualized use of history. Typical postmodern themes are simulacra and virtual reality, in such films as *Blade Runner* (Ridley Scott, 1982), *SimOne* (Andrew Niccol, 2002), or *The Matrix* (Andy Wachowski and Lana Wachowski, 1999): in the postmodern society, images are worth more than reality. Yet postmodern scholars seem to dwell on a handful of outstanding suitable examples and selected characteristics in order to validate their theoretical framework; at the same time, they seem to carefully omit most of the average productions that escape their classification, or those formal traits that may confute their argument.[10] For example, Laurent Jullier identifies *Star Wars* as the inaugural film of the postmodern cinema because it is the first remarkable product of the new spectacle-based aesthetics.[11] *Star Wars* can surely be seen as a key film in the creation of the New Hollywood, in the sense that it was the first global manifestation of the new horizontally integrated distribution based on merchandising and on the exploitation of every possible corner of the world market.[12] *Star Wars*, as mentioned in chapter 4, also relies heavily on the pastiche of previous films, genres, and music; the concept of pastiche is central to the postmodern aesthetics.

However, if the film might have some characteristics that can correspond to postmodernist conceptualizations, it is debatable that *Star Wars* was also a turning point in terms of "postmodern" style and form. A close formal analysis of the film tends to show the contrary. Stylistically, *Star Wars* is based on traditional editing techniques and classical shot/reverse shot alternation to make the narrative flow linearly, not to mention its inclusion of classical-style music. The narrative form is extremely classical too: there is a hero with a clear-cut personality, a precise goal, and strong motivations; and the narrative is built around causality and "stairstep construction," as in the "canonical story format."[13] Finally, its themes are anything but postmodern: the film is about one of the most classical themes of all, the archetypal hero's journey.[14] *Star Wars* seems to lack any postmodern characteristics, apart from those pointed out by Jullier: the film leans on prominent spectacular moments; it indulges in playful quotations, patent intertextuality, and metalanguage; it boasts striking special effects. These allegedly postmodern characteristics, however, were already present in some classical Hollywood films, such as *Hell's Angels* (Howard Hughes, 1930) and *King Kong* (Merian C. Cooper and Ernest B. Schoedsack, 1933), with their striking special effects; *The Adventures of Robin Hood* (Michael Curtiz and William Keighley, 1938) and *The Wizard of Oz* (Victor Fleming, 1939), with spectacular key moments; *Three Ages* (Edward F. Cline and Buster Keaton, 1923) and *A Night in Casablanca* (Archie Mayo, 1946), using playful quotations and intertextuality; and *Show People* (King Vidor, 1928) and *Hellzapoppin'* (H. C. Potter, 1941), employing metalanguage. If so-called postmodern films are actually only partially postmodern, it is even more difficult to convincingly apply this label to embrace indiscriminately an entire period of the whole film industry. A film like *Back to the Future* (Robert Zemeckis, 1985) is a typical product of the New Hollywood cinema, but it can hardly be called postmodern.[15] The main problem with postmodern arises from the number of areas in which the term itself is controversially used: there is one postmodern in economy, one in philosophy, and one in sociology; it seems that theorists of the various disciplines cannot agree on a shared definition.[16]

Since the term lacks a clear-cut stable meaning, although topical and widely diffused it might be, "postmodern" will not be used herein, in order to avoid confusion.[17] Indeed, if we thought of *Star Wars* as a postmodern film and of New Hollywood as a postmodern aesthetic trend, consequently John Williams—who became famous thanks to *Star Wars* and was one of the principal New Hollywood composers—would be a postmodern composer. The problem is that the postmodern label has been applied to composers such as

Ennio Morricone, Hans Zimmer, and, in art music, Luciano Berio.[18] It is obvious that Williams's idiom is very different from Morricone's and Zimmer's, not to mention Berio's. In this book, New Hollywood is considered not as a new style but as a period in Hollywood history characterized by a transformation of its industrial, commercial, and distribution practices and structures. In this period, a number of films were produced that overtly paid homage to the classical Hollywood tradition and imitated that style, and these can be tagged as "neoclassical." One of such neoclassical films is *Star Wars*, a revival of classical genres, with some emphasis on spectacular elements that can be called at most "hyperclassical." Likewise, Williams acted in these films as a *neoclassical composer*, since he has paid homage to classical Hollywood music and revived that style.[19]

Neoclassicism Takes Form

Williams's neoclassicism can be spotted particularly in his collaborations with neoclassical filmmakers such as George Lucas and Steven Spielberg, and became a dominant trend from 1975 to 1983.[20] In the same way as the "neoclassical era [began] not with its full flowering in *Jaws* (or *Star Wars*) but piecemeal, spread across films and studios," so Williams had already shown a penchant for neoclassical scoring before these two landmark films.[21] Besides the 1960s corpus of films that we have already considered, a previous artistic relationship must be mentioned, because it produced two remarkable early examples of neoclassicism. Between the late 1960s and early 1970s, Williams started a four-film collaboration with the director Mark Rydell. "Mark Rydell is very comfortable with music. He is a pianist himself, he loves music, it's very good to work with him on a certain kind of scene in a movie," says Williams.[22] The collaboration resulted in *The Reivers* (1969), *The Cowboys* (1972), *Cinderella Liberty* (1973), and the later *The River* (1984). The first two, *The Reivers* and *The Cowboys*, stand out in Williams's early canon as the first two neoclassical scores, both having been instrumental in signaling the composer to a wider attention and producing seminal consequences for Williams's career.

The Americana symphonic score for *The Reivers* earned Williams his first Oscar nomination for "Best Original Score." *The Cowboys* was one of John Wayne's last Westerns and carried on the Hollywood Western music tradition, employing a full symphony orchestra, galloping rhythms, syncopation, and pentatonic scales in the manner of Jerome Moross's *The Big Country* (William Wyler, 1958) and Elmer Bernstein's *The Magnificent Seven* (John Sturges, 1960). Attesting to the importance and musical quality of *The Reivers* and *The Cowboys* is the fact that the composer has adapted concert pieces from both scores.[23] More important, then-emerging filmmaker Steven Spielberg approached Williams in 1972 and later hired him on his first feature-length film—*The Sugarland Express* (1974)—because he was a keen admirer of both *The Reivers* and *The Cowboys* and had listened to the LPs so many times he wore them out.[24] Spielberg recalls:

> I'm a soundtrack collector and I collected scores of great composers. . . . I had a huge collection. And for many years there was like a drought. A lot of the great old composers like Dimitri Tiomkin and Max Steiner were no longer writing music anymore. . . . There was just a real loss of pure symphonic film music. And then when I heard *The Reivers* and *The Cowboys* I said, "My God, this guy must be eighty years old!" . . . I really thought, "Maybe he's some guy who's eighty years old, who maybe wrote the greatest scores of his life." And I wanted to know who this guy was and I met this young man named John Williams. . . . I was amazed! You know, "It's a rebirth, film music is back. It's alive! Hallelujah!"[25]

Yet, though important they might have been, the scores to *The Reivers* and *The Cowboys* cannot be said to have been groundbreaking for the neoclassical trend. Both are period films in which a more classical-style score would have hardly been an unexpected event. The score that really launched Williams's neoclassicism was *Jaws* (1975), the second entry of his collaboration with Steven Spielberg, because it was the first instance in which a fully neoclassical score was applied to a dramatic contemporary story. The score played a central role in the film's success and in turn benefited from its association with a film that enjoyed an unprecedented diffusion.

Here Comes "Bruce"

Williams was the ideal and obvious choice to score *Jaws*; not only had he just started a novel work relationship with Spielberg, but at that time, with *The Poseidon Adventure, Earthquake,* and *The Towering Inferno* on his resume, he was also the go-to choice for disaster-movie scores. Indeed, in terms of film genre, *Jaws* was somehow in the "disaster movies" category that was fashionable at that time, adopting many of its conventions.[26] In this case, the deadly threat is not determined by a lightning-stricken about-to-crash plane, or a transatlantic cruise liner turning upside-down, or an earthquake hitting Los Angeles, or a skyscraper on fire but by a great white shark eating islanders. *Jaws* indeed has some narrative conventions of the disaster-movie genre: a threat by an irrational and unstoppable natural element—fire, water, earthquakes, in this case a dangerous predator—looms on a large group of people; the protagonist warns the local authorities in due time but the authorities do not listen to him or her and take action only when it is too late.[27] Sharing the concise and gripping narrative premise of many disaster movies, *Jaws* was what Justin Wyatt calls a "high-concept" product, "one in which the story could be summarized in a couple of sentences and conveyed for advertising through a single iconic image. As an uncomplicated idea, it could then be used as the centerpiece for a wide marketing scheme that included the manufacture and sale of related products."[28] *Jaws* was also preceded by the wide success of the best-selling book it was based on. This likely guaranteed a "ready to use" large base of potentially interested viewers already familiar with Peter Benchley's novel. To maximize this advantage, a strategy was orchestrated consisting of an aggressive and never-seen-before advertising campaign and a theatrical distribution based on "saturation booking": the film opened in 464 North American theaters simultaneously.[29] *Jaws* was conceived as, in Thomas Schatz's words, a "hyper-efficient entertainment machine . . . supported by an unprecedented TV network ad blitz. An 'event' film and prototype summer blockbuster, *Jaws* redefined the profit potential of a major movie hit and spawned a multimedia franchise via sequels, reissues, licensed merchandise, theme-park rides, and myriad other tie-ins."[30] *Jaws* soon became the highest-grossing film thus far, with its $129.5 million in box office revenues, a watershed in Hollywood history.[31] For most historians, "the release of *Jaws* . . . constitutes the true birth of New Hollywood."[32] If the film went so smoothly at the box office, its production was anything but smooth. The making of *Jaws* was so troubled that the project was even on the verge of being aborted and never reaching the theaters.[33]

Several technical and logistical problems plagued its making, mainly due to the choice of shooting as many scenes as possible out to sea on location, for realism's sake, rather than in a more controllable studio tank. The biggest hitch and a major cause of hindrance for the progress of the shooting was "Bruce," the mechanical shark named after Spielberg's lawyer.[34] A pneumatically operated puppet, Bruce cost $750,000 and sank like a stone as soon as it was put into the ocean for the first time.[35] Its mechanics jammed continuously, and the shark—when not sinking—was unreliable and mostly unusable. The estimated budget of $8.5 million quickly climbed to $11 million. The 55-day production schedule ended up exceeding 150 days.[36] Exasperated crew members had come up with a sarcastic moniker for the derailing film project: "Flaws."[37] In order to keep up with the schedule despite the absence of the leading character, Spielberg resorted to various vicarious elements to signal its presence: piers torn and dragged away; air barrels previously fixed to the beast's back that emerge on the surface to indicate the presence of the shark underneath, and so on. These solutions were complemented with point-of-view shots: the camera substituted for the monster's eyes, and consequently the monster's body could be kept conveniently off-screen. In the film's 124-minute running time, the shark can be just glimpsed at 60 minutes and finally shows up only at 78 minutes, the total screen time being only 4 minutes.[38]

Music, in particular, ended up being the fundamental device to give substance and presence in those scenes in which the shark puppet was absent due to technical indisposition. With the actual shark unavailable, music had to take up the protagonist's role; it stood in for the shark, in a very physical way, as noted by numerous scholars. For K. J. Donnelly, Williams's music "does not merely signify [the shark's] presence, it *is* its presence."[39] In a film with several false alarms, the music is consistent with its function of incarnating the beast to the point that, as Jerrold Levinson notes, it is "the only reliable signifier of the shark."[40] When the shark is not around, music is also absent. The shark motif is constructed and employed so effectively—with an "extraordinary visceral impact"—that music is not merely *representing* the shark; the shark is actually *in* the music, as Giorgio Biancorosso has theorized: "I hear in the music (particularly through the motive's rhythmic acceleration) the shark's approach, its upward motion, its intention to attack and its strategically orientated motion towards its prey."[41] The music also fulfilled another important role: not only giving the shark a physical presence but giving it a *credible* menacing presence. A crucial doubt haunted the director and producers: in the few shots in which it appeared, would the fiberglass-and-rubber puppet really look credible and therefore perceived as a truly menacing shark?[42] As admitted by Spielberg himself, it was Williams's score that made the puppet credible and truly frightening: "I think that his score was clearly responsible for half the success of the film."[43] This is the first element that links the *Jaws* score with the classical period: the same thing had happened with the score for *King Kong*. The producers of *King Kong* similarly feared that the stop-motion-animated puppet would cause laughter instead of fear. And similarly, it was Max Steiner's score that saved the day. And, incidentally, as *King Kong* had been the opening score of the classical style, so *Jaws* is the opening score of the neoclassical trend. Besides these historical parallels, what makes *Jaws* a neoclassical score?

Let's start from the beginning, with Williams watching the film for the first time in the "spotting session," when the composer is shown a rough cut of the film as a basis for discussion about which scenes need music and what kind of music. Williams recalls the first time he watched *Jaws*.

I knew about the novel. . . . I don't think I read it, but Peter Benchley's book was very, very popular. I remember seeing the movie in a projection room here at Universal. I was alone; Steven was in Japan at the time. I came out of the screening so excited. I had been working for nearly 25 years in Hollywood but had never had an opportunity to do a film that was absolutely brilliant. I had already conducted *Fiddler on the Roof*, and I had worked with directors like William Wyler and Robert Altman and others. But *Jaws* just floored me.[44]

After "spotting" the film, Williams began to plan his work: "Most of the discussions I had with Steven at that point were about the shark. The challenge was to find a way to characterize something that's underwater with music rather than with sound effects."[45] Unlike *Piranha* (Joe Dante, 1978), where the voracious fish are characterized by a sort of excited high-frequency buzz, Spielberg wanted a musical identifier and looked for a musical idea that could be the aural equivalent of the predator.

What Does a Shark Sound Like?

Sometime later, Williams invited the director to his studio and played the main theme at the piano. This is Spielberg's recollection:

I had actually cut in one of John's own pieces of music for the opening titles. That was John's title theme from Robert Altman's film *Images*. So I cut in a section that was a lovely piano solo with some very ominous strings in the background that would probably have been wonderful for a movie about a hunting. And I thought it was playing against the obvious primal feelings that run very deep through *Jaws*. When Johnny heard it, though, he just didn't go for it at all.[46]

He continues,

I expected to hear something weird yet still melodic. But what he played instead, with two fingers on the lower keys, was *dun, dun, dun-dun, dun-dun, dun-dun*. At first I began to laugh, and I thought "John has a great sense of humor!" But he was serious—that was the theme for *Jaws*. So he played it again and again, and suddenly it seemed right. Sometimes the best ideas are the most simple ones and John had found a signature for the entire score.[47]

Williams simply explained to Spielberg: "The sophisticated approach you would like me to take isn't the approach you took with the film I just experienced."[48] This is a testament to the composer's acumen in identifying a film's true essence, and also to the importance of "experiencing" a film by *watching* it, not by reading scripts beforehand—which may produce misleading preconceptions, as I discuss in the next chapter.

Unlike the "weird melody" in line with the tradition of thriller music that Spielberg expected—dissonant and harmonically eerie, as the more tonal passages of the score for *Images* are—Williams opted for a closer musical equivalent of the shark, a primitive pulsation with no melody at all. Indeed, melody is a product of artistic civilization, which by its nature brings traces of history and culture. Williams elaborates on this:

> I fiddled around with the idea of creating something that was very . . . brainless, . . . like the shark. All instinct . . . Meaning something [that] could be very repetitious, very visceral, and grab you in your gut, not in your brain. Remember, Steven didn't have the computer shark. He only had his rubber ducky, so the simple idea of that bass ostinato, just repeating those two notes and introduce a third note when you don't expect it and so on. It could be something you could play very softly, which would indicate that the shark is far away when all you see is water. Brainless music that gets louder and gets closer to you, something is gonna swallow you up.[49]

Williams came up with the primitive rhythmic simplicity of an *ostinato*, that is, a brief repeating and hammering fragment, more rhythmic than melodic (see figure 3). Those three repeated bass notes recall the heartbeat, the primordial rhythm of life.[50] Their seemingly unstoppable constant and mechanical repetition effectively represents the shark: a primitive yet proficient killing machine, moved only by the instinct for eating.

Figure 3. John Williams, the shark ostinato (mm. 12–14), from *Suite from Jaws* (© 1975 BMI), published by USI B Music Publishing, administered by Songs of Universal Inc., printed/distributed by Hal Leonard, "John Williams Signature Edition," 04490414. Used in compliance with the US Copyright Act, Section 107.

In addition to characterizing the nature of the monster, the shark's motif performs another important function within the film, a function that Spielberg's "weird melody" could hardly have carried out. Being an ostinato, the shark motif can be more easily shortened, prolonged, or repeated in loops as required by visuals, so to become the aural equivalent of the shark's *movement through space*. Williams commented, "I thought that altering the speed and volume of the theme, from very slow to very fast, from very soft to very loud, would indicate the mindless attacks of the shark. Steven was a bit skeptical, but when the orchestra performed the piece, it worked better than we had anticipated."[51] Music is often the only sign of the presence of the monster that can be perceived, since the monster itself is off-screen for most of the time. Williams plays fair with the audience, since the shark motif is not used to cheat when the shark is not around but is played only when it is present. Bribitzer-Stull reminds us that "the absence of a given leitmotif can be as meaningful a clue to audiences as its presence."[52] For example, in the fake-fin prank scene, visually we can be led to take it as a real fin, but there is no music accompanying it, thus signaling that the shark is actually not there. On the contrary, in the same sequence, the music anticipates the real shark being spotted in the estuary. The shark's motif does not just perform the function of classical leitmotiv but is also a peculiar type of Mickey-Mousing: the music adheres perfectly to the spatial movements of the beast. But, unlike the classical Mickey-Mousing that replicated the on-screen movements, in this case it mostly indicates *off-screen* movements.

Consider Chrissie's death scene at the beginning of the film: it is the music that conveys the "obscene" violence and horror of the underwater off-screen attack—*ob scene* being Latin for "off-stage." Chrissie undresses and decides to take a nude night swim in the sea. A point-of-view shot looking up from the abyss shows us the body of the girl on the surface—as in the opening titles, we are seeing through the eyes of a mysterious sea creature. We hear a watery harp *arpeggio* evoking the waves, then two of those ominous low notes, which we have previously identified with the sea creature. The notes become louder and repeat faster and faster as the creature approaches the girl and points at its prey. Then, the narration reverses the perspective and cuts to Chrissie on the sea surface. Suddenly, something we cannot see starts pulling her down: the action is marked with a violently *sforzando* horns rip, a kind of *rrrrrruhah!* That is the shark's bite; the music conveys both the shark's fury and Chrissie's pain. She screams while she is tossed around. We do not see what is happening beneath the surface, but we can easily imagine the horrible scene of the shark tearing its victim. Frantic shrill violin writing, violent percussion, and repeated horns "bites" depict the off-screen/obscene violence. The scene takes shape in our imagination through music, which fulfills both a spatial perceptive and an emotive function.

The shark motif replicates the shark's movements on both the horizontal and the vertical axes. Horizontal trajectories are rendered through variations of dynamics and tempo: when the music slows down and the volume decreases, we know that the shark is slowing its pace; when the music speeds up or the volume increases, we know that the shark is attacking. Movements on the vertical axis are rendered through variations of orchestral texture: when the writing gets thicker, we know that the shark is coming to the surface; when the writing thins down to dark timbres only (contrabasses, cellos, bassoons), we know that the beast is plunging into the dark abyss. For example, consider the pier scene in which two islanders try to hook the shark, with the only result that the pier is torn away and they fall into the water, risking being eaten up. When the shark bites the bait and points offshore, dragging along the torn pier to which the bait was fastened, the shark ostinato starts, played by contrabasses and cellos. The ostinato keeps playing at the same level and speed during the tearing off of the pier and the falling into the water of the two men, one of whom is pulled offshore along with the pier. At one point, the pier stops and suddenly reverses, indicating that the shark is now pointing to the swimming islander. Violins and violas abruptly join the cellos and contrabasses in playing the ostinato, followed by the horns menacingly presenting the second motif associated with the beast, the "shark motto." The music's speed and volume increase as the shark chases the man who is frantically trying to reach the shore and come out of the water. The man succeeds, and the shark has to retreat. The music deflates, gradually decelerating and turning into a single sustained bass note that closes the scene: the shark has gone back into the abyss.

Another function of the score is to further separate the two worlds—the shark below and the humans above—and this is accomplished by using the timbres of the orchestra. The monster shark lives down, below the water surface; humans live above the surface. The difference between the humans' world (lit by the sun) and the shark's world (the abyss in which darkness reigns) is marked by the contrast between the shark music (mechanical, low pitched, with dark timbre) and the human music (melodic, higher pitched, and with the bright timbres of violins, flutes, and trumpets). The *Jaws* score has the important emotive function of creating suspense, anxiety, fear. Yet its

most successful contribution consists in its embodying the shark and skillfully
tracing its movements both on screen and off-screen. The score is particularly
outstanding for its spatial perceptive function; it is a high-class application of
the Mickey-Mousing technique.

Jaws's Neoclassicism

The first neoclassical element of the *Jaws* score is the recovery of classical techniques such as Mickey-Mousing and leitmotivs. Besides the Mickey-Mousing
tracing of the shark's movements, *Jaws* also has a number of other explicit sync
points embedded in the overall orchestral writing. In the beach scene when
the young Alex Kintner is cut to ribbons along with his yellow Lilo, a shriek-
ing violins upward glissando strengthens the zoom-in / track-out *Vertigo*-like
shot that captures Brody's horrified reaction. In the pond scene, a low flut-
ter by the brass replicates the victim's blood coming to the surface. When
the shark passes by Brody's son—in a point-of-view shot of the beast—music
underlines its swimming toward and then away from the boy respectively
with an upward and then a downward harp *glissando*. During the barrel chase
out to the sea, music marks the actions with accents when the shark is har-
pooned, with a perfectly synchronized cymbal clash when one of the barrels
hits the water surface, and with descending scales when the barrels are dragged
down. In one scene, Quint is gathering up one of the barrel's lines. The shark
abruptly emerges, and out of the silence the music punctuates the scaring surprise with a violent horns rip. Quint gets his hands cut by the rope, the painful scratch being stressed by a rapid and biting piccolo upward scale. When
the shark submerges again, this is marked by a downward scale of the contrabasses, followed by an acute upward scale led by the piccolo mirroring the
shark's fin splashing water over the boat.

As for leitmotivs, they are employed throughout the score, with particular
variety in the second half of the film, whereas the first half is dominated by
the shark motif and violent or eerie music passages. One theme is a broad
melody, which can be heard when the shark hunters' boat *Orca* is seen leaving the harbor, then across the whole second half of the film, and over the
end credits in a serene rendition for strings. This is the principal "human"
melody that contrasts the primitive pulse of the shark motif. It can be associated with the man-versus-the-beast struggle. Another theme is a buoyant
hornpipe-like tune, which can be heard again when the *Orca* leaves. It is associated with sea life and punctuates the humorous and bright moments of the
shark hunt. Another recurring theme that can be heard during the shark hunt

is a heroic fanfare, which conveys the excitement and adventurousness of the deed. Williams combines the elements of his leitmotivic palette with dramaturgical ingenuity and subtlety. The kitchen-table scene between Brody and his youngest son offers us an intimate family moment away from the aquatic horrors. Brody ponders on the shark that menaces his community, a frown of concern and a sullen look on his face. Next to him, his little boy observes his father's expressions, apparently amusing to the little kid, and he imitates them. When Brody takes notice of the affectionate mimicking, he momentarily puts his worries aside and engages in a father/son game of grimaces and face mirroring. Williams scores it with sweet and tender music, communicating the warmth of home and family: a restrained and sparse harp, piano, and vibraphone minimalist writing. It is a temporary musical respite from the other violent and horrifying episodes of the score. Yet Williams casts a shadow on this little parental digression with a reminder that the shark menace still looms over: in the background of the tender music, a sustained low note by the contrabasses emerges threateningly. Another example is the use of the ancient sea shanty "Farewell and Adieu to You, Spanish Ladies." It is introduced diegetically when Quint prepares to leave for the shark hunt: to show off his familiarity with all things maritime, the insolent and overconfident mariner sings it, smugly. Quint uses music to taunt the "rookie" marine biologist Hooper. Later in the film, too stubborn and proud to desist, Quint ignores Brody and Hooper's advice to slow the boat down. Instead, defiantly, he pushes the throttle to the limit as he sings "Farewell and Adieu to You, Spanish Ladies," this time angrily. The sea shanty at this point has been established as a musical signifier of Quint's flaunting of seafaring confidence. Yet the engine soon breaks down, as predicted by the others. The group is thus stranded in the open sea, with the boat slowly sinking. A defeated Quint goes below deck to look morosely at the irreparable damage and massive leaking, and Williams reprises "Spanish Ladies" nondiegetically, transforming it into a leitmotivic quip. As Quint contemplates the disaster, an impudent flute cites Quint's sea shanty, an episode of poetic justice. It is the narration that now uses music to taunt Quint, throwing salt on the wounds of the mariner's self-assurance and supposed mastery.

There is also a second leitmotiv associated with the shark. We have already considered the ostinato indicating the movements of the beast, which is heard only when the monster is around. The second leitmotiv is a horn-and-tuba motto associated with the shark when someone talks about it or just thinks of its menacing presence, as in the scene in which Brody reads a book on shark attacks (see figure 4). The central musical interval of the shark motto—the second and third notes, from G to C-sharp —is the tritone or augmented fourth, a dissonant interval traditionally associated with evil, the *diabolus in musica* (see also chapter 9).

Figure 4. John Williams, the shark motto (mm. 16–18), from *Suite from Jaws* (© 1975 BMI), published by USI B Music Publishing, administered by Songs of Universal Inc., printed/distributed by Hal Leonard, "John Williams Signature Edition," 04490414. Used in compliance with the US Copyright Act, Section 107.

The shark motto is also subtly used during the Indianapolis story sequence, which is a good example of proficient dialogue (monologue, actually) underscoring. Quint starts recounting his dreadful experience as a survivor of the USS *Indianapolis*, sunk during World War II. (The crew floated around in the ocean for four days. Only 317 men survived, out of 1,196, many having been eaten by sharks.) Quint's tale of the sinking begins without music, the serious faces of the listeners conveying the mood for the dramatic shipwreck being told. Then Quint's tale focuses on an inside tragedy within the shipwreck: the shark attacks that the survivors had to sustain in the following days. On the words "very first light, sharks come cruising . . . ," an ominous bass pedal point sneaks in from the silence, followed by a *piano* grating layer of dissonant high strings. During the monologue, low harp tones and aqueous arpeggios reverberate within the music texture, as to depict something moving in the abyss, below the surface. Strings writing provides more chilling effects through sinister gliding motions. Then Quint tells that at a certain point he saw a friend of his floating nearby and, thinking he was asleep, he reached him to shake him awake. "He bobbed up and down in the water just like a kind of top. Upended. Well . . . He'd been bitten in half, below the waist." At the beginning of this line, the shark motto can be heard, to anticipate Quint's macabre discovery and its cause.

Another neoclassical trait is the revival of the dialect used in the classical period, that is, the late-romantic symphonic dialect. *Jaws* is actually a film with two spirits: the thriller and the adventure. The first one dominates the first two acts: discovery of the shark; attempts to solve the problems from the land. Then, as the *Orca* boat leaves the harbor for the shark hunt, we switch gears: the third act, all in the open sea, is about the tracking down of the shark and the development of a bond between the hunters, while the final act is the climactic confrontation with the beast. While "experiencing" the film in the screening room, Williams had grasped this adventurous tone and the film's two macro stories: in the first, the shark is the protagonist; in the second, it is the group of hunters. While there are Debussyan touches in the score—for example, the liquid harp arpeggios and French "Impressionism" scales used in some underwater sequences—Korngold is the composer whose voice can be heard loud and clear in the fanfares and orchestral flourishes written for the seafaring hunting scenes. One of Williams's felicitous intuitions was that of emphasizing the adventurous spirit of the film. Spielberg reports: "When I first showed *Jaws* to John, I remember he said: 'This is like a pirate movie! I think we need pirate music for this, because there's something primal about it—but it's also fun and entertaining!'"[53] What did Williams mean when he spoke of "pirate music"? Here are Williams's words: "When I first saw *Jaws*, it was clear to me that it would require an action/adventure score. . . . For *Jaws*, I imagined something big and operatic, something very theatrical."[54] Evidently, the action/adventure score that Williams had in mind referred to the old Warner Bros. pirate films boasting Korngold's operatic scores. The barrel chase sequence in the open sea, for example, is scored with lush symphonic music and heroic fanfares: "It suddenly becomes very Korngoldian, . . . you expect to see Errol Flynn at the helm of this thing. It gave us a laugh," says Williams.[55] As a sign of the composer's neoclassical tastes, Williams admits having a special fondness for this sequence: "My own favorite cue in *Jaws* has always been the barrel chase sequence, where the shark approaches the boat and the three heroes think they have captured it. The music accelerates and becomes very exciting and heroic. Suddenly, as the shark overpowers them and eventually escapes, the music deflates and ends with a little sea-chant called 'Spanish Lady.' The score musically illustrates and punctuates all of this dramatic outline."[56]

And yet another neoclassical trait is the use of the symphony orchestra as a musical means. Among the early 1970s films set in the present time and designed to hopefully become box office hits, *Jaws* was the first one employing a symphonic score and having no theme song. A significant example is the montage sequence showing the flocking of tourists to the island to celebrate the Fourth of July. This ninety-second sequence would have been the ideal showcase for a marketable song, perhaps in the style of the Beach Boys' surf music—a choice that would have been clever from a commercial point of view and would have also been interestingly motivated by the contrast between the cheerful tone of the music and the deadly danger looming over the tourists. Instead, the montage is accompanied by a Baroque-dialect piece for strings, solo trumpet, and harpsichord. From under the serene and formal surface of the piece, the shark ostinato emerges played by cellos and contrabasses, offering a kind of black-humored comment on the impending menace. This choice also cleverly expresses in music one of the narrative themes: the city council refuses to close the beaches, preferring to ignore the menace rather than risk jeopardizing the Fourth of July tourism revenues. As in the music, a formal and pompous surface states that everything is fine so as to conceal the pending danger. Moreover, as in the old times, the music also carefully underscores the dialogue lines interwoven to the montage—by sustaining them with a thinner texture—and lets the trumpets play in full stride over the dialogue-free segments, revealing a second-by-second tailoring of the musical writing. Another very "non-pop" choice is the use of *fugato* writing for the sequence in which the hunters' trio sets up the shark cage.[57] The relentless complexity of the fugato provides the right compelling drive and anxious excitement for the elaborate and risky trap that the shark hunters are preparing.

Jaws was the first commercial film since the end of classical music style to discard pop music and modern style, and opt for a revival of past models. Eventually, this choice proved to be a good one. The film broke box office records, and Williams won his second Oscar, his first one for original music.[58] Moreover, as *King Kong* did, *Jaws* demonstrated once again the important contribution that nondiegetic orchestral music could give to film narration. Critics acknowledged the fact and, even before *Star Wars*, praised Williams's symphonic restoration: "Williams has been highly instrumental in trying to bring back to the movies the full symphonic score, with all its potential for pleasurable manipulation and its intimations of life larger than life. This was an important part of what we got from the movies once, and there are many signs that many [of] us want it back again."[59]

Williams expanded his canvas with *Jaws 2* (Jeannot Szwarc, 1978) and produced another neoclassical work, cleverly avoiding a copycat score. Only the shark ostinato survives from the 1975 film score; the shark motto is not used. The shark ostinato is less present and less manipulated than in the first installment, probably because the shark is much more visible, the director being more interested in on-screen horror than in off-screen menace. On the other hand, Williams provided new symphonic set pieces for the montage sequences, this time sounding like Prokofiev in the spirited and youthful music for the catamaran race, or in the sardonic and angular trumpet melody played during the crowded beach sequence, named "The Menu" on the LP album.[60] The film has two scuba-diving sequences in which French "Impressionism" harmonies are prominent. In the opening one, after liquid harp arpeggios accompany the underwater descent, the two scuba divers find the wreck of the *Orca*, and Williams quotes the "Man-versus-the-Beast" theme from the previous film, confirming musically that what we are seeing is that very boat. The other sequence has the weightless moves of the scuba divers scored with a graceful waltz-like harp piece, titled "Ballet for Divers" on the LP album. The score features heroic fanfares again, during the catamaran race and, more prominently, during the end credits to appropriately mark the successful outcome of another man-versus-the-beast heroic deed.

Williams has repeatedly confirmed the importance of the film for his career: "*Jaws* was the first major film opportunity that I had. . . . With Spielberg, it was the beginnings of our relationship really, and a lot of opportunity came my way as a result of it, including the *Star Wars* films. Spielberg introduced me to George Lucas and he was directly responsible for that relationship developing. The success of the *Star Wars* films brought unbelievable opportunities. I went to Boston and conducted the orchestra there for 15 years as a direct result of that."[61] The score to *Jaws* can be seen as a veritable turning point in his career, also stylistically. Mark Richards noted:

> It is with this score that Williams's main themes begin to be exceedingly tailored to their particular association, fusing a wealth of musical techniques that as a whole conjure up a very specific mental image. Also consider that the number of films he scores per year drops in 1975 from four or five in 1972–1974 to only two, and in the years following, the number almost always falls into a range of one to three. For all the above reasons, I understand *Jaws* as a stylistic watershed in Williams's career.[62]

The wide success of *Jaws* not only launched the neoclassical trend but also established Williams as the neoclassical composer par excellence.

CHAPTER 8

Williams's Neoclassicism

Style and Habits

I n art-music historiography, neoclassicism was a trend that brought back the clarity of past forms as opposed to the excesses of contemporary music.

[It is a] musical trend that arose in the second half of the nineteenth century (with the Bach revival promoted by such composers as Brahms and Max Reger) and gained full visibility in the 1920s as a reaction against post-Wagnerian thematicism and chromaticism and with the purpose of the stylistic re-creation of clear-cut pre-Romantic forms. Neoclassicism can be placed within those twentieth-century artistic movements inspired by the ideals of objectivity, rationality and concreteness, as opposed to those of subjectivity and irrationality typical of Romanticism and in large part inherited by Impressionism and Expressionism.[1]

For example, the musicologist Guido Salvetti writes the following about Igor Stravinsky's neoclassicism in *Pulcinella* (1920):

The modifications of the original music were not aimed at the deformation of the model: Stravinsky just added some canon-like dissonant passages, major seconds to some perfect chords, in a cadence he placed the chords built on the V and I degrees simultaneously, shifted a bar's accent on the weak beat, and of course, invented a personal orchestral color. . . . This Stravinskyan "neoclassicism" was characterized, even in its early days, by the dual aspect of both the respectful reconstruction and the irreverent parody. . . . The huge variety of cultural references resulted in a huge number of musical "tips of the hat" where once again the whole history of music is leveled on a ground where everything can be reused and enjoyed anew.[2]

What Salvetti writes about Stravinsky's *Oedipus Rex* (1927) in the following passage could be also said of the neoclassical nature of the score to *Star Wars* (George Lucas, 1977): "Neoclassicism is even better understood in this sense: it is the escape from the present and the plunging into the eternal dimension of Myth, where Time and History lose any perspective."[3] The decision to choose this kind of operatic music for *Star Wars*—very unusual for a sci-fi film—also followed the desire to evoke a common musical heritage that would reinforce the mythic dimension of the narrative. These neoclassical traits are also acknowledged by the musicologist Sergio Miceli.

> There are some characteristics that distinguish Williams from everyone else. . . . Williams has proved to be able to take on the most representative stylistic traits of his generation while smoothing their excesses by drawing inspiration from the second and even first generation of Hollywood film composers. To put it another way, in a work of synthesis rather than innovation, Williams has skillfully recovered leitmotivic functions, more extensive and complex thematicism, together with thematic interplay and implicit symbolism. The most significant difference if we compare his work to that of his predecessors consists in the complete absorption of blues and jazz influences, which causes his scores to sound much more up-to-date. As for the direct borrowing from the art-music repertoire (the other side of the coin) they are numerous but very blurred and well integrated, which is precisely due to Williams's extraordinary skillfulness in music assimilation. . . . In short, the fusion of different stylistic traits, from both art and popular music, had already been accomplished . . . but nobody had ever weighed and mixed the ingredients so carefully. To all of this, Williams has also added an ironic and playful spirit which was undoubtedly favored by the narrative nature of the films.[4]

In art music, neoclassicism is the revival of past forms and styles updated through the hybridization with twentieth-century harmonic progressions and dissonances, and reworked through an ironic mannerist exaggeration of certain traits. As such, neoclassicism performed a bridging action, as explained by Hermann Danuser: "Neoclassicism—especially that of the 1920s—can be understood as striving for a new unity between classicism and modernity in music by recourse to the past."[5] In film music, similarly, Williams has revived and updated the classical Hollywood music style by bridging the past with the present, inaugurating a neoclassical trend within the broader eclectic style of the New Hollywood.

Neoclassicism in Film Music

As with the classical style, neoclassicism in film music is not just a matter of reviving the old-fashioned symphonic language. As this book has maintained throughout, the concept of style as applied to film music should be a broader one, a four-tier combination of language, techniques, musical means, and functions. The more a score revives as many as possible of these four classical stylistic elements, the more it can be called neoclassical. For clarity's sake, consider three almost coeval pirate films, all clearly looking back on the 1930s swashbuckler models: *Pirates* (Roman Polanski, 1986, music by Philippe Sarde), *Hook* (Steven Spielberg, 1991, music by John Williams), and *Cutthroat Island* (Renny Harlin, 1995, music by John Debney). Each film has a full-blown symphonic score that harks back to the classical Hollywood scores. In *Pirates* and *Cutthroat Island*, music is also given a prestige symphonic treatment: Sarde's score is performed by the Orchestre de Paris, while Debney's is performed by the neoclassical-trend signature orchestra itself, the London Symphony Orchestra. However, upon watching the films, listening to their scores, and comparing them, it is clear that the most neoclassical one is Williams's. His score has a number of clear-cut and very recognizable leitmotivs each appearing as its related character appears on-screen, features decidedly Korngoldian fanfares, and, above all, displays an overtly higher classical adherence to the visuals—a prominent spatial perceptive function. This is evident if we pay particular attention to the sword-fight scenes, the pièce de résistance of the swashbuckler genre. Sarde's score displays a refined writing that convincingly refers to the Golden Age models, but the composer's techniques are decidedly more steeped in the European tradition. His treatment of the sword-fight scenes consists of music having its own flow, without the classical "catching the action"—no musical accents or gestures hit the many clashes of the blades, lunges, and stunts. Also, there is not a strong network of leitmotivs. Debney's score is more action-oriented, but it is also more similar to the heavy action music in the eclectic style (à la Hans Zimmer) than to the classical-style balletic scoring. Its perceptive function is more temporal than spatial. We hear a lot of pounding rhythms to sustain the pace of the scenes, overwhelming bass tones that act as a background for the sound effects, while explicit sync points between the music and the visuals are mostly underlined with emphatic cymbal clashes, in the form of isolated stingers. On the contrary, in the sword-fight scenes in *Hook*, the score is closely tailored on the visuals in a balletic way, as openly admitted by Williams:

When Peter Pan manages to fly, the orchestra plays music that reminds us of a very fast dance of a ballet. The same in the Ultimate War sequence. The music follows the rhythm of the picture, underlines the action. Somebody makes an intense move and the orchestra follows him with an emphasis, like the strings. Somebody else is dreaming and the orchestra describes the sense of this dream. In other words, my music for *Hook* doesn't abstain from that of a cartoon, where the music has to be attached in the picture.[6]

The music for *Hook*, in Williams's description (balletic, cartoonlike . . .), is a neoclassical reprise of the type of scoring one would find in the classical Hollywood, which Williams confessed he is quite fond of.

Way back, I used to go to the movies on Saturday with my sister. . . . I loved several things, but mainly I loved the music I could hear in films, which one couldn't hear anywhere else. I loved certain kinds of scenes. Obviously the love scenes, where you have a very expressive, lyrical and melodic piece of music. I also loved action-adventure scenes . . . , particularly sword fight scenes. First off, no one ever got hurt. They were choreographically expert. And the sword fights always had great music. Swashbuckling stuff! You could see Errol Flynn and Basil Rathbone doing their great turns. The other thing I loved was the cartoons, with all that quick music.[7]

In the music for *Hook*—and in other neoclassical scores such as *Star Wars* and *Raiders of the Lost Ark* (Steven Spielberg, 1981)—one can hear Williams reaching back exactly to those models. In the final assault on Captain Hook's ship and the following denouement duel between Peter Pan and the pirate leader, somersaults are replicated with woodwinds whirls, whip pans are accompanied by harp glissandos, lunges are stressed by woodwinds runs, and musical accents precisely hit the moves and gyrations of the duelists. Both Sarde's and Debney's score have some neoclassical traits, but only Williams's score is outright neoclassical.

Williams's old-fashioned style is acknowledged by a direct witness of the Golden Age, Lionel Newman (Alfred's brother): "He writes for films the way one would write an opera; he develops the characters dramatically through the music he writes. What he does enhances the film; he doesn't just write musical sequences [*closed musical numbers*], the way so many others do."[8] However, these classical stylistic traits are handled in a neoclassical way, in Miceli's words: "The nineteenth-century symphonic model is still present but now it is more credible and appropriate to the times since it has been revised to become more flexible, efficient but also more ironic and metalinguistic. . . . Unlike the previous 1930s and '40s musical themes, Williams's themes are designed to showcase the devices and techniques of musical rhetoric through the playful use of quotations, which are not taken literally but in their spirit."[9]

Williams's Neoclassical Style

The basic dialect employed in these neoclassical scores is late Romanticism, but compared with those of Steiner and Korngold, Williams's idiom is more influenced by the twentieth-century dialects. For example, episodes of polytonality and atonality are frequently found, and jazz chords color the symphonic texture: for example, the frequent use of thirteenth chords or syncopated rhythms—think of the march for *1941* (Steven Spielberg, 1979). Williams was also influenced by Copland's Americana dialect—pandiatonicism and quartal harmony—especially in his American themes: for example, John Quincy Adams's trumpet theme in *Amistad* (Steven Spielberg, 1997).[10]

Williams's harmonic progressions are typically nonfunctional, that is, the chords are not employed to serve a set of prescribed functions within the tonal system, and are not linked to each other following the patterns and hierarchical relations of the classical grammar of tonal music.[11] For example, a chord would not resolve but would bring the harmony toward a different tonal center, or would only serve to add an unexpected harmonic detour, a patch of musical color. Pandiatonicism typically employs the notes of the diatonic scale freely without conventional resolutions and without the standard chord progressions; unlike the traditional functional tonality, the chords built on the scale degrees are not assigned fixed functions and different grades of importance. "Hedwig's Theme" and "Fawkes the Phoenix," respectively from *Harry Potter and the Sorcerer's Stone* (Chris Columbus, 2001) and *Harry Potter and the Chamber of Secrets* (Chris Columbus, 2002), are two examples of themes with pandiatonic passages, as well as the "Journey to the Island" theme from *Jurassic Park* (Steven Spielberg, 1993). Pandiatonicism allows instantaneous key changes, and the frequent shifts and unexpected modulations from one tonality to others in Williams's music are powerful attention catchers, like sudden color changes in the lighting of a room. Musically, they are very useful in keeping the interest level high; cinematically, they are very effective in stressing noteworthy twists in the narrative or events in the visuals. When analyzing the Indiana Jones theme (more famously known as *Raiders March*) in chapter 9, one can see how strikingly the sudden use of a D-flat-major chord within a

C-major key gives a bright refreshing twist to the tune. Quartal harmony, on the other hand, builds chords not as juxtaposed thirds—as traditional harmony does—but as juxtaposed fourths. For example, the model of the "Main Title" from *Star Wars* is Korngold—namely *Kings Row* (Sam Wood, 1942). Williams, however, "Americanizes" Korngold, employing quartal chords and choosing to close the musical phrase with a chord progression typical of the Americana dialect used in Westerns: for example, in Jerome Moross's *The Big Country* (William Wyler, 1958)—the major triad built on the flattened seventh degree resolves to the dominant chord, as noted by Mervyn Cooke.[12]

Music theorists and musicologists have in recent years (finally) devoted their attention to the analysis of the Williams idiom. For example, Cooke has stressed that Williams's music, more than through the usual associations with Wagnerian opera, should be instead considered more akin to ballet music: "Williams's film scores are replete with echoes of the music of two of the greatest twentieth-century Russian ballet composers, Shostakovich and Prokofiev, both of whom (significantly) were also resourceful film composers whose output for theatre, cinema and concert hall shared common traits."[13] Mark Richards has examined the most recurring types of themes, "based on eight-bar models that divide into discernible halves of 4+4 bars, each half usually containing two short ideas of two bars each. Though this type of thematic structuring has been the norm for the majority of Hollywood film history, Williams's themes include variation more frequently than is typical for Hollywood films."[14] Richards has also discussed the composer's typical variation techniques and classified them into a four-period subdivision of his film-music production. Ian Sapiro has closely investigated the "Williams sound," describing the subtleties of his orchestrations and the typical use of each instrument—for example, the trademark Williams brass sound:

> It is the way that the brass is orchestrated that gives these themes Williams's distinctive sound. In several scores including those in the *Star Wars* and *Indiana Jones* series he features the trumpet section playing a theme in unison, giving the music a bravura that would be missing from a solo line, and Williams is also unafraid of using a wide pitch range without changing between instruments in the brass section. During the "Bike Chase" sequence in *E.T.: The Extra-Terrestrial* . . . Williams takes the horns up to a D_5 (a written top A), and the trumpets and trombones up as far as Ab_5 and Ab_4 respectively, meaning that he can present unbroken melodic lines in each instrument and thereby retain timbral coherence within phrases.[15]

More refined tools and definitions than those I have sketched here have been applied for the study of Williams's nonfunctional harmonic progressions: for example, Frank Lehman's neo-Riemannian approach to triadic chromaticism or Tom Schneller's "modal interchange."[16] Schneller explains:

> Many Williams themes open with a tonic–subdominant progression (sometimes grounded on a tonic bass pedal) and conclude with a cadence on the tonic or dominant. This sturdy diatonic framework is typically enriched by one or more chromatic "surprise chords," usually preceding the cadence. The result strikes a balance between the familiar and the unpredictable. . . . In major keys, Williams frequently replaces diatonic minor and diminished chords with major triads borrowed from the Aeolian, Mixolydian, Lydian or Phrygian modes. . . . [These] sonorities tend to be "color" chords that fleetingly import the flavor of the Phrygian or Lydian modes into an otherwise diatonic setting. The elimination of minor and diminished sonorities through modal interchange results in a major key on steroids—a simple but effective procedure in heroic passages of Williams' film and ceremonial music.[17]

The most characteristic mode in Williams's music, the musical fabric of his heroic and uplifting themes—what Lehman calls "soaring wonder"—is the Lydian mode, "because of its brightening of the already positively valenced major mode, an intensification of its upward tendencies."[18] Schneller also notes that "its characteristic buoyancy, which conveys a visceral sense of 'lifting off,' results from the unexpected suspension of the usual gravitational forces that condition melodic movement in major. . . . This denial of normative, functional resolution marks the progression as an extraordinary harmonic event and thereby intensifies its affective impact. . . . Given its implicitly levitational trajectory, the progression lends itself to suggesting, among other things, the physical sensation of flight."[19]

Zooming out and returning to more general issues of film-music style, if we consider the influences in Williams's music, we find both within the aforementioned first-generation composers—Korngold and Steiner, above all—as well as within the second generation: Herrmann, Waxman, and Rózsa. Besides bridging Hollywood's musical present with Hollywood's musical past, Williams has also blended the idioms of Hollywood's first generation with those of the second generation. Parts of *Jaws* (Steven Spielberg, 1975) have timbres, motifs, and modules that recall Herrmann's concise writing: the effective simplicity of the shark ostinato and the violent strings writing of Chrissie's death evoke *Psycho* (Alfred Hitchcock, 1960). This Herrmannesque modernist influence coexists with extended themes, richly orchestrated textures, and solid musical structure à la Korngold, and also with Steiner's precisely descriptive Mickey-Mousing. Harmonically, Aaron Copland is again a major influence as for harmonic choices, and the IV–I progression and plagal cadence frequently used by Williams—for example, in the main theme from *Jurassic Park*—are also typical of Copland's Americana modal sound.

When it comes to the influences from art music, Williams is often linked to Richard Wagner, especially for his penchant for using leitmotivs extensively. In this sense, as a master of the cinematic leitmotiv, it is natural that Williams has been linked to Wagner.[20] Nonetheless, besides the use of the leitmotiv technique and the continuous musical accompaniment, *Star Wars*—the work that is largely considered the most Wagnerian and *Ring*-like—does not sound very Wagnerian in terms of melodies and harmonies, and it is not Wagnerian in Williams's intention: "The instrumentation of *Star Wars* . . . might sound Wagnerian to some people; it doesn't to me."[21] Alex Ross has recently asked Williams directly about this supposed kinship with Wagner, and Williams has dismissed the weight of such influence: "'I don't really know the Wagner operas at all. If Mr. Hanslick were alive, I think I'd be sitting on the side of Brahms in the debate.' (The Viennese critic Eduard Hanslick campaigned for Brahms and against Wagner in the late nineteenth century.) 'People say they hear Wagner in *Star Wars*, and I can only think, It's not because I put it there.'"[22] Perhaps, if Wagnerian echoes are to be looked for in Williams's scores, some could be found in the farewell scene in *E.T. the Extra-Terrestrial* (Steven Spielberg, 1982), which might be reminiscent of the longing "unending melody" technique used in *Tristan und Isolde* (1865), or in the *Parsifal* (1882) ethos of the Grail theme for *Indiana Jones and the Last Crusade* (Steven Spielberg, 1989). Definitely more influential than Wagner have been such Russian composers as Sergei Prokofiev and Dmitri Shostakovich—think of the "March of the Villains" for *Superman: The Movie* (Richard Donner, 1978), or the "Parade of the Ewoks" from *Return of the Jedi* (Richard Marquand, 1983)—and the music of the British twentieth-century school such as Ralph Vaughan Williams, William Walton, Benjamin Britten, and Edward Elgar. The most prominent examples of the latter are *Jane Eyre* (Delbert Mann, 1970); more recently *War Horse* (Steven Spielberg, 2011); and the "Throne Room" music for the epilogue of *Star Wars*, which owes much to Walton's coronation march *Orb and Sceptre* (1953). Claude Debussy's ethereal "Impressionism" has also been an influence: think of the mermaid music for *Hook*, the séance scene music for *Family Plot*

(Alfred Hitchcock, 1976), and the "Fortress of Solitude" sequence in *Superman: The Movie*. Richard Strauss's orchestral grandiosity is the model, for example, of the end-credits music for *Close Encounters of the Third Kind* (Steven Spielberg, 1977), or of the "Planet Krypton" heraldic music for *Superman: The Movie*; while there are traces of Gustav Mahler's and Anton Bruckner's monumental and tragic Romanticism in the music for the more recent *Star Wars* films—for example, the elegy written for the Jedi immolation sequence in *Star Wars: Episode III—Revenge of the Sith* (George Lucas, 2005)—or in the melancholic final music for *Minority Report* (Steven Spielberg, 2002). Asked directly about his models, Williams replied, "I was crazy about Stravinksy and the Soviet composers . . . the super-moderns of the time. . . . Bartok was another from that same period that I was very much enamored with. But I always filled it in with the nineteenth century: Berlioz—fantastic!—and Brahms, of course. . . . And I always loved jazz when I was a kid. . . . Billy Strayhorn and Ellington, and the extension of those through people like Alex North."[23] On another occasion, he mentioned additional points of reference: "In the film world, I would have to mention again Alfred Newman and Bernard Herrmann but also Korngold—the great Viennese composer who went to Hollywood in the early years—he was a great hero of mine and Franz Waxman—and many, many others. In the concert field, there were, again, so many. I have to mention William Walton, a great favorite of mine—I admire his film and concert music. Walton was held in very high esteem in Hollywood. I like Elgar too, and all the Russian composers."[24] More recently, he seems to have turned more to the classical "classics," namely Joseph Haydn: "one of the all-time great musical talents. Without Haydn, we probably wouldn't have Mozart or Beethoven."[25] As to the use of the orchestra, in general, Russian "Impressionism"—Nicolai Rimsky-Korsakov and Igor Stravinsky's first works—seems to be a primary model for Williams. In his scores, there is a keen attention for a coloristic and inventive use of timbres, and such recurring traits as high-pitched woodwinds runs, prominent harp glissandos, glistening touches of the celesta, and the constant presence of the piano used either for adding color to a melody or to reinforce the percussion section.[26]

As for techniques, one of the most prominent traits of Williams's writing is, again, the extensive use of leitmotivs. Williams is a gifted melodist; he has an instinct for finding just the right musical equivalent for a film or a character, a knack for translating it into clear-cut themes with a strong identity that get instantly fixed to the listener's memory, and an outstanding dramaturgic sensibility in varying the themes vis-a-vis the narrative progression of the film.[27] According to Williams, "So much of successful film scoring relies on a gratifying melodic identification for the characters. . . . I try to draw on something that marries very well with what I'm seeing."[28] Finding the right, "inevitable" themes thus seems the very first step in Williams's modus operandi, and this is the result of a substantial amount of work, as he explains.

> I spend a lot of time on those melodies that will sound very simple or inevitable when they're heard. . . . It's weeks of tinkering around with various approaches and different ideas and trying to manipulate one or the other to make it feel like it lives or wants to belong in the film in a very natural way. It's not easy for me, and I spend more time doing that than orchestrating or developing or doing contrapuntal workouts of the material—once I have the material, all those other things are relatively easy.[29]

The creation of recognizable melodies and their skillful combination into a leitmotivic network allows Williams's scores to be a proficient musical retelling of the film's narrative. Themes and musical motifs associated with characters or concepts and their manipulation for narrative purposes are consistently present in virtually all his work, even in more experimental scores such as *Close Encounters of the Third Kind*.

The musical manipulation of leitmotivs also implies good skills in the theme-and-variation technique.[30] Says a reviewer: "Even more impressive, though, are the myriad ways in which he transforms the arching lines of that main melody, fragmenting and poisoning them as the mood turns from triumphant to ominous. The terse, tense music in 'Jurassic Park' isn't fundamentally different from the soaring stuff. Mr. Williams, for all his lyrical lavishness, is an expert at recycling, at making a given theme do many different things in the course of a film."[31] For example, the "Darth Vader" theme is widely used as the militaristic and threatening "Imperial march" in *The Empire Strikes Back* (Irvin Kershner, 1980). When Darth Vader, in *Return of the Jedi*, eventually repents and gives his life to save his son, Williams sensitively penned a benign variation of Vader's theme gently played by a solo harp. The intrinsic modal ambiguity of the theme (G minor / E-flat major) is now shifted toward a redeemed major mode by thinning down the harmonic backing. We have already mentioned how Darth Vader's theme is also astutely hidden within Anakin's theme to suggest the child's dark future in *Star Wars: Episode I—The Phantom Menace* (George Lucas, 1999). So is the theme of Emperor Palpatine, artfully anticipated within "Augie's Great Municipal Band," a joyful piece for chorus and orchestra that accompanies the celebration in the closing scene of the same film. A close listening reveals that the cheerful major-mode theme is, meaningfully, a variation of the minor-mode sinister Emperor's theme already featured in *Return of the Jedi*.[32] As our heroes celebrate what appears to be a victory to the sound of diegetic festive music, Senator (and future Emperor) Palpatine is there. Apparently, he celebrates with them the defeat of the Dark Side; actually, what he secretly celebrates is the smooth progress of his own power-grab plans. Frank Lehman describes it as "a deliciously cynical little musical Easter egg: While the good guys think they've won the day, everything, including the soundtrack, is actually proceeding according to the villain's design. George Lucas wanted Palpatine's rise to echo the ascents of real-life tyrants. 'Democracies aren't overthrown,' he claimed in a 2005 interview, 'they're given away.'"[33] Williams also masters the Mickey-Mousing technique, which in Williams's case is usually not pushed to the extremes as in Steiner's, but when needed, Williams can be very Steineresque: in the opening train-chase sequence of *Indiana Jones and the Last Crusade*, there is, on average, one explicit sync point every six seconds.[34] Another classical technique that Williams can handle proficiently is the dialogue underscoring (see especially chapters 2 and 6), the shaping of the musical phrasing around the phrasing of the dialogue and visual action. Explains Williams:

> Film music is, very broadly put, an accompaniment to dialog and to action. And there are rare moments when the orchestra can take full stage. And so it would be something like examining an opera score and taking away all the vocal parts and just having the accompaniment played. So that when one is writing for film, one needs to bear in mind that we're accompanying people speaking and we don't have 100 percent or 80 percent even of the listeners' attention but we're finding a register, a tessitura, a place in the orchestra, low, high, soft, loud, whatever, that will fit the tempo of the dialog and the register of the dialog and the intensity of it or action and bear that in mind with every measure we're writing.[35]

A typical Williams technique that is connected with the macro-emotive function is what I call "gradual disclosure of the main theme." The main theme is first presented gradually across the film, in the form of progressively longer melodic fragments, instead of directly in its entirety. This technique can be traced back to Wagner's musical theater, in what Bribitzer-Stull calls "presentiment."

One way composers make music memorable is by repeating it; specifically, by ensuring that the music playing during the critical moment when the association is formed is itself a repetition. Thus we find Wagner, and others, "previewing" (or, more accurately, "prehearing") associative music in advance of the dramatic moment of feeling needed to form the association. . . . John Williams seems particularly fond of this technique. . . . Thus, even before associational meaning becomes clear, both emotion and memory can be primed by musical premonitions.[36]

After introducing a fragment in one scene, evoking it again later in another moment, reprising the same fragment now enlarged with a new bit, the final exposition of the theme in its entirety comes only at a strategic point in the narrative. Typically such a strategic point is a scene requiring a strong emotional response from the viewers. Williams explains:

What is so important is an hour and a half or ten reels of preparation to that moment. . . . In the first reel we only heard two notes, in the third reel we heard four, in the fifth reel we heard six manipulated, in the tenth . . . and so on. But in the twelfth you hear all twelve coming. So, to the audience, you've created an expectancy to deliver something that's not only very emotional but is also inevitable. It's a moment that had to happen.[37]

Having been prepared throughout the previous part of the film, the viewers can easily recognize the theme when it is presented in its entirety and be gratified by the long-awaited full statement of the familiar theme. In Williams's hands, this "gradual disclosure of the main theme" not only produces an emotional arc and a satisfying sense of payoff and fulfillment when the arc reaches its climax. It also shapes film scores that have a rare organic quality, a formal cohesiveness, an extended design that Schneller calls "teleological genesis": "The opportunity to use sophisticated formal strategies like teleological genesis in film music is entirely dependent on the structure of the narrative. . . . But it takes a composer of particular musico-dramatic sensitivity and skill to recognize the potential for employing such a structural approach. . . . Few composers have been as consistently adept as Williams at negotiating this delicate balance between musical and filmic form."[38] Perhaps the best instance can be found in *E.T. the Extra-Terrestrial*. Its score demonstrates, within the film, dramaturgical effectiveness and emotional impact, while at the same time it possesses, outside the film, a rare stand-alone musical form—as can be seen in *The Adventures on Earth*, discussed later. Through its gradual disclosure, the *E.T.* main theme—fragments of which are presented throughout the first half of the film is completely stated by the full orchestra only in the spectacular and emotionally uplifting sequence of the bicycle flight over the moon. Locally, the gratification produced in the viewers by recognizing and finally hearing the long-delayed presentation of the full melody is projected onto the images, thus amplifying their emotional impact and performing a micro-emotive function.[39] This "gradual disclosure of the main theme" technique also works globally, performing a macro-emotive function on the whole film's form: it casts onto the entire film the sense of cohesion and unity given to the score by the recurrent thematic reprises and their development and formal closure. In *Jaws*, the technique circumscribes the whole shark-hunt final act: what I have called the "Man-versus-the-Beast" theme is heard for the first time when the *Orca* leaves the harbor; it is presented in fragmentary ways throughout the sea hunt; and it appears in its complete form only after the shark is killed, over the end credits, enhancing the sense of fulfillment for the man having defeated the beast.

Last, as for the musical means, Williams is evidently fond of the symphony orchestra: "The symphony orchestra itself is one of the greatest inventions of our artistic culture. Fabulous sounds it can produce and a great range of emotional capabilities."[40] Jack Sullivan notes, speaking of the film *War Horse*:

> As usual, Williams is obsessed with the sound of the orchestra and the quality of the solos: the score is "very performance-dependent. We need to get a magic moment from the flutist, . . . and the string orchestra that follows it will need to create something special. . . . The sound of *War Horse* is something you really can't synthesize with a computer or overlay with a new technology. This is a lyrical film that requires a lyrical response not only in the writing but in the performance from the orchestra. . . . So those recording sessions were more like playing at a concert than they were recording a score for a film."[41]

From *Star Wars* on, Williams's orchestra has been considerably bigger than the classical studio orchestras. This is another trait that can be called neoclassical—or "hyperclassical," in Bordwell's words—being an augmentation of classical traits.[42]

Williams's Neoclassical Attitude

Besides stylistic traits, there are also a number of habits and practices that link Williams with classical Hollywood music.[43] Williams commented, "My own preference is not to read scripts. It's like when you read a novel: you envisage the locales, you cast the players in your mind. That's the reason, I think, why people are so often disappointed by film versions of novels they have read—they don't conform to their preconceptions. So I'd rather not read scripts, and I tell producers that I'd rather go into a projection room and react to the people and places and events—and particularly the rhythm—of the film itself."[44] Compare Williams's words to Max Steiner's:

> I write what I see and what I hear and the way the character affects me. That is why I have a rule I have had all my life. I never . . . I never but never read a script. I have had one or two bad experiences. I read a script and I think this is the greatest script I ever read and I see the picture and it is the most horrible thing you ever saw. The characters are changing and you build up an image of characters when you read a script. On the other hand I have read scripts that were so terrible I wouldn't touch them. But when the picture came out, I loved it. So I decided I'd wait until I see the picture. . . . [Producers] say to me, "Shall I send you the script?" and I say, "Hell no, I don't want to read it," because I know it will steer me all wrong . . . good or bad.[45]

Besides the fact that written pages can evoke images that can be disappointingly different from the film version, this choice can be explained in stylistic terms too. Says Williams, "You really can't get that off the page of script. . . . There may be one page of script that could be five minutes of film, or five pages of script that's 30 seconds of film. We need to see it."[46] Composing music from a screenplay is possible in those cases in which the music is written prior to the film, as in the Leone/Morricone collaboration or when explicit sync points between music and visuals are not required, as in the modern style—for example, in Nino Rota's scores.[47] If, on the one hand, the music has to fulfill only a cognitive or emotive function, the composer can acquire the needed information by reading the script and discussing it with the director. On the other hand, if the score is also supposed to follow the images tightly and perform a significant spatial perceptive function, the composer must necessarily work from a film's cut in order to conform the music to the visuals second by second. To write in the style in which Williams writes, the script is not enough to communicate the complex audiovisual qualities of the film. "It's more a stimulation that comes from the whole visual presentation, all the textural aspects and the rhythmic aspects of what the film means, the editing speed, the whole kinetic of the film and the atmosphere of it. It's more than just seeing a picture; it's experiencing an event in time and visuals that

eventually translates into time and sound—i.e., the music," as Williams further clarifies.[48] The comparison of the work-in-progress score and the film cut
is a continuous process: "In the film work I look at the film a lot. There is
a cutting room, a viewing room so to speak, within the building I work in,
and I can look at a scene I am working on for two or three days and see it as
often as I need to see it. I can write a few bars, then go look at it."[49] It is like a
tailor working on a suit: one has to repeatedly check and recheck to make
sure that the measurements are adhered to as the sewing and cutting proceed:
"The test of a good score . . . is that you hardly even notice it. It's like a good
tailor. You don't want to know how he sewed it, you just want to know that
it holds," argued Williams.[50] And this statement, again, sounds much like
Steiner's "[music should fit] a picture like a glove."[51]

Williams's typical work routine is reported in a 1984 article.

> Williams—along with the producer, the director, the film editor, and the music
> editor—"spots" the film, that is, they decide when the music should start and
> stop. The exact spot, precise to one-third of a second, is marked on the film.
> Then the music editor writes out a detailed cue sheet—a chronological listing of
> every event and sound effect that happens during the parts of the film that will
> be accompanied by music. With the cue sheet as his guide, Williams composes
> about two minutes of music each day. He is allowed four weeks to write the
> music for an average feature film which requires about 60 minutes of music. . . .
> Most film cues are from a few seconds to two or three minutes long, so the film
> composer often adopts a piecemeal approach, concentrating on two minutes of
> film at a time. "When I come in in the morning, I like to look at the sequence
> that I'm going to work on that day, so it's fresh in my mind. . . . I look at my
> assignment for the day on the Moviola (a machine that reduces the movie to a
> four-inch wide viewing screen), mark up the cues sheet, restudy just that bit of
> film, and then work on it. I may check the clip again later in the afternoon. . . .
> There are many extra-musical problems. The biggest one is having the music
> co-exist with a lot of noises. It should be conceived orchestrally with these things
> in mind. You not only need to study the film, you need to study the sounds
> associated with the film in these areas and try to create a marriage between the
> orchestra and those sounds."[52]

As for the writing itself, Williams still uses—and has always used—an old-
school modus operandi. Unlike the next-generation composers and some
same-age composers—Jerry Goldsmith, for example—Williams does not use

synthesizers, MIDI, or any other technological implements to compose his music: "My musical education is such that it pre-dates all of that and although I know a little bit about it, I haven't developed the skills. I use the piano, that's my old friend in music."[53] He also uses "antique tools. Not even a pen these days. Pencil and paper. . . . And I find that at least for me pencil and paper introduces a process of working that's as much part of it, it becomes part of the conceptual routine or process of working. It's tangible. It feels good to hold a pen or pencil in your hand and dirty up paper. I suppose it must seem to young composers a completely antediluvian or old-fashioned way of doing it."[54] He further explains, "It's an influence that would be hard to quantify, but I think methodology is intimately connected to result. . . . It's something you do with your hands, so there's an aspect of craftsmanship involved, even penmanship."[55]

On the recording stage, Williams, unlike most contemporary film conductors, does not use too constrictive technical aids.

> Williams conducts with the film projected on a screen behind the orchestra and a clock in front of the podium. Timings are marked in the score at least every other bar. Other mechanical aids, like a "streamer" which shows up on the screen as a band of light followed by a bright flash at the crucial moment help maintain stop-watch precision. Many composers rely on click tracks (a variation on the metronome) that let the conductor and the orchestra members hear a beat that has already been synchronized with the movie. But Williams finds the unrelenting beat coming through the headphones too confining for musical expression. With the clock to mark off the moments that must be matched exactly, he prefers to allow his musicians some flexibility in between those key points.[56]

In the old days, the click track was employed by Steiner to allow his very tightly synchronized scores to be recorded in less time and as precisely as possible. Williams, on the contrary, typically conducts freestyle as Korngold did, which is a more complex method to achieve the perfect synchronization but allows the music to flow more freely and to sound less mechanical.[57] He also prefers to record the entire orchestra together as if during a concert—"the best sound, for me, is the live performance—the best we ever hear is on the soundstage or in the concert hall"—instead of employing multitracks and overlaying (the separate recording of sections of the orchestra that are then mixed together later), as is often done in contemporary work routines.[58]

Williams explains, "The orchestra and the performance are more important than the usual electronic assemblage of tracks. . . . We capture a moment of expression with the orchestra like you would in the theater or a concert. This is a modus operandi that is probably almost extinct with other people."[59] Williams's experience as a concert conductor has been fundamental: "I did so much live performance, especially in Boston but also elsewhere, that I began to have a different, and maybe more sophisticated, feeling about the orchestra and its way of breathing, its way of moving and so on. And that's a subtle thing but I think I'm, in my mind as I am writing, much more of a conductor than I was before."[60] As a concert conductor would do, he also resorts more to live in-orchestra balances than to postrecording mixing and registering.

> John is really mixing his own soundtrack when he's up there on the podium conducting, and he's making initial choices as to which instruments are louder than others. . . . There was this one section where the brass was playing and John (who knows every single person's name in that orchestra) called out to three people by name and said something like, "Mark, on bar 63, from beat two to beat six, can you not play please. I just want a little more clarity with two instruments instead of three. Thank you." So they backed up and did a pick-up on that bar and that gentleman dropped out for those few beats. . . . In the end, it really is John who is creating that mix.[61]

In chapter 6, I stressed the importance of Williams's apprenticeship during the final years of the studio system and his training in fast-paced television productions. His work habits seem to have been influenced by those past experiences, as it seems that he prefers to compose in a work environment somewhat reminiscent of the old music departments. Being no longer in-house employees but freelancers, most Hollywood composers have their studios at home (e.g., Danny Elfman, but Jerry Goldsmith also used to compose at home) or at their own musical company (e.g., Hans Zimmer).[62] Howard Shore's studio is located in New York, far away from the Hollywood studios. On the contrary, Williams has routinely worked in an office located in some film studio or production company throughout his career. He had had an office in the 20th Century Fox studios for twenty-five years, until he moved to Spielberg's Amblin compound at Universal Studios in 1987 (Amblin is now within the DreamWorks SKG facilities). However anecdotally this might sound, it somewhat attests to Williams's fondness for the old days: "We knew it was, say, Warner Bros Orchestra, because unlike now, where you have one or two honored freelance groups recording everything, it wasn't the same people playing on every film. . . . In the isolation of a few miles across Los Angeles you had inspirational individuality coming out of these studio systems."[63] He adds, "We had a music department table where we all went every day for lunch. We'd sit around and between ordering sandwiches, we'd talk about your problems and my problems, this dreadful director and that hateful producer, and we'd got a better cellist here than they have across the street— the kind of inside stuff that really puts you in touch with how things work. Every studio had that, but it's all gone now. Every composer works at home. We don't even know each other any more. We're not connected."[64]

Another similarity with classical Hollywood composers is Williams's already mentioned career in concert music both as a composer and as a conductor, whereas modern-style film composers typically have a parallel career in songwriting or pop music—apart from some exceptions like Rota and Morricone. Among the film composers who have also produced a considerable amount of concert music are Korngold, Waxman, Rózsa, Moross, and Herrmann. Williams's concert pieces are unusually numerous for a film composer of his generation: more than twelve concertos, one symphony, and somewhere around thirty other works comprising celebratory fanfares, orchestral miniatures, and solo or chamber pieces.[65] Williams also has a sustained parallel career as a concert conductor, as did Alfred Newman, who used to conduct the Hollywood Bowl Orchestra; Franz Waxman, who founded and was musical director of the Los Angeles International Music Festival; and Bernard Herrmann, who spent his last decade mostly as a conductor in London.[66] Newman, in particular, seems to have been a role model for Williams: "[As for conducting skills], of film composers, though, Alfred Newman was the best I've ever seen or heard: he was a magician with an orchestra, could get amazing effects. And such a disciplinarian, in the most natural and simple way."[67]

Even more unusual is Williams's care in adapting concert suites from his film scores. This is another element linking him to the classical period, whose film composers mostly came from theater or concert music and were used to that medium, whereas modern-style composers had radio stations and the record market as the primary target for their film music outside the films. Even Steiner, noted for the fragmentary structure and highly functional nature of his film works, showed some concern for the structural solidity of the music:

Even though the themes [of *Gone with the Wind*] are popular it's written in symphonic style. I tried to be as musical as possible. It's in itself a serious work, in itself. The score is symphonic, even if it is in a popular vein here and there. [Of course it can be played in concert halls,] sure. It has been. It has been played everywhere. I played it with the New York Philharmonic. There was just another one with the London Symphony, and now they are going to do it in Tokyo. . . . I have made a suite out of it.[68]

On arranging film music for concerts, Williams has stated: "If I can take the music out of the sound track and have it almost resemble music, this is a minor miracle, and a double asset. . . . If I write a 100-minute score, there may be 20 minutes that could be extracted and played. The other 80 minutes is functional accompaniment that could never stand on its own and was never intended to."[69] Although Williams underplays it, his particular care for concert versions is proved by the fact that he is the only film composer whose numerous concert suites can easily be found for sale in authoritative full scores.[70] Jack Sullivan goes as far as to say that "Williams envisions his projects as cinematic concerts."[71]

Like his colleagues of the past—particularly Rózsa, Waxman, and Herrmann—Williams often uses musical forms similar to those of art music: the *scherzo* in *Jane Eyre*, *Dracula* (John Badham, 1979), and *Indiana Jones and the Last Crusade*; the *fugato* in *Jaws*, *Black Sunday* (John Frankenheimer, 1977), and *Harry Potter and the Prisoner of Azkaban* (Alfonso Cuaron, 2004); set pieces for chorus and orchestra like the carols in *Home Alone* (Chris Columbus, 1990), "Gloria" in *Monsignor* (Frank Perry, 1982), and "Exsultate Justi" in *Empire of the Sun* (Steven Spielberg, 1987); and quasi-ballet music for action scenes, for example in *Jurassic Park*, of which the composer says, "[It is] a massive job of symphonic cartooning. You have to match the rhythmic gyrations of the dinosaurs and create these kind of funny ballets."[72] In the classical period, this attention to the solidity of the musical form on the part of classically trained composers can be explained by the hope that the best bits of a film score might be extracted and thus have a life outside the films.[73] Likewise, from the outset Williams inserts traditional forms when writing his film scores, so that he can obtain—with a minimum of changes—stand-alone pieces for concert presentations.[74] For example, he might add a coda to close a passage left open in the film score, as in the case of "The Asteroid Field" from *The Empire Strikes Back* or "The Lost Boys Ballet" from *Hook*.[75] From the score for *Harry Potter and the Sorcerer's Stone*, Williams adapted an eight-movement children's suite in the spirit of Benjamin Britten's *The Young Person's Guide to the Orchestra*, op. 34 (1946).[76] An example of the musical solidity of Williams's compositions is the finale of *E.T. the Extra-Terrestrial*, which was adapted with the mere removal of a few central measures into the symphonic poem *Adventures on Earth*.[77] Sergio Miceli thus praised the piece: "Thanks to its thematic concatenations, the piece alludes convincingly to the musical macro-forms of the nineteenth and early twentieth centuries . . . showing a musical legitimacy rarely to be found in film-music adaptations. . . . These same forms were also able to cope with and satisfy each narrative need in their natural place—that is, the film—and this is a proof of the overall quality of the composer."[78] Moreover, Williams has often employed famous or well-known concert soloists to play on his film scores: the violinist Isaac Stern in *Fiddler on the Roof* (Norman Jewison, 1971), the violinist Itzhak Perlman in *Schindler's List* (Steven Spielberg, 1994), and the cellist Yo-Yo Ma in *Seven Years in Tibet* (Jean-Jacques Annaud, 1997).[79] The involvement of these illustrious guest stars, mostly planned at the beginning of the compositional process, has led to a conspicuous quantity of film-music pieces for solo and orchestra, all of which are practically ready for concert presentation as well.

Besides concerts but still outside the cinema, Williams has accomplished another fusion between classical and modern practices. He carefully supervises the creation of the film-music album to be marketed, which is typical of the modern-style composers, while also striving to have a musical form as solid as possible, which is characteristic of classical-style composers. Following Mancini's example, Williams records selections from the film score expressly rearranged for the albums in order to have a better musical solidity and closure. The track list of the album does not reflect the order in which the pieces were presented in the film, but here the list meets criteria of musical variety and balance aimed at an autonomous music experience.[80] The LP album of *Star Wars* is a clear example: the track "The Little People Work" follows "Ben's Death / TIE Fighter Attack," in a reverse order compared to the film. The "Main Title" of *Star Wars* on the album is different from that in the film: "I combined part of the end title with the opening music to give the beginning of the record the feeling of an overture."[81] If we compare the 1982 LP album of *E.T. the Extra-Terrestrial* (40 minutes, MCA Records MCLD 19021, 1982), which has pieces expressly rerecorded for the album, with the 1996 CD containing the music used in the film's soundtrack (78 minutes, MCA Records MCAD-11494, 1996), we notice that the pieces on the 1982 LP albums were considerably adapted and expanded for a better listening experience. For example, on the CD with the original music track, the music for the Halloween sequence and the following bicycle flight over the moon (titled "The Magic of Halloween") lasts 2:53 while on the album the corresponding track "E.T.'s Halloween" lasts 4:07. Williams included additional phrases to get a more extended musical development that closed the piece more formally, while the film version stops abruptly with the bicycle landing. Similarly, the music in the montage sequence of *Jaws* lasts 1:30 in the film—and on the original music track CD (Decca MCAD-11494, 2000)—while on the CD album (MCA Records MCD01660-MCAD1660, 1975), the piece is humorously named "Promenade (Tourists on the Menu)" and was expanded to 2:46.[82]

Besides inheriting stylistic traits and habits from the past, Williams as a neoclassical composer has also become the target of some of the old prejudices that used to surround classical Hollywood composers. Russell Lack, in his film-music book, drags up the old bromide claiming that using an orchestrator is necessarily a symptom of artistic incompetence: "In foregrounding the symphonic score, Williams is siding with tradition, but his very tight working schedules mean that he works extensively with orchestrators. . . . One might argue that his celebrity is due more to the films he has scored rather than the scores themselves, which whilst stirring enough are hard to single out as distinctively his own since they are so varied, due in part to Williams' frequent use of a variety of different orchestrators and arrangers."[83] Working under "very tight working schedules" is something that any composer in Hollywood is used to, Williams being not an exception: "A standard contract for his movie compositions gives him three months to create a score. A Lucas or Spielberg epic might require 120 minutes of music. A little calculating and presto. Williams must compose forty minutes of original score a month, or 10 minutes a week, or two minutes every day (assuming he rests on the weekend, which he often does not)."[84] As discussed in chapter 2, the use of orchestrators is a traditional aspect of the Hollywood practice aimed to optimize labor time, and I have also argued against the necessary equation of orchestrators with ghostwriters. In Lack's statement there appears to be a lack of research, as he seems to ignore both the Hollywood tradition and Williams's specific work method. Williams had not used "a variety of different orchestrators" but collaborated for more than twenty years with Herbert W. Spencer (1905–92)—from *A Guide for the Married Man* (1967) to *Home Alone* (1990). Williams commented:

[Spencer's] been my first choice for a very long time. He's an expert orchestrator but he's also a guy I can live with for the length of time it takes to do a picture. It's more of a personal thing. . . . We know each other very well, so I suppose we do [create a form of shorthand]. He knows my idiosyncrasies. In doubling, for example, you may want to lean on something, to be à "2" or à "3" or whatever, and sometimes Herb will be in the next room and pound on the piano and say, "How much do you want that B flat? Three or four horns, or six?" And I may remember there's a great sword whack on the soundtrack, so I say, "Six!" That sort of thing. We have a great relationship.[85]

Williams had with Spencer a long and trusting collaboration—recalling that between Korngold and his orchestrator Hugo Friedhofer—which guaranteed an even and stylistically homogeneous output.[86] After Spencer's death, Williams began consistent collaborations with a few recurring names: John Neufeld, Alexander Courage, Conrad Pope, Eddie Karam, William Ross, many of whom had served as Spencer's associates and assistants. Williams, like most Hollywood composers of the past, needs the help of orchestrators to meet deadlines: "Without the orchestrator's help, Williams estimates that his daily output would be cut in half."[87] Nonetheless, his sketches are so detailed that using a different orchestrator would not affect the results in terms of idiom and orchestral texture. Williams clarifies the point:

I don't want to minimize the contribution of orchestrators but, on the other hand, I try to be *very* careful about my sketches so that I get just what I want: winds on two or three staves, horns, brass, low brass, piano, percussion, etc., in the middle, and then three or four staves for strings, so that on eight or ten staves you can get almost a note-perfect accurate score. But the sheer labor of laying it out in full score for symphony orchestra would greatly slow me up, so here orchestrators help. When you consider that *Star Wars* had some 90 minutes of orchestral music and had to be written in some six-plus weeks . . . about half the length of an opera. Well, to do that without even stenographic help from an orchestrator would be physically impossible. On *Star Wars* I used four: Herb [Spencer] was contracted to do it and he receives the credit (he must have done about 500 of the 800-or-so pages of score), but Arthur Morton, Angela Morley and Al Woodbury also helped a lot. I even did some sequences myself, so I hope that it's a compliment to my sketches that you can't tell who did what![88]

The Boston Pops percussionist Patrick Hollenbeck debuted as an orchestrator after Williams had asked for his help on *Indiana Jones and the Last Crusade*: "When I got out there I heard these horror stories of orchestrators being handed a page with a title, a key signature and a number of bars and nothing else on it; so orchestrators have developed a mystique as, allegedly, 'the secret composers,' and in many cases it may be true—but not with John Williams. With him, orchestrating means taking his notes from the little green paper and putting them in the big yellow paper."[89]

Williams is fully capable of orchestrating his works, schedule permitting: he personally orchestrated the scores for *Fiddler on the Roof* (Norman Jewison, 1971), *Jane Eyre* (Delbert Mann, 1970), *Cinderella Liberty* (Mark Rydell, 1973), *The Missouri Breaks* (Arthur Penn, 1976), and *Images* (Robert Altman, 1972)—not to mention his concert music, which is self-orchestrated.[90] Williams's works are consistent with his overall idiom and orchestral sound, as Kathryn Kalinak points out: "Such detailed sketches and long-term collaborations leave little room for deviation and insure a consistency in terms of the Williams sound."[91] In the most recent film projects, the figure of the orchestrator has somewhat been bypassed. With notation software, it is no longer necessary for copyists to have a hard copy of the full score from which to write down the single parts; parts can be extracted directly from the digital file of the full score. An "orchestration-impaired" composer would still need a collaborator to turn the tentative sketches into a complete and musically accurate document from which the information can be read and inserted into the software. The completeness and accuracy of Williams's sketches make it possible to send them directly to the music-preparation company: "The music library then transfers these directly to a computerized score from which instrumental parts are made. . . . We can reprint parts, edit as needed, change the bowings, etc.," explains Williams.[92]

After having traced this overview of Williams's neoclassical style, in the next two chapters I examine one of the peaks of Williams's film output and of Hollywood's neoclassical scoring, *Raiders of the Lost Ark*.

CHAPTER 9

Raiders of the Lost Ark
Background

A Neoclassical Film

May 1977. Mauna Kea Hotel, Hawaii. Steven Spielberg and George Lucas are on vacation together. *Star Wars* is just coming out in theaters. Lucas, thinking it would be a commercial flop, decided to flee California, away from the expected box office disaster—which, on the contrary, would soon turn into one of the biggest hits of all time. The two filmmakers and close friends are on the beach, working on a gigantic sand castle, and George shares with Steven an idea he had had on the shelf for some time: a story, or rather a series of adventures, whose protagonist is a fearless archaeologist who travels the world in search of treasures.[1] This, allegedly, was the quasi-legendary moment in which *Raiders of the Lost Ark* and the Indiana Jones saga were born, a saga that would develop over the next decades into four feature films—*Raiders of the Lost Ark* (1981), *Indiana Jones and the Temple of Doom* (1984), *Indiana Jones and the Last Crusade* (1989), *Indiana Jones and the Kingdom of the Crystal Skull* (2008)—a TV series, *The Young Indiana Jones Chronicles* (1992–93); and a possible fifth feature-film long rumored for some ever-shifting release date. Lucas, story author and executive producer with his film company Lucasfilm Ltd., relied on his friend Steven Spielberg to direct all the films of the series. Spielberg accepted the task enthusiastically, as he saw in it the chance to somewhat fulfill one of his long-standing desires: to direct a James Bond film.[2]

Actually, the two series are very different. The James Bond films are firmly set in the contemporary world and, since the first films and up to those realized in the twenty-first century, they have always been a showcase for the trends and habits of the society of the time. They flaunt the fads of the day in terms of cars, clothing, men's and women's hairstyles, technology, musical tastes, and the state of the art in current film style. Armed with the futuristic gadgets of Dr. Q, Bond is committed to protecting Western civilization;

Bond lives in the present day and is concerned in the future of his society. Indiana Jones, armed with his PhD in archaeology, is committed to retrieving ancient relics and is interested in past societies, not merely because he is an archaeologist—the past is his job—but because his adventures are set in the 1930s. Rather than being immersed in a contemporary and up-to-date context like Bond, Indiana lives in a "vintage" past.[3] Said Spielberg: "[That was a] period where adventures could happen, a romantic time when it took a little longer to get around the world by air than it does today, a period without advanced technology, where the cleverness of the individual against the enemy was what mattered. So it wouldn't use laser guns and light sabers and James Bond weaponry."[4]

As had happened before with *Star Wars*, the idea was to pay homage to the classical Hollywood genre films. Particularly, inspiration was drawn from B-movies like *The Masked Marvel* (Spencer Gordon Bennet, 1943) and serials like *Don Winslow of the Navy* (Ford Beebe, Ray Taylor, 1942) and *Blackhawk: Fearless Champion of Freedom* (Spencer Gordon Bennet and Fred F. Sears, 1952). Even more so than in the *Star Wars* case, all those involved in the film seemed to have the nostalgic wish of recovering not only those past genres but also their old-fashioned style.[5] When the film came out, the catchphrase on the posters and billboards was "The return of the great adventure." A reporter from the set noted: "It became clear that the majority of people making *Raiders* . . . had a core of romanticism several inches in diameter."[6]

George Lucas described the idea behind the film: "The essence of *Raiders* is that it's a throwback to an older kind of film. It's a high-adventure film vaguely in the mode of the old Saturday afternoon serials. Actually the serials were C-movies and I would say that *Raiders* is an old-fashioned B-movie."[7] Steven Spielberg directly declared his love for classical films: "I went back and looked at my favorite films from the 1930s and 1940s and thought how quickly and cheaply they were made. I think I'm basically a reincarnated director from the 1930s."[8] Compared to *Jaws* (1975) and *Close Encounters of the Third Kind* (1977), Spielberg's style for *Raiders* was more direct and strictly functional, "a model of stylish economy."[9] Even the screenwriter Lawrence Kasdan expressed his fondness for old adventure films: "Adventure films were absolutely at the heart of my love of movies. . . . Everything in the movie resonates from other movies. That's the feeling we were after. It doesn't take itself too seriously."[10] In the same spirit, Harrison Ford gave life to the main character, as the actor has commented: "[The film is] really about movies more than it's about anything else. It's intrinsically designed as a real tribute to the craft."[11]

Drawing from the Oldies

Throughout *Raiders* it is no surprise to find not only a number of influences but also outright quotations from B-movies and serials.[12] For example, the hero pursued by an indigenous tribe comes from *Too Hot to Handle* (Jack Conway, 1938); the fight against the Nazis comes from *Spy Smasher* (William Witney, 1942); the hero using a whip comes from *Man with the Steel Whip* (Adreon Franklin, 1954); the Arab disguise used by Indiana when he infiltrates the archaeological site comes from *Lawrence of Arabia* (David Lean, 1962); the animated map showing the route of the journeys is from *Casablanca* (Michael Curtiz, 1942), which also inspired the sequences set in Cairo and Indiana getting drunk à la Bogart after losing Marion; and the finale with the crate containing the Ark stocked in a huge warehouse is a nod to *Citizen Kane* (Orson Welles, 1941). As for the main character's look and nature, Spielberg said: "He's a remarkable combination of Errol Flynn from *The Adventures of Don Juan* [Vincent Sherman, 1948] and Humphrey Bogart as Fred C. Dobbs in *The Treasure of the Sierra Madre* [John Huston, 1948] . . . villainous and romantic all at once."[13] Two other films also seem to have had more than a little influence on the character and look of Indiana Jones: *King Solomon's Mines* (Compton Bennett and Andrew Marton, 1950) and *Secret of the Incas* (Jerry Hopper, 1954). As in *Raiders*, the male leads—Allan Quartermain and Harry Steele, respectively—are rugged adventurers who initially are quite rough with and definitely impolite to the woman with whom they are forced to travel but end up falling in love with her. In *King Solomon's Mines*, when the female lead's elegant dress proves to be totally inadequate for a trip into the jungle, Quartermain ungracefully tears it off, as Indiana will do with Willie's in *Indiana Jones and the Temple of Doom*. In *King Solomon's Mines*, there is also a capuchin monkey called Lulu, which is very similar to the monkey that Jones meets in Cairo. Also, the huge rolling boulder that traps Quartermain and his fellows in a mine cave resembles the one we see in *Raiders*—though another rolling-boulder line of ancestry can be traced back to *Journey to the Center of the Earth* (Henry Levin, 1959), in which Professor Lindenbrook and his team narrowly escape from being crushed by a gigantic rock. In *Secret of the Incas*, the river escape on a yellow dinghy is similar to that of *Indiana Jones and the Temple of Doom*. Moreover, the precise spot where the Inca treasure is hidden is indicated by a ray of sunlight reflected from a mirror placed in a precise position at a precise moment of the day, a trick that will be reprised for the Ra medallion and the map room in *Raiders*. Above all, in *Secret of the Incas*, the protagonist's look is very similar to Jones's: dark-brown leather bomber jacket; wide-brimmed fedora hat; a revolver in his belt; and his name, *Harry* (Steele), sounds very akin to *Henry* (Jones.)

Raiders of the Lost Ark can be defined as a neoclassical film because of its many explicit and ironic quotations of past works and its retrieval and update of previous stylistic options. For example, the film mocks the time-honored cliché of the hero knocking out an enemy to steal his uniform so as to inconspicuously mingle with the crowd. In this case, Indiana punches a Nazi soldier, but when putting the stolen uniform on, he realizes that it is so small that he cannot even button it up. Unlike the low-budget films by which it was inspired, *Raiders* is intentionally naive and flimsy-looking. It is well grounded in a deep appreciation and knowledge of classical cinema to the extent that sometimes it even borders on a philological approach. In line with this, the protagonist here is not just the explorer/adventurer type like Quartermain, Steele, and Dobbs but also a scholar, a professor of archaeology passionately splitting his life between the study of the past and the recovery of its relics. The same happens for Lucas and Spielberg. As cinephiles, they know and admire the classical Hollywood films; as "archaeologists/directors," they attempt to recover that style. Lucas and Spielberg are correctly regarded as two of the main promoters of the recovery of classical narration based on linearity and causality in the New Hollywood cinema.[14]

The Film's Synopsis and Form and the Scope of the Analysis

Professor Henry "Indiana" Jones has just come back to the college where he teaches archaeology, after a daring adventure in South America, during which he had recovered a golden idol, immediately stolen from him by his rival Belloq. Some representatives of the US government come to inform Jones that Hitler is on the trail of important archaeological artifacts near Cairo and they ask for Jones's help. Interpreting the information, Jones realizes that Hitler is looking for the Ark of the Covenant, whose immense power would be a massive threat in the hands of the dictator. The archaeologist then accepts the task and leaves. The first step is to retrieve the headpiece of the Staff of Ra, a medallion capable of indicating on a three-dimensional map the place where the Ark is buried. However, the medallion belongs to Abner Ravenwood, Jones's old mentor, who is now in Nepal. There, Jones meets Abner's daughter, Marion, who runs a tavern in the Himalayas and has inherited the medallion upon her father's death. Since Jones and Marion had previously been involved in a love affair gone awry, she is not happy to cross paths with

Jones and is only willing to swap the headpiece for a large sum of money. Meanwhile, the Nazis reach the bar, led by the unctuous and vicious Toht. Jones saves Marion and succeeds in retrieving the medallion. The tavern is destroyed by a fire, and Marion has to reluctantly follow Jones, hoping to gain a reward for her loss. The next stop is Cairo, where the Nazis have already found the room with the three-dimensional map of the ancient city of Tanis—Belloq is the head of the excavation site. Since they do not have the medallion, they cannot locate the spot where the Ark is buried. In Cairo, Jones is welcomed by his friend Sallah, one of the excavators hired to search for the Ark. In order to get the medallion, the Nazis kidnap Marion and attempt to kill Jones. With the help of Sallah, Jones manages to sneak into the excavation site. He enters the map room and, thanks to the medallion, identifies the exact point where the Ark is buried—the Nazis have a partial copy of the headpiece and are digging in the wrong spot. That night, Jones and Sallah find the "Well of Souls," a large tomb that houses the Ark and is crammed with poisonous snakes. However, the Nazis discover the clandestine operation and steal the Ark, encapsulating Jones and Marion in the tomb to what looks like a certain death. The two manage to escape; Jones, after chasing the truck carrying the Ark, succeeds in stealing it from the Nazis. Jones and Marion board Capt. Katanga's ship with the Ark, but the Nazis find them, take the Ark, and get hold of Marion again, handing her to Belloq, who has fallen in love with her. Jones has managed to avoid being captured and sneaks into the Nazi submarine. The U-boat emerges on an island in the Aegean Sea, and the Ark is carried through a gorge to be opened during an ancient Hebrew ritual. Threatening to destroy the Ark with a bazooka, Jones blocks the convoy and calls for the release of Marion. Belloq knows that Jones is bluffing and does not comply with him. Indeed, Jones is reluctant to blow up the Ark and eventually surrenders. Together with Marion, Jones is taken to the site of the opening rite. The rite begins and when the lid is removed, the Ark is revealed to contain nothing but sand. Belloq's disappointment soon turns into surprise when light and smoke start pouring out of the Ark. Jones warns Marion to keep her eyes shut: fire leaps out from the Ark and strikes down the Nazi soldiers, while some Angels of Death kill Toht, Belloq and the Wehrmacht colonel. Jones and Marion, who kept their eyes closed, are the only survivors. The Ark is handed over to officials in Washington, who exclude Jones from any research on it and even refuse to reveal the place where it is kept. Jones leaves the building in bitter disappointment, complaining about the bureaucrats' obtuseness. He finds Marion waiting for him outside the building, and she tries to cheer him up. Meanwhile, the Ark is locked in an anonymous wooden crate and stored in a vast warehouse full of hundreds of identical crates, probably to be lost again.

The most interesting formal characteristic of *Raiders* is the way in which the classical narration merges with episodic and freer modalities typical of serials and B-movies, as detailed by Warren Buckland:

> It is also clear that *Raiders* itself tells a story, a story which is structured according to the principles of the serial format that operated in B-movie adventure films in the 1930s and 1940s. . . . It can thus be divided into six distinct episodes, each of which is relatively self-contained, and each of which ends in a series of rapid dramatic actions and/or in an unresolved cliff-hanging sequence. . . . As is the case in most serial narratives, causal motivations appear at times to be suspended; it is unclear, for instance, precisely how Jones escapes from the Nazi Submarine. . . . However, a single plot-line linked to the search for the ark of the covenant, and an antagonistic relationship between the hero, Jones, and the villain, Belloq, link each of these sequences together.[15]

Under the episodic and spectacular appearance of the film's surface, in its deeper structure we recognize the solid pillars of classical narration. Each character unambiguously shows his psychological traits; their actions are and remain consistent with their psychology and are motivated by clear reasons. Each action is oriented to the achievement of a known scope/object, and this pursuit linearly guides the chain of actions to the end of the story. Actions, typically, are ordered along a well-constructed progression and linked by cause-and-effect relations. For example, in order to find the Ark, Jones needs the medallion of Ra, and in order to find it, he has to ask for Marion's help. Marion hates Jones and will give him the medallion only in return for a significant amount of money. When the Nazis attack, Jones manages to save her but not her tavern, which ends up being destroyed. Therefore, Marion, though detesting Jones, cannot do anything else but follow him in the quest, demanding a part of the reward as compensation for the loss of her tavern.

Marion's character is introduced according to the classical standards. Her character traits are straightforwardly defined from the very first moments of her first appearance, and they remain unchanged throughout the story. We first meet Marion in her tavern in the Himalayas while she is challenging a burly Nepalese to a drinking contest. From the beginning, the narration shows Marion as a tough, tenacious Katharine Hepburn–like woman. The narrative device of the drinking contest is not only functional to introduce the character but also has a compositional motivation, which will be revealed later when Belloq tries to get Marion drunk in the hope that she will inadvertently give away some information about the medallion. Unlike the viewers, Belloq does not know that Marion is used to hold her liquor masterfully, and his scheme will be thwarted, ending up with *him* instead getting drunk and being caught off-guard. We are not just informed that Marion is a tough woman but we are also given a piece of information that we use later in the story: this is the classical device of planting a "setup," which later blossoms into a "payoff."[16]

The same dual function is found in the episode in which Toht the Nazi—moments after having threatened Marion with a red-hot poker—brands the palm of his hand in grabbing the red-hot medallion. Apparently, the motivation for this action could be seen as a "karmic" balance punishing the evil Nazi, which also serves as comic relief, with Toht screaming hysterically and frantically running out of the tavern to shove his hand into the snow. Later, we discover that this comic gag was also a setup motivated compositionally. Why do the Nazis have the medallion of Ra if it is in Jones's possession? They had a copy made from the firebrand on Toht's hand, as the narration reveals when Toht displays it during an open-palm Nazi salute: here is the payoff. There are also some dialogue hooks typical of classical narration where a line of dialogue anticipates what will happen in the next scene, serving as a bridge to smooth the transition.[17] For example, after the escape from the Well of Souls, Sallah informs Jones that the Ark has just been loaded onto a truck. Jones looks at his Egyptian friend and asks: "What truck?" Immediately after, we see *the* truck leaving the excavation site and Jones chasing it on horseback.

Raiders is a neoclassical film inasmuch as it resorts to some staples of the classical narration form. Similarly, John Williams's neoclassical score supports the narration through an extensive use of leitmotiv and Mickey-Mousing, and the typical function of the classical music style: the spatial perceptive function. The film/music analysis in the following pages is concerned with the formal functions of film music; hence, an interpretive reading seeking to unearth the "symptomatic meanings" of the film is not the main focus here.[18] *Raiders* has been frequently listed among the right-wing "Reaganite entertainment" films, a by-product of the hard-body machismo and conservatism of the Reagan era.[19] As such, it has been accused of possessing and communicating a regressive and even authoritarian ideology.[20] Undeniably, *Raiders* flaunts many racial/racist stereotypes: South Americans as cowards, lazy, and petty; Arabs as untrustworthy, threatening, and deceitful; French as womanizing hedonists; along with overt celebrations of American superiority, as in the famous scene in which Jones looks down on an imposing Arab showing off his primitive scimitar and simply shoots him down with his stars-and-stripes revolver—the advanced Occident beats the underdeveloped Orient.[21] The film could be similarly accused of patriarchal paternalism, if not sexism.[22] Despite the initial portrayal of Marion as a strong, independent woman, she does quite little in the film aside from being the male protagonist's love interest, being abducted by the male villains, and then being rescued by the titular male hero. Marion is portrayed mostly as a passive female figure, a classic "damsel in distress."[23] These stereotypes are part of the classical conventions imported in the film's neoclassical "package" along with the fake exoticism of the scenery and the other traits of those past films that are this film's models. Such rough-cut stereotypical characters, for instance, were copiously present in the genre cinema and B-movies that inspired *Raiders*, like the Mexicans in *Treasure of the Sierra Madre* (John Huston, 1948) or the Indians in *The Naked Jungle* (Byron Haskin, 1954), employed as immediately recognizable one-dimensional figures representing a specific ethnic or social group—something similar to the typage one finds in Soviet cinema: stock characters that communicated in an immediate and even caricatural way the social class they represented.

The Score: Its Main Themes and Motifs

In 1981, after having composed the music for the film, Williams thus described his work: "It is a wonderful adventure film in the style of the '30s—like a Bogart-Bacall film set in the Middle East. It has an 80-minute score which I wrote in December and January and which I recorded with the London Symphony Orchestra in February. It's all in the manner of Max Steiner . . . things like the hero's theme and the big love theme."[24] Like the two biggest neoclassical examples that preceded *Raiders*—*Star Wars* and *Superman: The Movie* (Richard Donner, 1978)—the music plays a major role. And the distinguishing features of the classical style are similarly recovered: leitmotiv, Mickey-Mousing, thematic development, use of the large symphony orchestra, and late-Romantic dialect. However, compared to the other two films, the score for *Raiders* stands out for its more frequent and emphasized use of Mickey-Mousing and for its meticulous reenactment of old Hollywood musical clichés—indeed "all in the manner of Max Steiner." About the Indiana Jones films, Williams recalls that "there was nothing I had to take too seriously musically. They were theatrical and over-the-top."²⁵ He further explains, "We have the Nazis, you know, and the orchestra hits these 1940s dramatic chords, . . . seventh degree of the scale on the bottom, which is a kind of an old signal of some evil, militaristic doer. We just unabashedly did that just for the fun of it. I mean, for the camp fun of it. It's admissible, it seems, in the style of a picture like this."²⁶

The intra-opus style is more straightforward and simpler in terms of harmony than *Star Wars*. For *Raiders* the model was not so much Korngold's operatic grandeur as Max Steiner and his highly functional idiom aiming to illustrate each image and catch each action musically. It was not a "space opera" but a homage to the low-cost adventure B-movies. Williams consequently made his writing more direct and essential in order to mirror in music that straightforward and stripped-down film style. The music is still emphatic and heroic and—like *Star Wars* and *Superman*—Williams recorded it with the London Symphony Orchestra, showcasing once again the brilliant sound of its principal trumpet, Maurice Murphy: possibly, nobody has ever equaled Murphy's incisive vigor in playing the Indiana Jones theme. Yet, from a harmonic point of view, the writing is simpler, and from a melodic point of view, the themes have a more hummable quality—compare "Leia's Theme" from *Star Wars* to "Marion's Theme" from *Raiders*.

The first Indiana Jones theme is the famous one that opens the concert version called *Raiders March*.²⁷ From here on, it will be called "Indy 1" because this is the principal leitmotiv associated with the Indiana Jones character. From a harmonic point of view, it is built on the simple alternation of I and V degrees—tonic and dominant—with a twist in the eighth bar: a chord built on the flattened second degree, a sort of Neapolitan chord in major mode. If compared to the I–IV–I harmonic progression that characterizes *Star Wars* and *Superman*, this I–V–I progression sounds less modal and more diatonic— that is, more popular. As for the melodic component, it is clear that a good leitmotiv is one capable of revealing musically many traits of a character. On the "Indiana Jones Theme," Williams commented:

> A piece like that is deceptively simple to try to find the few notes that will make a right leitmotivic identification for a character like Indiana Jones. I remember working on that thing for days and days, changing notes, changing this, inverting that, trying to get something that seemed to me to be just right. I can't speak for my colleagues but for me things which appear to be very simple are not at all, they're only simple after the fact. The manufacture of those things which seem inevitable is a process that can be laborious and difficult.²⁸

A comparison can be made with "Luke's Theme" from *Star Wars*. The theme opens with the perfect fifth upward leap played by the trumpets—the perfect-fifth upward leap being another of Williams's idiomatic traits typically employed to depict heroism, as in *Superman*. The following downward triplet of contiguous notes is like a run before the minor-seventh jump to the high B-flat. The high B-flat is sustained for two beats across two measures—as to depict a sustained heroic effort—and the minor-seventh introducing it is a larger interval than the fifth. A telling anecdote about the care Williams put into crafting and chiseling his themes is how he rewrote "Luke's Theme": "I went around for weeks with Luke Skywalker's theme slightly different: the top B flat as only *one* beat. Then one day, driving home from the studio (and I'd already scored one sequence with the theme like that), I suddenly thought how much better it would be with *two* beats on the top note."[29] This combination—minor-seventh jump and two beats of sustained high B-flat—signifies a victorious achievement. From B-flat, the melodic line goes down to F—a perfect-fourth downward leap—which is the inversion of the upward perfect fifth. The triplet and the minor-seventh leap are restated, and the theme closes with a triplet that brings the music to rest on the second degree (C). Luke's theme speaks of heroism and victorious high achievements, which are confirmed twice by the repetition of the minor-seventh jump. Not a single note descends below the starting point (B-flat above the middle C) from which the heroic melodic journey has begun (see figure 5).

In the Indiana Jones theme, the heroic traits are also present, but their nature is more uncertain and ironic, and the overall tone is less idealized and a little more braggart. Here, the theme does not open with a perfect-fifth upward leap—Williams's trademark for "pure heroism." It opens with a cheeky dotted rhythm followed by a perfect-fourth leap to the tonic. The perfect-fourth

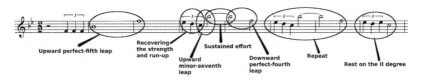

Figure 5. John Williams, "Main Title" (mm. 3–10), from *Star Wars: Suite for Orchestra* (© 1977 BMI), published by Bantha Music and Warner-Tamerlane Publishing Corp., administered by Warner-Tamerlane Publishing Corp., printed/distributed by Hal Leonard, "John Williams Signature Edition," 044900057. Used in compliance with the US Copyright Act, Section 107.

leap, unlike the perfect-fifth leap (from the tonic to the dominant), sounds like a closure (the return to the tonic) rather than a start (separation from the tonic.) The music seems to be saying: "Here it is, I have heroically completed my mission." However, as the film repeatedly demonstrates, Jones is not at all infallible and indestructible. In a scene where Marion starts kissing and cuddling Jones on the bed—after a day of jeopardy faced together—rather than seeing a passionate love scene, we see Jones falling asleep, aching and exhausted. The narration is sharply ironic in showing us not a hero who is always elegant and as well groomed as Bond but a man covered in mud, scratches, and bruises who typically manages to get himself out of trouble quite clumsily. At the beginning of *Raiders*, when Jones puts a bag of sand on the security mechanism on which the idol is placed in order to block the trigger, he smiles proudly for having shrewdly avoided the ancient alarm system. "I made it," his smile seems to say. His self-satisfaction soon turns into fear when he realizes that he has miscalculated, and the bag is not heavy enough to stop the device. He cannot but fall back on a hasty and rather unheroic flight. Similarly, in the leitmotiv, after the first perfect-fourth leap ("I made it!"), the melodic line contradicts it by going down a minor seventh, even below the starting note. Then the opening dotted rhythm is repeated but stops after a minor second (the minor second being the smallest move in the scale). As with the film narration, the music also takes Jones's heroism ironically down a peg or two. Nonetheless, Jones is stubborn and not inclined to giving up altogether: we expect him to win in the end. Indeed, the melody goes on, repeating the dotted rhythm starting from a higher note (G) and jumping up to the high F. It is a better result but still not enough: this jump to the high F is a *diminished*-fifth leap, that is, "incomplete heroism," if we take the *perfect*-fifth leap as the musical equivalent of heroism. The next musical gesture restates the dotted rhythm, starting from A—a position higher than the previous G starting point—followed by three contiguous notes on the scale, played well marked, as to suggest Jones's determination to achieve his goal. The melody reprises from the initial position (E), repeating the dotted rhythm and the fourth leap. This time, however, the line continues its rise through contiguous notes, replicating an octave higher the same notes previously heard as an ironic gesture of defeat, now transformed into a successful progression, which stops on the high F that had been previously reached "imperfectly" through the diminished-fifth leap. At the moment in which the high F is finally achieved, the harmony presents a bright chord on the flattened-second degree: this has the function of stressing in an emphatic way the conquest of that position. Then, there are two bars in which the trumpets do not play in unison as they have done so far but in vigorous chords and performing four leaps covering a major sixth, sounding even more heroic than the heroic perfect fifth (see figure 6). It is a tongue-in-cheek depiction of the heroic gesture, a swaggering celebration of victory after many defeats, "a heroic theme that swells when things are going well for our hero, the kind of music that makes the audience want to cheer."[30]

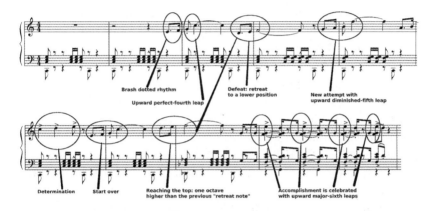

Figure 6. John Williams, the Indiana Jones A theme (mm. 3–12), from *Raiders March* (© 1981 BMI), published by Bantha Music and Ensign Music Corp., administered by Ensign Music Corp., printed/distributed by Hal Leonard, "John Williams Signature Edition," 044900015. Used in compliance with the US Copyright Act, Section 107.

That this leitmotiv is in the march form, as in *Superman* and *Star Wars*, is a further neoclassical element because, as Williams comments, it evokes memories of and feelings for the past.

> This isn't a period of time many people associate with march music. That seems to belong to Sousa's period, but I must enjoy writing marches. One friend I have worked with for years has said, "John's happy to write a march at the drop of the foot." Of course each of my marches was written to meet some musical film requirements. . . . A good march does get the blood up, and it might take a clever musicologist or sociologist or combination of the two to explain why this is true. . . . One of the most significant aspects of a march is the nostalgia involved. In a way it might be similar to baseball in that everyone who goes to a game surrenders a part of contemporary life. . . . The ballpark takes us back to the eras of our parents, grandparents, and great-grandparents, who had a very

different sense of time. I believe the days seemed to be longer because the pace was slower. If people had three hours to kill, they went to a ballpark, ate hot dogs, and waited for somebody to hit the ball, knowing it might never happen. Today people go to the ballpark and surrender to a kind of regression that leads back to an earlier time in this country. I think that the Sousa march and the swingy march—the kind of marches the Bill Finegan and Glenn Miller bands played— go to some place in the American soul and are part of what defines us as a nation.[31]

A further note on the Indiana Jones theme: Following the aesthetics of the serials, when the main theme is introduced for the first time (at the end of the opening South American jungle sequence), it is immediately presented in its outright nature of heroic theme, without following the classical tradition requiring a gradual introduction of the protagonist and his evolution over the course of the narrative. A comparison with *Star Wars* and *Superman* can make the point clearer. In both cases, the main theme is presented in the opening credits as an anticipation of the musical goal to be reached; we hear it again much later but only when the protagonist has attained a certain degree of evolution on the "heroism scale." In *Star Wars*, after the opening title sequence, we hear the main theme again when we see Luke on Tatooine for the first time. The narration tells us here that the "Main Title" theme is Luke's leitmotiv, but it is played as a horn solo, and then reprised by the woodwinds in a light orchestration—still an "immature" version. Only when Luke rescues Princess Leia from the prison and, pursued by the imperial guards, crosses a chasm with her in his arms, we now hear his leitmotiv played heroically by the trumpets: Luke has taken the first step toward his heroic maturity. Similarly, we hear the *Superman* theme again, played by the trumpets, when Clark Kent emerges from the spiritual retreat of the "Fortress of Solitude," no longer a youngster and ready to be a superhero. As for Indiana Jones, the narration does not show the evolution he has made to become what he is now but introduces him directly as he already is: a shrewd hero (see chapter 10). Moreover, Luke's and Superman's leitmotivs are presented in the opening credits and only later associated with a particular character. Therefore, they are also perceived as the signature musical theme of the film in a more pronounced way and as musical equivalents of the idea of the hero in general, besides the particular heroes featured in those films.[32] On the contrary, in *Raiders* the main theme is not presented in the opening title sequence, but it always appears when Indiana Jones shows up. Undoubtedly, it has ended up being associated with the film in the minds of the viewers, but it is primarily Indiana Jones's "personal" leitmotiv. Again, *Raiders* is not about *the* hero's journey but about a hero's journeys; the music has to represent not heroism but one type of heroism. This may also explain why the Williams-trademark heroic perfect-fifth upward leap, which is the basis of Luke's and Superman's leitmotivs, is not used for Indiana Jones.

Indiana Jones also has another theme (featured in the *Raiders March* as the B theme), which is linked not so much to the main character as to his reckless stunts. The Indiana Jones leitmotiv previously discussed appears in the films orchestrated in more subtle ways as well—for instance, for woodwinds with an emotive function. The best example is perhaps the warm cello rendition that can be heard at the end of *Indiana Jones and the Last Crusade* when Jones's father holds out his hand to pull his son out of the rift into which he is about to fall. On the contrary, the second theme, "Indy 2," usually played by brass, is employed in action scenes. It is akin to "Indy 1" as it opens with the same dotted rhythm and has the same alternation of upward heroic leaps and downward retreats (see figure 7).

"Marion's Theme" acts as the film's love theme and recalls those of classical Hollywood. It is played by violins or flutes ("female" instruments) and sounds outright "romantic" thanks to the opening major-sixth emotional leap to the whole note and the languishing rhythmic dilatation given by a triplet of quarter notes—three notes played on two beats (see figure 8). Williams commented, "I used to love those old romantic themes in Warner Bros. films like *Now, Voyager*. For the love story between Indiana Jones and Marion I thought that the music could be like one of those '30s themes and that would contrast well with the humor and silliness, even if it is inappropriate emotionally."[33] The harmony is chromatic and more complex if compared to the leitmotiv of Indiana Jones, and it serves to add to the tough Marion character a gloss

Figure 7. John Williams, the Indiana Jones B theme (mm. 28–32), from *Raiders March* (© 1981 BMI), published by Bantha Music and Ensign Music Corp., administered by Ensign Music Corp., printed/distributed by Hal Leonard, "John Williams Signature Edition," 044900015. Used in compliance with the US Copyright Act, Section 107.

Figure 8. John Williams, Marion's theme (mm. 68–75), from *Raiders March* (© 1981 BMI), published by Bantha Music and Ensign Music Corp., administered by Ensign Music Corp., printed/distributed by Hal Leonard, "John Williams Signature Edition," 044900015. Used in compliance with the US Copyright Act, Section 107.

of feminine charm, which she may lack: here the Hollywood musical clichés of feminine strings and sentimental music are projected onto the character in order to make her appear more feminine. It also creates a musical contrast with Jones's "masculine" theme and gives body to that sense of nostalgia for lost love that is barely mentioned by the film narration.

Finally, the last major leitmotiv is the one associated with the Ark.[34] It is a motif whose dynamic range and color go from the muted trumpets in low register backed by *tremolo* violins when the Ark is mentioned for the first time to the brass *fortissimo* with chorus when the Ark is opened. The mysterious and ominous tone of the Ark leitmotiv is given by both the minor-mode harmonic instability between distant keys (C minor and F-sharp minor, in the transcription reproduced here) and the nature of the melodic intervals. The motif moves downward within a perfect fifth from G to C, touching the "dreaded" augmented-fourth interval—the tritone. Once considered a "forbidden" dissonant interval called *diabolus in musica* (the devil in music), typically it has been associated with disturbing, ominous events.[35] The Ark is a magnificent and powerful object, but it is also a treacherous and deadly one, and the leitmotiv is built in such a way as to prefigure this doubly, dangerous nature—the menacing augmented-fourth "hidden" within the perfect fifth (see figure 9).

Figure 9. John Williams, the Ark motif, from the *Raiders of the Lost Ark* film score as heard in the film and CD releases (© 1981 BMI), published by Bantha Music (ear transcription). Used in compliance with the US Copyright Act, Section 107.

Part of the neoclassical quality of the score is given by the extensive almost wall-to-wall use of music, as happened in the old days. The total duration of the film's narrative from the beginning of the first shot to the beginning of the end credits is 106:20. The end credits sequence—which is external to the narrative—lasts 3:50. The film's total running time from the first frame with the Paramount logo to the end of the end credits is 110:20. On film support at 24 f/s (frames per second), the total running time of the narrative would be 110:50, the total running time of the film 115 minutes. Music accompanies the narrative for 67:17, plus 3:50 of end-credit music. Moreover, there are 4:29 of diegetic music, mostly featured in the Cairo sequences. The nondiegetic score covers 71:07 of the film, that is, 65 percent of it. However, watching the film, the impression is that the percentage of musical presence is higher. This is probably given by the particular exuberance and obtrusiveness of the musical writing, by the primary role that the narration gives it, and by the presence of very long sequences in which the music never stops—as in the first twelve minutes of the film, where the music is present for 11:17.

The music is scored for Williams's typically large symphony orchestra, augmented with a women's chorus, an ARP synthesizer, and a Fender Rhodes electric piano when mystical, eldritch, and arcane hues need to be added. "Orientalism" and ethnic colors are evoked by the occasional use of a cimbalom to imitate the qanun (a Middle Eastern box zither), an autoharp in lieu of the kinnor (an ancient Hebrew lyre), and a sistrum (an Egyptian rattle). In the next chapter, I will provide a thorough look at how Williams's score operates within the film, scene by scene.

CHAPTER 10

Raiders of the Lost Ark
Analysis
The Return of Max Steiner

Opening: A South American Jungle

Like all chapters of the series, *Raiders of the Lost Ark* opens with the Parmount logo, a mountain, which dissolves into a visually similar form.[1] In this case, the Paramount mountain becomes a real mountain, the profile of which is then blocked off by the entrance of a character donning a fedora hat and coming into the frame facing away from the camera. We find out later that the man with the hat is the protagonist. At the moment, we can only recognize in him the typical "explorer type." Viewers in 1981 were familiar neither with Indiana Jones nor with Harrison Ford, who at that time was not as well known as he is today. The man is leading an expedition in the jungle; with a superimposed title, the narration informs us that we are in "South America, 1936." We know the time and the place, and we are already in the midst of an adventure.

This opening is striking for one element that differentiates it from classical films and from the other two neoclassical models, *Star Wars* (George Lucas, 1977) and *Superman: The Movie* (Richard Donner, 1978). In the classical period, the opening title sequence was a fixed presence and had some recurring features.[2] The names of the cast and crew were shown on a background and with graphics that anticipated some narrative themes or visual motifs of the film—like the falcon's image in *The Maltese Falcon* (John Huston, 1941). More-over, there used to be a short musical overture presenting the main musical themes of the score: sticking to our *Maltese Falcon* example, the opening titles are accompanied by Adolph Deutsch's mysterious and menacing music. Neo-classical films like *Star Wars* and *Superman* begin with a memorable extradie-getic title sequence that serves as a frame to the film narrative. *Superman* even has a metalinguistic prologue that bares its comic-book origin. *Star Wars* does not have classical opening titles—cast, crew, and so on—but has an opening sequence anyway, telling the backstory through crawling titles of striking visual impact. Even *Jaws* (Steven Spielberg, 1975), which is the least overtly neoclassical of these three films, has a memorable opening title sequence. In all these cases, the music brings the viewer into the film, starting its overall macro-emotive function of unifying the narrative. Oddly enough, a neoclassical film like *Raiders* has no extradiegetic opening title sequence and no musical overture. George Lucas explained:

> The idea was that instead of starting off the film slow, we would start off fast. The whole thing in serials is that they always recapped what happened before. I didn't wanna make it that much of a serial. So I said, "The fun part is if we take the last episode or last film, and start at the climax." You take that—the best part of a movie you haven't seen—then stop, then you start a new movie 15 to 20 minutes in. It was kind of an outrageous idea at the time.[3]

Following the aesthetics of serials, *Raiders* was not designed as a single, stand-alone film but as a portion of a larger series of adventures, not only open to more episodes to come featuring Indiana Jones but also in continuity with the past films with Harry Steele, Alan Quartermain, Tarzan, and others.[4] So, we are deliberately thrown into the middle of the action. As soon as the Paramount logo dissolves into the real mountain, the music starts to accompany the expedition. First, it denotes the exotic location, using clichéd percussion instruments typically associated with the idea of wilderness and uncivilized locales. The suspense builds through a very slow, barely tonal melody for flute in the low register and sustained high-pitched dissonant notes of the strings, creating a sense of anxiety due to the music stasis.[5]

Next, a native who is taking part in the expedition finds an effigy of a threatening deity behind the vegetation and flees in terror, causing the desertion of the other natives as well. The music emphasizes the frightening discovery with a startling dissonant trumpets stinger in perfect synchronization. It is already clear that we should expect from the score a prominent use of the old-fashioned Mickey-Mousing technique. Indeed, shortly after that, another explicit sync point—a muted trumpets *sforzando* and a tam-tam rub—directs our attention to a poisoned dart stuck in a nearby tree. When Satipo, one of the guides, says concernedly that the Hovitos (a dangerous local tribe, we infer) are probably on their trail, the dialogue underscoring presents menacing, low-pitched trombones minor chords. The association between low-pitched trombones minor chords and "villains" will be a recurring idea throughout the film. This association of the minor mode with dramatic events and the low register with darkness and menace are old musical conventions.[6] It is also a well-established cliché in film music, already used in the silent era.[7] For brevity, henceforth these chords will be called "villains' chords."

The expedition party arrives at a river, and the other guide treacherously tries to shoot the man with the hat: a low-pitched turn of the contrabasses is brought out to anticipate the man's criminal intent. The man with the hat hears the gun hammer clicking and with a rapid whip crack—highlighted by a burst of repeating notes by the trumpets—he disarms him and makes him flee. Then, the man with the hat emerges from the shadows with a menacing look in his eyes; here we see his face for the first time. When he comes out of the shadows, a marked downward scale of trombones minor chords is heard, which increases the menacing nature of his look. Interestingly, the villains' chords are used here for the man with the hat. We do not know anything yet about his intentions and nature, and the music plays on this ambiguity, choosing to use those chords instead of the character's leitmotiv.

The two remaining members of the expedition—Satipo and the man with the hat—arrive at the treasure cave. The music texture gets thinner to make room for the dialogue between the two men. They enter the cave, the music becoming almost a background noise–like atmospheric patina: low-pitched piano notes, soft tam-tam roll, and high-pitched cluster effects of the violins creating a reverberating "cavernous" sound.[8] The musical texture presents sparse *pianissimo* movements by the strings: low-pitched *tremolo* chromatic scales, contrabasses and violins *pizzicato*. They do not correspond to any visible movement *yet* but seem to suggest the presence of an unknown something, moving off-screen. As anticipated by the music, a horrified Satipo points at something on the shoulders of the man with the hat. A *fortissimo* bow slap by the contrabasses is heard in synchronism with the cut to the man with the hat, revealing that he is covered in tarantulas. This musical gesture is followed by a creeping, almost aleatory high-pitched violins *pizzicato*, which mimics the movement of the legs of the spiders and emotionally heightens the viewer's shudder of revulsion at the sight of the spiders on the protagonist's neck. Soon, Satipo realizes that many more tarantulas are on his shoulders too. The emotive function of music here is to depict Satipo's repulsion, which is accomplished through an upward violins *glissando* of high-pitched dissonant chords, a musical equivalent of a shiver running down the spine.

Once they get rid of the spiders, the two move on to the treasure room. The music—with a prevalent spatial perceptive function—plays throughout the whole sequence, catching each action: explicit sync points punctuate the spear trap snapping shut and the gruesome view of the corpse of an unlucky explorer, the snapping of the whip around a beam, the collapsing of the beam while Satipo is crossing over a bottomless pit, and a poisoned arrow hitting the torch held by the man with the hat. The music also has an emotive function: a strings *tremolo* creates tension over the fate of Satipo being on the verge of the bottomless pit and a slow atonal strings arpeggio projects its tonal uncertainty onto the images, making the success of the expedition feel uncertain.[9]

In order to take the golden idol away from its pedestal, the man with the hat has to remove it without triggering the weight-activated security mechanism, and to do so he has devised a plan to swiftly substitute it with an equally heavy bag of sand. The atonal arpeggios are superseded by equally uncertain harmonic progressions, a dynamic *crescendo* and a thickening of instrumentation. Music is now gaining momentum and building the cinematic suspense. When the man quickly replaces the idol with the bag, the musical progression stops with a rapid upward scale duplicating the swift movement of his hand. Everything seems to have gone fine. However, a sustained high-pitched strings note can still be heard—*not* a good omen. Indeed, in spite of the sand bag, the pedestal of the idol lowers—wrong weight!—and the cave begins to collapse. The man with the hat is forced to make a hurried retreat, accompanied by hectic music characterized by rapid high-pitched repeating notes of the trumpets when a rolling boulder chases the man with the hat. Here, the main function is temporal perceptive: the music emphasizes the pace of the frenzied escape and supports the speedy rhythm of the editing. The man with the hat manages to escape and jumps out of the cave at the very last minute, the disloyal and greedy Satipo having found a deserved death. The music accompanies the hasty, final rush of the retreat with a *crescendo* chord played *fortissimo* by the whole orchestra. The chord stops abruptly and makes way for a contrasting silence when we unexpectedly see the menacing Hovitos waiting outside and surrounding the man with the hat.[10] The Hovitos are led by Belloq, a treasure hunter and archenemy of the man with the hat, whose name is finally revealed: "Dr. Jones," as Belloq calls him. Belloq takes the idol away from Jones and incites the Hovitos to kill him.

The music, which has been silent for only fifty-nine seconds, resumes to provide accompaniment to Jones's escape. The musical piece opens with a sinister horn motif played as Belloq laughs wickedly. So far, the music has maintained a sort of ambiguity about the nature of the man with the hat. The narration has now revealed his name and in the previous scenes has shown that he is not only a grave robber but also a man of principles: after all, he saved Satipo from falling into the bottomless pit. Moreover, now we know that Belloq is the real villain. According to the black/white Manichaeism of the popular Hollywood cinema, if Belloq is the villain, then Jones must be the hero. The music confirms this inference, emphasizing Belloq's laugh with a dark horn motif. Jones is revealed as the hero of the narrative, but what kind of hero is he? The music does not accompany his escape from the Hovitos with a powerful rhythmic section or vigorous action music but with a bumbling strings *pizzicato*, awkward *staccato* accents by muted trombones, and funny gestures of the piccolo clarinet. The music casts a comic emotional overtone onto the chase, giving an ironic image of Jones, a resourceful and brave adventurer but quite far from being the traditional infallible hero. When Jones swings on a vine to reach the seaplane that is waiting for him but instead plunges into the river, we hear the main Indiana Jones leitmotiv ("Indy 1") for the first time, played by the trumpets, with only its first four bars repeated twice; the full theme will be stated only much later in the film. An upward high-pitched trumpets gesture celebrates the success of the daredevil retreat.

Jones's plane finally flies away from the hostile Hovitos. The narration taunts him again, downplaying his heroic status: Jones is rumpled, soaked through, and his fedora now resembles a bowl-shaped wet rag. Then he realizes with horror that a python is crawling on his legs and shouts to the pilot, almost whimpering, that he hates snakes. (Jones's reptile phobia is introduced as a gag, but once again it is also a setup that will have its payoff later in the sequence of the Well of Souls.) The pilot reassures him by telling him that it is Weggie, his pet python, and invites Jones to be a man: "Come on, show a little backbone! Will ya?" The music accompanies the scene, presenting for the first time the secondary Indiana Jones leitmotiv ("Indy 2") during the python gag. As we have seen, "Indy 2" will be used throughout the film to underline the heroism of Jones's feats. Here the musical irony is given by the presentation of the heroic motif over a gag unveiling one of Jones's weak spots, thus stressing once again his fallible, comically human side. Then, "Indy 1" is taken up by the trumpets when we see the plane flying into the sunset, and the episode set in the South American jungle is over. A diminished coda for strings with a cadence resolving to the tonic reinforces the closure effect and bridges the cut to the establishing shot that opens the next scene: the austere exterior of a college.

At Home: Getting Ready for a New Mission

We soon discover another facet of Jones: his second life as an archaeology professor. Two government officers come to see Dr. Jones: they inform him and Brody, the dean of the college, that the Nazis are on the trail of the Ark of the Covenant. Jones opens a bulky book to show the officers what the artifact is expected to look like. As soon as the book is opened, we hear a "pedal point," a sustained low-pitched note of the contrabasses that conveys a sense of threat and uneasiness to the scene. This is another classical musical cliché: the low-pitched pedal point denotes a pending threat; and as such, it is employed throughout the film. When Jones shows an illustration of the Ark with lightning bolts coming out of it to exterminate the enemy armies, we hear for the first time the Ark motif, emerging over the pedal point. In film music, orchestration is as important and significant as the melody and harmony. The Ark motif is played by muted trumpets, backed by a vocalizing female choir singing *sottovoce* and by *tremolo* violins: the *tremolo* gives a shivering sense of threat to the melody, indicating that the Ark is a powerful and dangerous object indeed. The use of the mute in the trumpets aptly represents the latent power of the Ark. In the scene in which the Ark is finally found, its leitmotiv will be played without any mute: from that moment on, the menace will be a real one and the power of the Ark liable to be unleashed at any moment. As for the vocalizing female choir, it is an interesting musical choice that foretells what will be found *inside* the Ark. The scene closes with "Indy 1" played interrogatively by a clarinet backed by a low-pitched pedal point: Jones is going to be involved in a dangerous new quest.

The next scene moves to Jones's house and shows him packing for the expedition, with Brody paying a visit. The first thing to do is retrieve the Ra medallion, the key to the exact location of the Ark. This means that Jones has to get in touch with Marion. Just before Jones mentions her name to Brody, the music introduces Marion's theme, played by the flute. The narration anticipates that we will soon meet the heroine. Brody reminds Jones that Marion will be the smallest of his problems and advises him to be careful when dealing with the Ark. Here, the music—following the classical dialogue underscoring technique—moves from Marion's leitmotiv to the Ark's, played again by ominous muted trumpets. This further presentation of the Ark motif is not only functional in emphasizing the danger mentioned by Brody but is also useful to strengthen the identification of this musical motif with the Ark and fix it in the viewers' memory.

Jones embarks on a plane, accompanied by "Indy 1" in a minor mode: a new risky adventure is about to begin. Then, the music points our attention to a black-clad passenger who spies on Jones from behind a magazine: the use of the villains' chords immediately identifies the nature of the character. In the following air-travel montage, the music gives cohesion and links the unfolding images, until the animated line on the map (as in *Casablanca*) reaches a red dot: Nepal. Immediately, ethnic colors and mannered Orientalism are added to the music: bells, gongs, and a hint of pentatonic scale, following a classical and typically Steineresque use of ethnic musical clichés or quotes of national anthems to set the locale.

Nepal: Meeting Marion and Retrieving the Medallion

Jones meets a resentful Marion in her tavern. It is interesting to note that Marion is presented without her theme; we shall discover why later. When Jones states that he will come again the next day and leaves the tavern, Marion pulls the medallion out of her neckline. We hear a sinuous theme: the melody is chromatic and is played by a solo English horn—both of these choices give the melody a Middle Eastern flavor consistent with the medallion's Egyptian origin. Furthermore, some traits in the melody and harmonization are akin to the Ark motif, and in this way the music reminds us of the connection between the two artifacts.

After Marion has put the medallion away, the door opens and some not-very-friendly-looking thugs led by a sinister black-clad man—reminiscent of the slimy criminals played by Peter Lorre—enter the tavern. The music accompanies this entrance with the villains' chords, strongly marking their downward move and accentuating the dissonant seventh at the bottom of the chord in the manner of Steiner. The downward move of the musical line emphatically ends on the close-up of Toht, the black-clad Nazi—"he is the worst of all," the music seems to be saying. This downward trombones figure is followed by a low-pitched pedal point supporting a snare drum rhythmic pattern and martial repeating notes played *piano* by the trumpets. Toht is not wearing a Nazi uniform, but we can readily imagine that he is one of them; yet the music, in accordance with the "excessively obvious" classical style, makes sure that we understand Toht's nature. Toht mellifluously asks Marion about the medallion. Marion, in response, puffs the smoke of her cigarette into Toht's face. The cigarette puff is duplicated by a high-pitched upward scale by the harp and the celesta. Here Williams is overtly quoting a famous episode of Steiner's Mickey-Mousing. In *The Informer* (John Ford, 1935), Katie, the reluctant prostitute, is puffed some smoke into her face by a potential customer, the action being scored by Steiner with the very same musical gesture. Toht opts for strong-arm tactics and threatens Marion with a red-hot poker: a piercing chromatic upward movement by the trumpets marks the entrance of the firebrand into the frame from the lower off-screen zone. The trumpets *crescendo*, rising proportionally with the approach of the firebrand toward Marion's face, is suddenly interrupted by Jones's whip crack that disarms Toht. The musical Mickey-Mousing closely follows the action and culminates in an upward scale by the trumpets duplicating the visual upward movement of the flames propagating from a curtain ignited by the firebrand that has been tossed away, here reprising the association of the hot sound of the trumpets with fire. A *crescendo* with strings tremolo and triangle trill announces the battle. When we hear the first gunshot, the music stops and the sequence proceeds without music. When the fight is over and the villains momentarily defeated, the music resumes on Marion telling Jones that he will have the medallion provided she becomes his business partner, and now we hear the opening bar of the medallion's theme. During the following travel montage, "Indy 1" is presented in major mode—the first stage of the adventure has been successfully completed, Jones has the medallion—and is followed by Marion's theme: Marion has joined him in the adventure.

(Mis)Adventures in Cairo

Arabic-like chromatic music accompanies the visit to Sallah's house and the introduction of the capuchin monkey that will accompany Marion and Jones on the streets of Cairo. Then Jones sets eyes on Marion—she has dismissed her masculine clothes and is now wearing more feminine apparel—and we hear Marion's theme. On closer observation, "Marion's Theme" is not actually her leitmotiv but Jones's love theme for her. As we have seen, the theme is not played when Marion is introduced—she is alone in that scene—but only in the scenes in which she is with Jones, or in those in which Jones is thinking of her.

In the next sequence, Jones and Marion are taking a stroll in the streets of Cairo: instrumental Arabic-sounding diegetic music can be heard and, although the source is not visible, the music volume rises or lowers as the two characters move around, which suggests an intended diegetic source. Besides setting the "local color," the diegetic music serves here to define the position of the characters in space. The point of highest volume is the square, but the same music can be heard also from the room in which the villains are preparing to attack: thus the music locates the room in the environs of the square. A different diegetic vocal music is present in the scene under the arcade between the thug with the monkey and the Nazis, separating the indoor arcade space from the outdoor square space.

The nondiegetic music resumes; we hear the villains' chords when one of the Nazis appears under an arch, and the diegetic music gradually tails out. A suspended dissonant harmony increases the suspense: unlike the viewers, Jones and Marion are unaware that they are about to be assaulted. When two local assassins—announced by a timpani roll *crescendo*—start the attack, a balletic musical sequence begins. Williams explains:

> I look at it as a kind of musical number that has a beginning, a middle and an end, and try to calculate a series of tempos, and a series of changing tempos. I will try to design it almost in the same way as you would a balletic number, which may contribute a certain aspect of fun and adventurousness in this Harrison Ford character. The music may sound serious but it's not really, it's more theatrically conceived and hopefully always has an aspect of fun or even camp about it.[11]

The music keeps up the fight pace (temporal perceptive function), punctuates each action and piece of narrative information (spatial perceptive function), and gives the sequence a comic overtone through the use of humorous Prokofiev-like melodies (micro-emotive function). Mickey-Mousing is glaring: when the narration cuts on the villains, trombones minor chords are played; when Marion stuns one of the assassins with a frying pan, a downward scale by strings and piano comically underlines his fall; when the monkey searches for Marion, comedic *pizzicato* violins punctuate the action; when the villains abruptly stop and turn back because they have located Marion's hiding place, a theatrical trombones *sforzando* acts as a stinger to mark their reaction; when an Arab intimidatingly brandishes a scimitar, his appearance is dramatically stressed by brass minor chords, while an Oriental motif for horns—punctuated by exhibitionistic repeating chords—accompanies his spinning the scimitar with threatening skill; when Jones in turn looks at him unimpressedly and quite condescendingly, strings *pizzicato* accentuates the comical effect of Jones's unexpected reaction; the musical phrase closes, resolving to the tonic when Jones simply shoots him down with his gun. Marion is trapped into a big basket, abducted, and loaded onto a truck. Jones shoots down the truck driver to rescue Marion: an exuberant trumpet fanfare

stresses the heroic act. Unfortunately, the death of the driver causes the over
turning of the truck and its explosion: Jones's heroic act has (supposedly)
killed Marion. This is what Jones believes and what the narration tries to
make us believe as well. Dramatic chords and the desperate minor-mode rendition of Marion's theme by strings topped by a piercing *sforzando* final note
by the horns "manipulate" our emotion and belief about what we have just
watched.

The music calms down and leads us into the next scene, in which Jones
sits alone at a bar table while trying to soothe his grief with alcohol, like Rick
in *Casablanca*. Marion's theme is played mournfully by the woodwinds. When
two Nazis arrive—we recognize them as the people behind the assault—to
take Jones with them, the villains' chords are played softly by the bassoons and
not by the more menacing trombones. In terms of musical form, this makes
the music more homogeneous, since all the instruments used here are woodwinds. From a narrative point of view, music may imply that Jones's grief
makes everything else of no importance to him, as his suicidal attitude seems
to confirm in the next dialogue scene: "Do you want to talk to God? Let's go
see Him together. I've got nothing better to do."

Later, Sallah takes Jones to visit an old sage, to decipher the inscription on
the medallion. The scene begins with a muezzin chant heard in the distance,
then enters a low-pitched pedal point by the contrabasses, indicating that a
threat is looming. Indeed, we see the thug with the monkey sneaking into the
room, accompanied by an Arabic motif for English horn. A turn by the flutes
points our attention to the appearance of a red bottle from his sleeve and a
high-pitched violins trill marks the man pouring a poison over some dates in
a bowl. Meanwhile, Jones and Sallah are engaged in a conversation with their
host—the cimbalom and the sistrum can be heard within the orchestral texture to provide ethnic touches.

When the old sage mentions "The Hebrew God," wind suddenly begins
to blow through the open window, swinging the lamps in the room. Beneath
the sound of the wind, "noise-like" music can be perceived: violins playing
artificial harmonics in super-acute register and tam-tam rolling *pianissimo*.
One of the themes of the film is the loss of faith, archaeological in a narrow
sense and religious in a broader one. In the conversation scene after Marion's
"death," Belloq tells Jones that they are not so different from each other:
"Archaeology is our religion, yet we have both fallen from the purer faith." In
the first act of the film, Jones tells Brody, who has just warned him to beware
of the powers of the Ark, "I don't believe in magic or superstitious hocus

pocus. I'm after a find of incredible historical significance and you're talking about the boogeyman!" At the beginning of the film, we see Jones as a grave robber, plundering a temple whose finds will be sold to Brody's museum. Jones's archaeological faith is indeed similar to Belloq's: it is just an exciting search of objects having historical and economic value; objects that have been deprived of their original, deepest cultural/religious significance. Jones equals religion and faith to magic and superstition. For him, the Ark is just an object of inestimable value and a desirable prey. The mysterious Ark motif has already suggested that the Ark does possess some kind of supernatural power. Here, the sudden wind blowing when the Hebrew God is named is a further signal in this sense. The mysterious music hidden beneath the sound of the wind suggests the presence of God: as the Bible says, "a sound of a gentle blowing."[12] In this scene the music, besides having the emotive function of increasing the concern for this strange phenomenon, also has the cognitive function of providing a clue as to how the faith theme will be an important one in the development of the narrative.

After the wind episode, still in the old sage's house, we see Sallah sing a Gilbert and Sullivan song to celebrate the successful deciphering of the medallion, while Jones takes a date from the bowl and throws it in the air to swallow it up.[13] We see a slow-motion detail of the date floating in the air. Sallah's song stops abruptly, and a timpani roll amplifies the perception of time dilation given by the slow motion. The timpani roll ends with a sharp hit perfectly in sync with Sallah's hand catching the date in midair, instants before it falls into Jones's mouth. Piercing chords by the violins accompany Sallah turning his head to point at something on the floor. The chords continue on the cut to the monkey lying dead—we have seen it eating a date earlier in the scene. The scene ends with a high-angled full shot showing a ceiling fan rotating in the foreground and the monkey corpse on the carpet in the background. The music duplicates the movement of the fan blades with fast circular turns by the celesta.

Digging Up the Ark

Once the precise height of the staff on which the medallion must be inserted has been obtained, Jones can finally sneak into the excavation site and enter the map room, which houses a miniature replica of the ancient town of Tanis. When sun enters the map room, the medallion is supposed to channel its rays onto the replica to indicate the spot in which the Ark is buried. As soon as Jones goes down into the room, a long musical sequence begins. It starts with the Ark motif, played by flutes in the lower register and muted trumpets, backed by the harps (doubled by the crystal-y sound of the Fender Rhodes piano) and a low-pitched pedal point by the contrabasses (augmented with the ARP synthesizer to make the acoustic basses sound "less normal"). The score closely follows the cross-cutting upon which the sequence is built, alternating between the inside of the map room (where the Ark motif is heard) and the outside, where Sallah keeps watch over the entrance: here the music is militaristic, with rhythmic snare-drum patterns and minor-mode trombones fanfares. The cross-cutting music helps to further separate and make a comparison between the two sets: the inner Egyptian room, where a supernatural power is hidden, and the outside Nazi camp, where a worldly power is flaunted. Jones deciphers the inscriptions over the replica to find out where the pole must be inserted. The music reprises those atonal arpeggios that we have already heard when Jones was trying to bypass the traps in the South American temple at the beginning of the film. When Jones finally finds out which is the right hole, an upward chord progression follows Jones turning his head toward the entrance of the room. The narration cuts to the detail of the bright sunlight starting to filter through and the progression resolves to a piercing brass chord played right on the editing cut. When Jones inserts the pole, the Ark motif starts over, played *forte* by the full orchestra, with a vocalizing female choir rising from the orchestral texture and coming to the fore in the second reprise of the theme. (Notice that here, again, female voices *emerge* from the instrumental texture of the Ark motif.) An orchestral *crescendo* of harmonic progressions resolves to the tonic when the sun hits the medallion and a beam illuminates the burial spot. Sallah helps Jones climb out of the room.

Jones wanders around the camp disguised as an Arab—coherently, we hear a "disguised" Arabic-like version of "Indy 1" played in minor mode by the English horn—and enters a tent. Inside he finds Marion alive, and a stinger followed by a Steiner-like musical pause underlines his surprise. Jones is dressed in an Arab outfit and his face is covered: for this reason, the music presents ominous low-pitched notes. The music here is focusing our emotion on Marion, who has not recognized him and fears that the stranger may have evil designs on her. When Jones uncovers his face, Marion's theme is played liberatingly. However, the musical phrase is soon suspended by an interrogative modulation that suggests Jones's thoughts: he has just realized that freeing Marion means disclosing his presence in the camp and jeopardizing the recovery of the Ark. Between Marion and the Ark, Jones chooses the Ark and, after trying to explain his motive, he leaves her inside the tent.

With the help of Sallah and a group of diggers, Jones starts working on the site indicated on the replica. When the upper trapdoor opens, Sallah and Jones look down into the dark pit—the "Well of Souls." The score presents a high-pitched chromatic scale by *tremolo* violins, a "creeping" music gesture, quite fitting, as we are about to see. Indeed, Sallah asks Jones why the floor is moving. They throw a torch down to the bottom of the well—the fall is duplicated by a downward flute scale—and realize that the chamber is crammed with poisonous snakes. The music presents slow *glissando* clusters by the violins with the emotive function of heightening the repulsive images of the reptiles. We hear high-pitched circular woodwinds scales, mimicking the snakes coiling up. The narration cuts back to Jones, who pulls his head out of the trapdoor and lies down, dejected: "Snakes. Why did it have to be snakes?" The music once again mocks the hero, with a comical downward trombones *glissando*. Here is the payoff of the gag of Weggie the python in the first act: that episode was not only a comic relief but also served to inform us of Jones's phobia.

The narration cuts to the tent where Marion is imprisoned. Belloq enters and unbinds her. He soon proves to be well behaved and friendly. We understand that he wants to flatter and seduce her in order to obtain information on the medallion . . . and maybe also obtain something else—after all, Belloq is French and, as we have seen, stereotypes abound in the film. Belloq offers her a tray with food and water. Marion glances at a knife among the cutlery on the tray: the music points our attention to the potential weapon with a bright triangle tinkle, suggesting Marion's scheming thoughts. A low-pitched pedal point plays under the whole scene and increases the suspense over Marion's fate and the success of her escape, despite the tone of the conversation being friendly and relaxed. When Belloq presents her with a white dress and asks her to wear it, a romantic gesture of the violins underlines the gift. Marion goes behind the room divider and Belloq peeps at her reflection in a mirror while she is taking off her brassiere. The music repeats the romantic gesture of the strings, with an added upward woodwinds trill to mark the growing excitement of the man. A stronger trill accompanies Marion coming out from behind the screen and displaying herself wearing the dress. The scene closes with Marion putting her old dress on the table to hide the knife: the music switches to low register again. As previously happened, Marion's theme never appears in this scene—and similarly will not in the next two—confirming that it is the love theme between Jones and Marion rather than Marion's own leitmotiv.

The entire night sequence is based on a cross-cutting between the Well of Souls and Belloq's tent. In the Well of the Souls, the music continues to enhance the sense of disgust for the reptiles and to duplicate their creeping, coiling movements. A few examples: When Jones lands in front of a cobra, muted trombones increase the comical effect of Jones's disgusted grimace with a slow upward *glissando*. When we see a close-up of the cobra, we hear an upward arpeggio, which recalls that of the shark motto in *Jaws* (see chapter 7)—not for tuba and horns but for flute and oboe, aurally evoking the snake charmers.

In the tent, the seduction goes on, and Belloq fills two glasses with a strong liquor. He wants to get Marion drunk in order to obtain the information he needs. The suspenseful low-pitched pedal point is still there. Unlike Belloq, we know that Marion is an experienced drinker. A light violins *pizzicato* accompanies the toast, and a bold turn of the clarinets underlines Belloq swallowing his glass with a smirk on his face. Marion answers by emptying her glass at a single stroke, and a turn of the flutes answers to the clarinets. A *pizzicato* comically emphasizes Belloq's surprise. This time it is Marion's turn to fill the glasses, and we realize that she is already leading the game. The score closes the scene with the low-pitched pedal point, still reminding us that, although partly comic, Marion's plan is a risky one. In the following tent scene, the low-pitched pedal point is gone. The two contestants are both drunk, apparently. Marion goes on pouring the liquor. Funny gestures by the clarinets and trombones mimic the uncoordinated movements of the drunks. Suddenly, Marion grabs the knife from the table and points it at Belloq: a low-pitched stinger stresses the surprising twist. Belloq's reaction is a fit of laughter, and Marion does the same while she backs away toward the exit. We hear again comical gestures in the score, but the low-pitched pedal point reemerges so as to warn us of an impending danger. A close-up shows Belloq looking at the entrance to the tent: his smile fades from his face. Marion bangs against Toht, blocking the exit behind her, and the villains' chords mark his appearance. When Toht picks up his bag and pulls out a menacing black object with chain inserts, a dramatic brass low-pitched *crescendo* heightens the suspense and seems to confirm our impression that we are about to see a torture scene. When the object is revealed to be simply a hanger for Toht's coat, the comic effect given by the sudden contradiction of our expectations is enhanced by the deflating of the musical *crescendo*. Proverbially, "the mountain has brought forth a mouse."

In the meantime, Sallah has joined Jones, and the two lift the Ark out of a large stone sarcophagus. As soon as the profile of the object emerges, the Ark motif is stated by the horns, to which unmuted trumpets playing *forte* are added when the Ark comes completely out of the sarcophagus. Earlier, the Ark was hidden—muted trumpets—and now the object has been brought to light and its power is a real threat. When the Ark is placed into a wooden crate, we hear a disturbing atonal vocalizing female choir.

Losing the Ark / Getting the Ark / Losing the Ark Again

A new day has come and Belloq, out of the tent, notices the clandestine excavation and summons all the soldiers. In the Well of Souls, Sallah is climbing to the exit accompanied by a spirited version of the Ark motif. When it is Jones's turn to grasp the rope, the rope falls back into the Well—a dynamic *crescendo* by the trumpets duplicates the falling movement. When the rope touches the ground, the *crescendo* stops and leaves room to a low-pitched pedal point. Another *crescendo* accompanies the upward whip-pan to the top, which stops on the image of Belloq tauntingly greeting from above: "Hello!" A *piano* note by the trombones serves as a coda for the tailing-out of the music to make room for the unaccompanied dialogue. The music starts again dramatically when Toht arrives and throws Marion down into the Well. Mickey-Mousing closely duplicates the following events, such as Marion's fall, Marion clinging to the teeth of an Anubis, a tooth of the statue cracking, a snake coiling up inside the shoe that Marion has lost during the fall, the tooth finally breaking apart, Marion's falling into Jones's arms, and her landing in front of a cobra. The Nazis take the Ark, and the two are locked into the Well, apparently sentenced to death. To flee the place, Jones understands that he has to tear down one of the walls. The music starts with a rhythmic pattern expressing Jones's determination and Mickey-Mousing marks the action. Jones climbs onto one of the huge Anubis statues, makes the statue swing, and manages to detach it from its base, causing it to fall and land on the wall, demolishing it—the trumpets play "Indy 1" while Jones "rides" the falling statue.

In the following scene, Jones tries to get hold of an airplane and engages in a fistfight with a mechanic. Again the music treats the action as a ballet. The fists are emphasized by trumpets stingers and woodwinds runs, while a brass *ostinato* serves as rhythmic drive across the action—the brass *ostinato* also recalls the rotating propellers of the plane, which are an extra pending danger that will play a key role in the outcome of the fight. Jones has knocked down the mechanic and is now climbing on the wing to get rid of the pilot. Unfortunately, he is stopped by another, much more robust mechanic, who assertively motions him to step down from the wing to engage in a fist fight. The rhythmic ostinato stops and gives way to a middle register pedal point by the horns, on which the oboe and clarinet play a weary minor-mode version of "Indy 1." This reinforces the ironical image of the hero reluctantly giving the brawny mechanic a tired nod, as if to ask him to be allowed some time to climb down from the wing. Once on the ground, the musical *ostinato* suddenly resumes when Jones, with a trick, distracts the man and unfairly kicks the rival between the legs. The mechanic takes the blow—and the others to follow—as if he were impervious to pain and indestructible. Meanwhile, Marion knocks out the pilot, who collapses onto the control stick, thus making the plane move in circles. When the control stick lowers, a new musical section begins, serving as a frame for the sub-episode of the sequence. Now Jones must not only get rid of the burly mechanic but also pay attention to not being crushed by the wheels of the aircraft or being cut to ribbons by its rotating propellers. There is more: a wing strikes a tanker truck, causing a leak from which fuel begins to spill out onto the tarmac; a high-pitched flutes trill focuses our attention on this narrative event that will trigger a chain reaction. Jones sees a gun on the ground and runs toward it; we hear the trumpets starting to play "Indy 1." When the mechanic blocks his way to the gun, the melodic line of "Indy 1" is suddenly diverted by an abrupt modulation. When Marion sees a military truck passing by, we hear for the first time a minor-mode march, which will be henceforth associated with the Nazis. If Jones had to deal with single enemies like Belloq, Toht, or some Nazis in civilian clothes generically marked by the villains' chords, now he has to steal the Ark from the Wehrmacht itself. Marion uses the aircraft machine gun to shoot the truck and other approaching enemies. However, during the shooting, some fuel cans explode, causing a fire. A shot of the fuel flowing onto the runway is highlighted by fast and flowing strings scales. Jones realizes that Marion is locked in the cockpit and that the airplane could explode at any minute. He climbs onto the fuselage, accompanied by a heroic version of "Indy 1" played by the trumpets. However, the melody stops again after four bars: the mechanic has climbed onto the plane and diverts Jones from rescuing Marion. The fistfight continues on the plane, backed by dramatic Mickey-Mousing. The fuel is now about to reach the fire, and the music emphasizes the danger with an alarming high-pitched trill of the woodwinds. The seemingly invincible mechanic gets accidentally killed by the airplane propellers—a convenient narrative turn to eliminate the mighty opponent. Jones is now free to save Marion, a last-minute rescue before the plane explodes. "Indy 1" played by horns accompanies the rescue, stopping at the fourth bar and repeating the same half phrase twice.

Jones and Marion meet Sallah, surprised and happy to see them alive. Sallah informs Jones that the Ark was loaded onto a truck to be taken away. The next sequence shows Jones chasing the truck on horseback. Once again, the long musical sequence (7:44) treats the chase like a ballet. The uninterrupted musical accompaniment, besides creating a unified perception of the frenzied editing of the sequence, supports the action with extensive Mickey-Mousing embedded in a relentless ostinato. During the sequence, the score also develops and weaves cells of the various leitmotivs, and switches from one to the other, directing our attention to the various related characters—for example, the "Nazi march" when we see the convoy escorting the Ark, and "Indy 1" over the shots of Jones riding his horse. In this sequence, we hear "Indy 2" for the second time in the film, after its ironical use in the initial python-on-the-airplane gag. This time, "Indy 2" accompanies an episode in which Jones does "show a little backbone": the theme is used when Jones takes possession of the truck and rams the Nazi car; when Jones—after having being thrown in front of the moving truck and dragged under the vehicle—skillfully succeeds in climbing back on board; when Jones takes back control of the truck and pushes the Nazi car off the road. Arriving in Cairo, Jones hides the truck in a safe place. The success of the mission is celebrated by the horns playing "Indy 1" but still limited to the half phrase: the battle is won, the war not yet.

Jones, Marion, and the Ark embark on Captain Katanga's ship. After having been buried alive, almost beaten to death by a stout mechanic, and thrown out of a speeding truck, Jones—covered in bruises and scratches—can finally lie down and rest. Marion takes care of him; from dressing his wounds, the action soon progresses to kissing. We first hear Marion's theme for solo flutes when she offers to take care of the beaten man. Then, the theme is repeated by the flutes backed by the strings. A cell of Marion's theme warmly played by cellos is heard when it is clear that the nurse is about to become the lover. When Marion kisses Jones on the lips, the theme is restated by the violins, and then the full orchestra soars with a passionate *crescendo* leading to a repeated sweeping arpeggio in triplet rhythm. Suddenly, the crescendo stops and the music deflates: Jones has fallen asleep. The score has created a sort of musical *coitus interruptus*. The comic effect of this scene is obtained by first building expectations—through the use of romantic, passionate musical clichés like the love theme by strings, the thickening of the instrumentation, the yearning effect of the triplet rhythm—and then frustrating those expectations, which provokes laughter, serving as an emotional outlet.[14] The image of the sleeping Jones is accompanied not only by a musical deflation but also by a delicate motif played *piano* by the celesta, imitating a music box that winds down, as the final notes of a lullaby.

The narration takes us to the cargo hold in the ship's hull, where the Ark is stowed. A slow tracking shot moves forward to the wooden crate, marked with a Nazi swastika. An insert shot shows a rat behaving oddly, as if affected by an invisible force. The tracking shot completes its movement and stops on the detail of the swastika, which is suddenly burned out by some heat emanating from the inside. As in the scene in which a mysterious wind blew through the house of the Arab sage, here we perceive again some musical presence beneath the low-frequency noise of the ship engines.

The next morning, the ship is seized by a Nazi U-boat; they retrieve the Ark and kidnap Marion. Jones has managed to hide, and Katanga justifies his absence by telling the Nazis that he killed him to keep Marion for himself. The Nazis search the ship without finding Jones, so they believe Katanga's story and go back to their submarine. Indeed, even Katanga and his men have no idea where Jones might be. Then the music presents "Indy 2" played by the strings, as to anticipate that a feat of heroism is about to take place. Indeed, one of Katanga's men looks overboard and says, "I found him," pointing at something off-screen. The music duplicates his pointing gesture with a woodwinds run, which leads to a cut to Jones climbing onto the U-boat. Reaching the upper deck, Jones salutes Katanga and his men, accompanied for the first time by the complete presentation of "Indy 1"—including the "show-off modulation"—in the form of an exuberant march, with its bold major-sixth leaps emphasizing the cheers of Katanga and his crew.[15] Here, the music celebrates the hero and distracts us from concentrating on the implausibility of Jones swimming toward and climbing onto a U-boat. In such moments, the music has the scope of diverting our attention from the narrative logic and directing it to the spectacular and emotional qualities of the scene. The effect is achieved by Williams's typical technique of "gradual disclosure of the main theme," discussed in chapter 8.[16] After recurrent presentations of the first semiphrase only, "Indy 1" is heard here in its entirety for the first time. The recognition of a familiar melody finally heard in its full form has a resulting effect of gratification that attaches to the visual, and the music also projects onto the scene a sense of coherence deriving from the cohesion of the score—thus masking the weakness of the narrative logic.

Opening the Ark

The U-boat arrives at some Mediterranean island and docks in a hidden military base. Jones disembarks and spies on Marion and Belloq from behind some crates. We hear "Indy 1" played by the clarinets and flutes in low register, backed by the low-pitched pedal point by the contrabasses. Two *pizzicato* notes by the contrabasses pinpoint a soldier in a long shot being suddenly pulled away behind some crates. Having knocked him out, Jones steals his uniform. During the gag in which Jones discovers that the uniform is too tight for him, the comic effect is strengthened by "Indy 1" played by the clarinet and reprised in canon-like imitation by ironic contrabasses *pizzicato*. "Indy 1" is then interrupted when another soldier arrives. His legs threateningly enter the on-screen space and create a frame-in-the-frame of Jones's face—our hero has apparently been trapped. A minor-mode trombones chord and martial repeating notes by the trumpets accompany his unexpected arrival. Yet the soldier does not recognize the impostor and believes he is just a shabby recruit. He yells in German, evidently ordering Jones to tidy up. Jones plays along, smiling embarrassedly and proving his compliance by combing his hair. The music presents a comic version of "Indy 1" backed by violins *pizzicato*. The gag ends when Jones suddenly kicks the soldier down, catches his hat in midair, and dons it: an upward run by the clarinets comically duplicates his catch. Then, Jones mingles effortlessly with other soldiers, and—in case viewers might have missed something—the music draws our attention to his presence among the Nazis by presenting a cell of "Indy 1" played by a solo clarinet as he passes by.

In the next sequence, the Ark is brought into a gorge. The Ark motif arranged as a minor-mode march accompanies the soldiers on the trek. Jones is at the tail of the line of soldiers: the music indicates his presence with "Indy 1" played by the horns. Jones breaks away from the convoy and hides behind some crates: a harp *glissando* reinforces our perception of his abrupt movement and serves as a musical bridge to the reprise of the Ark motif when the narration cuts to the next shot. Jones appears on an upper ridge saying "Hello!" and threatens the soldiers below with a bazooka. His elevated position mirrors the previous scene with Belloq looking down from the trapdoor of the Well of Souls and similarly saying "Hello." A telling *crescendo* precedes Jones's appearance, and a thinning of the music makes room for Jones's cue, while a stinger emphasizes the surprise of the soldiers. The music inconspicuously tails out under the dialogue.

Now on the mountain's plateau, the Ark is placed on a stone altar, around which we see Toht, the Wehrmacht colonel, and Belloq, who is dressed as an ancient Hebrew priest. Before them, soldiers are filming the event with swastika-branded cameras. Jones and Marion are on the side opposite the altar, tied to a pole. At the beginning of the scene, wind blowing through the plateau can be detected: we can hear the wind's whisper and see Belloq's clothes move. The score presents not the Ark motif but a high-pitched pedal point by the strings and some chromatic Oriental-flavored gestures by the woodwinds, backed by the autoharp in lieu of the biblical kinnor lyre. After Belloq has uttered some ritual formulas, the Ark is opened. Disappointingly, instead of wonderful treasures and the Tablets of the Law, the Ark contains nothing but sand. The colonel raises a handful of it, which begins to slide through his fingers. The music emphasizes the sand sliding with silvery high-pitched notes by the piano, arpeggios by the autoharp, and the cascading sound of the Mark Tree.[17] This musical choice recalls a scene in *The Treasure of the Sierra Madre* (John Huston, 1948) in which Steiner's music stresses the pouring of gold dust into scale pans in the same way: for that gold dust, Dobbs (Humphrey Bogart) will lose his life. Here, there seems to be not only a tribute to Steiner but also an anticipation of what will soon happen to Belloq and his comrades: like Dobbs, they will lose their lives while attempting to get hold of an ineffable treasure.

Suddenly, the electrical equipment mysteriously begins to break down: the Ark motif enters played by the trumpets. A weird light appears from the bottom of the Ark; fog starts to billow out of it and envelop the area. Jones observes the ominous phenomena in astonishment. Evidently remembering the biblical episode of Lot's wife—"look not behind thee!"—he urges Marion to keep her eyes squeezed shut.[18] Spirits with gorgeous feminine faces come out of the Ark and start to float around, with fast-flowing strings runs duplicating the spirits' flight. The musical choice of the angelic vocalizing female choir often heard under the Ark motif is now clear: the music was anticipating what would emanate from the Ark. The Nazis stare at the fascinating spirits that suddenly turn into Angels of Death. Bolts of lightning spring out from the Ark and strike each soldier to the ground. Belloq, the colonel, and Toht scream in terror and explode, implode, and liquefy, respectively. Flames envelop the entire plateau and the adjoining gorge, destroying everything in it. A column of fire rises from the mountain up to the sky and then returns into the Ark, on which the lid finally falls. The only survivors are Jones and Marion: God's Fire has spared their lives as it happened to Lot during the destruction of Sodom and Gomorrah.[19]

Once again, the music in this scene represents the presence of God. While previously it was an almost unnoticeable presence hidden beneath the wind sound and the ship's engine, now God's power is unleashed and his presence evident. Williams said: "For the opening of the Ark, I wanted to try and evoke a biblical atmosphere."[20] He certainly succeeded. During the terrible demise of Belloq, the colonel, and Toht, the score states a peremptory horn motif, which may be called the Wrath of God motif (see figure 10). This horn motif has an ancient flavor given by musical intervals that can be played using the natural harmonics of the instruments.[21]

Figure 10. John Williams, the Wrath of God motif, from the *Raiders of the Lost Ark* film score as heard in the film and CD releases (© 1981 BMI), published by Bantha Music (ear transcription). Used in compliance with the US Copyright Act, Section 107.

Moreover, the shofar—one type of ancient horn—is the ram's horn used in Hebrew liturgy and mentioned several times in the Bible. In the book of Exodus, the very sound of the horn indicates the presence of God: "There was thunder, lightning and a thick cloud on the mountain. Then a shofar blast sounded so loudly that all the people in the camp trembled. . . . Mount Sinai was enveloped in smoke, because *Adonai* descended onto it in fire— its smoke went up like the smoke from a furnace, and the whole mountain shook violently. As the sound of the shofar grew louder and louder . . ."[22] Jones, who previously professed not to believe in superstition and magic, discovers a supernatural facet of life that he had never considered. The themes of (archaeo- logical) faith and (religious) Faith, introduced since the first act as an open question, find here a possible answer. Maybe this experience has taught Jones that the archaeological finds are not just trophies to win and sell but are sym- bols that must be respected. In life there is much more than what one can see, feel, and touch. Set free by the Divine Fire, Jones and Marion embrace each other, and we hear Marion's theme, which closes the scene and the adventure with an authentic cadence (V–I) and a slow upward harp arpeggio. All ended well . . . or maybe not. On the cut leading to the epilogue, the musical line goes up a half step, contradicting the closure effect of the authentic cadence.

Epilogue

There is still something pending: What will become of the Ark? In Washington, Jones is informed by some bureaucrats that the relic is being kept in a safe place and studied by their qualified "top men," which excludes him. Outside the building, Marion asks him the reason for his disappointment. Jones insults the bureaucrats: "They don't know what they've got there." Marion tries to cheer him up: "But I know what I've got here." She invites him to go for a drink together. Again, we hear Marion's theme. Jones offers his arm to her, and Marion's theme is reprised by the strings—violins and cellos, female and male reunited. The lost Ark has been found and lost again, but during this adventure, Jones has retrieved something else: a lost love. This scene confirms our previous claim that Marion does not have her "own" theme. Marion's theme is actually the projection onto her of Jones's love for her—the romantic idealization of the beloved woman.[23] From this perspective, the music can also prompt a feminist interpretation: in the patriarchal Hollywood cinema, the woman is only a passive object of desire and "gaze" for the male protagonists, in this case Jones and Belloq.[24] Therefore, even if she is the film's co-protagonist, she does not have an identity of her own—that is, her own musical theme— as the male lead has. As previously clarified, my analysis was intended to be mainly formalist and not to dwell on ideological readings. Notwithstanding, it is worth pointing out this ambiguous placement of Marion's theme as a good example of how a film score—and a classical-style film score in this case—can also serve a cognitive function that singles out connotations and paves the way for further interpretative analysis. Marion's theme is indeed far too romantic to express her down-to-earth nature, and it is probably for this reason that Williams called it "inappropriate emotionally." It could be debated, then, whether Williams wrote a theme that unproblematically treats Marion in the traditional sexist way or if, by deliberately assigning an overromantic, "inappropriate," and characterially incongruous theme to her, he subtly invites us to reflect on the classical representation of the heroine as a subordinate appendix of the hero.

What has happened to the Ark? This is the last narrative question still left open. While Jones will probably never know, the omniscient narration provides the viewers with the answer, as happens in *Citizen Kane* (Orson Welles, 1941). We are shown that the Ark is locked in an anonymous crate and stored in a huge warehouse full of identical crates. Probably the much-sought-after relic will eventually get lost again, and the Ark motif accompanies it being pushed on a trolley through the stacks of crates. Interestingly, on the CD album, this final track closes with a *crescendo* leading to a *forte* authentic cadence by the full orchestra: thus, the piece closes sharply. In the film, on the contrary, the closing tonic chord is cut and the crescendo is overlapped by a suite starting exactly at the beginning of the end credits and accompanying their crawl.[25] The cut of the closing tonic chord and the sudden shift to "Indy 1," the "signature tune" of the series, seems to avoid a sharp closure of the film narrative, which is in line with the lack of opening titles in this film—the opening titles being the other strong element that typically frames a film narrative. Following the aesthetics of serials once again, the narration seems to reject a sharp closure effect as if it were telling us that the adventures of Indiana Jones are not over.

Conclusion

Ian Freer commented: "Few concerns are closer to Spielberg than film lore, and it is this respect and passion for the craft that gives *Raiders* its soul. Indeed, what ultimately separates *Raiders* from the action pack is affection, not only for the genres and staples it is parodying but for the sheer delight in yarn spinning. The mark of all great cinema, *Raiders* joyously reaffirms why we love movies in the first place."[26] The score is a fundamental element of the vintage quality of this film. The use of clichés, techniques, and dialects from the past is dealt with by Williams with similar respect and passion for the film-music craft and with an equal fondness for the past masterpieces. "To discern a '30s mood and express it isn't like doing a pastiche. A pastiche is not that difficult. What is not easy is taking it a stage further and doing the real thing, with some sincerity," says Williams.[27] The *Raiders* score manipulates the perception of cinematic time by supporting the rhythm of cutting and heightening the pace of the staged actions. It fulfills a micro-emotive function, not only giving the proper romance to love scenes but also stressing the sense of revulsion for snakes and other unpleasant images or adding further comedy and irony to the gags. It also performs a macro-emotive function, since it makes the narrative seem more cohesive and its episodic nature more unified. In a careful analysis, this extroverted and illustrative score fulfills an important cognitive function as well: it suggests the presence of God and outlines the stages of development of the theme of Faith. A good classical-style score is not merely "plastering movies with bits of what we know, rather than revealing an unseen dimension," as superficial critics of Williams and Hollywood music in general claim all too simplistically.[28] Above all, the *Raiders* score is "an object lesson in how to mirror screen action in memorable music."[29] Its core is precisely the classical spatial perceptive function—Mickey-Mousing, stingers, and leitmotivs—fulfilled at many different levels and with such a virtuosity and inventiveness that *Raiders of the Lost Ark* can be said to be one of the finest examples of neoclassical film scoring, as John Williams can be said to be the greatest heir to Max Steiner.

CHAPTER II

Dark Neoclassicism

The "Sublime" Score to *Dracula*

In the period between 1975 and 1983, in which Williams produced the best examples of his neoclassical scoring, the composer also worked on a genre that he has rarely tackled: horror. Compared to other colleagues of similar standing, such as Jerry Goldsmith or Ennio Morricone, who have produced remarkable scores within this genre—for example, Goldsmith's Oscar-winning *The Omen* (Richard Donner, 1976) or Morricone's *The Thing* (John Carpenter, 1982)—horror is conspicuously absent in the Williams filmography. He has scored many thrillers, and there are surely moments that can be qualified as "horror" in the *Indiana Jones* films (Steven Spielberg, 1981, 1984, 1989, 2008), *Jaws* (Steven Spielberg, 1975), *Close Encounters of the Third Kind* (Steven Spielberg, 1977), *Jurassic Park* (Steven Spielberg, 1993), and *The Witches of Eastwick* (George Miller, 1987). Yet none of these are proper *horror* films, according to Noël Carroll's definition—which I adopt.[1] Williams's only contribution to the genre is for the 1979 adaptation of *Dracula*, directed by John Badham. The wider attention that works such as *Jaws*, *Star Wars* (George Lucas, 1977), and *Superman: The Movie* (Richard Donner, 1978) have received, as a result of not only the outstanding quality of the music but also the stellar box office successes, has caused the neglect of other works that are not at all inferior. One such underestimated and largely unknown work is precisely the *Dracula* score. It deserves a chapter on its own because it illustrates a realization of the neoclassical approach that is quite different idiomatically from the heraldic major-mode fanfares of *Star Wars* and *Superman*. Also, in his only foray into horror territories, Williams faced the difficult task of tackling one of the most complex and most staged/filmed monsters of the horror literature, Count Dracula, which came heavily encrusted with a solidly established baggage of associations, connotations, and clichés.

Dracula, the "Sublime" Predator/Seducer Monster

Volumes and articles have been written in astounding quantity on Dracula
and vampires: the historical origins of the legend, its medical explanations, its
sociocultural connotations, and its possible interpretations have all been extensively surveyed.[2] Similarly, the presence of the vampire and, more specifically, of the Transylvanian count in cinema has been charted and examined in
a conspicuous number of monographs.[3] I shall only pinpoint here an aspect
that makes Dracula a monster more complex than others: it is a strongly fascinating creature, scaring and alluring at the same time. Dracula brings death
but also eternal life; his bite means damnation yet has also long been a metaphor of raw uninhibited sexual intercourse.[4] The monsters of horror narratives are potent mirrors and barometers of the sociocultural context in which
they flourish; they are the reflection of—and a reflection on—that specific
epoch of time; they are "meaning machines."[5] First appearing in the late Victorian era, Bram Stoker's Dracula monster reflected a number of more or less
conscious social worries. One of the most cited sees Dracula as a symbol of
the sexual liberation intimated by the agenda of the "New Woman," one of
the first feminist movements.[6] Freudian interpretations have considered the
vampire as a symbol of the spontaneous drives of the id (the unconscious
stratum of the psyche) revolting against the stifling "castrating" values and
norms imposed by the superego (the regulatory censor of the psyche). This
threat/liberation and fear/attraction dualism of the vampire has often been
interpreted using the concept of *unheimlich* (translated as "uncanny," it literally means "unhomely"). *Unheimlich* is said of an object or situation that causes
some repressed thought, desire, or belief to attempt to reemerge from the
unconscious into the conscious.[7] This attempted return of the repressed trig-
gers a feeling that is at the same time one of familiarity (and hence of attraction
and comfort: once we used to know the repressed) and one of unfamiliarity
(and hence of threat and repulsion: the return of the repressed is a threat to
the status quo). Dracula is *unheimlich*, both alluring and scaring.

   This "uncanny" repellent/attractive dyad can also be accounted for through
an aesthetic category central to that Gothic literature of which *Dracula* is
one of the late products, Edmund Burke's "sublime," as described by Anne
Williams: "Like Freud's late theory of the pleasure principle and the death
instinct, love and fear—the beautiful and the sublime—function in Burke's
Enquiry as the two contrary passions of the human soul."[8] While the beautiful is the fruit of pleasure and has a relaxing effect on the nerve system, the

sublime is the fruit of the fear of pain: "Whatever is fitted in any sort to excite the ideas of pain and danger, that is to say, whatever is in any sort terrible, or is conversant about terrible objects, or operates in a manner analogous to terror, is a source of the sublime . . . the strongest emotion which the mind is capable of feeling."[9] We experience a taste of the sublime whenever we face something that makes us realize how finite and small we are within the universe. "Anything that threatens our existence is capable of evoking terror and hence the sublime," in Burke's own definition.[10] The sublime is a category not as stable and pacified as the beautiful but a contradictory and dynamic one. "The sublime arouses our astonishment and admiration. We enjoy those things which are simply good and beautiful in nature; they are pleasurable and edifying; they create an impression that is tranquil enough for us to enjoy without disturbance. The sublime, however, works on us with hammer-blows; it seizes us and irresistibly overwhelms us," explains Johann Georg Sulzer.[11] The sublime includes notions of trespassing and transformation, as noted by Anne Williams: "The word 'sublime' comes from the Latin for 'under the threshold.'. . . . In chemistry, 'to sublimate' means to change state."[12] The sublime is a source of attraction because it discloses a larger-than-life and not fully graspable dimension; at the same time, it is a source of fear because it intimates the fatal transformation that might be incurred if the threshold is crossed. The sublime is an ideal category to account for the fascination elicited by vampires and by the radical change of existential state they cause.

Before Bram Stoker's novel, British literature had offered two more polarized incarnations of the vampire: John Polidori's Lord Ruthven, the protagonist of *The Vampyre* (1819); and Varney, of the "penny dreadful" serial *Varney the Vampire, or, The Feast of Blood* (1845–47). Lord Ruthven, based on Lord Byron, was an amoral libertine bestowed with an irresistible charm. Varney, on the contrary, was a wretched type, cursed into being a monster—and described as such, also physically. In Ruthven and Varney, we find two characterizations—the irresistible sexually charged seducer and the beastly lethal predator—that Stoker fused into a more ambiguous character but that have coexisted, as part of the vampire's uncanny/sublime allure, for ages: Lilith in Jewish mythology is described as an infant-killing vampire demon but also as a seductress; the Latin/Greek *lamiae* and *empusai* were similarly interested in both having sex with their victims and on feasting on their flesh and blood; and Balkan and Slavic folklore similarly features revenants who are both sex-thirsty and blood-thirsty.[13] All the subsequent Dracula adaptations had to pick a position on the spectrum enclosed between the two poles: fear of the beastly predator, on the one side; and attraction for the charming seducer, on the other. F. W. Murnau's *Nosferatu* (1922) and its horrifically ugly Count Orlok leans strongly toward the beastly predator side; Hammer's series with Christopher Lee (starting with *Horror of Dracula*, Terence Fisher, 1958) lies midway, depicting a handsome vampire but more a violent predator than a seducer; Bela Lugosi's Rudolph Valentino–like portrayal foregrounded the suave seducer rather than a predator; Francis Ford Coppola's *Bram Stoker's Dracula* (1992) leaned emphatically toward the "sweet prince" with a tragic backstory. John Badham's 1979 version, starring Frank Langella, is one of the most effective in keeping the two poles in balance. And if Woijeck Kilar's score to Coppola's film is, according to James Deaville, one of the key factors to make the "beauty of horror" emerge in that Beauty-and-the-Beast redemption tale, John Williams's score to Badham's film is a primary agent in the materialization of the "sublime of horror" that Dracula incarnates.[14]

John Badham's 1979 Adaptation

Badham's *Dracula* is the film adaptation of the 1977 Broadway revival of the Deane/Balderstone stage play based on the Stoker novel.[15] The film was co-produced by Universal, the first studio to release an official version of *Dracula* back in 1931 (directed by Tod Browning), based on the same 1927 Deane/Balderstone reduction. The 1979 film, therefore, can also be considered a remake of the 1931 film.[16] Like the 1970s cycle of vampire films—*Martin* (George A. Romero, 1977), *Rabid* (David Cronenberg, 1977), and the spoof *Love at First Bite* (Stan Dragoti, 1979) in the US, and *Nosferatu: Phantom der Nacht* (Werner Herzog, 1979) in Europe—Badham's was in line with the "sympathetic vampire" revisionist trend that downplayed the monstrous and accentuated the tragic and sorrowful side of the character.[17] While many will certainly be familiar with the Dracula story, a brief summary is in order to delineate how the classic narrative was reshaped for this specific film.

> The film opens with a storm and a shipwreck on the shores of Yorkshire: Dracula has arrived to take possession of Carfax Abbey, which he has bought through the solicitor Jonathan Harker. He is rescued (pretends to be rescued) after the storm by Mina Van Helsing, a guest of Dr. Seward's, the director of Whitby's mental asylum. Invited to dinner at Seward's, Dracula meets his solicitor, Harker; and, most importantly, Harker's fiancée, Lucy, the daughter of Dr. Seward. Dracula is clearly attracted to the unconventional "hot-blooded" woman, and he seems to be reciprocated. That night, Dracula visits

Mina, whom he had previously hypnotized, to feed on her blood. Of weak and sickly constitution, Mina dies the morning after. As Mina's father, Professor Van Helsing, is on its way to attend the funeral, Lucy accepts a dinner invitation at the count's residence. There, the two discover they are kindred spirits and kiss passionately. When Van Helsing arrives, he soon realizes that a vampire is behind his daughter's weird death. Since she has turned into a vampire, Van Helsing has to exorcise her corpse by removing her heart. Meanwhile, Dracula visits Lucy during the night and, unlike in Mina's case, she is not hypnotized but consensual. In a majestic love scene, they exchange blood and Lucy is chosen (and chooses) to become Dracula's "best beloved one." Van Helsing identifies in the count the vampire, and soon his attempts at destroying him conflict with Lucy's love for Dracula. Imprisoned, for her own safety, in a cell of her father's asylum, she is rescued by Dracula, and the two sail to Dracula's homeland to become forever united. Van Helsing and Harker manage to board the ship on which the elopers have embarked. In the final confrontation, Van Helsing is the one who ends up impaled by Dracula, but in a last-ditch effort, he manages to pin a cargo-lifting hook into Dracula's shoulders. Harker releases the lever and the vampire is hoisted outside the cargo hold, hanging on to the mast in full light to be disintegrated by the sunrays. As a dejected Lucy lies on the floor, Dracula's cape suddenly detaches from the hook and flies away. An enigmatic smile appears on Lucy's face.

The count is depicted as a lonely tragic figure; his first appearance is in the form of a wolf—as in "a lone wolf." Later in the film, the iconic Dracula line, "Listen to them—the children of the night. What music they make!" is meaningfully changed. In the book, it is said by the count to Harker in appreciation of the sinister howls of the wolves that surround the castle. When Harker responds with a disagreeing expression on his face, the count adds: "Ah, sir, you dwellers in the city cannot enter into the feelings of the hunter."[18] In the book, the wolf is akin to the count because both are hunters, predators. In Badham's film, the line becomes "Listen to them. Children of the night. What sad music they make. So lonely, like weeping." The wolf is, here, akin to the count because they both roam the earth in a sad state of loneliness. Instead of a puzzled look from the counterpart Harker, in the film we have Lucy, Dracula's love interest, who replies, "I think it's a wonderful sound" and expresses her appreciation for the night: "So exciting! Night was made to enjoy." Dracula has found a kindred spirit, and he is reciprocated.

In the novel and in other films, the quest of Van Helsing and the vampire hunters is characterized as one of salvation of the wickedly manipulated girl. Here, the narration brings to the fore the "vampire as a liberator" element and turns the heroine from a passive victim—subjugated by a male vampire, on the one hand, and rescued by the male "Crew of Light," on the other— into an active decision maker in charge of her own life. When the count tells her, in an apologetic tone, "You must forgive me for intruding on your life," Lucy answers, "I came of my own accord." The film presents an inversion of the female characters—Lucy is the protagonist, Mina a character of secondary importance—that is inherited from the US stage play.[19] Interestingly enough, the 1931 film was based on the same US stage play but kept the characters' roles as they are in Stoker's novel. This inversion acquires particular significance in Badham's adaptation. In the novel, Lucy is the more sexually uninhibited and modern of the two, and here she is promoted to protagonist, while the more conservative Mina is demoted and depicted from the outset as sickly and sheepish. In the film, Lucy is introduced as about to graduate and embark on a career in a law firm, and Mina, commenting upon Lucy's soon-to-start professional career, says, "You're much braver than I am, taking on all those men like that." Mina has no love partner, while Lucy appears relaxed in her effusions with her fiancé, Jonathan. When their kissing gets too prolonged, her father, Dr. Seward, quips, "Enough! Save it till after you're married!" Like in the novel, Dr. Seward (as the other male protagonists do) represents the good old family values, but his portrayal here is satirical. He is inept at medical science—"not wholesome" is the only comment he can offer about the teeth marks on Mina's neck—and he lacks sensitiveness; while Lucy is too distraught to eat after Mina's death, he has no restraints in gorging on eggs and bacon, the yolk spilling on his beard. Van Helsing comes off as a frail old man, much different from the assertive and determined figures of most other films, and the only motive that keeps him fighting the vampire is to exact revenge for his daughter's death. Harker, the fiancé, is portrayed as faux open-minded: he is described as "fancy," he works in London, and he sports the only motorcar in Whitby. Yet he reveals his true old-fashionedly jealous and possessive nature when Lucy shares a dance with the count. Dracula is the towering hero in the film, much more imposing, majestic, and overwhelming than any of the other characters: he is "sublime." He has noticed the exceptional creature that Lucy is—"She's stronger than most women," he says—and he is offering her a "sublimation," to cross the threshold to free up her potential. The vampire hunters are the antagonists, if not the villains, that try to thwart the liberating transformation in order to maintain the conservative status quo.

Unlike most of the 1970s adaptations, Badham's sets and costumes are firmly traditional, merely moving the setting from the Victorian 1897 to the Edwardian 1913. The box office reception was lukewarm—arguably because the film was perceived as too traditional within the competing contemporary vampire series of films.[20] Yet praise from the critics' circles precisely stressed its fidelity to the spirit of the Gothic tradition: "There have been so many Draculas . . . that the tragic origins of the character have been lost among the gravestones, the fangs and all those black cloaks. This 'Dracula' restores the character to the purity of its first film appearances. . . . John Badham hasn't updated Dracula, thank God. What he has done, though, is concentrate a little more fully on the tragedy of having to live forever."[21] The Gothic feel in Badham's film is achieved visually through the centrality that is given to nature. "Nature may be sublime or beautiful, nurturing or destructive," notes Anne Williams, and it is in nature that the sublime typically manifests itself.[22] The film opens with a sea-storm sequence like those one finds aplenty in the paintings of William Turner and others who translated into images the sublime as theorized by Burke. The film, unlike the 1931 adaptation, is not set in London—at the time the emblem of modernity—but entirely in the Yorkshire moors, like Emily Brontë's *Wuthering Heights* (1847), another supernaturally tinted story of doomed love that is central to Gothic literature.[23] The film's open ending is also in line with the Gothic tradition.[24] Janet Maslin of the *New York Times*, in a not entirely positive review, noted: "One of the most impressive things about *Dracula* is its soundtrack. John Williams has contributed yet another ravishing score."[25] Indeed, music is as central as the scenery and cinematography to configure the Gothic sublime in the film.

Dracula by Williams

Williams has thus described his reaction to the film: "It's a wonderful subject for music, really, for the sweep of the kind of romance and areas that we are uncertain about, an odd world that we're attracted to but we're a bit afraid of at the same time. The magnetism of the unknown, mixed with the erotic aspects of the story made it for me a very romantic piece in many ways."[26] One key point here is "erotic/romantic," which creates a link with the metaphors of sexual liberation and transgressive love that have long been associated with Dracula and vampires: for example, in the influential pre-Romantic vampire story, Goethe's 1797 ballad "The Bride of Corinth."[27] The other element stressed by Williams is the "odd world that we're attracted to but we're a bit afraid of at the same time." This sounds very close to the very definition of the sublime (and the uncanny). How did Williams translate these two guiding aspects—the erotic/romantic and the sublime—into music? John Badham provides an indication coming from his first meeting with Williams: "He confessed that he had never seen a vampire movie of any sort before. . . . How fortunate to have the pre-eminent film composer of the day arrive with no advance notion of the kind of ketchup and thunder music that prevails in the horror film genre."[28] With "ketchup and thunder music," Badham refers to what the standard reference was at the time for vampire music: James Bernard's scores for the Hammer films.[29] Bernard's theme for Dracula has been described by Timothy Scheurer as "not a melody, but a progression of relentless dark chords suggesting terrible evil."[30] Famously, the Dracula theme was also written so as to spell rhythmically the very name of the count, a sort of hyperexplicit stalking leitmotiv for a horrific predator. There is nothing romantic in Bernard's Dracula (see figure 11).

Figure 11. James Bernard, the Dracula motif, from the *Horror of Dracula* film score as heard in the film and CD releases (© 1958 ASCAP), published by Universal Music (ear transcription). Used in compliance with the US Copyright Act, Section 107.

Bernard's scores, moreover, are neatly bipolar: on the one side, we have distinctly horror-sounding dissonant music; on the other side, we have serene and pastoral consonant music to depict the world of humans and the redeeming (socially acceptable) conjugal love. In Hammer's films, according to Isabella van Elferen, "The use of leitmotifs provides audiences with clear indications of which movie character is good and which evil, and when these respective characters are going to appear."[31]

Horror music, in general, has long been patterned along this dichotomy: "On the one hand, there must be music to underscore the normal, stable or functional and, on the other hand, there must be musical motifs that signify the abnormal, unstable or dysfunctional," Scheurer explains.[32] The typical stylistic devices of horror music, as listed by Philip Hayward, are "dissonance, . . . atonal elements, including dramatic and unpredictable intervallic leaps and

meandering melodies that emphasize minor seconds and tritones . . . an ostinato . . . , a stalking topic," as well as the "stinger," an abrupt *fortissimo* dissonant chord that punctuates some sudden visual shocks, "the ultimate horror
sound."[33] In its designated function to shock the audience, horror music is,
alongside science fiction music, "one of the prime genres for the exploration of (what was once characterized as) musical avantgardism."[34] The music
for the Hammer films featured all these elements, to the point of constitut-
ing a "musical reference bank for future horror-film composers," borrowing
Michael Hannan's formulation.[35] Even if Williams's *Dracula* score does include stingers and dissonance, however, he did not employ "musical avantgardism" but resorted to the idiom of the musical Romanticism, typically
associated with romance but also closely linked to the concept of the sublime, which was an "important facet of Romantic thought and composition,"
as stressed by Leonard B. Meyer.[36] Moreover, Williams took some departures
from the horror-music routines that made his music sound Gothic more
than horror. Because of the Manichean good (consonance) / evil (dissonance)
demarcation of Bernard's and other horror-film scores, they cannot be called
Gothic music, according to van Elferen: "Since fear and desire are twin impulses, Gothic spectres are simultaneously dreadful and appealing. . . . Gothic
is located in a perpetual and self-perpetuating in-between. It inhabits a radi-
calised liminality characterised by the destabilising force of pervasive ambivalence. . . . Gothic music is a journey into the uncanny."[37] A psychoanalytical
approach is adopted here, employing the concept of the *unheimlich*. As we
have seen, what is shared between this concept from psychoanalysis and
Burke's sublime is a similar state of uncertainty and suspension between attraction and repulsion. So we can say that Gothic music is also *a journey into the
sublime*; after all, as pinpointed by Anne Williams, "the uncanny is Freud's
theory of the sublime."[38]

While the Gothic in music is not so much a matter of a specific compositional style as one of "its *functionality* within the larger context of Gothic
narration," some idiomatic traits have nevertheless been singled out as Gothic
by van Elferen: "timbres like that of the 'spectral' high-pitched violin, of the
'transcendent' female choir," as well as the use of the pipe organ.[39] This
instrument is generally associated with the horror genre but is particularly
evocative of Gothic atmospheres, as described by Julie Brown: "The instrument's clear religious associations enable it to serve as a musical sign of religious ponderings . . . , esoteric knowledge . . . , and possible death followed by

funerals. . . . The organ's usual location—inside churches and cathedrals, near crypts alludes to the space of the Gothic novel."[40] Williams's usual full symphony orchestra—the London Symphony Orchestra, once again—is precisely augmented with an ethereal-sounding women's choir (mostly performing "Ah" in up-and-down minor-second vocalizes), and a pipe organ also adds an esoteric color. When Mina meets Dracula in the cave, the organ suddenly appears to ominously mark the initiation-like moment of Dracula touching the hand of his future victim. In the finale, as Van Helsing confronts Dracula, the organ provides extra gravitas and a religious tone. In general, more than the brass and harshly dissonant chords present in Bernard's and others' horror-film scores, in Williams's we find a prevalence of less unsettling dissonances and a predominance of the strings, arguably the principal color of what is considered "romantic" music. Strings are recurrently used in their extreme "spectral" higher registers but also in dark drones by the celli and contrabasses, and we also find tone clusters, artificial harmonics, and slithering glissandi—devices already used in *Close Encounters of the Third Kind*.[41] The effects produced by the combination of these strings techniques are "creepy," disturbing, and suspense-building rather than outright scary as in Bernard's compositions. If the score in general has a Gothic spirit in its being "simultaneously dreadful and appealing," and also has Gothic colors ("spectral high-pitched violin," "transcendent female choir," and organ), it is in the main theme, Dracula's theme, that Williams translates the idea of the Gothic's sublime into music.

The Dracula theme is presented at the beginning of the film, over the opening titles. On a black screen, we hear a wolf howling, and then the music starts *pianissimo* with high-register tone clusters of the strings. As a circle of white mist—another form that Dracula can take, besides the wolf and the bat—grows out of the black to invade the screen, the tension of the music builds up with slow glissandi of the celli emerging from the depth of their lower register and gradually creeping up in tessitura and volume. After having heard the wolf howling and seen the mist spreading, here comes Dracula's other vicarious shape: a bat (see figure 12). The bat's entrance is announced by the piccolo prefiguring the Dracula motto and *sforzando* notes of the muted trombones—the piccolo and trombones are timbres at the extreme ranges of the orchestra, away from the "normal" middle range, and thus used to communicate a sense of threatening abnormality. As the bat flies into the mist tunnel, the horns play a musical motif, like an introductory motto for Dracula.

Figure 12. Screenshot of bat and mist tunnel in the opening titles from *Dracula* (© 1979 Universal Pictures Limited). Used in compliance with the US Copyright Act, Section 107.

In itself, this motto is already indicative of the different direction taken by Williams, if compared to Bernard's "Dra-cu-la" motto. Bernard's motto was characterized by the augmented fourth/tritone (the *diabolus in musica*), an unmistakable signifier of danger and fear. Williams had used the tritone both for the secondary shark motto in *Jaws* and for the Ark motif in *Raiders of the Lost Ark*, to mark the lethal nature of the sea "monster" and the arcane threat posed by the religious artifact (see chapters 7 and 9). This time, Williams opts for a more ambiguous solution: a first inversion of an augmented chord with an added major seventh (A♭aug^{M7}) (see figure 13). The augmented fifth in the chord tends toward the dissonance but is not as gratingly dissonant as the clusters employed by Bernard are. Moreover, as William Rosar confirms, it "had a long tradition in theater and program music of being associated with supernatural subjects."[42] It was also used in the French "Impressionism"—notably Debussy—for the creation of dreamlike suspended atmospheres. While the tritone has a history of sounding unequivocally evil, the augmented fifth has magical and supernatural but not outright evil implications. The magical nature of the augmented fifth is charged with darker hues by the presence of the "horror trope" minor-second interval (G/A-flat) created by the inversion of the major seventh. The Dracula motto communicates an in-between quality of supernatural allure and threat.

As the film's title, "Dracula," emerges from the mist tunnel, the main theme starts exactly on its appearance—much like what happens in *Superman: The*

Added major seventh

A-flat major
(1st inversion)

Augmented fifth

Figure 13. John Williams, the Dracula motto, from the *Dracula* film score as heard in the film and CD releases (© 1979 BMI), published by USI B Music Publishing (ear transcription). Used in compliance with the US Copyright Act, Section 107.

Movie or in *Star Wars*. Musically, Williams introduces Dracula as the film's hero. The main theme, unlike Bernard's, is a melody, in the key of C minor—in line with the traditional somber/dark associations of the minor mode—and is designed to incorporate both aspects previously alluded to by Williams: the erotic/romantic and the sublime, attraction and fear. The theme opens with a dotted rhythm (signifying determination, as in the Indiana Jones theme) and an upward leap, as in many Williams main themes; it does not reach a perfect fifth (as in the clear-cut heroism of *Star Wars* and *Superman*) but goes beyond to hit a major seventh. The interval of the leap is a dissonant one: the major seventh is the inversion of the minor second—the most dissonant interval and horror music's trademark, as we have seen—that was present in the Dracula motto. The inversion of the minor second into a larger interval at the same time mitigates its dissonant nature (making it less "horror") while also retaining an association with the "horror" minor second. After a rapid four-note turn (*gruppetto*) that seems to evoke the swift gyrations of the bat's wings and Dracula's cape, the theme drops down an octave—back into the darkness from which it originated—and then marks the somber minor-mode setting by ending forcibly on the third degree of the C-minor key, the E-flat.[43] The theme is restated over an aerial shot of a dilapidated castle perched over a cliff—unequivocal Gothic imagery. Then, the theme expands and jumps up, covering a minor tenth—C to the E-flat in the higher octave. This motion creates at the same time a melodic stretching and restates once again the minor-mode (hence dark) nature of the theme by repeating the C to E-flat motion. After this, the stretching of the theme continues through chromatic permutations, reaching up higher and higher in register, while at the same time the orchestral texture, the dynamics, and the momentum increase climactically. The musical stretching and climax build across a series of chromatic

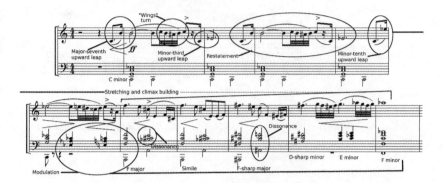

Figure 14. John Williams, the Dracula theme, from the *Dracula* film score as heard in the film and CD releases (© 1979 BMI), published by USI B Music Publishing (ear transcription). Used in compliance with the US Copyright Act, Section 107.

modulating passages until the theme reaches the climax's peak at the end of the opening credits (see figure 14).

Williams sets the romantic/erotic tone by implementing the techniques typical of the music of the Romantic period, not only chromaticism—used in Romantic music to weaken the musical syntax and thus express a longing feeling of "openness" and "ongoing process"—but more specifically what Leonard Meyer calls "stretching," "statistical climax," and "apotheosis."[44] The music of the Romantic period is preponderantly based on secondary "statistical" parameters (expression) rather than on primary "syntactical" parameters (form).[45] The ideal that is pursued is not the beautiful but the sublime, so not so much "form" or "quality" (say, as in a Haydn symphony) as "size" and "quantity" (as in a Gustav Mahler symphony).[46] This can be achieved by developing a melody through "stretching" (for example, making the intervals increasingly wider) or by stretching secondary parameters (for example adding "discordant harmonies and widely spaced sonorities").[47] Climaxes are buildups, "points of intense and complex activity," "intensifications" of the statistical parameters (dynamics, agogics, density of orchestration . . .), and the apotheosis that typically follows such climaxes is a reprise of the theme in "powerful statements of majestic affirmation," as Meyer explains.[48] By combining these Romantic techniques with a subtle use of modernistic dissonance and atonality, Williams adds to the erotic/romantic element one of an "odd world that we're attracted to but we're a bit afraid of at the same time," to restate the composer's own words, thus producing the ambiguous quality of the sublime.

Melodic Stretching, Climax, and Apotheosis:
The Sublime in Dracula's Score

If an element of neoclassicism in the score is the symphonic writing, Williams's signature prowess in performing a spatial perceptive function through the Mickey-Mousing technique is also showcased throughout the film. During the storm sequence, Dracula's hand suddenly breaks out of his wooden box to slain a sailor's throat, and this is punctuated by a "peekaboo" horns rip; in the scene in which Dracula hypnotizes Mina, his hypnosis-releasing move of the fingers is highlighted by a glissando on the harp. In the love-scene montage, within the developmental melodic flow, Williams manages to insert flutters of the flutes and piccolo to mirror the moves of the bat that is seen flying in the background. Another neoclassical element is the extensive use of the leitmotif technique. While the Dracula theme is utterly preponderant in the score, there are a limited number of secondary motifs too. One is associated with Van Helsing and his vampire hunt. Interestingly, it is an ostinato: the typical musical trope for the stalker is used here not for the monster (*Jaws*'s shark motif is an ostinato) but for the monster hunter, further clarifying who the hero is and who the antagonist. The repetitive structure of the ostinato communicates the professor's unremitting resolve to destroy the monster. In the scenes in which Van Helsing dissects his own vampirized daughter, the ostinato is combined with a hint of a fugato, which in Williams is often used to score the progress of some operation carried out with unflinching determination—as in the shark-cage assembly in *Jaws* or the bomb search in *Black Sunday* (John Frankenheimer, 1977). Williams titled the piece for this quasi vivisection "Van Helsing's Solution," which further pinpoints the "Dracula is a problem that must be fixed" attitude of the scientist (see figure 15).

Figure 15. John Williams, "Van Helsing's Solution," from the *Dracula* film score as heard in the film and CD releases (© 1979 BMI), published by USI B Music Publishing (ear transcription). Used in compliance with the US Copyright Act, Section 107.

The first two measures of Dracula's theme are initially employed as a leitmotif, Dracula's identifier, and thus presented when he appears, or is mentioned, or is investigated. In the opening storm sequence, the theme is played by the horns as we see an oblong box in the ship's cargo old. When the narration closes in on the delivery address on the box—"Count Dracula, Whitby, Yorkshire, England"—the trumpets spell out the theme again, and the theme is reprised powerfully by the trombones at the end of the storm sequence. When, in Carfax Abbey, the count "welcomes" Renfield, we hear the themes played by bassoons. Later in the film, as Van Helsing is researching vampire literature, the narration cuts to a vampire-bat illustration in one of the professor's books: as we see the drawing, Dracula's theme is played by the horns—a situation reminiscent of *Jaws*, when the horns play the shark motto as Brody looks at shark photos in a book. In all these instances, music consolidates the association between the leitmotif and its character.

Mina too is given a specific musical treatment. After witnessing the shipwreck that coincides with Dracula's arrival, she runs to succor him in the cave: we hear not horror music but a mysterious piece in which fairy tale–like "Impressionist" whole-tone scales and augmented fifths recall the Dracula motto. She is fascinated by the weird discovery and touches the stranger's hand. He, in turn, gently but deliberately takes her hand: on this detail shot, exactly as Dracula's fingers close on Mina's hand, the music climaxes with a solemn *tutti* chord in minor mode, colored by an ominous organ—fascination *and* horror. This musical piece is presented again, virtually identical, as Dracula appears at night to vampirize Mina. As the "Impressionist" music flows and Mina looks at the count with a mix of fear and desire, the mood is more fantastical/sexual than horror, until the same *tutti* minor-mode chord resounds as a sound bridge when we cut to the next scene. The mortal bite is kept off-screen, and it is the music that communicates what is happening as a consequence of the previous encounter in the cave: in Jean-Marie Lecomte's interpretation, "the vampire's sensual hand caressing Mina's on a moonlit beach is a visual metonym that ushers in a more desirable Death. The hand of death grasps the willing hand of life: Mina is sick and dying and her Keatsian self is 'half in love with easeful death.'"[49] Mina also has her own leitmotif. This feeble-sounding phrase is heard in the scene in which Dracula pays a dinner visit to Dr. Seward's house. In the dialogue between Mina and Dracula, we hear Mina's motif played by the flutes and the bassoons, as if to symbolize the connection between the delicate woman (flute) and the dark prince (bassoon). Her leitmotif is later highlighted during Mina's funeral, played by a solo trumpet.

An element of interest in the musical dramaturgy is that Dracula's theme is never heard in conjunction with Mina, while it is omnipresent in his scenes with Lucy. The nocturnal visit to Mina is a vampire's repast; the visit to Lucy is a love pledge. Mina is a victim without a choice, while Lucy "makes a conscious, existentialist choice to rebel against her father and lover. Badham makes it clear that Lucy (unlike Mina) is never under a spell and is determined to follow her own light and be Dracula's lover," as Lecomte stresses.[50] Dracula's own kindred woman is Lucy, and only during his relationship with her do we hear his theme, because only in Lucy does he have a personal investment. On the other hand, Lucy has no musical theme because she is bound to get fused with Dracula as if into a single entity, to be sublimated into something else. There is a pro and a con in the sublime. She has freely chosen to unite with the count, something astonishing and larger than life—"You will be flesh of my flesh, blood of my blood," that is, Dracula's love pledge. Yet the sublime is also something in which it is likely to get annihilated—Dracula's pledge continues, "You shall cross land or sea to do *my* bidding," a promise not of tranquil equality in the relationship but of a disturbing fusion and abandonment on her part.

As the romance between the count and Lucy develops, Dracula's theme undergoes a transformation: before meeting Lucy, the first two measures of the theme have been used as an identifier for the character, highlighted in its dark and threatening qualities by trumpets, horns, trombones, and bassoons. After meeting Lucy, Dracula's theme is more frequently played by oboes and flutes, shifting its color to more seductive nuances. Also, we hear incremental fragments of the stretching and climax part of the theme, beyond the initial measures used as the character's identifier. Williams employs his "gradual disclosure" technique, which in this case is not of the main theme—as in *E.T.* or *Indiana Jones*—but a gradual disclosure of the erotic climax. After their intimate dinner, Lucy and Dracula kiss, and we hear Dracula's theme played tenderly by flutes. Then he lustfully gazes at Lucy's neck—we hear ominous low-register celli—and yet he soon redirects his bite to her ear, turning it into an affectionate nibble, as the Dracula theme is reprised by the violins. When Lucy confirms her personal choice to be involved—"I came of my own accord"—they resume kissing as the theme is stretched and inflated into a foretaste of the "statistical climax."

The Dracula theme receives a full development—and the statistical climax a full disclosure—in the night encounter between Lucy and Dracula, which Williams titles "Love Scene." This scene is the plot's midpoint, and this pivotal position is signaled both visually and musically. Here the musical climax peaks into an apotheosis of Dracula's theme. Exactly as Dracula bites Lucy on the neck, Williams reprises the Dracula motto that opened the film, and visually we see the same tunnel of mist. In the opening credits, the mist tunnel is in cold blue tones and traversed by the lonely bat; in the love scene, it is of a bright red. More important, the image of the bat is now intercut with the silhouettes of Dracula and Lucy, tangled in their lovemaking: "one flesh" (see figure 16).

There is not a lonely bat but the two lovers united under the vampire-symbolizing bat. After the apotheosis that powerfully restates Dracula's theme for full orchestra—as heard over the opening titles—there is another climax that, unlike the minor-mode resolution heard at the beginning of the film, leads to a massive, orgasmic *tutti* C-major chord. In the following musical abatement—like a *petite mort* after the orgasm—the Dracula theme is repeated by flutes backed by a dreamy harp glissando.[51] Yet the essence of the sublime is attraction *and* repulsion. After the lovemaking, Dracula cuts his own chest to make Lucy drink his own blood, in a sort of unholy communion, or the vampire's baptism: "one blood." Williams accompanies this moment of horror with shrill figurations of the high-pitched violins backed by pounding timpani hits, and as Lucy drinks the blood, a low-pitched minor-mode *forte* chord closes the scene and seals Lucy's crossing into the sublime world of vampiric curse.

The climax/apotheosis structure of the love scene is paralleled in Dracula's demise, thus carrying out the score's macro-emotive function of connecting the narrative's hinges into a unified whole. As Dracula struggles to free himself from the hook in the cargo hold, the orchestra surges to a climax that resolves to an apotheosis when Dracula is hoisted to the top of the mast, as a sort of blasphemous crucifix—apotheosis also means "divinization." Dracula's theme is played here again in full stride, as he desperately tries to shield himself from the lethal sunrays. The presentation of Dracula's theme is interrupted by a harmonic progression of unrelentingly pulsating chords backed by timpani—as if to articulate a countdown in the vampire-dispatching ritual—and colored by the organ. This is followed by furious blasts of the brass, fragments of the love-scene climax, and the final deflating statement of Dracula's theme. Music abates as Dracula succumbs—a real, *grand mort* this time. The narration cuts to an unnaturally tinted shot of the sun surface, which in its round shape recalls the mist tunnel at the beginning of the film and in the midpoint love scene: unlike in those instances, the orchestration here is rarefied, with no basses or middle range, almost colorless, dominated by algid high-pitched violins and organ arpeggios. As we cut to Lucy, who has lost her vampire look and is freed from the count's contamination, music launches

Figure 16. Screenshots of the mist tunnel in the love scene (red in original) from *Dracula* (© 1979 Universal Pictures Limited). Used in compliance with the US Copyright Act, Section 107.

into another climax, starting with a foregrounded note of the chimes—like the bell used at the end of Modest Mussorgsky's *Night on the Bald Mountain* to signal the coming of the day that dispels the forces of the night, to name just one instance. The brief climax resolves as we see Harker, the legitimate fiancé, sitting next to the restored Lucy. A chord mirrors the full-orchestra C-major chord to which the love scene peaked; this is not passionate, full-bodied, and orgasmic but a sparse *religioso*-sounding chord by high-pitched violins and organ—the sound of piety and purity.

Music makes room for silence as Lucy looks around, confused and dispirited. She lays a hand on Jonathan's shoulder, to which he replies with a look of ill-concealed contempt. Suddenly, a flapping sound catches Lucy's attention and she looks up. The music resumes to replicate, with flutters of the flutes, the motion of Dracula's cape flying away, and a musical atmosphere of suspense is built as Lucy stares with an indefinite expression. As we cut to the cape gliding away in the distance, we hear a wolf howling, like the one that opened the film; then we cut back to Lucy and zoom in on her reaction. A subtle smile of relief and hope illuminates her face (see figure 17). On Lucy's reaction shot, we hear the return of the Dracula theme played by a horn with a F-major harmonization, to which an augmented fifth is soon added (evocative of the augmented fifth in the Dracula motto), and then the music resolves to an A-major chord, which connects this moment to the major-mode resolution of the love scene. Soaring scales of the woodwinds accompany the flight of the cape as we move seamlessly into the end credits.

Dracula and *Swan Lake*: An (In)conclusive Hypothesis

The music for the end credits opens up a hypothesis about Williams's inspiration for this score. Badham reports: "His initial fix on it after looking at it and thinking about it for a while was *Tristan and Iseult* . . . a great tragic love story."[52] In Wagner's *Tristan und Isolde* (1865), surely, we have one of the most celebrated musical settings of a doomed love story, with the opera being an almost continuous climax that only resolves as the lovers finally reunite in death, on a higher plane—in the apotheosis of the final Liebestod (love/death) scene "Mild und Leise." Yet, if references have to be found for Williams's *Dracula*, I do not think that *Tristan* would be the most relevant. The score surely has chromatic passages but does not have the never-ending-melody quality inspired by Wagner that we find, for example, in Herrmann's *Vertigo* (Alfred Hitchcock, 1958). The recurring idiomatic trait in Williams's score, more than continuous chromaticism, is the sudden unprepared appearance of major-mode chords in an otherwise minor-mode setting—as in the love scene

Figure 17. Screenshots of the "happy ending" from *Dracula* (© 1979 Universal Pictures Limited). Used in compliance with the US Copyright Act, Section 107.

and end credits. In more recent interviews, Williams gives other cultural references: "[*Dracula*] makes us reflect on the idea that eternal love comes only after death. . . . As in *Romeo and Juliet*, the lovers have to die together to be together. We have this idea in our culture that love is eternal."[53] The *Romeo and Juliet* reference is a better fit than *Tristan*: while in both dramas there is an enamored couple whose love is impeded by their belonging to opposing factions, in Wagner's the two protagonists turn from enemies into eternal lovers because of a love potion they inadvertently drink. In Badham's film, as in *Romeo and Juliet*, there is no magic that compels Lucy to go against her family to join the supposed enemy, Dracula. More important, the *Romeo and Juliet* reference connects the score to a past model that I argue is more relevant than Wagner: Tchaikovsky. More than Wagner's paroxysmal yearning, in Williams's *Dracula* there are echoes of Tchaikovsky's Slavic melancholia and of the alternation of longing apotheoses and despondent abatements—mood swings, we could say—traceable in Tchaikovsky's music.

We have seen how the 1979 film can be considered a remake of the 1931 version. In her analysis of the earlier film, Alison Peirse notes the weakness of the screenplay, devoid of a proper hero and populated by sapless characters. Her conclusion is that the count is the hero.

> If Dracula is the protagonist, then this film is a tragedy. Classically, a tragedy contains the noble hero, the tragic flaw, the inevitable fall. Count Dracula is our noble protagonist. . . . Dracula's flaw is built into his essence: he is undead. . . . In England he meets Lucy and Mina, and it is here that his desires will spiral out of control. It is his murder and vampirism of Lucy and his pursuit of Mina that leads to his "catastrophic fall." In line with this approach, it makes sense to view Van Helsing—who does not appear until almost halfway through the film—as the antagonist. . . . Although supernaturally powerful, Dracula is undone by his unquenchable thirst for the blood of a young woman. . . . It's counter-intuitive to think of Dracula as a tragic hero, brought down by his desire for two English women, but it accords with Universal's marketing of the film: the poster tagline was *The Story of the Strangest Passion the World has Ever Known!*[54]

In the film's opera scene, Lugosi/Dracula enigmatically admits, "To die, to be really dead. That must be glorious. There are far worse things awaiting man than death." Dracula is trapped in an eternal-life loop. In Badham's remake, the concept of loneliness and sadness is unpacked in the "children of the night" dialogue, but Lugosi's line is also augmented in Badham's dinner scene in which Dracula confesses to Lucy, "There are worse things than death. You must believe me. I have buried many friends and I, too, am weary. I'm the last of my kind." Frank Langella's performance, like Lugosi's, shuns the showy flaunting of vampire fangs but resorts to the hypnotic magnetism of the gaze, a mix of seduction and threat (see figure 18). Also, both actors had previously donned the count's costume in theater productions (in 1927–30 and 1977–80, respectively), and both films are direct adaptations that brought the actors from the stage boards to the film set. The two films are closely related. I suspect that, despite Badham's claim that Williams had never seen a vampire film before, the composer must have been familiar with the 1931 film, particularly after the 1960s TV revival of Universal's horror classics. And the only nondiegetic musical piece featured in the 1931 film is from Tchaikovsky's *Swan Lake* (1875–76): the Swan theme from Act II, Scene 10. Over the years, this specific piece has become so associated with Lugosi's Dracula—and had already been reused in *Murder in the Rue Morgue* (Robert Florey, 1932) as a Lugosi musical identifier—that the documentary *Bela Lugosi: Hollywood's Dark Prince* (Kevin Burns, 1995) showcased it, and Howard Shore quoted the piece as Lugosi's theme in his score for *Ed Wood* (Tim Burton, 1995).[55]

The choice of the Swan theme for the 1931 *Dracula* can be due to its already established presence in silent-cinema anthologies under the category of "misterioso music."[56] Yet its contemporaneous use also in *The Mummy* (Karl Freund, 1932), a horror film tinged with doomed/eternal love nuances, might indicate a rationale other than the mere use of a well-tested piece from the silent-film repertoire. The music supervisor at Universal, Heinz Roemheld, was European educated, and it is highly probable that he was familiar with the libretto of the Tchaikovsky ballet. *Swan Lake*, a tragic love/death story, is about Princess Odette, who, under a curse by the evil magician von Rothbart, lives as a swan by day and only turns human by night—like Dracula, she is a shape-shifter, and cursed to be fully herself only after sunset. When Prince Siegfried—who has never found true love and is about to be forced into an arranged marriage by his family—is about to kill a swan with his crossbow, he witnesses the transformation of the animal into Odette. The cursed princess tells him that only the pledge of eternal love by someone who has never truly loved can break von Rothbart's spell. Siegfried and Odette fall in love, but at a costume ball, von Rothbart tricks Siegfried into declaring his love to Odile, the sorcerer's daughter magically disguised as Odette. Everything is lost, and Odette and Siegfried decide to die together, leaping into the lake. The sacrifice breaks the spell and Odette and Siegfried ascend to heaven, where they

Figure 18. Comparison of the gazes of Bela Lugosi and Frank Langella, screenshots from *Dracula* (© 1931 Universal Pictures Corporation) and *Dracula* (© 1979 Universal Pictures Limited). Used in compliance with the US Copyright Act, Section 107.

will be united in eternal love—a literal apotheosis that is rendered musically by Tchaikovsky through a full-orchestra triumphant transposition to major mode of the melancholic minor-mode Swan theme. The ballet, as can be seen, has parallels with the Dracula story as told by Badham and Williams: Dracula is somewhat like Odette, a lonely, love-deprived, cursed outcast; Lucy is somewhat like Siegfried, bound by family obligations and forced into a marriage.

The 1931 film features a condensed version of the *Swan Lake* piece in which six parts can be identified. Part 1 (measures 2–6) features the B-minor Swan theme played lamentingly by the weeping sound of the oboes (see figure 19).

Figure 19. Part 1: Swan theme played by oboes, from Pyotr Ilyich Tchaikovsky, *Swan Lake* (1895 score, public domain), "Act II, Scene 10," mm. 2–6.

This is the current, doleful condition of the cursed outcast. Then the music jumps to measures 30–33 (part 2), where we have an A-major passage that expresses longing and hope through the stretching and climax techniques (see figure 20).

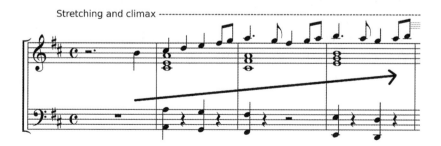

Figure 20. Part 2: Climax, from Pyotr Ilyich Tchaikovsky, *Swan Lake* (1895 score, public domain), "Act II, Scene 10," mm. 30–33.

The climax reaches its peak by jumping to measures 34–37 (part 3), in which the sudden transition to C major, the alternation of major and minor chords, and the hypnotic quality of the repeating triplet figures inject a sense of mystery and magic but also of a melancholic uncertainty between happiness and sadness (see figure 21).

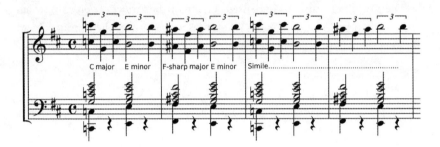

Figure 21. Part 3: Major/minor mode oscillation, from Pyotr Ilyich Tchaikovsky, *Swan Lake* (1895 score, public domain), "Act II, Scene 10," mm. 34–37.

Then, we have a modulating section with prominent brass chords (part 4, measures 38–47) whose climax leads to an apotheosis-like *tutti* repetition of the Swan theme (part 5, measures 52–59), followed by an abatement in which the music deflates as the Swan theme is repeated by the celli, basses, and bassoons to finally die out (part 6, measures 64–70).[57]

My contention is that Williams's score has in Tchaikovsky an idiomatic model but it also nods to *Swan Lake* as used in the 1931 film. A similar structure to that of the abridged Swan theme can be detected in Williams's end-credits music. We have the oboes playing the Dracula theme with the same lamenting mood (part 1). Then, as the music is launched into a climax and stretching (part 2), we suddenly reach a modulating passage (part 3), which, if not in structure (no triplets here), is similar in its repetitive pattern and major/minor-mode alternation (see figure 22).

Figure 22. Parts 2 and 3: Climax and major/minor mode oscillation, from John Williams, "End Credits," from the *Dracula* film score as heard in the film and CD releases (© 1979 BMI), published by USI B Music Publishing (ear transcription). Used in compliance with the US Copyright Act, Section 107.

This modulating passage is followed by another modulating bridge for brass (part 4), which acts like a condensed version of Tchaikovsky's (see figure 23).

Figure 23. Part 4: Modulating brass chords, from John Williams, "End Credits," from the *Dracula* film score as heard in the film and CD releases (© 1979 BMI), published by USI B Music Publishing (ear transcription). Used in compliance with the US Copyright Act, Section 107.

After this, we have the apotheosis-like restatement of the Dracula theme (part 5). This is followed by the musical abatement (part 6), which dies away much as Tchaikovsky's "Scene" does (see figure 24).

Figure 24. Part 6: Musical abatement, from John Williams, "End Credits," from the *Dracula* film score as heard in the film and CD releases (© 1979 BMI), published by USI B Music Publishing (ear transcription). Used in compliance with the US Copyright Act, Section 107.

I do not claim that the two pieces have musical sections that are similar *note-wise*, but I see in them a kindred nature. This potential connection, besides being a possible homage to the 1931 predecessor, would also be a plausible comment upon the elusive cape-flying ending. By evoking *Swan Lake* and its final love/death apotheosis, Williams may give us a hint of what is likely to happen next. In his own words, "in the end of *Dracula*, we have a sense that this love, even if one of them dies, is still there and that they will eventually live it out together in its eternal form. I think somewhere in there lies the *secret* of what the music is conveying."[58] The "secret" conveyed by music might be the veiled reference to *Swan Lake*, turning the death-only apotheosis of Dracula into a delayed love/death apotheosis: unlike in *Swan Lake*, Lucy cannot ascend with him right now, but her smile suggests that she will be looking forward to the moment when they will be finally reunited.

The 1970s saw a revival of interest for the vampire figure and the decade's films, in Deaville's assessment, "unlike the Hammer Studios Dracula films, which featured predictable horror-genre music, . . . displayed a variety of musical approaches, ranging from . . . atmospheric assemblage of stock music . . .

to Donald Rubinstein's 'Baroque-jazz' contemporary score to *Martin*,"[59] Williams's approach is, once again, neoclassical even when serving darker stories. He steers away from not only Hammer's horror clichés but also the modern approaches, instead looking back to the music of the 1930s and 1940s horror films by Universal. The characteristics of the music for the Universal horror cycle are summed up by Rosar:

> the frequent use of the whole-tone scale and augmented triads . . . a marked tendency toward melodic chromaticism. . . . Dissonant, chromatic chords . . . and numerous instances of chromatic progressions. . . . Orchestrally, the use of the organ to color the orchestration. . . . [Quotations of] music from the repertoire of composers of the Romantic period (as exemplified by Liszt and Tchaikovsky). The style of the music composed for these films is also predominantly influenced by composers of the Romantic period and by the "Impressionist" school of Debussy and Ravel. . . . Unlike many of today's horror films which present the viewer with unrelenting horror both visually and on the sound track, reflected in the music with a continuous stream of weird musical sounds, the scores to Universal's films also contain music of considerable beauty and pathos. This music reflects those elements in the films which form a strong dramatic contrast to the horror and create sympathy for the characters.[60]

All these traits, as we have seen, are well present in Williams's *Dracula*, a score that provides the film with "a poignancy and lyricism that underlie even the dramatic and terrifying moments, and at the same time embodies the power, passion and horror of the Dracula figure incarnate in a single musical statement," according to Randall Larson.[61] Williams has produced only one score for the horror genre, but the result succeeds in capturing all the complexity of the Gothic sublime and of the Dracula tradition, while also demonstrating the versatility of Williams's neoclassicism.

CHAPTER 12

Reviving the Hollywood
Music Classics beyond the Films

E ach year the Boston Symphony Orchestra—one of America's "Big Five" orchestras—turns into the Boston Pops Orchestra for the spring/summer season.[1] The programs of the Pops concerts feature light symphonic pieces, spanning from famous opera overtures to selections from operettas, ballet suites, American marches, standard songs, concert extracts, and symphonic arrangements from the latest Broadway hits. The Boston Pops' mission is to bridge the gap between the classical and the popular repertoires and to introduce the concertgoing custom and the sound of a symphony orchestra to wide audiences. Founded in 1885, the Boston Pops—nicknamed "America's Orchestra"—has become one of the country's principal musical institutions, a world ambassador of American culture, and perhaps one of the most widely known orchestras because of its extensive presence on television, radio, and in the record market. The conductor who brought widespread fame to the orchestra and forged its unmistakable identity was Arthur Fiedler, who led the Pops from 1929 until his death in 1979. Fiedler refurbished the traditional three-part program to feature the classics of the symphonic repertoire (e.g., overtures, ballet suites, symphonic poems) in the first part, a soloist from either classical or popular music in the central part, and the most lightweight popular repertoire (cheerful marches or beloved songs in orchestral arrangements) in the third part. He opened the door of symphonic concerts to the Broadway musical repertoire, which increasingly took the place of traditional selections from operas and operettas, to jazz, as well as the Beatles' songs and disco-music hits; in his own words: "There's nothing wrong with playing light music. You don't always read Milton, Shakespeare, and Schopenhauer. You can enjoy Mark Twain."[2]

Fiedler's Boston Pops albums would sell a total of close to fifty million copies. He also pioneered the multimedia expansion, launching local live radio broadcasts in 1952, which then expanded to reach national diffusion in 1962. In 1967 the Pops moved to television, and from 1969 to 2004 it was featured in a regular, nationally aired TV program, *Evening at Pops*; with about 250 episodes in those thirty-five years, it made the Boston Pops the only orchestra in the world with such a visibility.[3] On 4 July 1929 Fiedler had inaugurated the free outdoor Esplanade Concerts on Boston's Charles River Esplanade, a tradition he carried on annually with increasing success. The 4th of July 1976 concert—celebrating the bicentennial of the Declaration of Independence—totaled an attendance of more than four hundred thousand people, marking the record for the largest audience for a symphonic concert at that time.[4] When Fiedler died, on 10 July 1979, at the age of eighty-five—having led the Pops for a staggering fifty years—the BSO management was left with a daunting task: to find a successor to this iconic figure.

John Williams from Hollywood

After a lengthy search for candidates and a painstaking short listing, on 9 January 1980 John Williams was appointed as the nineteenth conductor-in-residence of the Boston Pops Orchestra. Although he was the least experienced in concert conducting among the front-runners, Williams had scored the highest grade among the short-listed conductors in the assessment questionnaires filled out by the orchestra's members.[5] In May 1979 Williams had appeared as a guest conductor twice with the Boston Pops, and those two concert performances must have been favorably impressive to the musicians. Williams accepted the offer: "Nobody could successfully succeed Arthur Fiedler, and some professional conductors might actually damage his or her own career by trying. . . . I had nothing to lose, and I could gain the joy of experiencing a live audience, which we don't have in the studio."[6] In the peak of the neoclassical trend that he launched, Williams's success in bringing back the old-fashioned symphonic sound to mass audiences was arguably the major factor in signing him for the Boston post. One commentator observed: "Perhaps the most fortunate result of Williams' later movie scores is the way in which they exposed the general movie audience to the symphonic sound. In this way, he is similar to Fiedler, whose televised performances with the Boston Pops brought symphonic sound to the TV masses."[7] The current Boston Pops conductor, Keith Lockhart, elaborates on the significance of that appointment: "That changed the viewpoint of the way film music was perceived in the broader world of orchestral music. . . . That's not his music specifically; it's taking a Hollywood composer seriously enough to give him a position in the

world of orchestral music, which is the starchiest and most rigid of all performing arts."[8] Indeed, that was the first time in which a prominent and
highly successful Hollywood composer was given the leadership of such an
important musical institution.[9]

The initial reactions to Williams's appointment were generally positive,
some even enthusiastic. For instance, André Previn, then conductor-in-
residence of the London Symphony, explained:

> Anybody who thinks John Williams is just a Hollywood musician is completely
> wrong. He is such a good musician, so thorough, so completely schooled. John
> is damned fortunate at this stage of his career that the job at the Pops should
> open. . . . At the same time, the Pops is lucky that John is available. He is a first-
> class pianist, and he knows a terrific amount of music. . . . He can make superla-
> tive arrangements of pop materials, and he can edit, fix, handle anything that
> comes up in someone else's arrangement, make it better, and all in a matter of
> minutes. . . . He is also a very efficient conductor; the players of the London
> Symphony Orchestra, who have recorded several film scores with him, are full
> of admiration. They say there's no nonsense about him, that he knows what he
> wants and he knows how to get it.[10]

Jaws producer David Brown commented upon Williams's election: "His
appointment to the Pops lends great prestige to the entire movie industry."[11]
Similarly, the reviews of his inaugural Boston concert on 29 April 1980 were
largely favorable: "A new era began tonight for the Boston Pops Orchestra
as John Williams, the award-winning film composer who was named the Pops
conductor three months ago to succeed the late Arthur Fiedler, put down
his baton at the end of his first public performance and was greeted with a
sustained roar of applause."[12] However, this trespassing from the commercial
film music into the "sacred" concert hall territories did not pass unnoticed by
some "cultural guardians," who chastised the outrageous affront. The most
bitter reaction came from Jordan N. Whitelaw, producer of the TV series
Evening at Symphony, who commented: "Williams made no impression on me
whatsoever. His music shouldn't happen to a dog."[13]

The Boston Pops post was a unique chance for Williams to advance a further step in his effort to revive classical Hollywood music. From such a prestigious podium, he could contribute in creating a canon of Hollywood music
and disseminate the best pieces in live concerts, radio and TV broadcasts, and
orchestral albums. Williams had the opportunity to crack the "iron curtain"

that had been keeping film music out of concert programs on the grounds of prejudicial points. Film music can be a source of legitimate music and an important repertoire from which symphonic pieces can be drawn for symphonic popular programs as those of the Boston Pops. In the first press conference, Williams described his plans for the Pops and the goals that he wanted to achieve, one of which was that "it is possible that I can bring prestige to the best film music by presenting it in a concert format. Only one half of one percent of the music written in the nineteenth century is anything we ever hear today; surely there must be at least that percentage of good music written for films."[14] To give film music a better recognition did not simply mean to increase the amount of film music in concert programs—Fiedler programmed film music too—but it meant to have a more attentive care for quality.

Fiedler used to choose film music written in a pop language, something akin to the pop song repertoire. He looked for something accessible that could fit the third part of the programs, reserved for what he called "gumdrops."[15] Fiedler preferred new pieces with a recent successful performance in the easy-listening record charts—"Lara's Theme" from *Dr. Zhivago* (David Lean, 1965, music by Maurice Jarre) and "Gonna Fly Now" from *Rocky* (John G. Avildsen, 1976, music by Bill Conti), to name two—or marketable songs featured in a film's soundtrack: for example, "The Way We Were" (lyrics by Alan and Marilyn Bergman, music by Marvin Hamlisch, from *The Way We Were*, Sidney Pollack, 1973) and "Raindrops Keep Falling on My Head" (lyrics by Hal David, music by Burt Bacharach, from *Butch Cassidy*, George Roy Hill, 1969). After the unprecedented sales of the *Star Wars* symphonic album, from 1978 on, there was an obvious increase in the quantity of film music presented in the Fiedler programs. There was also a slight change in preference for pieces that were notable for being prominent examples of film music rather than for being prominent hits on the pop charts. Concerts featuring more numerous film-music selections were held in both the 1978 and 1979 seasons. From a *quantitative* perspective, in those seasons Fiedler did give more importance to film music. However, from a *qualitative* perspective, things remained unchanged: Fiedler's preference was again for pop language and easy-listening sounds. Regardless of the origin of the music, whether from Broadway, Hollywood, or pop music top-ten charts, Fiedler would have all the new pieces arranged according to his idea of popular music and conformed to the standard Pops sound, which in his final years consisted of a thick sound either loudly showy and band-like or old-fashioned and sentimentally bel canto–like. In 1978, for example, Fiedler programmed the main theme from *Star Wars* not in its original orchestration but in an arrangement titled "Theme and Dance [!] from Star Wars." The arrangement starts with a band-like rendition of the main theme in which the canon-like structure of the opening fanfare was elided, as well as every sign of contrapuntal writing, and showy cymbal clashes were gratuitously added all over to spice it up. Then, an incongruous Spanish-sounding bridge is introduced, leading to a Charleston-like version of "Cantina Band," the diegetic piece that can be heard in the background during the Mos Eisley scene in the film.[16] When Fiedler chose to play film music, he chose it not as film music but as a subgenre of the up-to-date pop genre, fitting for the third part of the program.

On the contrary, Williams's approach to film music was quality driven. He would search the film-music repertoire not merely to find trendy pop pieces but to find musically interesting pieces. Film music is seen as an art to be taken more seriously and as a repertoire that could provide musically legitimate material. The first sign of this different view was the placement of film-music entries in Williams's programs. He began to include film-music pieces in the first part too, which was traditionally reserved for the art-music classics. This apparently inconspicuous change actually had a groundbreaking meaning: now film music was put on the same level with concert music. The 7 May 1980 concert did not open with music from the opera or ballet repertoire but with Erich Wolfgang Korngold's overture to The Sea Hawk from his film score for the 1940 Michael Curtiz swashbuckler. Williams also approached film music with an unprecedented philological care. Unlike previous cases like "Theme and Dance from Star Wars," Williams presented the original versions—not only for film-music classics like Korngold's but also for contemporary works like those by Jerry Goldsmith.[17] If the originals were not available, Williams would commission new arrangements based on the author's authentic orchestration reconstructed from surviving orchestral parts and from the film's music track. For example, Williams commissioned Alexander Courage to reconstruct Conrad Salinger's original orchestration of "Singin' in the Rain" and premiered the piece on 12 May 1981. Courage was only one of the top orchestrators and arrangers that Williams brought along from Hollywood, the others being Angela Morley, Morton Stevens, Sid Ramin, Eddie Karam, and Herbert Spencer.

"Artistic and Creative Differences"

In a brief press statement on 13 June 1984, Williams announced his resignation from the Boston Pops due to "artistic and creative differences between myself and the orchestra."[18] According to a widely spread rumor, the inciting incident was that during the rehearsal of 12 June, some players in the orchestra had hissed at Williams's new piece *America, the Dream Goes On*.[19] In the following days, more reports were published in the newspapers, adding details about the notorious demotivated and careless attitude of the orchestra members during Pops rehearsals. It emerged that such low morale and bad attitudes were inherited from and had been constant since the final decade of the Fiedler era.[20] After receiving apologies from and meeting with the musicians, on 3 August, Williams withdrew his resignation. His concern, he stated, had been not so much the orchestra discipline as their low morale, and the "artistic and creative differences" were over the status of popular music: "The high point of my music year is coming to Boston. . . . To them, it's playtime, but to me it's serious. I wanted to express my musical goals pretty high. It was kind of an attitudinal disagreement."[21] Williams then called a number of assemblies with the orchestra members. Many were worried that playing the light repertoire could weaken their technique and affect their skills. In response, Williams launched a series of changes to make the orchestra members feel more gratified when playing in the Pops.[22] Musicians welcomed Williams's return and were particularly pleased with his involvement in listening to their complaints and proposals, and in trying to accommodate their needs.[23] The biggest innovation was a new clause, which would allow BSO players to opt not to play in the Pops, thus transforming the orchestra into a more motivated and cooperative group.[24] Williams also carried on with his policy of featuring musically interesting, high-quality arrangements, with reciprocally satisfying results: "The biggest thrill I've gotten out of Boston is when some players have come to me after the season and said, 'That was great, we had a real stretch, and the brass players had a wonderful blow, and we got to Tanglewood [BSO's summer season] in better shape than ever before, because of what the Pops repertoire was able to do for us.' That is the biggest praise I could get."[25]

After the 1984 crisis, Williams led the Pops for another nine seasons, in which he disseminated the classical film-music canon through the PBS TV show *Evening at Pops*, dozens of best-selling orchestral albums, tours around the United States, and three trips to Japan (1987, 1990, 1993). At the end of the 1993 season, though, Williams left the demanding job to concentrate more on composition and private life.[26] *Boston Globe* music critic Richard Dyer described Williams's overall contribution:

> The statistics on his tenure are pretty staggering: 13 seasons [*sic* 14], more than 300 concerts [ca. 600 in fact], six national or international tours, 24 premières

and commissions, 28 CDs and nearly 50 television shows. Along the way, Williams has brought some of the leading artists of several musical worlds to the Pops. . . . Williams took from Fiedler what worked: the shape of the program, the mix of music, putting the spotlight not only on celebrities but on members of the orchestra and young musicians. Williams improved discipline and morale and raised the standard of performance.[27]

In the 1994 season, Williams agreed to lead the Pops during the transition period as its conductor emeritus, leading most of the concerts and helping the committee as a musical consultant in its search for a successor.[28] In 1995 Keith Lockhart was named twentieth conductor-in-residence of the Boston Pops, while Williams has since maintained a steady relationship with the institution, appearing several times each year with the title of "Boston Pops Laureate Conductor."

Williams's Multimedia Experiments

Since his retirement, Williams has specialized in multimedia forms of concert presentation, which have become the trademark of his concerts. Film clips are projected onto a big screen above the stage as the orchestra plays the related music live. The resulting experience is one that combines the live music performance with the visual or audiovisual prerecorded medium; in these concerts, the soundtrack is generally completely discarded from the projected clips, but sometimes parts of the dialogue or sound effects are kept and played through the hall's sound system. Film music, performed as concert piece, progresses from an ancillary to a leading role, allowing the listeners to concentrate on the music without the distractions from the images and the other elements of the soundtrack. On the other hand, in such a setting, film music loses part of its essence. When film music is separated from its visual counterpart, one cannot fully appreciate the specific work beyond the strictly musical one. A good film composer has to be not only a good musician but also as precise as the finest tailor while "measuring" and "cutting" the music onto the film, and as acute and visual sensitive as a portraitist while he "paints" on the musical canvas what he sees on the screen.[29] Restoring this audiovisual coupling in the concert halls may prove a good way to enhance the experience and provide a truly "specific" concert presentation of film music.[30]

Although cases of audiovisual film concerts have been occurring since the early nineties (for example, the 1992 *David Lean Tribute* at the Royal Albert Hall in London conducted by Maurice Jarre), Williams and the Boston Pops have been regularly performing such "multimedia film music" since 1993 with unmatched sync precision, variety, and flair—"the most immaculate sync," as Angela Morley praised Williams's conducting of these multimedia concert pieces.[31] On 12 May 1993, in "A Gala Celebration for John Williams," the farewell concert for his last season as conductor of the Pops, Williams launched his experiments and surpassed in quality and virtuosity the previous attempts. During the event, he and actor Richard Dreyfuss teamed up to treat the audience with a special surprise: a demonstration of how film music works. After a few introductory words by Dreyfuss, the "Barrel Chase Sequence" from *Jaws* was screened without music. The same footage was then screened again, but this time with music, performed live and in perfect sync. Following this, a spectacular eight-minute medley of Williams's most famous themes from *Star Wars* to *Superman* to *Indiana Jones* to *E.T.* was played, accompanied by clips from the related films. Particularly spectacular are those cases, like the "Barrel Chase Sequence," in which an entire scene or sequence from a film is presented with its original score played live. The re-creation of the audiovisual coupling that once happened in the controlled and secluded setting of the recording stage—where retakes are possible and frequent in case of lost synchronization—is now reenacted in the "unsafe" setting of the concert stage, before an audience, without the possibility of adjusting a bad synchronization. Williams has since become one of the most accomplished conductors of multimedia film-music presentations.

On 16 March 2002, on the occasion of the twentieth anniversary of *E.T. the Extra-Terrestrial*, Williams extended this form of multimedia presentation to an entire film. With the Recording Arts Orchestra of Los Angeles, he conducted the full score live throughout the film, something often performed with silent films but unheard of with such a complex and musically rich sound film. One offspring of Williams's duodecennial experiments in multimedia was *Star Wars in Concert*, a multimedia road show that debuted on 1 October 2009. It featured music from the double trilogy performed by the Royal Philharmonic Orchestra and Chorus conducted by Dirk Brossé. The package was complemented by *Star Wars* actor Antony Daniels (C3-PO) as narrator, projected clips from the films, smoke and laser-light effects, and a coherently spaceship-shaped stage. The next development has been to turn Williams's multimedia experiments into packaged shows that could be rented to any interested orchestra. The technological advancements of digital projection and sync-aiding software made it possible to set up such shows more easily than in the past.[32] Thus the number of presentations of entire films accompanied live has skyrocketed in the last ten years, with "Film Concerts" of *The Lord of the Rings* (trilogy), *Harry Potter* (saga), *Back to the Future*, *Gladiator*, Hollywood classics like *Singin' in the Rain* and *The Wizard of Oz*, as well as the most beloved works by Williams.[33] *Variety*'s Jon Burlingame reports: "After years of looking down their collective noses at film music as unworthy of performance alongside, say, Beethoven or Wagner, orchestras from the Chicago Symphony to the New York Philharmonic are jumping on the bandwagon, playing classic film scores 'live to picture' in growing numbers. 'It's gone from an occasional novelty to being a vital part of the concert-going experience,' says Brian Grohl, pops program manager at the Hollywood Bowl."[34]

Williams's Legacy

After his retirement, Williams's innovations and the repertoire he built during his tenure are still part of the Boston Pops concerts. Film music remains a staple of the Pops programs, as well as multimedia presentations. In 2006 a fixed panoramic screen—covering the entire length of the stage—was installed in Boston Symphony Hall, replacing the temporary "Film Night" setting. Now an integral "multimedia" part of the Pops stage, the screen is also used by the present Pops conductor, Keith Lockhart, for multimedia performances of non-film music too, in order to enhance the experience.[35] Lockhart has also become—along with David Newman and Richard Kaufman—one of the most experienced and active conductors of the live-to-film concerts in the US: the Pops season now regularly includes at least one "Film Concert" each year. John Williams's conductorship of the Boston Pops and his commitment to legitimize film music in concerts have had a large influence on other orchestras as well. As for other Pops orchestras in the US, an evident increase in their number and activities during and particularly following Williams's tenure is evident.[36] In particular, the Cincinnati Pops and the Hollywood Bowl Orchestra—the former launched during the final years of Fiedler's tenure and the latter established in the final years of Williams's—are both very active in the promotion and live presentations of film music.

The Cincinnati Pops (founded in 1977) is second only to the Boston Pops as far as television and record-market exposure and international reputation. Its founder, Erich Kunzel, appeared thirty-seven times as a guest conductor of the Boston Pops between 1977 and 2009 and followed the Bostonian model closely. In 1984 Kunzel recorded his first film-music album, *Star Tracks*, devoted to Williams's music for *Star Wars*, *Superman*, *Close Encounters of the Third Kind*, *Raiders of the Lost Ark*, and *E.T.*, all in the wake of the commercial success of

Williams and the Pops' 1980 space-music album, *Pops in Space*.[37] In 2005 on the release of the final episode of the second *Star Wars* trilogy, Kunzel conducted a series of concerts centered on Williams's scores for the six films.[38] The Hollywood Bowl Orchestra was founded in 1991 and its conductorship given to John Mauceri, who had regularly appeared as a guest conductor of the Boston Pops (twenty-six times between 1979 and 1994). Mauceri soon proved to be in line with Williams's belief that each genre of music requires respect and care and that film music is a legitimate repertoire for concerts. In Mauceri's first album with the orchestra (*Hollywood Dreams*), pieces from the art-music repertoire are presented side by side with film music, with composers spanning from Arnold Schoenberg, Igor Stravinsky, and Sergei Prokofiev to Williams, Max Steiner, Alfred Newman, Erich Wolfgang Korngold, John Barry, Franz Waxman, Leonard Bernstein, and even selections from *The Wizard of Oz* (Victor Fleming, 1939, music by Harold Arlen and Herbert Stothart). Mauceri also shares with Williams the same philological accuracy and search for the originals when dealing with film music.[39]

Film music has increasingly become a frequent feature in the programs of both major and minor orchestras. Beginning in November 1991, *Film Score Monthly* has had a column listing all the concerts featuring film music around the world.[40] The variety that can be perceived reading through the issues of the magazine, far too wide to be reported here, has further spiked in recent years. For example, a film-music concert was held during the Atlanta Olympics in 1996, on 26 July.[41] A prestigious tribute to the classical Hollywood composers was paid by the US Postal Service in 1999 with the issuing of six commemorative stamps portraying Max Steiner, Erich Wolfgang Korngold, Alfred Newman, Franz Waxman, Bernard Herrmann, and Dimitri Tiomkin in the Legends of American Music series, thus acknowledging Hollywood film music as an important part of the American heritage.[42] On 11 September 2004 Michael Tilson Thomas opened the symphonic season of the San Francisco Symphony Orchestra with a program featuring Bernard Herrmann's suite from *Vertigo* (Alfred Hitchcock, 1958) along with Debussy's *La Mer* (1905), Copland's *Danzón Cubano* (1942), and Gershwin's *An American in Paris* (1928).[43] Beginning with the 2003–4 season, the Chicago Symphony started a series of recurring concerts titled "Friday Night at the Movies."[44]

Abroad as well, one can observe many signs of a "détente" in the so-called cold war between applied film music and absolute art music. In 1992 Zubin Mehta and the Israel Philharmonic recorded Franz Waxman's *Carmen Fantasy* from his film score for *Humoresque* (Jean Negulesco, 1946) alongside music by

Paganini and Saint-Saëns.[45] In London, the Royal Academy of Music in collaboration with the British Film Institute (BFI) dedicated the eleventh edition
of the International Composers Festival to film music (16–22 June 1996).[46]
In 2004 the London Symphony Orchestra celebrated the first centennial of
the "powerful relationship between music and the movies" with an American
tour presenting film music concerts.[47] In Italy, on 10 October 2004, Leonard
Rosenman was celebrated by the Roma Sinfonietta at the Rome Auditorium
with a program of his film works.[48] In Leipzig, Germany, the prestigious
Gewandhausorchester played Bernard Herrmann's film works on 23 January
1998 (the overture from *The Man Who Knew Too Much*, a suite from *Marnie*,
and the prelude from *North by Northwest*).[49] In Spain, on 4 and 7 November
1998, Jerry Goldsmith was invited to conduct two concerts in Seville with the
Real Orquesta Sinfónica.[50] In Warsaw, Poland, Elmer Bernstein was invited to
conduct a concert on 25 May 2000 within the "Viva Arts Festival."[51] On 8 June
2010 the Wiener Philharmoniker played a selection from *Star Wars* along with
music by Josef Strauss, Liszt, and Holst during its annual "Sommernachtskonzert" outdoor concert in the park of the Schönbrunn castle. In 2015 Simon
Rattle and the Berliner Philharmoniker devoted the Sommernachtskonzert
at the Waldbühne to a program of Hollywood classics that included music
by Bronislau Kaper, Miklós Rózsa, Scott Bradley, Erich Wolfgang Korngold,
Jerome Moross, David Raksin, Alfred Newmann, and Williams—it was the
first time that the highly regarded German orchestra tackled the film-music
repertoire this extensively.[52] If one reads through the archives of London's
renowned BBC Proms, an increasing presence of film music alongside concert pieces from the canonical repertoire can be noticed, to the point that film
music has now become a regular ingredient. For example, in the concert of
10 September 2005, the suite from Korngold's *The Sea Hawk* was presented
along with pieces by Purcell, Handel, and Elgar; in the concert of 24 July 1999,
Williams's "Main Title" from *Star Wars* shared the stage with Haydn, Stravinsky, Prokofiev, and Saint-Saëns. A number of special concerts centered
on the film-music repertoire have also been increasingly held, like "Hollywood" conducted by Carl Davis on 31 July 1999; the Elmer Bernstein concert
on 14 August 2001; the English film-music-themed concert on 14 July 2007; or
the numerous appearances of the John Wilson Orchestra.[53] In Denmark, the
Danish National Symphony Orchestra has recently launched a series of film-
themes programs. Ensembles specializing in film music have been founded
(for example, the Swiss 21st Century Symphony, or the Film Symphony
Orchestra in Spain) and annual film-music festivals enjoy a steady success—

the Filmucité in Tenerife, the Hollywood in Vienna (where the Max Steiner Film Music Achievement Award is assigned), or the film-music concerts and seminars at the Film Fest Gent in Belgium (also home to the World Soundtrack Awards). Even in Italy, where the concert-music circles have long been characterized by a highbrow disdain for all things popular, Williams's music has not only been increasingly admitted into the programs, but entire concerts are being devoted to his music—for example, the recurrent *Star Wars* concerts conducted by Simone Pedroni with the Milan Symphony Orchestra. Lockhart, who is also the principal conductor of London's BBC Concert Orchestra, concludes:

> I think because of John Williams there has been an explosion in the way that orchestras all over the country and the world have embraced film music. . . . I think it is a recognition by the orchestral world that the world of film scores is the popular interface with the world of orchestras. It's kind of like opera was at the beginning of the seventeenth century, or like ballet scores during the nineteenth century. . . . So in a way, if the light classical music of the nineteenth century was Von Suppé overtures, Rossini and Delibes, that sort of thing, the light classical music of this century, from 1930-something on, is film music.[54]

As to Williams, after his retirement from the Pops, he has remained an active and much sought-after conductor. He has been a regular guest conductor for the major American orchestras, and in addition to his longtime annual appearances at the Hollywood Bowl with the Los Angeles Philharmonic, Williams has enjoyed steadfast collaborations with the New York Philharmonic and the Chicago Symphony, bringing film music to those prestigious concert stages too. In 1996 Williams was invited to conduct a concert at the Royal Academy of Music in London; in 1998 he held a film-music composition seminar at the revered Tanglewood Music Center; and in 2003 he collaborated with Leonard Slatkin, the conductor of the National Symphony Orchestra in Washington at that time, in the organization of a film-music festival in Washington, DC, titled "Soundtrack: Music and Film."[55] The festival ran from 21 January to 1 February and consisted of six film-music concerts, conferences, and panel discussions moderated and animated by Slatkin and Williams themselves and by the film-music historian Jon Burlingame and the famed film director Stanley Donen.[56] In 2009 Gustavo Dudamel, newly appointed artistic director of the Los Angeles Philharmonic, invited Williams to conduct three film-music concerts, in the first part of the symphonic season, titled "Music from the City of Angels," acknowledging Hollywood film music as a major Los Angeles contribution to the music repertoire. Among the new-generation conductors, Dudamel is, with Stéfane Denève, one of the most ardent promoters and admirers of Williams's work. Denève considers Williams's music "first class" and has brought his music, for both film and the concert stage, all over the world, from the podium of the Philadelphia Orchestra to that of Rome's Accademia di Santa Cecilia, often inviting the composer to share the conducting duties with him.[57] Dudamel has made Williams's film music a staple of his repertoire, frequently including it in his programs, and dedicated two entire Los Angeles Philharmonic concerts to the composer, in 2014 and 2019. Dudamel also got to guest-conduct the studio orchestra during the recording of *Star Wars: Episode VII—The Force Awakens* (J. J. Abrams, 2015), and commented, "It was such a privilege to stand next to this genius and conduct this music I've been in love with all my life."[58] Williams's film music works in the film—which is something people have long realized—but it also works on the concert stage: it is good music to play. Lockhart, a deep connoisseur of the classical repertoire and of Williams's, explains:

> John's music is very demanding, and it's demanding in a good way. There are film composers whose music is difficult to play especially in live-concert situations because, honestly, they are less skilled composers. There are difficulties because of the inadequacy of the material. Occasionally you see things with other composers that are simply unplayable. I mean, it might be assemblable in a studio environment where you can patch soundtrack cues together from many takes into one. Or they're demanding just because they are exhaustively repetitive, or something like that. On the other hand, there is a kind of musical difficulty that arises because the composer knows the orchestra well enough to write to the full extent of performers' abilities. And John's music is demanding in this last sense. When you look at the symphonic repertoire, at, for example, Gustav Mahler . . . you see things that were written absolutely to the limits of the players' individual technique. But nobody would ever argue that Mahler symphonies were "unplayable," because the composer has a mastery and knowledge of the instruments they are writing for. . . . The basic thing is that, as opposed to a lot of other film music, John's music is extremely involved and highly difficult, and actually requires the same amount of rehearsal time one might give to a piece in the more core classical repertoire. But on the other hand it also bears a fruit, artistically, that's worth the difficulty. One of the other things that makes his music particularly different is its integrity. It's possible to

do film-music concerts of almost anybody's music. . . . But rarely is there somebody whose music is able to sustain enough interest if you take the film away, that is compelling enough to perform it on its own for a live audience. That to me is what distinguishes Williams's music.[59]

Lockhart's positive assessment is now largely shared, even by orchestras that, up to a few years ago, would have never touched film music. According to the annual "Classical Music Statistics" by Bachtrack.com, in 2019 Williams was the most performed living composer, surpassing Arvo Pärt.[60] The 2020 Princess of Asturias Award for the Arts—one of Spain's top accolades—was co-assigned to Ennio Morricone and John Williams "in recognition of the fundamental value of musical composition for film," praising Williams for transferring "the spirit of the Viennese symphonic tradition to Hollywood blockbusters."[61] On 18 and 19 January 2020 Williams conducted the Wiener Philharmoniker in two concerts that can be rightly called historic. It was the first time that a "film composer" was invited to the celebrated Goldener Saal of the Musikverein in Vienna—the venue of the annual New Year's Concert, a hall whose acoustics are considered among the very best in the world—by the prestigious (and notoriously traditional) Vienna orchestra to perform an entire program of film music. Joining Williams was the virtuoso classical violinist (and Williams enthusiast) Anne-Sophie Mutter as soloist. The concert was reviewed favorably even by the *Wiener Zeitung*, once the rostrum of the nineteenth-century musicologist Eduard Hanslick, one of the promoters of "Absolute Musik" and a defender of the purity of the musical beauty against the contamination from extramusical references or practical uses.[62] On 18 November 2020 Williams was awarded the coveted Gold Medal of London's Royal Philharmonic Society, defined as "one of the most privileged honours in the world of music."[63] Launched in 1870 in celebration of the centennial of Beethoven's birth and since then "awarded internationally for the most outstanding musicianship," its roster of recipients includes such eminent musicians as Johannes Brahms, Edward Elgar, Sergei Rachmaninov, Richard Strauss, Arturo Toscanini, Serge Prokofiev, William Walton, Igor Stravinsky, Herbert von Karajan, Leonard Bernstein, Pierre Boulez, and many others who cannot be all listed here.[64] The motivation for Williams's induction in the Gold Medal ranks is the fact that he "dedicated his life to ensuring orchestral music continues to speak and captivate people worldwide" and "for his shining achievements introducing millions to orchestral music who may otherwise never have encountered it."[65]

In 1993 *Boston Globe* music critic Richard Dyer had already noted: "The main reason Williams took the job in 1980 was to win greater recognition for the artistic legitimacy of his life work in film and the life work of many of his colleagues. Whether he succeeded in that aim (it's too early to tell), he certainly brought film music out of the background and into the limelight."[66] John Williams's conductorship of the Boston Pops has been an integral part of his commitment to revive classical Hollywood music, a facet of his double life as a composer/conductor that proved seminal in the creation and acknowledgment of a canon of the Hollywood music classics. The invitation of Williams to Vienna—an event also celebrated by the classical recording-label par excellence, Deutsche Grammophon, with the release of the CD and Blu-ray *John Williams Live in Vienna*—can easily be seen as the ideal point of arrival of Williams's multidecade commitment to the cause of quality-driven film music and its dissemination. It can be argued that now film music has eventually secured a legitimization and an acceptance into the concert-music repertoire. This was made possible in large part by John Williams's groundbreaking work, not only as the renowned talented and successful composer but also as a committed and pioneering conductor.

Closing Remarks on Neoclassicism and Today's Hollywood Music

U ltimately, the impact of neoclassicism was quite limited. In Jeff Smith's words, "despite a major revival in the Korngold-styled scores of John Williams, Romanticism's hold on film scoring was further weakened by the incorporation of rock, folk, and soul elements in the 1960s and 1970s, and electronics, minimalism, and even New Age elements in the 1980s. By the 1990s, Romantic-styled film music was still being composed, but it was merely one stylistic option among many."[1] In the first two decades of the 2000s, besides the aforementioned idioms and stylistic options growing in importance, the hierarchy of the three elements of the soundtrack—sound effects, music, and dialogue—underwent a remarkable reshaping. During the classical period, dialogue's "intelligibility" was the primary preoccupation, and sound engineers made sure that priority should be given to dialogue, then to the accompanying music, and then to ambient sound and dramatically salient sound effects.[2] In the 1970s, technological innovations like the Dolby system allowed for a more detailed recording and reproduction fidelity of the diverse sound components.[3] The term "sound designer" was introduced in that decade to identify the person in charge of supervising the now exceedingly more nuanced balance of sonic elements—one of these new figures was Ben Burtt, whose work on the first *Star Wars* trilogy was pioneering.[4] Yet, in such 1970s and 1980s films as *Star Wars* (George Lucas, 1977) or *Raiders of the Lost Ark* (Steven Spielberg, 1981), the sound component and the music component still remained largely distinguishable. John Williams was the one in charge of penning and dramaturgically developing Darth Vader's leitmotif or the Ewoks' march or the Ark's theme; Ben Burtt was the one in charge of devising the sound of Darth Vader's respirator or of the Ewoks' language or of a pit full of slithering snakes. K. J. Donnelly correctly remarked that "music and sounds have never been really separable."[5]

Yet it could be said that it was at this point, in the 1970s and 1980s, that music and sounds had reached a position of parity and equal importance, paving the way to a truly "integrated soundtrack," to use today's definition.[6] In more recent years, that equilibrium has broken, with "music" in the traditional sense slipping down in importance to the lowest position.

Laurent Jullier has identified, in what he calls "film concert," a predominant characteristic of contemporary cinema, which consists in "the prevailing of the sound dimension over the visual one: the soundtrack embraces the viewer and occupies the frequency spectrum almost entirely."[7] The Digital Audio Workstations (DAW) used for sound design were first developed to compose music; most sound engineers have a musical background, and the increasingly refined sound-reproduction technologies implement high fidelity and spatialized sound to an unprecedented extent, allowing for the minutest detail to emerge. Contrary to what could be expected with these seemingly favorable environments and conducive technologies, the role of music in the contemporary Hollywood "film concert" is anything but dominant. There is a large quantity of music, surely, but its role has mostly been demoted to that of an anonymous background. To use an actor's simile, if in the past music happened to have the chance to land protagonistic roles in the foreground, now there is much music in the background, as there are many extras packed in the background of crowd scenes. Film music is primarily designed so as to dovetail with the sound effects, to serve as a kind of binding substrate for or a supplement to the sound-effect track.[8]

That film music could not expect to have the viewer's full attention and a foregrounded position in the mix is not a novelty, of course, and sound effects have long posed audibility problems for music.[9] Yet this "competition" between music and sound effects has intensified in the 1990s. The composer Danny Elfman, whose scores for *Batman* (Tim Burton, 1989) and *Dick Tracy* (Warren Beatty, 1990) follow a neoclassical approach, had already voiced the discontent in a 1995 interview: "Contemporary dubs to my ears are getting busier and more shrill every year. The dubbers actually think they're doing a great job for the music if a crescendo or a horn blast occasionally pops through the wall of sound."[10] Twenty years later, there seems to be no more competition: sound effects have apparently gained the upper hand. Digital technologies have made it possible to mix hundreds of effect tracks—with sound engineers producing sound mixes of remarkable architectural complexity to create a surrounding and hyperrealistic aural "super-field."[11] Sound effects are often so intrusive that it is not only music that has to fight for audibility: even dialogue seems to be often sidelined by clashes and explosions, or given a position so secondary in the mix that the choice results as detrimental to comprehension and audibility—as some lamented in particular as to Christopher Nolan's *Tenet* (2020).[12] From the year 2000, we could individuate a new period in Hollywood film-music historiography. If 1978 opened a period that, after James Wierzbicki, can be called "eclectic style," I submit that the current post-2000 period could be called "sound design style."[13] Danijela Kulezic-Wilson, one of the foremost specialists in the current film-sound aesthetics, has declared that "sound design is the new score."[14]

In the final decade of the "eclectic style," elements of pop, electronic, and minimalist music were already superseding neoclassical scoring, and increasingly significant and widespread signs of a technological and stylistic change could be detected around the year 2000.[15] Hans Zimmer can be considered the leading figure in today's "sound design style." Zimmer, active since the late 1980s, has proven to be endowed with astute musico-dramaturgical acumen and a keen understanding of audiovisual narration. He has successfully blended the three leading film-music trends of that decade—minimalism (e.g., Philip Glass, Michael Nyman), electronic music (e.g., Vangelis, Tangerine Dream), and the use of large symphony orchestras (e.g., John Williams, Jerry Goldsmith)—into a recognizable and personal style that includes well-distinguishable "Zimmerisms."[16] The two most defining characteristics of Zimmer's approach are probably teamwork and computer technology. Zimmer's modus operandi is openly collectivist, his policy being that of having a pool of talents that is coordinated by himself acting more as a music producer, talent scout, and sound designer than as a composer in the old sense—the one who writes down the notes on paper—in a "collaborative atmosphere—often unabashedly friendly to ghostwriting," as Frank Lehman remarks.[17] In *Pirates of the Caribbean: On Stranger Tides* (Rob Marshall, 2011), Hans Zimmer is listed as the film's composer, but if we read through the end credits, we can spot as many as seven "additional music" composers, and the result is seamless, a testament to the well-homogenized collective work. As to style, as Lehman notes, Zimmer is a "maximal minimalist" whose very direct music has no virtuoso-writing pretensions that would require aural foregrounding:

> Zimmer's musical vocabulary is limited and mostly quite conventional; he seemingly has little interest in harmony outside the tonal Common Practice, and certainly not with genuine avant-garde or modernist idioms. His cues are often thickly scored, but without being finely wrought contrapuntally.

Countermelodies are fleeting, genuine independence of lines is rare (but not nonexistent), and often the middle range of the orchestra is treated purely as a vehicle for static sustained chord tones (if it is filled at all). . . . The composer's predilection for digital augmentation can yield a distinctly overproduced sound, where every detail is manipulated somehow and the individuality of component parts is sacrificed for a holistic impression of busy loudness.[18]

Like commercial techno music, this is music that is "felt" more than listened to, having a strong, visceral, and immediate impact on the listener, even bodily—as when one can feel the soundwaves of a subwoofer pounding on their belly. Such music blends very effectively with the aggressive sound design of contemporary cinema and is, allegedly, "loved by directors, producers and cinema-goers worldwide."[19] Among academics, such visceral music is an ideal object of study within the current discourses about "embodiment," "immersion," "haptic experience," and "materiality," as well as for phenomenological approaches to media studies.[20] Yet, in terms of concrete output, the "Zimmer School"—his epigones more than Zimmer himself—often sounds as if mechanically applying a prescribed style to all films instead of responding more discernibly to the demands of the single film. "Zimmer's commercial influence, which is enabled by a literal company of like-minded and well-networked composers, cannot help but institute a degree of uniformity of sound and style," notes Lehman.[21] Standardization is as old as Hollywood, but one of the characteristics of the top old Hollywood composers, versatility, seems to be now seriously on the wane, in favor of "a slick but somewhat anonymous style that fits seamlessly with risk-averse corporate film-making," in Buhler and Neumeyer's words.[22] In *Sherlock Holmes: A Game of Shadows* (Guy Ritchie, 2011), in the sequence at the Opéra de Paris, we even witness the "Zimmerization" of the diegetic performance of Mozart's *Don Giovanni* (1787): the original score was, evidently, too terse for today's standards and was subjected to a thicker and louder reorchestration to make it compliant with the now generally prescribed sonic style. The same happens in the NBC miniseries *Dracula* (2013), whose "maximal minimalist" music is by Trevor Morris: at the party in Dracula's mansion in episode 1, the diegetic late nineteenth-century acoustic chamber orchestra that accompanies the dances has the exact same Zimmer-like sound as the nondiegetic music, without any consideration for making the diegetic music consistent with the period set designs and costumes—which are not so "steampunk" as to motivate a synthetic sound coming from the acoustic diegetic orchestra too. The application of a trendy sound seems to override more specific and divergent needs that the single film might have. This sameness might be an ingredient of the success of Zimmer and his epigones: to have found a ready-made and successfully employable sonic style that perfectly reflects the technology-determined formulas of today's Hollywood: "Part of Zimmer's appeal to filmmakers is specifically that he is not as stylistically chameleonic as, say, John Williams (who can do a convincing Zimmer impression, though I have not yet observed the reverse). Zimmer cannot help but speak in his own, immensely distinctive voice," comments Frank Lehman.[23]

Film music is now more about *designing* soundscapes rather than *composing* music in the traditional meaning of the term. An example of this "sound design style" from the Christopher Nolan / Hans Zimmer collaboration is *Dunkirk* (2017): a continuous soundscape envelops the film and it is often difficult (and pointless) to tell which is music and which is sound effects—for example, in the beached trawler sequence, with the music's clocklike tickling blended with the sound of the bullets piercing the hull. To achieve such sound-design quality, today a composer must work with music software, DAWs, and digitized sound samples. With computer technology, the process of music production has considerably quickened. On the one hand, this makes composition easier, allowing for time-saving workarounds—for example, automatically extracting parts from a digital full score. On the other hand, in a vicious circle, producers and executives have immediately exploited the time-saving qualities of the new technologies to further compress the time they grant composers to deliver the music. In the old days, the motto of Warner Bros. cofounder Jack Warner was "I don't want it good. I want it Tuesday," proverbial as to the producers' typical preference for efficiency over quality. In the classical studio system, composers were generally required to write a score in eight to ten weeks; these days, two-hour-long scores can be commissioned within a three- to four-week deadline.[24] Producers now "want it *Monday*." As a time- and money-saving measure, composers are also required to prepare a preliminary MIDI (Musical Instrument Digital Interface) "mock-up" of the score. This is a computer-generated demo of the music rendered by VST (Virtual Studio Technology) instruments—audio samples either synthesized or recorded from a real orchestra. Mock-ups allow directors and producers to get a very precise idea of what the music will sound like before the (extremely expensive) stage of recording the music with a real orchestra, with a considerable savings of time and, hence, of money. All such digital routines mandate that film composers, if they want to stay in the business, have to be proficient with computer technologies, and tech-savviness might even result as more indispensable than classical musical training and education. "Music notation skills and traditional orchestration, while extraordinarily useful, are no longer required," admits Mark Kerins.[25]

Computer technology is now applied not only to music composition but to film editing as well, and this new process has had a considerable impact on the style of Hollywood's current film music. In the old days, a film's work print was assembled on a Steenbeck flatbed editor, cutting and splicing the physical pieces of positive filmstrip struck from the camera negatives. The edit thus obtained, which was "spotted" by the composer to prepare a cue sheet of the scenes and sequences to be scored, was a fairly locked version of the film: further corrections and last-minute second thoughts on the director's part would have been quite expensive and were done only if necessary—for example, after bad review cards from a test screening. With the use of editing software, today a film can be assembled in much swifter and more flexible a way: the footage is digitized and stored in the computer workstation. Tweaking or even massively modify the film's cut is virtually inexpensive, since replacing a scene with another, or moving one sequence to a different place, is a matter of a few minutes and much less labor, and no additional (and costly) film stock has to be used. As a consequence, a film is never really locked until distribution copies are prepared. The composer may spot one film and tailor the music to the footage that has been carefully measured; then, once the score is ready, the composer may be faced with a different film, which the music does not fit as it was supposed to. This fluid nature of the final cut can impact the style of the music.

If a musical cue written in a traditional fashion—eight-bar melodies, phrases, a developmental discourse, inner voicing, counterpoint, etcetera—has to be modified because the cut has changed, this may not be an easy and painless task. A proper rewrite might take more time than allowed, thus proving unfeasible. If there is no time for rewrites and rerecording, then it might be necessary to modify the music on the fly—on the recording stage—by bluntly excising some segments or structural elements to adjust to the new configuration of the cut. If already recorded, the music editor would chop off and paste the required bars to adjust the recording to the new configuration. In both instances, in the presence of a melodic phrasing and developmental discourse, such cuts would be noticeable—even as "earsores"—in their blunt interruption or corruption of the musical flow: for example, a previous eight-bar melody may no longer have time to complete its course and thus gets truncated. Edits on the music track to better conform music to film also happened in the past, but given the now decidedly more unstable and unpredictable state of the final cut, it is far more probable that the musical structure might be repeatedly tweaked until the last minute. The best way to cope with this is to *adapt* in a Darwinian way—survival of the fittest—and *adopt* a music style that is not so much flowing, developmental, or melodic as *modular*. Music is built in short repeating blocks—as in minimalism—or as a uniform static sound pad. This way, it is easily modifiable, by either the composer or the music editor, who can lift the now exceeding modules without the type of harsh aural impact that such elisions would have on a more articulated melodic flow. The flexible, trimmable, modular approach is the safest choice with today's film technology.[26] Once again, Zimmer pioneered this flexibility-driven convergence of music and the other departments determined by the shared use of digital workstations: in *Gladiator*, Kerins reports, "Zimmer tried working next to the picture editors, providing draft music cues as they went . . . , as well as by giving the editors raw music tracks not tied to specific moments, to use as they saw fit [in *Black Hawk Down* (Ridley Scott, 2001)]; in both cases, it was crucial that Zimmer could quickly create and output audio stems the editors could bring into their own systems and play with."[27]

Given the saturated sound mix, the film's potentially ever-changing editing, and the tighter deadlines promoted by computer-based composition and film editing, it is no surprise that elaborate formal writing and old-fashioned symphonic style have little place in today's film music. A flowing melody, a leitmotivic network, or a theme-variations approach would hardly find aural space within the thick layers of sound effects, and it would prove too inflexible for the ever-changing final cut. There is much music in contemporary Hollywood films, but music is not so much about melodies, phrases, and intramusical development—as in the old symphonic tradition and in the neoclassical style—as about providing a congenial sound pad onto which the sound effects can be inserted. It is not so much about the development of an extended musical discourse—as in the case of the leitmotif technique, for example—as about the creation of a musical atmosphere.

Neoclassical Film Music in the Sound Design Style

The symphony orchestra as a musical means seems to be the only neoclassical element that has really had some influence on contemporary Hollywood film music. Nonetheless, the sound might be *orchestral* but the language is often anything but *symphonic*. The terms "orchestral" and "symphonic" are not meant as synonyms here. "Orchestral" refers to the instrumentation of a piece of music, that is, an orchestra, more or less conforming to the traditional settings of a symphony orchestra (woodwinds, brass, percussion, strings in five groupings, keyboards, harps, etc.). "Symphonic" refers to the writing style of a piece of music: the instrumental sections in the orchestra are engaged in contrapuntal, harmonic, and timbral interplay with each other and, within each section, with other instruments of the same section (e.g., a dialogue between oboes and bassoons). A piece that is orchestral is not necessarily symphonic (for example, we can have swing music or a Beatles song arranged for orchestra). In the "sound design style," music can be surely called *orchestral*, because it is still played by large orchestral ensembles, but it is not *symphonic*. It is an orchestral texture resembling more rock/techno/pop music arranged for orchestra rather than symphonic music. Padded with synthesizers, digitally enhanced, and boosted with an enlarged percussion section, the symphony orchestra is still in use because it can produce a loud and massive sound, which can keep up with the level of the sound-effects volume and contribute to create the characteristic aural saturation of the contemporary "film concert." A very recent example that stresses how the dominant trend is orchestral but not symphonic is the third trailer for *Star Wars: Episode VII— The Force Awakens*. It features some of Williams's canonical themes arranged into a more contemporary sound. Frank Lehman has analyzed it: "Maximum volume and density at all times appears to be the desired impact, at the pronounced expense of orchestrational clarity. Far more in-line with practices of Hans Zimmer and his epigones than of the original model of Golden Age Hollywood, trailer three sounds assertively and symptomatically 'contemporary.' Observe the electronically overproduced textures, the crashing drums, the musicalized (mostly synthetic) sound effects. For better or worse, here, the *Star Wars* musical idiom is for once not pure symphonic throwback."[28] Trailers are, of course, designed to attract the largest possible audience by catering to the current tastes: if producers felt that the sound of the *Star Wars* music had to be updated for the final trailer, this is a meaningful enough, further sign that symphonic film music is hardly considered fashionable and appealing today.

Being part of an industry that dictates specific aesthetic, commercial, and procedural rules, composers not grown up and educated within the new sound-design culture but with a traditional musical training had to adjust and retool, willy-nilly. In the 1980s, James Horner was an emerging classically trained composer, being one of those practitioners who did not compose with the help of computers and showing neoclassical inclinations—for example, in *Star Trek: The Wrath of Khan* (Nicholas Meyer, 1982), *Krull* (Peter Yates, 1983), *Aliens* (James Cameron, 1986), and *Willow* (Ron Howard, 1988). However, after the success of *Titanic* (James Cameron, 1997) and the song "My Heart Will Go On," Horner appears to have retreated from his neoclassical outpost and opted for the secure shelter of "modern-style" commercial songs as pièce de résistance of the music track, as in *The Mask of Zorro* (Martin Campbell, 1998), *A Beautiful Mind* (Ron Howard, 2001), *Troy* (Wolfgang Petersen, 2004), and *Avatar* (James Cameron, 2009). Lately, Horner specialized in spectacular but mostly repetitive lengthy scores delivered at incredibly short notice, as for *Troy*, which he composed in less than a month after Gabriel Yared's dismissal.[29] In post-2000 interviews, he revealed a resigned disillusionment toward his own job.[30] A notable and widely successful symphonic set of scores of the early years of the twenty-first century was Howard Shore's majestic symphonic tapestry for *The Lord of the Rings* trilogy (Peter Jackson, 2001, 2002, 2003); yet, if Shore's works have a leitmotivic network, they do not perform a spatial perceptive function to such an extent as to be defined neoclassical. Moreover, this is an exception for a composer who is otherwise not famous for being neoclassical, as his scores for David Cronenberg's films clearly show.

The weakness of the neoclassical trend can also be seen in the fact that even George Lucas and Steven Spielberg, whose films marked the birth of this movement, partially conformed to the poetics of contemporary cinema. Despite continuing to work with Williams, both Lucas and Spielberg followed the trend of the moment. As reported by *Film Score Monthly*, in 1996 Spielberg appointed Hans Zimmer as head of the film-music department of his film studio, DreamWorks SKG, a choice that hardly seems to promote neoclassicism.[31] In the second *Star Wars* trilogy, particularly in *Star Wars: Episode III— Revenge of the Sith* (George Lucas, 2005), music has been given less importance in the new audio mix than in the previous trilogy. In action scenes, the music is drowned out by the overwhelming flood of sound effects: two hundred audio tracks constituted the starting point for the final mix.[32] During a lecture at the Thornton School of Music of the University of Southern California, Williams talked about the musical difficulties in coping with the seventeen-minute-long noisy battle at the beginning of that film.[33] Moreover, the making-of documentary on *Star Wars: Episode III* shows Kenneth Wannberg—Williams's longtime music editor—at the mixing console complaining about the excessive volume of the sound-effect track and trying to advocate a more relevant role for music: "It's noisy. I think the music should live a little bit more than it does. I mean, it just gets wiped out. The music is kind of a thread through that whole montage of cutting back and forth. . . . And it just gets lost."[34]

Lucas not only followed the new trend but also altered the sound balance of the classic trilogy. He tinkered with the first three films of the *Star Wars* saga in order to rerelease them in theaters in 1997 and on DVD in 2004. These versions, characterized by new CGI shots and various digital corrections, have received many complaints from the fans and caused the general perplexity of critics.[35] Williams's score was severely compromised, marginalized by a new audio mix, which gave such a predominant role to the new sound effects that the original music track is muffled in many points. One reviewer writes that "Williams' awe-inspiring *Star Wars* score has been severely mishandled on the new DVD," and a brief search on the internet shows how fans and critics are generally baffled and discontented: for example, "During the first part of the Death Star battle at the end of the film, John Williams' score has been reduced in prominence in the sound mix. . . . Lucasfilm says this was a deliberate creative decision and I absolutely hate it," or "The familiar Force theme trumpet fanfare that used to play right after Red Leader says: 'This is it!' and just as the X-wings start diving towards the Death Star's surface has been dialed back in volume so that it's almost inaudible—it's almost completely buried in the surround mix. . . . The sound effects definitely sound like they've been ratcheted up a LOT, to the point that they now overwhelm the dialogue and the music in a lot of scenes."[36] There have been so many protests that in 2006 Lucas decided to release a two-disc DVD set including both the 2004 "enhanced" version and the 1977 original one.[37]

Scores that can be called "neoclassical" are few in contemporary cinema and, significantly enough, Williams has even been called "The Last Movie Maestro" by the *Wall Street Journal* and "the last survivor of Hollywood music" by the French composer Bruno Coulais.[38] Indeed, the few scores that adopt some of the traits of the neoclassical style do so by treating such style almost as a venerable relic from the past. Those who employ it and its techniques are deliberately referencing the past: for example, Ludovic Bource's score for the silent-film revival *The Artist*, in which the tropes of silent-cinema music are nevertheless reappropriated through the lens of Hollywood's music history, neoclassicism included. If not in reference to the past, neoclassical traits are used as nods to a well-known cinematic corpus and tradition, as is the case with Michael Giacchino's score for the *Star Wars* spin-off *Rogue One: A Star Wars Story* (Gareth Edwards, 2016) and, more faithfully, with John Powell's *Solo: A Star Wars Story* (Ron Howard, 2018). Talking about this specific score,

Powell sounds like someone handling some museum artifact with a reverent sense of trepidation ("There were a lot of times when I froze and couldn't write because I was too worried. . . . I spent more time thinking than writing in this case") or someone who is embarking on some academic enterprise of applied philology ("This has taught me a lot about how elegantly John Williams writes. . . . It was like doing my master's degree").[39]

The most recent examples of outright neoclassical scores are all Williams's: *Indiana Jones and the Kingdom of the Crystal Skull* (Steven Spielberg, 2008), *The Adventures of Tintin* (Steven Spielberg, 2011), *The BFG* (Steven Spielberg, 2016), and the latest *Star Wars* trilogy. And yet even Williams, though maintaining a style generally grounded on neoclassicism, has modified some of his stylistic traits to better fit the current soundscape. As is true of any film composer, he has always shown a keen understanding and awareness of how music has to compete with a number of other cinematic elements. "One of the biggest mistakes a film composer can make is to assume that his music will have the audience's full attention. On the screen, there's always something that will compete with it. If it isn't the sound effects, or the dialogue, it's someone very attractive undressing," Williams once joked.[40] Though not having retooled to the new computer technology and still writing music with a piano, paper, and pencils, Williams is experienced and knowledgeable enough of the medium's current needs as to adapt to the contemporary "sound design style."

Already in the second *Star Wars* trilogy, Williams's music presents some stylistic differences from the previous ones. Prominently, the scores feature fewer memorable melodies—particularly in Episodes II and III—because the current mixes do not allow space for the same melodic flow and leitmotivic network as in the first trilogy.[41] The orchestration is also less thick—in the first trilogy the middle register was richer—with more isolated instrumental groupings and timbral effects placed in the higher and lower registers; a recurrent trait is the use of *fortissimo* accents by the piccolo and the xylophone, two of the few instruments in the orchestra able to pierce through the wall of sound effects. If music wishes to find its place in today's highly saturated sound mixes, it has to emerge more timbrally than melodically. In the prequel trilogy, battles and action sequences are scored more rhythmically and coloristically than melodically. Musical pieces have a looser form and act more as a background for the clashes of the battle and less as musical compositions on their own: for instance, the opening battle of *Star Wars: Episode III—Revenge of the Sith*. The shift from the more old-fashioned style of the first trilogy to the sound-design style of the second is particularly evident if *Star Wars: Episode I—*

The Phantom Menace (George Lucas, 1999)—melodically richer, with identifiable longer themes, and more similar to the classic trilogy—is compared to the subsequent episodes of the prequel trilogy, a shift that is perhaps the result of the re-editing misadventure that Williams experienced. In *Episode I*, Lucas decided to change the editing of the final battle after Williams had already spotted the film and written the music, meaning that the composer had to reconfigure the music as he was recording it: "If I hit the ground running, I can write two minutes of music a day. If I were to have started all over again on the last reel, I would be ready to record in July—with the picture already in the theaters! So I've been making the music fit as we go along. That's why I'm constantly telling the players to drop measures 7 to 14."[42] To avoid future inconveniences like this, Williams probably realized he had better opt for a less thematic approach.

In the third trilogy, Williams's music continues to follow the more modular and less thematic approach he developed for the second trilogy—"because of the tremendous noise of the effects in these films, I have gone for a very bright trumpet-drum preponderance"—but his usual work routine also had to be adjusted to the current practice.[43] As per the workflow of the digital convergence and perpetual trimming, editing and sound/visual-effect processing were made in parallel on one chunk of film at a time, not in separate and subsequent steps, as it used to be. Reportedly, for *Episode VII* Williams never saw the whole film in a more-or-less stable rough cut but was given the film piecemeal.[44] In the process, he had to modify or completely rewrite almost one hour of the 175-minute-long score because in the meantime the director, J. J. Abrams, had re-edited and made adjustments to the film, repeatedly. As a consequence, Williams worked on the score from December 2014 to November 2015, with the recording taking place not in a compressed series of days but in separate sessions scattered from June to November.[45] Explains Williams:

> George Lucas and J.J. Abrams have very different working styles. With George, who grew up with thirty-five millimeter film . . . his editing was constructed almost like Hitchcock. I mean the edit that I received was the edit we scored. In the case of J. J. Abrams, . . . we were making changes up till the very last minute. . . . Particularly in the beginning of the process, when I was working on the earlier reels, [Abrams] was with me on that but he also knew the later reels which I did not at the time. So he began to guide me towards developing a theme that would eventually mature in reel seven or reel eight—scenes that I may not have yet seen at all or at least not in their entirety at that point.[46]

The same happened with *Star Wars: Episode VIII—The Last Jedi* (Rian Johnson, 2017), which took almost one year again to score and record, and, even more radically, with *Star Wars: Episode IX—The Rise of Skywalker* (J. J. Abrams, 2019), which underwent such recuts (and reshoots) that the last recording session took place on 24 November 2019, a mere three weeks before the film's release (18 December), with the final mix executed under conditions that are not too difficult to imagine as rushed.[47] Moreover, as Williams could never watch the entire cut but had to be guided by Abrams's descriptions, the exactness of payoff of the "gradual disclosure of the main theme" and other instances of the macro-emotive function have probably suffered from the incomplete access to the film.

Besides the less momentous, climax-building quality of the scores for the third trilogy, stylistically Williams has nevertheless been able to maintain his trademark leitmotivic treatment, though applied to motifs, short melodic cells, and rhythmic figurations instead of longer themes and melodies—in line with the modular approach. For example, Kylo Ren's motif is much more concise if compared to the formal extension of Darth Vader's Theme. If Williams has often included some electroacoustic instrument (e.g., the Fender-Rhodes piano) or some synthesizer within his orchestra (e.g., Williams's celesta in his film scores is mostly a synth celesta), he has managed to resist electronic "sweetening" in postproduction and maintained the use of symphonic writing performed by an acoustic symphony orchestra. He explains:

> In this score, there are no drum machines or electronic tricks. It's just the orchestra. Which makes it a kind of anomaly in today's world. I mean, I think much of music which is done in contemporary films is fabulous. I've heard in prior years very adventurous and beautiful things that have been done that are non-orchestral. I wouldn't be able to do those things. But orchestras and films are brother and sister, it seems to me. And when we can offer a score that an orchestra can play, and there's room on the canvas for it, as there is in *Star Wars*, it's a bonus, and it's a privilege, and it's a treat.[48]

It is indeed a (rare) privilege. The exceptional nature of this process cannot be stressed enough: such year-long deadlines and constant availability of a (100-plus) orchestra to record the score piecemeal are luxuries that were granted to Williams because of the household name he has become and because of the asset he has come to be for the *Star Wars* franchise. Williams does not work with DAWs or offer preliminary mock-up demonstrations:

"I learned to write with a pencil and paper, which are still usable tools, but only, sort of, monk-ish elderly. . . . I still do it in this, what is to younger people a very primitive way of writing music note-by-note. . . . And so it's, kind of, like making home dough."[49] Such uncommon arrangements—including waiving the preparatory mock-ups—are like a tribute to the last survival of a species on its way to extinction, or allowing a master baker to make his own "home dough" instead of using an industrial kneading machine. But, as we have seen discussing the shift to a more modular writing approach, even Williams could not but adapt to the current "sound design style." And his music was given no special prominence but was handled as per the current sound-design standards and hierarchy: according to the classical violinist Anne-Sophie Mutter—a self-confessed film-music fan and a close Williams friend—the composer was as "enttäuscht" (disappointed) as she was when they discovered how music ended up drowned and muffled in the final mix of *Episode IX*.[50]

Conclusion

As a closing assessment of film music's neoclassicism, we can consider it a limited substyle within the larger "eclectic style," a substyle that has enjoyed a particular prominence in the 1975–83 period and has continued to be featured consistently mostly in the work of one composer. In general, the influence on contemporary film music and on the "sound design style" has been limited and circumscribed to the most superficial traits of some of Williams's work, such as the use of a large symphony orchestra and the thickness and loudness of the orchestral sound.[51] I argue that the real importance and stronger relevance of film music's neoclassicism has consisted in having drawn attention to the classical Hollywood musical heritage, also beyond the screens and into the concert halls. Apart from his commercial success and artistic achievements, John Williams is a key figure in cinema history, film-music history, and *music* history for his seminal role in bringing the classic Hollywood music style and its canon into the limelight, to the attention and consideration of audiences, orchestras, and scholars. The rediscovery of Korngold, Steiner, and Rózsa in the past four decades is also due to the fact that Williams, as a composer, revived some elements of their works in a period in which they were considered outdated; at the same time, as a conductor, Williams programmed the best of the film-music repertoire in a time when it was still strongly out of favor in concert halls. If the neoclassical trend has not, in the end, managed to bring symphonic film music back to today's cinemas, it has surely succeeded in bringing it into today's concert halls, including Vienna's Musikverein. The music critic Ned Lannamann has thus characterized Williams's contribution:

> Williams, perhaps more than any other contemporary musician or composer, has used the breadth of his influence to open up doors to the worlds of classical and film music to everyday listeners. His music, deeply infused in the subconscious of generations raised on *Star Wars* and *Harry Potter* films, satisfies in its own regard, but it simultaneously functions as a vital signpost to the monumental works of the past. He's like the best kind of professor; John Williams' career is a syllabus that opens the gates to a whole world of music. . . . This is a man with a studious and rich sense of the history of classical music, coupled with a deep and enduring affection for film.[52]

The importance of Williams's contribution has been perhaps more historical than stylistic. In the words of the composer and conductor—and Alfred Newman's son—David Newman, "He bridged the Old Hollywood and the New Hollywood . . . and he has done more than anyone to elevate the awareness of the art form of film music."[53] Williams has restored dignity to a neglected facet of the Hollywood tradition. Putting aside idiosyncratic tastes and old prejudices, scholars and critics are now widely acknowledging this fundamental contribution that Williams has given to film-music and cinema history.

As to the situation of film music in films, stylistically, Williams seems to be the only heir of the classical style of Korngold and Steiner, the very last survivor of the Hollywood music tradition. John Powell, while working on *Solo*, has called Williams "the film-scoring equivalent of Yoda," the pluricentennial Jedi Master of the *Star Wars* saga.[54] As in *Episode VIII*, the Sacred Jedi Texts are willingly destroyed, so it seems to happen in contemporary Hollywood with its film-music heritage. Some might not agree with my perhaps too pessimistic outlook. Today's music has a pop inclination and market orientation that might remind one of the "modern style" of the 1960s, when symphonic film music had been similarly replaced by more up-to-date and marketable idioms. And yet the seemingly deceased symphonic film music was resurrected after a decade: the same might happen again, as styles and history are cyclical. There is a difference, I argue, between the current condition and the 1960s. After the 1960s "pop craze," the neoclassical approach managed to revert that trend because compilation scores and pop scoring eventually proved less effective than symphonic scoring in terms of film/music dramaturgy. *Jaws* (Steven

Spielberg, 1975) and the subsequent neoclassical scores demonstrated that the traditional symphonic scoring was more "film-friendly" and more narratively flexible as a style of accompaniment. Contemporary scores, unlike those of the "modern style," *are* film-friendly, and they manage to be both appealing to today's musical tastes and fully functional to the aesthetic of today's films. A change in trend in favor of symphonic neoclassicism, as happened in the 1970s, does not seem foreseeable in the near future.

Some might rejoice and welcome this new course as refreshing and liberating: get rid of the past symphonism and make way for the new sound design. But the "eclectic style" had already made way for the new while at the same time allowing for a wider variety of idiomatic options: synths, pop, World Music, jazz, blues, atonality, minimalism, noise music, a more creative role for sound designers . . . and neoclassicism. The problem, I think, is that today's "sound design style" has the tendency—determined by the technological, industrial, and consequently aesthetic characteristics that I have discussed—to impose a uniform single approach and idiom, with the consequence of narrowing the idiomatic diversity and, possibly, discouraging creativity. Seemingly more open, refreshing, and liberating (and maybe also more "democratic" as computers make it easier for anyone to produce music), the current "sound design style" might on the contrary cause conformism and silence nonaligned voices. The "eclectic style" within which the neoclassical trend blossomed was pluralistic and open; the "sound design style" apparently not so much.

Appendixes

Peh! They're butchering the classics! . . .
Laser effects, mirrored balls . . .
John Williams must be rolling around in his grave.

> —Homer Simpson, attending a *Star Wars* concert (*The Simpsons*,
> season 6, episode 23: "The Springfield Connection")

John Williams at work, ca. 1981. Photograph by Samantha Winslow Williams. Courtesy of John Williams.

Appendix I
Williams's Versatility for Spielberg (and Others)

Neoclassicism is the style mostly associated with John Williams. However, he also possesses a chameleonlike ability to write in a number of diverse musical dialects and to adjust his personal idiom to the requirements of the film at hand. For example, Williams employed contemporary dialects and musical means in *Heartbeeps* (Allan Arkush, 1981) and *Space Camp* (Harry Winer, 1986). In the former, he used synthesizers and mixed them with his trademark orchestral sound, including fugato writing; in the latter, he adopted both synthesizers and 1980s pop-music dialects. Later, he also ventured into Asian dialects for *Seven Years in Tibet* (Jean-Jacques Annaud, 1997), for which he blended Tibetan chorus and Eastern scales with a Western romantic main theme featuring Yo-Yo Ma's lyrical cello solos. Williams would explore Asian dialects again—this time more deeply and substantially—for *Memoirs of a Geisha* (Rob Marshall, 2005). Williams explained that the major challenge was "to incorporate the grammar of Japanese music with what we recognize as Western harmonic and melodic idioms—to bring those two things together to create a third element that would seem at home in the film."[1] Japanese instruments—the koto, the Japanese zither, the Shakuhachi flute, the bamboo flute, the Shamisen lute, *taiko* drums—are blended with the timbres of the Western symphony orchestra. The writing also mimics the improvisational gestures of traditional non-notated music, in a way similar to the writing Williams had used for his Shakuhachi-inspired *Flute Concerto* (1969). Williams described his work on the *Geisha* score in detail.

> It's all written out, and we have wonderful drummers in Los Angeles who have kabuki instruments and taiko drums of all sorts—wood and metal, used in traditional Japanese theater—and they were all available to me. Although we

didn't do a lot of layering or overdubbing, we did some with the percussion, which gives it energy but also a kind of glow. There are koto bits and pieces in there—which is a Japanese thirteen-stringed instrument—and most of those are ghosted by a conventional Western chromatic harp, where you might have 70% of the energy coming from the koto and the rest coming from the harp, where you're not really even aware of it. But the combination of the two things gives the koto a kind of glow—it's different from a reverb; it's prettier than that. You could add any other instrument to do that, but the harp is very close to the koto, and it's fascinating because the koto's able to do a lot of things that the harp can't—and vice versa—because of the pedals and the tuning.[2]

That same year, Williams also worked on a completely different score for *Munich* (Steven Spielberg, 2005), switching to Middle Eastern timbres and scales. "It couldn't be more different from *Geisha* in ambiance and texture," admitted Williams.[3] Departing from the Eastern European Yiddish-influenced idiom associated with Jewish music that he had employed in *Schindler's List* (Steven Spielberg, 1993) and *Fiddler on the Roof* (Norman Jewison, 1971), Williams now adopted a Middle Eastern sound.

Musically, there are several things; one is, there are areas where we felt would benefit from certain atmospherics of the Middle East, Israeli music and some Palestinian music. That meant that some instrumental coloration, the use of an oud—which is a Persian instrument—and combinations of cimbalom, orchestral clarinets and so on that were used in an effort to create the atmosphere of Israel. When most of us think about Jewish music, we think in terms of the European experience of Russia, Poland, Germany and so on. . . . I felt what was needed . . . was a different expression of the locale and ambiance of Israel and Palestine itself, so instrumental coloration particular to the film was challenging.[4]

These two films alone, both from 2005, already signal the adaptability of which Williams is capable. Such versatility is amply on display in his multidecade artistic collaboration with Steven Spielberg.

The Spielberg/Williams Collaboration

The Spielberg/Williams collaboration is one of the longest-lasting relationships between a director and a composer and is perhaps also the most prominent, successful, artistically homogeneous, and harmonious. Alfred Hitchcock and Bernard Herrmann worked together for eleven years and produced eight films. Sergio Leone and Ennio Morricone for twenty years and eight films; Federico Fellini and Nino Rota for twenty-six years and sixteen films; François Truffaut and Georges Delerue for twenty-three years and eleven films; Sergei Eisenstein and Sergei Prokofiev for seven years and three films. Spielberg and Williams have enjoyed an artistic relationship that has produced twenty-eight feature films—excluding TV episodes such as *Amazing Stories* (1985/1987) or other short-film commissions, such as *Unfinished Journey* (2000) or *A Timeless Call* (2008). More noteworthy, from their first collaboration, *The Sugarland Express* (1974), to the most recent, *The Post* (2017), they have enjoyed an impressive forty-three years of artistic marriage.[5] Says Spielberg:

> I usually try to give him the book or the script to go on. Sometimes he reads it and sometimes he doesn't, depending on how busy he is. What John prefers to do is just talk a lot with me, before I even make the movie—about what the picture's about and how I see it. Then after I'm finished with the picture, I show John a very rough assembly. And then John, without really needing to hear any more from me because the film pretty much says it all, goes off and writes his themes. Then he performs sketches of the themes for me on the piano. I usually fall in love with all of his themes. I've often made a fool of myself sitting there weeping, hanging over the piano after he's played me something, either from *E.T.* or *Schindler's List*. Or I just admire what he's done. More often than not, the first thing he plays me is what goes into the movie. . . . I don't think there's been a single moment where we've had a disagreement about music. We certainly have a high regard for each other, but I just think that's about Johnny hitting the target in an uncanny way. . . . I call him Max. As a matter of fact, when I named my first child Max, that came from a nickname that I gave Johnny from the first time we met. It's a joke that sometimes his music reminded me of Max Steiner. And he would always laugh, so I got to calling him Max.[6]

Spielberg also remarked, "Without question, John Williams has been the single most significant contributor to my success as a filmmaker."[7]

Williams, in turn, says of his longtime associate: "Some directors feel as though they've failed if they need lots of music. It's cosmetic, even unwanted. Spielberg's aesthetic is a very fanciful one and is comfortable in the presence of music, so his pictures always offer the opportunity for lots of music."[8] About their artistic synergy, Williams has explained:

He comes to my office and I play things for him on the piano. In all these years, he's never said, "I don't like that. It's not, you know, try something else." By the time I get halfway through, I can see from his face muscles where I am with this thing. And he's enthusiastic about everything, even the things that we reject. Sometimes I'll do a scene with the orchestra and I frequently write two versions. And I know exactly which one he's gonna take. But it's part of the process that I need to go through to get somewhere between his thinking and mine that will meet. . . . I think one other thing that I would mention why the relationship with Spielberg is so lasting, he loves music. So many producers will go on the stage, we have a ninety-piece orchestra sitting there, it's very expensive, and they will worry: "When are we gonna finish? Let them go." It's more expensive if we go into overtime and people understand this. And at the end of our session, Steven will come to me. "Have you got any more? Play some more. Don't let them go." It's an almost physical joy.[9]

Moreover, both share a "neoclassical" appreciation of the traditional acoustic symphony orchestra over electronically enhanced or synthetic sounds, as Spielberg acknowledges: "I don't like electronic scores, so Johnny and I have been very Luddite about including full orchestras and full choirs in most of our films. . . . We don't like to use electronics to make music. I can always tell the difference between an orchestra and a synthetic orchestra. . . . I love orchestras."[10]

Close Encounters of the Third Kind (1977)

Having started their collaboration with *The Sugarland Express* and then consolidated it with the rousing success of *Jaws* (1975), the duo's third project, *Close Encounters of the Third Kind*, offered one of the most outstanding examples of combination and interplay of film and music in film history—and one of their finest achievements. The screenplay required that humans and aliens communicate through musical signals, in particular through a five-note pattern, which served as the musical identification of the mostly unseen aliens—as the ostinato did for the rubber shark in *Jaws*. Since the five-note signal was so central to the narrative and had to be ready before the shooting phase, Williams and Spielberg began working on the music long before the production started—something uncommon in Hollywood practice. In a 2009 interview, Williams said:

Well, *Close Encounters* is, in my experience at least, unique. The five-note motif that you mentioned was the result of a lot of experimentation, meeting with my friend Steven Spielberg. I think I wrote about 300-plus examples of five notes starting with all on one note and with no rhythmic variation, just interval-lic, that is to say pitch differences. And we settled on this one [five-note motif from the film] for whatever reasons. . . . It wasn't even a theme. It was more like a signal to incorporate in the orchestral material. . . . And I kept trying to say to Mr. Spielberg, "I need more than five notes to make this point. It isn't enough." And his point to me was, "It should not be a melody. It should be a signal." . . . So it was an interesting exercise for me in getting to the point, absolute minimal number of syllables, words, to use a literary analogy, perhaps, of saying it all in three words instead of allowing yourself five.[11]

Although completed in the same year, the score for *Close Encounters of the Third Kind* is diametrically opposite to that for *Star Wars* (George Lucas, 1977). As the latter is overtly operatic and exuberantly melodic, so the former is dissonant and avant-gardist. Its structure is an inventive musical journey from atonality to tonality. It begins with Pendereckian avant-garde tone clusters, then moves to Arnold Schönberg's expressionist atonalism, then to Claude Debussy's "Impressionism," and finally reaches a late-Romantic tonal grand finale à la Richard Strauss. The score closely follows the gradual evolution of how earthlings perceive the arrival of the extraterrestrial visitors.[12] At the begin-ning, the extraterrestrials are perceived as an unknown threat, then they are recognized as friendly messengers: "It starts really when the extra-terrestrials appear from the mother-ship: here the tone-clusters involve all the twelve notes of the chromatic scale. Then you take one strand away, then another, so the music grows more and more consonant, until you end up with a pure, liturgical E major."[13]

1941 (1979)

The film *1941* is a parody of war films and deals with the fear of a possible Japanese invasion spreading hysterically in Los Angeles after the Pearl Harbor attack. In this zany film, music itself is zany and excessive, flaunting a parodic tongue-in-cheek spirit, which helps the narration mock many targets. The heroic machismo of the war genre is spoofed with the bombastic march asso-ciated with Wild Bill Kelso, the deranged pilot played by John Belushi. Williams stated, "I felt, and Steven did also, that certain characters, I think especially John Belushi, should be characterized by a typical World War II American march, of the kind that I grew up with as a child and played with even in school. And that march has a kind of jazzy, almost southern swagger to it . . .

and the accents are tilted and the synch-ups are a little bit off, and it's a little bit impertinent in its character."[14] The 1940s dance music, particularly Benny Goodman's "Sing, Sing, Sing," was paid homage to in "Swing, Swing, Swing," Williams's diegetic piece for the jitterbug contest scene at the USO.[15] Old Hollywood romantic music is also given a memorable parodic treatment. In the first act, a Japanese sailor sees a naked blonde girl clinging to the periscope of his submarine; when he excitedly points at her, screaming, "Hollywood!" we hear an old-fashioned passionate melody for strings and horns that mocks Steiner's melodramatic music. Steiner is again the target of more tributes and parodies. When Wild Bill Kelso puffs his cigar, a synchronized upward harp glissando replicates the rising smoke just like Steiner's score does for an identical action in *The Informer* (John Ford, 1935). Another tribute to Steiner is the use of the German anthem *Das Deutschlandlied* to characterize the Nazi captain von Kleinschmidt, as Steiner did in *Casablanca* (Michael Curtiz, 1942) for Major Strasser. Like the film itself, the score also has a number of nods to other films. The traditional Irish polka "The Rakes of Mallow" is the basis for the music accompanying the fight at the USO, and it was similarly used by Victor Young for the fight scenes in *The Quiet Man* (John Ford, 1952).[16] Moreover, the beginning of the film includes a self-quotation of *Jaws* on the part of both the director and the composer. When a blonde girl removes her clothes and takes a night swim in the sea, we hear the famous low-pitched ostinato emerging from the silence, this time to surprisingly announce the arrival of a Japanese submarine.[17]

E. T. the Extra-Terrestrial (1982)

E.T. the Extra-Terrestrial, concerning the friendship between a boy and an extraterrestrial, is another masterpiece of Williams and Spielberg. The music is sentimental, tender, and emotional; harp, strings, and woodwinds are the prevailing orchestral colors. Music is the major force in turning what could have been a teenage sentimental film set in the Los Angeles suburbs into a poignant and universally affecting love story, as Williams explains: "In *E.T.* . . . there's a theme for the little alien creature and for the little boy, Elliott, who finds and hides him, and that theme is kind of like a love theme. It's not sensual in the way a love theme would be, but it develops as their relationship develops."[18] The "Flying Theme" from *E.T. the Extra-Terrestrial* is one of Williams's most famous creations.[19] It perfectly captures the miraculous power of friendship and love, and tangibly conveys the feeling of flying.[20] Explains Williams:

What do we have to do musically to accompany a thing like that? I looked for
the melody [*he sings the melody*]. , , , All these intervals reach up, up, up all the
time, to stretch the musical grammar, to give this kind of feeling. And then in
performance, [it's] the same thing. . . . [It requires] a kind of energy [to] make a
hundred-piece symphonic orchestra feel like it's gonna come right off the floor,
and not be all these heavy people playing violins. . . . You have a creature that
you can fly with, that's not of our own species, but of our own spiritual one-
ness, that we'd come together in joy and we'd go over the moon. Fantastic idea!
It needs great sweep in the music and great feeling of freedom. Freedom being
in this case the loss of gravity. We speed up, speed up . . . , we will lose gravity,
we're now in space, and we are finally free. And that's what the orchestra has to
give us . . . [what] the composer has to give us.[21]

Following his "gradual disclosure of the main theme" technique, Williams
carefully develops and gradually unveils the main theme across the first half
of the film, finally presenting it in full form and in perfect timing at the
moment in which Elliott and E.T.'s bicycle takes off in the night sky and flies
over the moon—an iconic film/music moment—and again in the film's grand
finale. According to Williams:

[The love theme] starts with a few notes, they look at each other—a little bit
uncertain. And it grows and becomes more confident, and more lyrical as E.T.
begins to communicate with the boy. At the end it's kind of a full-blown sort of
operatic aria when E.T. goes away. . . . In that scene their theme or love theme
. . . comes back. It's like, in a way, a moment in opera when two lovers are being
separated. I build to that kind of musical denouement.[22]

The film's finale consists of fifteen minutes with continuous symphonic
accompaniment, a memorable set piece that is one of the highest achievements of the art of composing for films.

That sequence involved a lot of specific musical cues. . . . So you can imagine in
the space of that 15 minutes of film how many precise musical accents are needed
and how each one has to be exactly in the right place. I wrote the music mathe-
matically to configure with each of those occurrences and worked it all out.
Then when the orchestra assembled and I had the film in front of me, I made
attempt after attempt to record the music to exactly all those arithmetic parameters. But I was never able to get a perfect recording that felt right musically and

emotionally. I kept trying over and over again and finally, I said to Steven, "I don't think I can get this right. Maybe I need to do something else." And he said, "Why don't you take the movie off? Don't look at it. Forget the movie and conduct the orchestra the way you would want to conduct it in a concert so that the performance is just completely uninhibited by any considerations of mathematics and measurement." And I did that and all of us agreed that the music felt better. Then Steven re-edited slightly the last part of the film to configure with the musical performance that I felt was more powerful emotionally.[23]

In this case again, Spielberg reversed the standard practice and cut the film to the music, so as to achieve a perfect fusion of image and music. Williams explains, "[There is] an intimate connection between picture and music that I don't think the greatest expert in film synchronization could quite achieve. There is an ebb and flow, where the music speeds up for a few bars, then relents, the way you would conduct for a singer in an opera house. There is something visceral, organic, about the phrasing. That last 10 minutes deliver something, emotionally, that is the result of the film fitting the music, and not the other way around, I am delighted to say."[24] Williams also quoted Victor Young's love theme from *The Quiet Man*. Elliott is in telepathic connection with E.T., who is at home watching *The Quiet Man* on TV. The boy feels the urge to kiss his blonde classmate at the exact time when E.T. is watching John Wayne kiss Maureen O'Hara. The kiss is scored by quoting Young's theme, followed by an arrangement of the E.T. main theme in the manner of the old Hollywood love themes—a brief neoclassical Williams moment.

Indiana Jones and the Temple of Doom (1984)

The second Indiana Jones film is set in India; this time Dr. Jones is fighting Khali's Thuggees. *Indiana Jones and the Temple of Doom* opens with a musical extravaganza: a flamboyant dance number on Cole Porter's "Anything Goes" arranged by Williams in a full-blown MGM-like sound, with lyrics sung in Mandarin. The score is generously tinged with exotic touches, such as the Eastern pentatonic scales in the opening Shanghai sequence, the ethnic instrumentation for the jungle and village sequences, and the Asian-flavored march associated with the slave children. The film's tone is darker than that of the first Indiana Jones film, and the music provides appropriate atonal chilling effects, as in the temple sequence, in which there is also a ferocious, unremitting ritual chant to accompany the Thuggee human sacrifice—a diegetic piece that Williams composed before starting to work on the film score and that Spielberg played on set during the filming of the sequence.[25] A new hero-ine sides with Dr. Jones in this second adventure, and Williams consequently wrote a new love theme, similarly old-fashioned and Warner Bros.–like but more tongue-in-cheek in its soaring sentimentalism than Marion's theme in *Raiders of the Lost Ark* (1981).

Empire of the Sun (1987)

After taking a break with *The Color Purple* (1985)—as producer Quincy Jones also provided the score—Williams reunited with Spielberg for *Empire of the Sun*, a World War II drama about a British boy separated from his family and interned in a prison camp after the Japanese invasion of Shanghai.[26] Strings and wordless chorus are the predominant features of a score with a dual nature. On the one hand, Jim's drama, the separation from his parents and the harsh life in the Japanese prison camp, is scored with dissonant and "anti-emotional" music. On the other hand, Jim's dreams of flight and his con-templation of the airplanes taking off from the nearby military airport—the only bright moments in his life of incarceration—are scored with uplifting tonal music for soaring strings and celestial voices. The liberation is scored with a baroque-like piece for orchestra and chorus singing in Latin: "Exsul-tate Justi," from Psalm 33; the piece is reprised in the end credits. The use of a hymn when Jim is finally set free is an interesting choice on Williams's part. It may fulfill a cognitive function: in earlier scenes, Jim had repeatedly pro-claimed his agnosticism. This particular musical choice might suggest that now he has finally found an answer to his religious search—to strengthen the point, during "Exsultate Justi," food capsules are dropped by American air-planes: like manna from Heaven.

Indiana Jones and the Last Crusade (1989)

In *Indiana Jones and the Last Crusade*, the third installment of the saga, Dr. Jones manages to unearth the Holy Grail and prevent the Nazis from seizing it, while also reuniting with his estranged father—brilliantly played by Sean Connery. Williams reprises the series' signature march, but the overall tone of the score is less bombastic and histrionic and more mature and restrained. One of the main points of interest is the father/son relationship, and a some-what melancholic mood about the passing of time can be felt throughout the film. Aptly, Williams's score features a tender theme for the father/son rela-tionship and a solemn, pastoral theme for the Grail, with touches of religious transcendence reminiscent of Wagner's "Good Friday Spell" music from

Parsifal (1882). However, the film certainly does not lack adventure sequences scored with thrilling music. The opening circus-train chase is a virtuoso Mickey-Mousing effort, having around fifty sync points precisely hit by music within the piece's five minutes; the boat chase in Venice is sustained musically for the action pace and the locale, featuring picturesque Italianate mandolin solos; the motorcycle chase is scored with a driving scherzo, humorously titled "Scherzo for Motorcycle and Orchestra" in the concert version.

Always (1989)

Williams provided the appropriate romantic overtones for *Always*, Spielberg's remake of *A Guy Named Joe* (Victor Fleming, 1943). Anticipating *Ghost* (Jerry Zucker, 1990), *Always* is similarly about a man's untimely dying and coming back in spiritual form to console his fiancée' and help her recover from the loss. Like *Ghost*, the key diegetic musical element is the two lovers' heart song, which here is "Smoke Gets in Your Eyes" (Jerome Kern / Otto Harbach, 1933), in the 1958 cover by the Platters. Williams provides the nondiegetic music, sentimental for the romance, poignant for the two lovers' parting, and soaring/dramatic for the firefighters' daredevil flights.

Hook (1991)

The idea of *Hook* was to pick up the story from the point at which James M. Barrie's *Peter Pan* (1911) ended, thus involving a grown-up Peter Pan (now Peter Banning), who has repressed the memories of his past and makes a living as a dull, workaholic lawyer. When Captain James Hook kidnaps his children, Peter has to cope with his past and travel to Neverland to rescue them. The film was originally conceived as a musical to be shot in 1985 and indeed has kept some characteristics typical of the genre: flamboyant scenery, quasi-dance numbers, and a foregrounded position for the music.[27] The score covers almost the entire film. Lush and imaginative, it is one of the best examples of Williams's neoclassicism and of his fondness for the music of Erich Wolfgang Korngold. Leitmotiv and Mickey-Mousing abound, and Korngold's idiom is a constant reference for the pirate scenes, especially in the grand sword fight in the final act, which is probably the best homage to Korngold's swashbuckling music ever done. *Hook* was not as financially successful as expected and received mostly negative reviews. The overall film has formal unevenness, some occurrences of wrong casting (Rufio, for instance), and for all its scope and budget, it indulges too much in childish moments. Consequently, Williams's score has not received the attention it should deserve. However, there

are a few outstanding film/music moments that stand out: the flight to Neverland (featuring early Stravinskyan writing and kaleidoscopic orchestration),
the arrival in the pirate town and the presenting of the hook (opening with
folk fiddles, moving to Smee's comical march, and closing with Hook's pompous entrance, accompanied by his *Flying Dutchman*–like theme and Korngoldian fanfares), Peter's recollection of his childhood and the recovery of his ability
to fly (a ten-minute music piece starting from Peter's frustration for not remembering his past and not being able to fly, moving through melancholia and
nostalgia as Tinkerbell helps him remember his childhood, and finally bursting into a joyful celebration as Peter finds his "happy thought" and takes off).

Jurassic Park (1993); *The Lost World: Jurassic Park* (1997)

The film *Jurassic Park*, based on Michael Crichton's 1990 best-selling sci-fi
novel, made up for *Hook*'s disappointing performance by breaking all box
office records. It concerns the inauguration of an amusement park on a trop-
ical island whose draw is live dinosaurs, re-created though DNA engineering.
For this adventure/thriller, Williams composed a multifaceted score: a jubi-
lant fanfare is heard on the arrival to the island, as if to symbolize the victory
of science over nature; majestic and almost reverent music is associated with
the leviathans of ancient history (the main theme recalls a hymn, the harmony continuously alternating between the first and fourth degrees of the
scale, the plagal ["amen"] cadence); South American percussion sets the right
locale for the jungle sequences (as when Dennis steals the embryos); and *Rite
of Spring*–like music is used for the action scenes. The score for the sequel, *The
Lost World: Jurassic Park*, is decidedly more action oriented. The previous film's
soaring main themes are reprised minimally—in the finale—and the score is
less melodic and uplifting, and more rhythmically driving and pounding, as in
the hunt sequence, or when the T-Rex visits San Diego.

Schindler's List (1994)

Right after *Jurassic Park*, Williams and Spielberg embarked on an ambitious
and completely different project, *Schindler's List*. For this austere black-and-
white drama about the Holocaust, Williams was assigned a demanding task:

> I felt writing this film was a particularly daunting challenge; nothing could
> be good enough to meet a story like this. What I was most conscious of was a
> desire not to melodramatize. . . . I felt this story required music that was gentle
> and loving. The orchestra of Richard Strauss, which was the orchestra of the

period, would have been the wrong noise for a film like this. The main theme, I felt, should be something like a Hebraic lullaby heard at your mother's knee— not actually a lullaby, but something original, created for the film.[28]

Williams had had a previous experience with the Eastern European Yiddish-influenced idiom of Hebraic music, for his Oscar-winning adaptation of the Jerry Bock / Sheldon Harnick Broadway musical *Fiddler on the Roof*, for which he also wrote additional music that featured the celebrated concert violinist Isaac Stern as the soloist. For that film, Williams had traveled to Israel, to conduct research into the Hebrew and Yiddish musical idioms at the University of Jerusalem.[29] More than twenty years later, Williams rehashed his familiarity with those idioms, a familiarity that had also been acquired through some of his past teachers and mentors, including Jewish émigré Mario Castelnuovo Tedesco, with whom Williams studied composition: "Anyone growing up in music as I have done has so many teachers who are Jewish; it's so much a part of what we know and what we do. Those modalities and peculiarities are very familiar to us," explains Williams.[30] The main theme is a minor-mode piece full of dignified poignancy and sweet melancholy for violin and orchestra. Williams turned to the Hebrew liturgy for one of the most devastating scenes, the corpses of the Jews gathered and burned over a huge pyre by Nazis, as reported by Richard Dyer: "Williams asked Rabbi [Bernard] Mehlman for a selection of appropriate texts from the Hebrew liturgy. 'He very generously made a collection for me, with translations; I chose one of them because I loved the thought it expressed: "With our lives, we give life." From this kind of horror, this kind of sacrifice, life can come. I set the words for chorus, and we recorded that in Toronto and in California.'"[31]

Amistad (1997)

Amistad is set in Connecticut in the first half of the nineteenth century and concerns the issue of slavery. A court has to decide whether some Africans who mutinied their traders are indeed slaves, and thus guilty of mutiny, or free men, and thus perfectly entitled to mutiny as self-defense. The overall design of the score replicates the encounter between the African and the Quaker American culture presented in the film. Two pieces stand out as representative of these two cultures: a noble piece for solo trumpet and orchestra, in Americana dialect, is the theme of the elderly president emeritus John Quincy Adams; while a cheerful piece for children's chorus singing in an African dialect celebrates the final liberation of the slaves. The composer relates the creative process:

For some of the scenes requiring an African texture, I felt that the use of children's voices would be particularly effective. . . . As I searched for a text of what the children might sing, I discovered in a volume of West African poetry, a poem by Bernard Dadié written decades ago, which was entitled *Dry Your Tears, Africa, Your Children Are Coming Home.* I was thrilled to discover this, however accidentally, as it seemed ideal for the final scene of this film. . . . The words of the song that I wanted to write would, of course, have to be sung in Mende, the native tongue of the Africans associated with this true story, and so with the help of a translator at the Sierra Leone embassy in Washington, D.C., I arranged to have the poem translated from English to Mende. After slightly adjusting the text to fit the musical phrases, and with Mr. Dadié's permission, and adding some generic phrases such as "sing a song of joy . . . hush child don't cry," it only remained to teach our children's choir to phonetically sing the song.[32]

A typical Spielberg/Williams moment is the trial sequence when, in a claustrophobic courtroom, Cinque—the leader of the African slaves—is anxiously trying to understand what the many witnesses for both the prosecution and the defense are saying about the Middle Passage. Music emphasizes the distressful state of Cinque, with atonal writing, echoing effects, and occasional distant and muffled ethnic percussion and vocalizes, as if to symbolize Cinque's thinking of the far homeland from which he has been violently abducted. At one point, music freezes on a suspenseful sustained note by the strings as we hear Cinque trying to say something. Everyone in the courtroom stops and looks at him. Cinque stands up and, showing his chained hands to the court, he screams repeatedly: "Give us free!" Williams music uplifts the moment by building a moving musical crescendo, starting with a vocalizing chorus singing *mezzo forte* the theme of "Dry your Tears, Afrika" and then, with an arresting modulation, reprising the theme *fortissimo* with the full wordless chorus and orchestra. Using his customary technique of gradual disclosure of the main theme, Williams introduces here only the melody of "Dry your Tears, Afrika," while the full choral version with lyrics will be foregrounded during the final liberation sequence of the Lomboko slave prison.

Saving Private Ryan (1998)

The war drama *Saving Private Ryan* focuses on D-Day and the Allied invasion of Normandy in 1944. The musical choices are characterized by sobriety: only one hour of music for more than two hours of running time. The music is absent in action scenes—as in the opening landing on Omaha Beach and in all the following battle scenes—and enters only in the pauses between one action sequence and another, having the function of framing those moments of re-flection. Says Spielberg: "Restraint was John Williams' primary objective. He did not want to sentimentalize or create emotion from what already existed in raw form. *Saving Private Ryan* is furious and relentless, as are all wars, but where there is music, it is exactly where John Williams intends for us the chance to breathe and remember."[33] The score has warm lyrical episodes for strings—especially for basses and cellos—and solemn parts for brass in which the trumpet and horn solos stand out for their intense pensive tone. Unlike Williams's usual practice, the score is composed of a dozen long pieces last-ing eight to ten minutes, and the music has no perceptive function but mainly an emotive function. Although there are a few recurring themes, the closed musical number technique is used instead of leitmotivs. The end titles are accompanied by the poignant "Hymn to the Fallen" for vocalizing chorus and orchestra, not present elsewhere in the film. It is a concert piece in its own right, dedicated to the memory of the fallen. The score was performed by the Boston Symphony Orchestra and the Tanglewood Festival Chorus and recorded at Boston's Symphony Hall.

A.I. Artificial Intelligence (2001)

The sci-fi tale *A.I. Artificial Intelligence* is based on a Stanley Kubrick project that Spielberg inherited upon Kubrick's death. The score has one part featur-ing atonal dialect and a sort of futuristic minimalism—with coloring touches of synthesizers and electric guitars—which is the musical equivalent of the "outside": the chillingly technological future world. The other part is based on a sweet lullaby for soprano and orchestra, which represents the "inside" of robot-boy David: his feelings, fond memories, and his yearning love for his lost human mother. The score presents a quotation of Richard Strauss's *Der Rosenkavalier* (1911), reportedly a homage to Kubrick, as he had planned to use the piece in the film, following his repertoire-compilation approach to film music.[34] Particularly memorable is the finale, in which David's deceased mother is temporarily resurrected and the robot-boy is given one last day to spend in her company. Williams's music employs the lullaby to score the sequence poignantly by maintaining the tone in a bittersweet equilibrium between David's happiness for having his mother back and his painful awareness that their time together is mercilessly ticking away.[35]

Minority Report (2003)

For the thriller *Minority Report*, set in a future hypertechnological society, Williams composed a homage to the film-noir genre, with many references to Bernard Herrmann's idiom. He explained:

> I wanted to do this in a film noir kind of way; the grandparent of the score is the work of my old mentor and friend, Bernard Herrmann, who scored so many films for Alfred Hitchcock. . . . Steven Spielberg and I wanted the musical atmosphere of an old Bogart film like *The Maltese Falcon*. Some elements of the music are not tonal and depict the futuristic aspect of the film, but the movie is also about nostalgia and memory, and that's where the film noir element comes in.[36]

After much violence and inhumanity bathed in film-noir shadows, the film closes with a peaceful and poignant adagio celebrating "a new beginning," reconnecting with nature after a dark age of technological oppression.

Catch Me if You Can (2002)

For the con-artist comedy/drama *Catch Me if You Can*, Williams jumped back to the 1960s comedies of the first period of his career and thus revisited his West Coast jazz background. The musical theme that accompanies the protagonist's escapades has an alternation of time signatures ($\frac{7}{8}, \frac{3}{4}, \frac{5}{8}, \frac{2}{4}$ . . .) reminiscent of the metrical oscillations of Dave Brubeck's "Blue Rondo à la Turk" (1959). The furtive main theme for alto saxophone is reminiscent of Henry Mancini's famous theme for *The Pink Panther* (Blake Edward, 1963) and is presented over a 1960s-like opening title sequence, which pays homage to the graphic designer Saul Bass. In Williams's words:

> The title sequence of the film was an opportunity to create something with finger-snapping, 1960s swagger, and I thought a jazz saxophone solo in the style of Art Pepper or Stan Getz would be perfect. . . . In a film setting, such as the title sequence, the musical events have to happen exactly in sync with the visual events. If someone were truly improvising, the music might not ascend or quicken exactly when it should. . . . This music is a two-part invention for bass and alto saxophone. The advantage of traditional notation is that there can be more tightly constructed counterpoint than when people improvise. If the players were improvising, the bass player wouldn't really know what the saxophonist

was going to do until it happened, but through traditional notation the piece sounds improvised even though it has carefully controlled counterpoint.[37]

The Terminal (2004)

A Frank Capra–like comedy, *The Terminal* centers on Viktor Navorsky, an Eastern European trapped in New York's JFK airport because his country's government has just been overturned and Viktor's visa and passport have suddenly ceased to be valid. While living in the terminal and waiting for a solution to his case from the US authorities, Viktor meets Amelia, a beautiful flight attendant with a very complicated sentimental life. We later discover that Viktor had traveled to New York to complete his late father's collection of jazz musician autographs. Viktor's Eastern European heritage, his encounter with American culture, and the jazz subplot made it possible for Williams to express this multicultural nexus musically. The score's intra-opus style ranges from klezmer to jazz to contemporary American minimalism; Williams also created a diegetic Slavonic anthem for Viktor's fictitious homeland, Krakozhia. Williams explained:

> I featured the clarinet, which is in the idiom of so many groups of Eastern and Southeastern Europe, but also the cimbalom, an instrument, I think, indigenous to Hungary, and it is played with hammers, and it would be part of the orchestral texture to suggest latitude and culture, and so on. And also the very subtle use of an accordion. . . . It is a nice point about the jazz being a subplot of the film. . . . And the only music that is somewhat related to that idiom is the music that I have written for Amelia, who in my mind is so American. There is something I and Steven would call a "love theme," and that is the theme that springs off in my mind—Amelia—in the texture of what it is. Which is a very kind of American-sounding piece, in contrast to Viktor's music.[38]

War of the Worlds (2005)

War of the Worlds, the remake of the 1953 classic by Byron Haskin, is a contrasting item in the Spielberg extraterrestrial-related filmography. After *Close Encounters'* childlike aliens and the amiable E.T., for the first time Spielberg chose to portray vicious extraterrestrials, probably as a consequence of the 9/11 events.[39] Accordingly, Williams's score is rather devoid of melodies. In his own words: "*War of the Worlds*, where we have this machine coming to bring aliens here that are so destructive, [is] an interesting deviation for Steven. It creates a different musical opportunity and a different role for the orchestra and for the music. And there are a few sections in there, a few cuts to the alien machine, where the orchestra does a grand gesture of a classic monster film."[40] Piercing dissonance, disorienting atonality, stalking rhythms, and frenetic percussion are the score's pillars, with the moments of respite making room for brooding trumpet solos.[41]

Indiana Jones and the Kingdom of the Crystal Skull (2008)

In the series' fourth chapter, *Indiana Jones and the Kingdom of the Crystal Skull*, Williams—besides using the "Indiana Jones" theme and the "Marion Theme" taken from the previous films—has composed new melodies that represent three decades of Hollywood music history. The theme for Matt, Dr. Jones's son, is a bright symphonic piece, which recalls Korngold's scores for Michael Curtiz's 1930s swashbuckling films; Irina's theme, for the ruthless female KGB agent, is a seductive and tortuous saxophone melody reminiscent of the old femmes fatales themes of the 1940s film-noir genre; and the Skull theme is a nod to the sci-fi music of the 1950s, with the synthesizer reproducing the trembling timbre of the theremin.[42]

The Adventures of Tintin (2011)

Part of the fascinating nature of *The Adventures of Tintin*, a computer-generated imagery (CGI) animation film, based on the comic books by the Belgian author Hergé, is its vintage flavor. *Tintin* is vintage not just because its tales and adventures are old-fashioned treasure hunts and puzzling mysteries; the vintage quality is also given by the detailed historical locales in which the stories are set and the characters move. In this film, one of the main "vintage-making" factors is the music. The score for *Tintin*—Williams's first animation film—has such a strong leitmotivic structure and use of Mickey-Mousing that it reminds of *Raiders of the Lost Ark* and can be highlighted as an excellent recent example of neoclassicism. If the Korngoldian references can be spotted in the pirate scenes and duels between Captain Haddock and Rackham the Red, Max Steiner's Mickey-Mousing technique is scattered all over the score, accompanying each jump, fall, and run of the characters—particularly those of Snowy, Tintin's white dog. Williams's score is also based on a network of interwoven and developed leitmotivs—one for Tintin; one for Snowy; one for the Thompsons, the detective twins; one for Haddock, the alcoholic sea wolf. Haddock's theme, for example, is presented as a faltering piece in minor mode comically played by bassoons when the captain is drunk; later in the film, when Haddock reforms and regains his dignity, his theme is rendered in major mode and played nobly by the horns. Moreover, Williams reinforces the film's vintage backgrounds by musically evoking the bygone days: in the main title sequence, Tintin's theme is presented in an early 1930s European jazz arrangement; the Thompsons' theme is played by the euphonium—very fashionable at the time and now a "vintage-sounding" instrument; and the accordion is used extensively to give a French nostalgia color all over the score.

War Horse (2011)

The drama *War Horse*, set in World War I, concerns the friendship of a young man, Albert, and his horse, Joey. Joey is sold to the British cavalry, employed in war actions, and switched to a number of diverse owners, to finally survive the war and be reunited with Albert. Williams's score is richly melodic, combining noble tones and foregrounded flute solos with strong hints of the British music dialect—for example, Ralph Vaughan Williams and Edward Elgar. The film's beginning has a continuous musical flow introducing us in Dartmoor in 1912, and then accompanying the newborn horse in his first shaky gait through the British moors—the horse's moves are mirrored by galloping gestures of the strings. Atonal passages provide the tense atmosphere for the battle scenes, while a noble and poignant brass chorale uplifts the moment when Albert and Joey reunite and go back home—in a *Gone with the Wind*–like sunset.

Lincoln (2012)

In *Lincoln*, a biopic of America's sixteenth president—who had the Thirteenth Amendment passed, thus outlawing slavery—the nearly three-hour film depicts with serene pace and a realistic attention to detail an intimate, anti-triumphalist portrait of Abraham Lincoln. Williams delivered a restrained score that covers only about one-third of the film's length. Dialogue is mostly not underscored and, contrary to other Williams presidential themes—such as John Kennedy's in *JFK* and John Quincy Adams's for *Amistad*—the leading solo instrument is not a celebratory trumpet but a pensive, intimate piano. Noble Americana dialect, nineteenth-century hymnal music, and spiritual-song inflections are the linguistic basis of the score—with a humorous episode featuring a spirited country fiddle in the searching-for-the-votes sequence. Jon Burlingame reports Williams's comments:

> "I thought that the music, in some fundamental way, should have the harmonic and melodic grammar of the 19th century," Williams explains. He started his

work near the end of the film, when Lincoln delivers his second inaugural address ("with malice toward none, with charity for all"), thinking that "if I could solve the inaugural scene, be supportive at the right level," he might find the key theme for the score. Once he and Spielberg decided on the music for that scene, however, the composer discovered that the film demanded different moods for different aspects of Lincoln's character and experiences: a sorrowful piano for the president's dead son Willie; a noble theme for the moment when black Americans are permitted inside the House of Representatives to witness the passage of the 13th Amendment outlawing slavery; a lighthearted fiddle for the shady work of political operatives; an elegy for a field of hundreds of dead Civil War soldiers; and others, six themes in all. "It's a tapestry, really, of thematic pieces original to the film," Williams says.[43]

The Unionist song "Battle Cry of Freedom" is jubilantly arranged for chorus and orchestra and featured when the Amendment is finally approved.[44] It must be noted that the score was performed by the Chicago Symphony Orchestra, which marked the famed orchestra's debut in film music.

The BFG (2016) and The Post (2017)

After skipping *Bridge of Spies* (2015, scored by Thomas Newman), Williams reunited with Spielberg for *The BFG* and *The Post*, the couple's latest two collaborations, which could not be more divergent in style and topic, an ulterior proof of both artists' versatility. The *BFG*—acronym for "Big Friendly Giant"— is based on Roald Dahl's novel of the same name, telling the story of a little orphan girl who travels to Giant Country and befriends one of its inhabitants, who is timid and friendly, unlike the others. Made for Walt Disney Studios, the film is a fantasy piece about the acceptance of diversity and the power of childhood—two classic Spielberg themes. Musically, the tapestry is reminiscent of *Hook* and the first two *Harry Potter* films scored by Williams. The score boasts memorable and perfectly bespoken leitmotifs—for example, one for Sophie, one for the flying Dreams, a menacing one for the not-so-friendly giants—as well as Williams's top-notch timbral and orchestral mastery, including virtuoso writing for the flutes and British-music touches for the scenes set in Buckingham Palace. The score presents all the neoclassical traits, including extensive use of Mickey-Mousing: almost each gesture while chasing and catching the flying dreams in Dream Country is punctuated with musical accents and mirroring gestures. Indeed, the balletic quality of the work is one of the highest in Williams's production. Says the composer:

I kept saying to Steven, "It is almost like a child's opera or a child's ballet." . . . When the BFG tries to capture dreams with his net, he does something that looks like a Ray Boulger or Fred Astaire dance. It's an amazingly musical and choreographic sequence, and it requires the orchestra to do things that are more associated with musical films. It's different [than usual] thematically and in orchestral texture. At least in my mind, more theatrical, you can almost feel there is curtain there. . . . And Steven never had anything this close to this stylistically.[45]

Spielberg, who before the remake of *West Side Story* (2021) and besides the opening number in *Indiana Jones and the Temple of Doom* had never directed a musical, has come very close in this case. Actually, he confirms in a different interview Williams's impression of the film, citing the exact same dream-catching choreography: "I think my favorite part of the filming is when the BFG and Sophie were chasing dreams in Dream Country."[46] Spielberg also offers a reference to the specific musical he had in mind while working on *The BFG*: "I got very excited that this was going to be a little girl's story, and that her courage and values was going to, in a way, turn the cowardly lion into the brave hero, at the end, which is what she turns the BFG into. I saw all kinds of *The Wizard of Oz* comparisons, when I was first reading the book. I said, 'Here's a real chance to do a story about Dorothy and the cowardly lion.'"[47]

Following this Disney quasi-musical fantasy was a completely different film, perhaps one of the most political, topical, and austere that Spielberg has made, *The Post*. The film is a journalism drama in the lineage of *All the President's Men* (Alan J. Pakula, 1976), telling the story of the fight of the *Washington Post* journalists against the Nixon administration and of how the *Post* finally managed to publish the incriminating Pentagon Papers. Already at work on the big-budget sci-fi film *Ready Player One* (2018), Spielberg decided that he wanted to put this story out first, and he made the film in a mere seven months, with preproduction limited to the bare minimum (no storyboarding, for example), and an unprecedented degree of theater-like improvisation left to the stellar cast, led by Meryl Streep and Tom Hanks.[48] The reason for the unusual haste was precisely a matter of "urgency" to counter the fake-news discourse and the attack on the "bad/loser" media instigated by the Donald Trump administration, with clear parallels made with the cover-ups of the Nixon administration depicted in the film, as explained by the director: "The level of urgency to make the movie was because of the current climate of this administration, bombarding the press and labelling the truth as fake if it suited them. . . .

I deeply resented the hashtag 'alternative facts,' because I'm a believer in only one truth, which is the objective truth."[19] The score is similarly austere and somber, running for less than forty minutes, based not on leitmotivic networks but on separate set pieces to accompany the montage sequences—not unlike what Williams had done with his scores for the Oliver Stone films. Burlingame reports: "Spielberg says that *The Post* was a rare instance in which he went to the recording sessions 'having not heard a note' in advance. He was in the middle of post-production on his next film *Ready Player One* when Williams needed to write and record. He praised the score's 'tremendous restraint, then coming right out and being strong musically when it needed to be.'"[50] Highlighted in the score are a series of piano solos, in Williams's words aimed at representing "the simple respect and maybe even nostalgia for integrity and tradition, wrapped together . . . quietly reflecting about a very powerful thing, the effective search for truth."[51] The climactic point in the score is the montage sequence in which, after much legal battling, the presses are finally set to roll to print and distribute the coverage of the White House's cover-ups. Over a propulsive minimalist pattern for strings, the horns create a build-up that climaxes into an uplifting and even heroic brass motif when the copies of the *Washington Post* are finally seen flowing out of the conveyor belts of the presses. These two recent collaborations perfectly encapsulate the two poles that have characterized Spielberg's filmography—the adventure/fantasy and the historical/committed drama—and the versatility that Williams has demonstrated when he has effortlessly and always effectively accompanied Spielberg in whatever project he was embarking on.

Williams's Eclecticism besides Spielberg (and Lucas)

Williams has lent his versatile skills to other directors as well. This section details some notable outcomes. *Black Sunday* (John Frankenheimer, 1977) is a thriller about terrorist attacks, in which a montage sequence—the inspection of the stadium in search of a bomb—stands out for a fugato, which reworks the previously introduced leitmotivs. *Midway* (Jack Smight, 1976) is a World War II drama about the famous battle in the Pacific Ocean and features the "Midway March"—a staple of the Williams march repertoire—in the style of John Philip Sousa, and the soaring "Men of Yorktown March."

Family Plot (1976)—Alfred Hitchcock's final film—is a suspense/comedy about a couple of swindlers who get involuntarily involved in a kidnapping. The film features baroque fugato for suspense sequences, Debussy-like "Impressionist" harmonies for the séances, and a lively main theme colored by a brisk harpsichord reminiscent of some of Williams's 1960s comedies such as *Fitz-willy* (Delbert Mann, 1967) or *How to Steal a Million* (William Wyler, 1966). Says Williams about his collaboration with the director:

> [Hitchcock] had had a long relationship with Bernard Herrmann, who was a great friend of mine at the time. The first conversation I had with Hitchcock, I was a bit sheepish because of my closeness to Herrmann. I didn't feel I could accept the assignment without either talking to Herrmann or understanding why it was that Hitchcock had broken off with him, which was one of those relationships in film that we all were hoping would continue. Hitchcock said to me, "No, no need to be sensitive about that because Mr. Herrmann and I have agreed not to work together again. I'm sure he'll be very happy if it's you, if it's not going to be him." I did ring up Herrmann and he said about the same thing. He said, "No, no, Hitch and I will not work together any longer but I am delighted that you will be doing this." . . . At one of our lunches, Hitchcock was describing a composer he'd hired to write a score for a film about a murder. He said he went to a scoring session and the composer had every double bassoon and tympani that was capable of making an ominous sound for the score. I said, "Well, Mr. Hitchcock, that sounds as if it was close to the mark," and he said, "No, you don't understand, murder can be fun."[52]

The Fury (Brian De Palma, 1978) has perhaps the most Herrmann-like score, with dissonant motivic writing and the eerie sound of the theremin. The principal theme heard over the main titles has a hypnotizing spiral quality, which resembles Herrmann's *Vertigo* (Alfred Hitchcock, 1958). As Williams acknowledged:

> I'd admired *Obsession*, which had a Herrmann score I liked very much, and I thought Brian [De Palma] had served Herrmann's music better than anyone in so many years. I wrote him and thanked him for that. Later I met Brian and it turned out he was a close friend of Steven Spielberg. One day he burst into my office at Fox and said, "Look, we're doing this picture called *The Fury* and, alas, poor Benny isn't with us and Amy [Irving—Spielberg's girlfriend] is the star— would you do the score?"—and I said, "With great pleasure."[53]

Also in 1978, Williams composed the score for *Superman: The Movie* (Richard Donner), which features one of his most famous concert marches and is arguably the first blockbuster superhero film. The score was recorded with the

London Symphony Orchestra, with extensive bravura playing by its legendary principal trumpet Maurice Murphy. One of such bravura trumpet pieces
is precisely the rousing main-title march, which introduces the score's centerpiece and principal leitmotiv. The Superman theme features the heroic and
trademark Williamsesque ascending perfect-fifth leap, which in this case even
spells the very name of the character it scores. Director Richard Donner
recalls:

> The first recording session for *Superman* was the opening reel of the movie,
> and those brilliant titles that were done by Richard Greenberg came flying onto
> the screen. It demanded special music, but you didn't have to say that to John
> because when the title "Superman" came flying in, John made the music say,
> "Su-Per-Man!" If you listen to just that one little piece, you can literally hear the
> music say, "Superman." It brought tears to our eyes. When he's conducting,
> you're usually looking at his back, because you are looking at the orchestra
> much like he is. But I would often go on the music stage, up behind drums and
> the top instruments, and watch John like the orchestra was watching him, and
> his face conveyed the whole movie. He must have studied acting because it was
> like he was living the entire piece. Very beautiful.[54]

An array of other themes populate the score. A heraldic motto built on the
dominant and tonic acts as an aural counterpart of Superman's "S" emblem—
we hear it as Clark Kent rips open his shirt to reveal the superhero's "uniform"
beneath, ready to take action and come to the rescue; *Thus Spoke Zarathustra*-
like "cosmic" music depicts the planet Krypton; pastoral Americana idioms
accompany the rural adolescence of the soon-to-be "caped wonder"; Debussy
harmonies create the mood for the hero's maturation in the Fortress of Solitude; an expansive love theme (which references Richard Strauss's *Death and
Transfiguration*, 1889) elevates the romantic exchanges between Clark Kent /
Superman and Lois Lane; and a comical Prokofiev-sounding minor-mode
march is heard as the villains scheme and plot against the hero and the world.

In 1982 Williams composed the music for *Monsignor* (Frank Perry), a drama
set in Italy during and after World War II and concerning a Catholic priest who
makes black-market business with the Sicilian Mafia and has a love affair with a
nun. This film—decidedly not well received—is worth mentioning for its score
(performed by the LSO), which features at least three noteworthy set pieces.
The first one (the main theme) is a minor-mode slow waltz for trumpet tinged
with a sense of doom and written in an Italianate dialect reminiscent of Nino

Rota's music for *The Godfather* films (Francis Ford Coppola, 1972–74). "The Meeting in Sicily" (thus titled on the LP album) is a sunny, lively orchestral showpiece that contrasts the prevalently darker mood of the score—in the following year Williams reworked it into a concert piece (*Esplanade Overture*). Finally, "Gloria" is a powerful piece for chorus, orchestra, and pipe organ written as a background for a solemn Mass sequence: the tonal church music is occasionally punctuated by strident dissonant chords—for example, in the organ introduction—so as to depict musically the priest's discordant morals behind the pious facade.

The Faustian comedy *The Witches of Eastwick* (George Miller, 1987) has a sardonically "satanic" score boasting a grotesque tarantella as the devil's leitmotiv, with appropriate strings scratches in the style of "witches' fiddles" and supernatural-suggesting synthesizer's coloring. It is also memorable for a classy scherzo for piano and orchestra written for the tennis-match scene, and a lavish love theme for the balloon scene, which can be heard only partially in the film, since its first part was replaced by Puccini's "Nessun Dorma."

Williams has also composed very intimate and restrained scores, which are often ignored by his detractors, who strategically focus on his allegedly "pompous" and "bombastic" scores of major "commercial" successes. Examples of what could be called "chamber music Williams" show up in *The Accidental Tourist* (Lawrence Kasdan, 1988) and *Stanley and Iris* (Martin Ritt, 1990), both of which feature lyrical piano solos, and the thriller *Presumed Innocent* (1990), again with prominent piano solos, atonal passages, and synthesizer touches.

Williams's collaboration with Oliver Stone for the controversial American trilogy formed by *Born on the Fourth of July* (1989), *JFK* (1991), and *Nixon* (1995) deserves a niche of its own. The core of the score for *Born on the Fourth of July* is an elegiac trumpet solo (played by Tim Morrison) backed by poignant string writing. "I knew immediately I would want a string orchestra to sing in opposition to all the realism on the screen, and then the idea came to have a solo trumpet—not a military trumpet, but an American trumpet, to recall the happy youth of this boy," says Williams.[55] As for *JFK*, the composer was involved in the project before shooting, and his music was later used to edit the film. Williams explains: "Actually what drove the idea was the fact that *JFK* had been made like a documentary film. . . . [It] was going to be edited more in terms of a documentary film than a live action drama, accompanied by a lot of narration, voice-overs, that had to be edited or cut. Oliver Stone and I thought that it might be a good idea to have set pieces of music, on which to build these segments of the film."[56]

In the blockbuster-film department, Williams also contributed to the success of the slapstick children's comedy *Home Alone* (Chris Columbus, 1990) and its sequel *Home Alone 2: Lost in New York* (Chris Columbus, 1992). He composed comedic cartoonlike scores with extensive Tom and Jerry–like Mickey-Mousing, enriched with original Christmas carols—"Star of Bethlehem," "Somewhere in My Memory," "Christmas Star," "Merry Christmas, Merry Christmas." In *Home Alone 2*, in particular, a tip of the hat to the music of Max Steiner must be pointed out. For the fake film noir *Angels with Filthy Souls II*—watched on TV by little Kevin—Williams penned a parody of Steiner's music for *The Big Sleep* (Howard Hawks, 1946). Director Chris Columbus reminisces:

> We were having some screenings of *Home Alone* around town, and the word got out that people were enjoying the movie, and so John's agent said, "I'd like to show it to John Williams." . . . He decided he wanted to write the score. . . . One of the things we were struggling with when we were adding temp music to the movie is having a comical score. A comical score is one of the most difficult things to write, because composers tend to overwrite for comedy. If you write something comedic for a comedy scene, it basically kills it. You have to know when to stay away from the moment and let the comedy play. With John, it was amazing how subtle it was. You don't have an overbearing comedic score. That taught me a lot. You have to let comedy breathe and accentuate just those special moments. When we first heard the movie's theme, I just thought, "This is one of those special themes that will hopefully live forever." And the theme carried over into the final moments in the movie, which are extraordinarily emotional. John's score beautifully accentuates the moment without making it overly sentimental.[57]

In 1992 Williams worked on Ron Howard's *Far and Away*, a nineteenth-century migration epic about a young Irish couple moving to America. He adopted the Irish musical dialect and colored the score with the sound of ethnic instruments—like the bodhrán drum—performed by the Irish group the Chieftains, and he once again paid homage to *The Quiet Man*.

> One of the films I admired the most when I was a very young person was a John Ford picture *The Quiet Man*. . . . I always felt that I would love to write the score, and this opportunity came along through Ron Howard. . . . I also had worked with the Chieftains in Boston about a year before this, when they came as guests and they played with the [Boston Pops] orchestra. There were Uilleann pipes,

bagpipes, these Irish things, penny whistles, fiddle. So I looked at Ron Howard's movie and thought it was a wonderful opportunity to bring in Paddy [Maloney]'s group, to give that particular flavor to the orchestration.[58]

Williams returned to an Irish setting with *Angela's Ashes* (Alan Parker, 1999). However, for this story of poverty and immigration, Williams did not resort to ethnic "Oirish" music but to a more universal dialect. The overall score, with prominent solo parts for piano and harp, alternates between restrained episodes and more expansive, hopeful impulses, with some humorous touches as well—for instance, the pizzicato writing for the telegram delivering scene. Explains Williams:

> Parker said he didn't feel that the music should be in the Irish idiom particularly, that it should be broader, more universal—an emotionally direct score. I thought that probably was a right decision. I found the film to be a kind of chamber piece in the sense that you had the father and the mother and the children—four or five principal parts. Obviously, the music shouldn't be scaled on a Strauss opera; it would have been too big for the film. So I felt that a chamber music approach with musical protagonists that would more or less match the acting ones might work. I wrote a score that featured the piano, harp, oboe and cello set in front of a string orchestra.[59]

A few words should also be said for *Rosewood* (John Singleton, 1997)—a drama set in the early nineteenth-century southern United States—with consistent solo parts for guitar, bass guitar, harmonica, piano, and featuring three a cappella spirituals: "Look Down, Lord," "Light My Way," and "The Freedom Train," a further demonstration of the composer's versatility.

At seventy, Williams opened the new millennium with another box office hit: the *Harry Potter* series, whose first three films he scored (*Harry Potter and the Sorcerer's Stone*, Chris Columbus, 2001; *Harry Potter and the Chamber of Secrets*, Chris Columbus, 2002; *Harry Potter and the Prisoner of Azkaban*, Alfonso Cuarón, 2004). Said Williams, "I wanted to capture the world of weightlessness and flight and sleight of hand and happy surprise. This caused the music to be a little more theatrical than most film scores would be. It sounds like music that you would hear in the theater rather than in the film."[60] Williams's musical tapestry for the trilogy is a very rich one, and only a few examples can be given here. The series' signature tune is "Hedwig's Theme," Hedwig being Harry's white owl. It can be heard at the beginning of each film—it is also retained in the subsequent five film chapters not scored by Williams. In the narrative, it is associated with the magical world of Harry and his friends. It is a music box–like ethereal melody, backed by kaleidoscopic harmonies, and played with silvery timbre by the celesta—a carillon-like sounding instrument notably used in Tchaikovsky's "Sugar Plum Fairy Dance" from *The Nutcracker* (1892). Indeed, the scores for the first two films hark back to the Russian school, with Tchaikovskyan melodies, Rimsky-Korsakov–like orchestrations, and timbres and colors reminiscent of Stravinsky's *The Firebird* (1910). Expansive and soaring Williamsesque flying themes abound—the broomstick rides and the magical bird Fawkes the Phoenix. A lively staccato woodwinds theme—"Nimbus 2000"—is associated with Harry's flying broomstick and with spells in general. A dark, satanic, slithery motif is the trademark for Voldemort and black magic—featuring the tritone, the *diabolus in musica* (see chapters 7 and 9). An odd duet, harp and contrabassoon, accompanies the heavy snoring of Fluffy, a two-headed monster dog. A noble, British-sounding brass theme acts as a musical signature for the "Hogwarts School of Witchcraft and Wizardry," while the Quidditch matches are scored with heraldic fanfares, kinetic action music, and a tight network of snippets from the various leitmotivs. The overall tone of the music changes radically in the third film, where only a couple of the old themes are kept—"Hedwig's theme" and "Nimbus 2000." The tone of the film is less childlike as Harry and his friends approach adolescence. The music accordingly becomes more experimental and varied. There are fugato episodes (in the Quidditch match), virtuoso solos (as the exhilarating flute solo in the butterfly flight scene), archaic instrumentation (crumhorns, recorders, fiddles), and medieval modal dialect (as in the music accompanying Hagrid's lessons). There is a Greensleeveslike theme for Harry and his memories of the past, chilling atonal writing for the Dementors (ghosts who feed on people's happiness, driving them desperate and mad), and an oddball Leonard Bernstein–like symphonic jazz piece accompanying the reckless trip of a magical "knight" bus. When Harry takes a long-awaited revenge by casting a spell on the nasty Aunt Marge, a Rossinilike waltz humorously accompanies her with appropriate *crescendo* as she inflates like a balloon, rises in the air, and floats over the rooftops of London. There is even a diegetic choral piece—"Double Trouble"—based on William Shakespeare's witch-spell scene from *Macbeth* (1605–8) and played on ancient instruments by the Dufay Collective.[61]

In contrast to the kaleidoscopic orchestral colors of the *Harry Potter* triptych, the Nazi Germany–set story *The Book Thief* (Brian Percival, 2013) recounts,

narrated by Death himself, how a young girl survives the regime, the depriva-
tions, and the war thanks to the comforting help of books. Says Williams:

> I loved the idea that through reading we can find peace and solace. Liesel is also
> a strong girl. She defends herself in the schoolyard. We discover that the life she
> leads is supported and made possible by words and by the power of literature.
> . . . One particular [musical] theme concerns the almost physical attraction that
> books hold for Liesel. She goes into the library and the books are very beautiful
> and irresistible to her. Another theme is how the messages of the Voice of
> Death are expressed musically. They maybe mournful but they are also filled
> with hope.[62]

As *Schindler's List* featured a prominent violin part, this score showcases piano
solos, to the point that Williams has adapted a piano-solo suite from it.[63]

This overview, which has no pretense of being a thorough account of Williams's production, has hopefully traced a fly-over trip across the remaining
major parts of his film work, in order to show that besides his neoclassical
scores, Williams is also a resourceful, versatile composer who has ventured in
the most diverse territories.

Appendix II
Film and Television Scores

Film titles followed by an asterisk (*) were nominated for an Academy Award (for Best Original Score unless noted otherwise). Film titles followed by a dagger (†) won an Academy Award.

SCORES FOR THEATRICAL AND TV FEATURE FILMS

Star Wars: Episode IX—The Rise of Skywalker, 2019,* J. J. Abrams
The Post, 2017, Steven Spielberg
Star Wars: Episode VIII—The Last Jedi, 2017,* Rian Johnson
The BFG, 2016, Steven Spielberg
Star Wars: Episode VII—The Force Awakens,* 2015, J. J. Abrams
The Book Thief,* 2013, Brian Percival
Lincoln,* 2012, Steven Spielberg
The Adventures of Tintin,* 2011, Steven Spielberg
War Horse,* 2011, Steven Spielberg
Indiana Jones and the Kingdom of the Crystal Skull, 2008, Steven Spielberg
Memoirs of a Geisha,* 2005, Rob Marshall
Munich,* 2005, Steven Spielberg
Star Wars: Episode III—Revenge of the Sith, 2005, George Lucas
War of the Worlds, 2005, Steven Spielberg
Harry Potter and the Prisoner of Azkaban,* 2004, Alfonso Cuarón
The Terminal, 2004, Steven Spielberg
Catch Me if You Can,* 2002, Steven Spielberg
Harry Potter and the Chamber of Secrets, 2002, Chris Columbus (music arranged by William Ross)
Minority Report, 2002, Steven Spielberg

Star Wars: Episode II—Attack of the Clones, 2002, George Lucas
*A.I. Artificial Intelligence,** 2001, Steven Spielberg
*Harry Potter and the Sorcerer's Stone,** 2001, Chris Columbus
*The Patriot,** 2000, Roland Emmerich
*Angela's Ashes,** 1999, Alan Parker
Star Wars: Episode I—The Phantom Menace, 1999, George Lucas
*Saving Private Ryan,** 1998, Steven Spielberg
Stepmom, 1998, Chris Columbus
*Amistad,** 1997, Steven Spielberg
The Lost World: Jurassic Park, 1997, Steven Spielberg
Rosewood, 1997, John Singleton
Seven Years in Tibet, 1997, Jean-Jacques Annaud
*Sleepers,** 1996, Barry Levinson
*Nixon,** 1995, Oliver Stone
*Sabrina,** 1995, Sidney Pollack (nominated for Best Original Comedy Score
    and Best Original Song)
Jurassic Park, 1993, Steven Spielberg
Schindler's List,† 1993, Steven Spielberg
Far and Away, 1992, Ron Howard
Home Alone 2: Lost in New York, 1992, Chris Columbus
*JFK,** 1991, Oliver Stone
*Home Alone,** 1990, Chris Columbus (nominated for Best Original Score and
    Best Original Song)
*Hook,** 1991, Steven Spielberg (nominated for Best Original Song)
Presumed Innocent, 1990, Alan Pakula
Stanley & Iris, 1990, Martin Ritt
Always, 1989, Steven Spielberg
*Born on the Fourth of July,** 1989, Oliver Stone
*Indiana Jones and the Last Crusade,** 1989, Steven Spielberg
*The Accidental Tourist,** 1988, Lawrence Kasdan
*Empire of the Sun,** 1987, Steven Spielberg
*The Witches of Eastwick,** 1987, George Miller
Space Camp, 1986, Harry Winer
*Indiana Jones and the Temple of Doom,** 1984, Steven Spielberg
*The River,** 1984, Mark Rydell
*Star Wars: Episode VI—Return of the Jedi,** 1983, Richard Marquand
E.T. the Extra-Terrestrial,† 1982, Steven Spielberg
Monsignor, 1982, Frank Perry

Yes, Giorgio,* 1982, Franklin J. Schaffner (nominated for Best Original Song) (main theme and song "If We Were In Love"; additional music by Michael J. Lewis)

Heartbeeps, 1981, Allan Arkush

Raiders of the Lost Ark,* 1981, Steven Spielberg

Star Wars: Episode V—The Empire Strikes Back,* 1980, Irvin Kershner

1941, 1979, Steven Spielberg

Dracula, 1979, John Badham

The Fury, 1978, Brian De Palma

Jaws 2, 1978, Jeannot Szwarc

Superman: The Movie,* 1978, Richard Donner

Black Sunday, 1977, John Frankenheimer

Close Encounters of the Third Kind,* 1977, Steven Spielberg

Star Wars: Episode IV—A New Hope,† 1977, George Lucas

Family Plot, 1976, Alfred Hitchcock

Midway, 1976, Jack Smight

The Missouri Breaks, 1976, Arthur Penn

The Eiger Sanction, 1975, Clint Eastwood

Jaws,† 1975, Steven Spielberg

Conrack, 1974, Martin Ritt

Earthquake, 1974, Mark Robson

The Sugarland Express, 1974, Steven Spielberg

The Towering Inferno,* 1974, John Guillermin

Cinderella Liberty,* 1973, Mark Rydell (nominated for Best Original Score and Best Original Song)

The Long Goodbye, 1973, Robert Altman

The Man Who Loved Cat Dancing, 1973, Richard C. Sarafian

The Paper Chase, 1973, James Bridges

Tom Sawyer,* 1973, Don Taylor (nominated for Best Score Adaptation) (arrangement of Richard M. Sherman and Robert B. Sherman's original songs and additional background music)

The Cowboys, 1972, Mark Rydell

Images,* 1972, Robert Altman

Pete 'n' Tillie, 1972, Martin Ritt

The Poseidon Adventure,* 1972, Ronald Neame

The Screaming Woman (TV film), 1972, Jack Smight

Fiddler on the Roof,† 1971, Norman Jewison (arrangement of Jerry Bock and Sheldon Harnick's original songs and additional background music)

Jane Eyre (TV film), 1971, Delbert Mann

Storia di una Donna [Story of a Woman], 1970, Leonardo Bercovici

Daddy's Gone A-Hunting, 1969, Mark Robson

Goodbye, Mr. Chips,* 1969, Herbert Ross (nominated for Best Score
    Adaptation) (arrangement of Leslie Bricusse's original songs and
    additional background music)

The Reivers,* 1969, Mark Rydell

Heidi (TV film), 1968, Delbert Mann

Sergeant Ryker, 1968, Buzz Kulik

Fitzwilly, 1967, Delbert Mann

A Guide for the Married Man, 1967, Gene Kelly

Valley of the Dolls,* 1967, Mark Robson (nominated for Best Score
    Adaptation) (arrangement of André Previn and Dory Previn's original
    songs and additional background music)

How to Steal a Million, 1966, William Wyler

Not with My Wife, You Don't!, 1966, Norman Panama

Penelope, 1966, Arthur Hiller

The Plainsman, 1966, David Lowell Rich

The Rare Breed, 1966, Andrew V. McLaglen

John Goldfarb, Please Come Home, 1965, J. Lee Thompson

None but the Brave, 1965, Frank Sinatra

The Killers, 1964, Don Siegel

Nightmare in Chicago (TV film, extended version of the *Kraft Suspense Theater*
    episode "Once upon a Savage Night"), 1964, Robert Altman

Diamond Head, 1963, Guy Green

Gidget Goes to Rome, 1963, Paul Wendkos

Stark Fear, 1962, Ned Hockman (composer of diegetic music; nondiegetic
    music by Ned Hockman)

Bachelor Flat, 1961, Frank Tashlin

The Secret Ways, 1961, Phil Karlson

Because They're Young, 1960, Paul Wendkos

I Passed for White, 1960, Fred M. Wilcox (music cowritten with Jerry Irvin)

Daddy-O, 1958, Lou Place

SCORES FOR TV SERIES, DOCUMENTARIES, AND SHORT FILMS

Dear Basketball, 2017, Glen Keane and Kobe Bryant (animated short)

Great Performances [*Masterpiece Classic*], 1971– (main theme, 2009–)

A Timeless Call, 2008, Steven Spielberg (documentary short)

The Unfinished Journey, 1999, Steven Spielberg (documentary short)

Amazing Stories, 1985–87 (main theme and episode scores "The Mission" and
   "Ghost Train," both directed by Steven Spielberg)

Land of the Giants, 1968–70 (main theme and episode score "The Crash,"
   1968)

CBS Playhouse, 1967–69 (episode score "Saturday Adoption," 1968)

The Ghostbreaker, 1967 (score for rejected one-hour pilot episode)

And Baby Makes Three, 1966 (score for rejected half-hour pilot episode)

The Kraft Summer Music Hall, 1966 (main theme)

The Tammy Grimes Show, 1966 (episode score "How to Steal a Girl Even if
   It's Only Me")

The Time Tunnel, 1966–67 (main theme and score for the pilot episode
   "Rendezvous with Yesterday," 1966)

The Katherine Reed Story, 1965 (short film)

Lost in Space, 1965–68 (main theme and five episode scores, 1965)

Who Goes There?, 1965 (score for rejected half-hour pilot episode)

Gilligan's Island, 1964–67 (nineteen episode scores, 1964–65)

Wayne and Shuster Take an Affectionate Look At . . ., 1964–65 (six episode
   scores, 1965)

Breaking Point, 1963–65 (episode score "Better than a Dead Lion," 1964)

Bob Hope Presents the Chrysler Theater, 1963–67 (eight episode scores,
   1963–67)

Kraft Suspense Theater, 1963–65 (main theme and twenty episode scores,
   1963–65)

The Eleventh Hour, 1962–63 (episode score "The Bronze Locust," 1963)

The Wide Country, 1962–63 (twenty-eight episode scores)

Alcoa Premiere, 1961–63 (main theme and seven episode scores, 1961–63)

Ben Casey, 1961–65 (episode score "A Little Fun to Match the Sorrow," 1965)

Checkmate, 1960–62 (main theme and forty-one episode scores, 1960–62)

Kraft Mystery Theater, 1959–63 (main theme, 1962–63)

Markman, 1959–60 (episode score "Woman of Arles," 1959)

Bachelor Father, 1957–62 (forty-four episode scores, 1959–60)

M-Squad, 1957–60 (eight episode scores, 1958–59)

Tales of Wells Fargo, 1957–62 (three episode scores, 1960)

Wagon Train, 1957–65 (six episode scores, 1958–64)

Playhouse 90, 1956–61 (episode score "The Right Hand Man," 1958)

You Are Welcome (documentary), 1954

General Electric Theater, 1953–62 (two episode scores, 1960–62)

Principal Early-Year Collaborations

The Great Race, 1965, Blake Edwards (pianist, music by Henry Mancini)

The Pink Panther, 1964, Blake Edwards (pianist, music by Henry Mancini)

Charade, 1963, Stanley Donen (pianist, music by Henry Mancini)

Hemingway's Adventures of a Young Man, 1962, Martin Ritt (pianist, music by Franz Waxman)

To Kill a Mockingbird, 1962, Robert Mulligan (pianist, music by Elmer Bernstein)

Breakfast at Tiffany's, 1961, Blake Edwards (pianist, music by Henry Mancini)

The Guns of Navarone, 1961, J. Lee Thompson (orchestrator and arranger, music by Dimitri Tiomkin)

Hatari!, 1961, Howard Hawks (pianist, music by Henry Mancini)

West Side Story, 1961, Robert Wise (pianist, music by Leonard Bernstein, arrangement and musical direction by Johnny Green)

The Apartment, 1960, Billy Wilder (pianist and Orchestrator, music by Adolph Deutsch)

The Magnificent Seven, 1960, John Sturges (pianist, music by Elmer Bernstein)

Studs Lonigan, 1960, Irvin Lerner (pianist, music by Jerry Goldsmith)

City of Fear, 1959, Irving Lerner (pianist, music by Jerry Goldsmith)

Gidget, 1959, Paul Wendkos (orchestrator, music by Arthur Morton)

Johnny Staccato (TV series), 1959–60 (pianist, music by Elmer Bernstein)

Mr. Lucky (TV series), 1959 (pianist, music by Henry Mancini)

Some Like It Hot, 1959, Billy Wilder (pianist, music by Adolph Deutsch)

The Twilight Zone (TV series), 1959–64 (pianist, music by Bernard Herrmann)

Bell, Book, and Candle, 1958, Richard Quine (pianist, music by George Duning)

The Big Country, 1958, William Wyler (pianist, music by Jerome Moross)

God's Little Acre, 1958, Anthony Mann (pianist, music by Elmer Bernstein)

Peter Gunn (TV series), 1958–61 (pianist, music by Henry Mancini)

Porgy and Bess, 1958, Otto Preminger (pianist, music by George Gershwin, arrangement and musical direction by André Previn)

South Pacific, 1958, Joshua Logan (pianist, music by Richard Rodgers, arrangement and musical direction by Alfred Newman)

Funny Face, 1957, Stanley Donen (pianist, music by Adolph Deutsch)

Sweet Smell of Success, 1957, Alexander Mackendrick (pianist, music by Elmer Bernstein)

Carousel, 1956, Henry King (pianist, music by Richard Rodgers, arrangement and musical direction by Alfred Newman)

Glossary

absolute music: Music that is *ab soluta* (untied), that is, composed for a stand-alone listening experience freed from any external influences and extramusical references. The term originated in the nineteenth century, within the philosophical framework of idealism.

applied/functional music: A musical rendition of a literary text, like a symphonic poem, or a musical accompaniment to an extramusical event, such as a ballet, an opera, or a film.

BMI: Broadcast Music Inc., one of the top music rights management agencies.

CGI: Computer-generated imagery.

cognitive function: An instance in which film music serves to clarify explicit or implicit meanings implied by the film, giving clues to understand denotations and to interpret connotations.

diegetic: Music or sound presented as originated from some source within the film's world. It can be heard by film viewers and by characters as well.

emotive function (micro/macro): Locally, film music serves to enhance an emotional tone already present in a scene or to provide one by transferring to the images its emotional component (micro-emotive function). Globally—by presenting the theme in the opening titles, then reprising it in variations throughout the film and finally presenting it again at the end of the film—film music performs a function similar to that of a frame in a painting and unifies the aesthetic experience of the film for the viewer (macro-emotive function).

"gradual disclosure of the main theme": A typical John Williams technique that has both a macro- and a micro-emotive function. The main theme is presented gradually across the film, in the form of progressively longer melodic fragments. The final exposition of the theme in its entirety comes only at a strategic point in the narrative, typically in a scene requiring a strong emotional response from the viewers. Globally, the gradual and coherent development of the music projects onto the film's form a sense of overall coherence (macro-emotive function). Locally, when the viewers finally hear the familiar theme presented in its entirety, the effect is a strong emotional gratification that attaches to that particular scene (micro-emotive function).

leitmotiv: In music dramas, and later in film music, the association and identification of a character, situation, or idea with a musical motif, which is reprised and developed narratively throughout the work.

Mickey-Mousing: A film music technique aimed at adhering closely to the visuals through a tight series of explicit sync points where musical gestures duplicate visual actions.

MIDI: Musical instrument digital interface. This technology allows a keyboard to be connected to a computer, which directly transcribes the music as one plays.

montage: A film-editing technique that serves to condense time, space, narrative, and conceptual information. It is mostly used to summarize in an emblematic sequence events that would otherwise require a lengthier presentation, or to convey concepts through semantically meaningful juxtapositions of images.

nondiegetic: Music or sound that is not part of the film's world. Film viewers can hear it; characters cannot.

pandiatonicism: An approach to composition that employs the notes of the diatonic scale freely without conventional resolutions. Unlike in traditional diatonic writing, the chords built on the scale grades are not assigned fixed functions and different degrees of importance.

"payoff": The moment in the film where the function of the "setup" is revealed and fulfilled.

quartal harmony: Chords are built not as juxtaposed thirds but as juxtaposed fourths, creating freer and more dissonant harmonic patterns than traditional tonal harmony.

"setup": The planting of a piece of information in the film whose function will be clear at a later moment—for example, a detail that initially seems to be of no importance is later revealed to be essential for a turning point in the plot.

spatial perceptive function: An instance in which film music serves to guide or modify the perception of the viewer by pointing his attention to a particular element within the framed space.

sync point: A moment in a film where a visual event and a musical event are precisely synchronized and perfectly matched.

tam-tam: A kind of large indefinite-pitched "gong" used in symphony orchestras.

temporal perceptive function: An instance in which film music serves to influence the perception of the pace of the film, by using its own rhythm to speed up or slow down the visual rhythm and the speed of the cutting.

tone clusters: Groups of contiguous notes played simultaneously and therefore sounding highly dissonant and perceived as "fastidiously" grating.

tritone: An augmented-fourth interval, slightly dissonant. It was known as *diabolus in musica* in medieval treatises.

typage: An immediately recognizable one-dimensional figure representing a specific ethnic or social group.

"villains' chords": Low-pitched minor chords played by the brass, mostly with the seventh degree of the scale on the bottom, recurrently used in Hollywood film music of the 1930s and 1940s.

Notes

Introduction

1. It must be said that Disney, being the producer, accrued to his name the nominations of each product released by his studio but was not directly involved artistically in every item. Each nomination that Williams has gotten was for a work that was entirely of his own direct creation; the creation of a single person, not a studio, makes the number of nominations even more impressive.

2. Stephen Moss, "The Force Is with Him," *The Guardian* (London), 4 February 2002. Williams's non-cinematic output is surveyed in Emile Wennekes, "No Sharks, No Stars, Just Idiomatic Scoring and Sounding Engagement: John Williams as a 'Classical' Composer," in *John Williams: Music for Films, Television, and the Concert Stage*, ed. Emilio Audissino (Turnhout: Brepols, 2018), 71–94. One of Williams's most refined concert pieces, his 1976 *Violin Concerto*, is thoroughly analyzed in Tom Schneller, "Out of Darkness: John Williams's *Violin Concerto*," in *John Williams: Music for Films, Television, and the Concert Stage*, ed. Emilio Audissino (Turnhout: Brepols, 2018), 343–74.

3. Geoffrey McNab, "They Shoot, He Scores," *The Times* (London), 25 September 2001.

4. Tom Shone, "How to Score in the Movies," *Sunday Times* (London), 21 June 1998.

5. Roberto Aschieri, *Over the Moon: La música de John Williams para el cine* (Santiago de Chile: Universidad Diego Portales, 1999); Peter Moormann, *Spielberg-Variationen: Die Filmmusik von John Williams* (Baden-Baden: Nomos, 2010); Alexandre Tylski, ed., *John Williams: Un alchimiste musical à Hollywood* (Paris: L'Harmattan, 2011); Andrés Valverde Amador, *John Williams: Vida y obra* (Seville: Editorial Berenice, 2013).

6. Tony Thomas, *Film Score: The Art and Craft of Movie Music* (Burbank, CA: Riverwood, 1991), 18.

7. On the origins and diffusion of this aesthetic criterion, see Carl Dahlhaus, *The Idea of Absolute Music*, trans. Roger Lustig (Chicago: University of Chicago Press, 1991). I discuss the implication for film music in Emilio Audissino, "Overruling a Romantic Prejudice: Forms and Formats of Film Music in Concert Programs," in *Film in Concert, Film Scores and Their Relation to Classical Concert Music*, ed. Sebastian Stoppe (Glücksstadt: VWH Verlag, 2014), 25–43. On the traditional critics' preference

for instrumental music over dramatic music, see David Neumeyer, "Introduction," in *Music and Cinema*, ed. James Buhler, Caryl Flinn, and David Neumeyer (Hanover, NH: Wesleyan University Press, 2000), 21.

8. See Mervyn Cooke, ed., *The Hollywood Music Reader* (New York: Oxford University Press, 2010), 83–92, 259–80, 317–26; and James Wierzbicki, Nathan Platte, and Colin Roust, eds., *The Routledge Film Music Sourcebook* (New York: Routledge, 2012), 79–82, 96–99; and Theodor W. Adorno and Hanns Eisler, *Composing for the Films* (1947; repr., New York: Continuum, 2007).

9. Williams quoted in T. L. Ponick, "Movie Music Raised to Its Rightful Place by Composer," *Washington Times*, 3 December 2004.

10. Martin Bernheimer, "Pop! John Williams on Philharmonic Podium," *Los Angeles Times*, 12 November 1983.

11. Chris Pasles, "John Williams Brings Bland Offerings to the Art Center," *Los Angeles Times*, 4 April 1988.

12. "Angela Morley in Private Interview, 1999," YouTube, April 12, 2020, 38:00, https://www.youtube.com/watch?v=A3Xb9XDDeA0. Morley was a frequent collaborator of Williams's, also doing "score preparation" work on *Star Wars*.

13. Neil Lerner, "Nostalgia, Masculinist Discourse and Authoritarianism in John Williams' Scores for *Star Wars* and *Close Encounters of the Third Kind*," in *Off the Planet: Music, Sound, and Science Fiction Cinema*, ed. Philip Hayward (Eastleigh, UK: John Libbey, 2004), 106.

14. Royal S. Brown, *Overtones and Undertones: Reading Film Music* (Berkeley: University of California Press, 1994), 187.

15. For example, Chloé Huvet, "*D'Un nouvel espoir* (1977) à *La Revanche des Sith* (2005): Écriture musicale et traitement de la partition au sein du complexe audiovisuel dans la saga *Star Wars*" (PhD diss., Université Rennes 2/Université de Montréal, 2018); Frank Lehman, "Scoring the President: Myth and Politics in John Williams's *JFK* and *Nixon*," *Journal of the Society for American Music* 9, no. 4 (2015): 409–44, Tom Schneller, "Modal Interchange and Semantic Resonance in Themes by John Williams," *Journal of Film Music* 6, no. 1 (2013): 49–74; and Konstantinos Zacharopoulos, "Musical Syntax in John Williams's Film Music Themes," in *Contemporary Film Music: Investigating Cinema Narratives and Composition*, ed. Lindsay Coleman and Joakim Tillman (London: Palgrave Macmillan, 2017), 237–62.

16. Jeremy Orosz, "John Williams: Paraphraser or Plagiarist?," *Journal of Musicological Research* 34, no. 4 (2015): 299, 318–19.

17. Emile Wennekes, "'What's the Motive?,' She Asked: Tales from the Musical Pawnshop," in *Liber Plurium Vocum: Voor Rokus de Groot*, ed. Sander van Maas et al. (Amsterdam: University of Amsterdam, 2012), 208.

18. Alex Ross, "Listening to *Star Wars*," *New Yorker*, 1 January 2016.

19. Anne Midget, "As a Classical Music Critic, I Used to Think the *Star Wars* Score Was beneath Me. I Was Wrong," *Washington Post*, 18 January 2019.

20. Maurizio Caschetto's website, the Legacy of John Williams, is a rich repository of original podcasts and interviews with classical musicians discussing John Williams's importance and influence. See https://thelegacyofjohnwilliams.com.

21. Ozawa quoted in Jon Burlingame, "A Career of Epic Proportion," *Los Angeles Times*, 3 February 2002.

22. Russ, "Listening to *Star Wars*."

23. David Vernier, "Magnificent Modern Maestro," *Digital Audio*, March 1988.

24. I have addressed Williams's versatility in Emilio Audissino, "John Williams and Contemporary Film Music," in *Contemporary Film Music: Investigating Cinema Narratives and Composition*, ed. Lindsay Coleman and Joakim Tillman (Basingstoke: Palgrave Macmillan, 2017), 221–36. Essays by international scholars investigating both major and less-explored works are collected in Emilio Audissino, ed., *John Williams: Music for Films, Television, and the Concert Stage* (Turnhout: Brepols, 2018).

25. Steven Spielberg, speech given at "John Williams 80th Birthday Gala," Tanglewood Festival, Lenox, MA, 18 August 2012.

26. Williams quoted in David Patrick Stearns, "2 Emmys, 4 Oscars, 15 Grammys . . . but, Hey, Who's Counting? Not John Williams, Hollywood's Most Honored Composer," *Arts & Entertainment*, February 1993, 22.

27. Moormann, *Spielberg-Variationen*; Jack Sullivan, "Spielberg–Williams: Symphonic Cinema," in *A Companion to Steven Spielberg*, ed. Nigel Morris (Malden, MA: Wiley-Blackwell, 2017), 175–94.

28. On Williams bringing back the symphonic style, see, most recently, Matthew Bribitzer-Stull, *Understanding the Leitmotif: From Wagner to Hollywood Film Music* (New York: Cambridge University Press, 2015), 272.

29. Kieron Casey, "An Interview with Todd Haberman," *The Totality* (blog), September 2016, http://www.wondrouskennel.com/2016/09/todd-haberman-interview-hans-zimmer-remote-control.html.

30. Emilio Audissino, *Film/Music Analysis: A Film Studies Approach* (Basingstoke: Palgrave Macmillan, 2017), v–vi.

31. See Kristin Thompson, *Eisenstein's "Ivan the Terrible": A Neoformalist Analysis* (Princeton, NJ: Princeton University Press, 1981); and Kristin Thompson, *Breaking the Glass Armor: Neoformalist Film Analysis* (Princeton, NJ: Princeton University Press, 1988).

32. Thompson, *Breaking the Glass Armor*, 10.

33. On cognitivism and narrative frames, see David Bordwell, "A Case for Cognitivism," *Iris* 9 (Spring 1989): 23.

34. Fred Karlin, *Listening to Movies: The Film Lover's Guide to Film Music* (Belmont, CA: Schirmer, 1994), 17–18.

35. "Miss Austria" was composed by Korngold in 1929 for his arrangement of Leo Fall's operetta *Rosen Aus Florida*.

36. The terms "intradiegetic," "extradiegetic," and "metadiegetic" are drawn from Gérard Genette, *Figures III* (Paris: Seuil, 1972). The application of Genette's categories to film music is discussed in Claudia Gorbman, *Unheard Melodies: Narrative Film Music* (London: BFI, 1987), 20–26. Gorbman renamed the extradiegetic level "nondiegetic level" and is credited for having established the terms as canonical tools of film-music analysis.

37. See Ben Winters, "The Non-Diegetic Fallacy: Film, Music, and Narrative Space," *Music and Letters* 91, no. 2 (2010): 224–44.

38. Adorno and Eisler, *Composing for the Films*, 2–3; Sergio Miceli, *Musica per film: Storia, Estetica, Analisi, Tipologie* (Lucca: LIM, 2009), 667–70.

39. James Buhler, "*Star Wars*, Music, and Myth," in *Music and Cinema*, ed. James Buhler, Caryl Flinn, and David Neumeyer (Hanover, NH: Wesleyan University Press, 2000), 33–57; Scott D. Paulin, "Richard Wagner and the Fantasy of Cinematic Unity: The Idea of the Gesamtkunstwerk in the History and Theory of Film Music," in *Music and Cinema*, ed. James Buhler, Caryl Flinn, and David Neumeyer (Hanover, NH: Wesleyan University Press, 2000), 58–84; Justin London, "Leitmotifs and Musical Reference in the Classical Film Score," in *Music and Cinema*, ed. James Buhler, Caryl Flinn, and David Neumeyer (Hanover, NH: Wesleyan University Press, 2000), 85–96; Bribitzer-Stull, *Understanding the Leitmotif.*

40. For an against-the-tide view of "wallpaper music," see Ben Winters, "Musical Wallpaper? Towards an Appreciation of Non-narrating Music in Film," *Music, Sound, and the Moving Image* 6, no. 1 (Spring 2012): 41–54.

41. Style in the *broader sense* is somewhat similar here to the concept of "paradigm" or "group style" as used in David Bordwell, Janet Staiger, and Kristin Thompson, *The Classical Hollywood Cinema: Film Style and Mode of Production to 1960* (New York: Columbia University Press, 1985), 5.

42. Leonard B. Meyer, *Style and Music: Theory, History, and Ideology* (Chicago: University of Chicago Press, 1996), 23–25.

43. Miceli, *Musica per film*, 616.

44. Bordwell, Staiger, and Thompson, *Classical Hollywood Cinema*, 33–35.

45. L. Meyer, *Style and Music*, 163.

46. L. Meyer, *Style and Music*, 327.

Chapter 1. A Chronicle of Classical Hollywood Music

1. Rick Altman, *Silent Film Sound* (New York: Columbia University Press, 2004), 199–201.

2. Tom Gunning, "The Cinema of Attraction: Early Film, Its Spectator, and the Avant-garde," *Wide Angle* 8, no. 3 (1986): 63–70.

3. I sum up the functions of music in silent cinema in Emilio Audissino, "'Behold the Newest Technological Sensation! With Music!' The Use of Music in the Silent Cinema," in *Music and the Second Industrial Revolution*, ed. Massimiliano Sala (Turnhout: Brepols, 2019), 429–47.

4. Altman, *Silent Film Sound*, 231–46.

5. Siegfried Krakauer, *Theory of Film: The Redemption of Physical Reality* (New York: Oxford University Press, 1960), 138.

6. Hitchcock quoted in Kristin Thompson and David Bordwell, *Film History: An Introduction*, 3rd ed. (New York: McGraw-Hill, 2010), 177.

7. Tony Thomas, *Music for the Movies*, 2nd ed. (Los Angeles: Silman-James, 1997), 139.

8. Michael Slowik, *After the Silents: Hollywood Film Music in the Early Sound Era, 1926–1934* (New York: Columbia University Press, 2014).

9. Roy M. Prendergast, *Film Music: A Neglected Art; A Critical Study of Music in Films* (New York: W. W. Norton, 1977), 23.

10. Barry Salt, *Film Style and Technology: History and Analysis*, 2nd ed. (London: Starword, 1992), 212.

11. In postrecording, the music track originally used on the set as a guide for the actors' singing and dancing is replaced with a definitive new version. See Fred Karlin and Rayburn Wright, *On the Track: A Guide to Contemporary Film Scoring*, 2nd ed. (New York: Routledge, 2004), 441–42. Dubbing is the mixing and balancing of the three separate dialogue, effect, and music tracks into a single, final soundtrack to be printed on the film's master. See Karlin, *Listening to Movies*, 56–62.

12. Prendergast, *Film Music*, 22–23.

13. If in the silent cinema the attraction was the moving-image technology, in the newborn sound cinema it was the sound-synchronization technology, and in its first years of sound cinema, the technological novelty was similarly paraded. Poetics similar to that of the cinema of attraction—the primacy given to the spectacular showcase of film-making novelty often at the expense of storytelling—have tended to reemerge in periods of technological innovation. See Wanda Strauven, ed., *Cinema of Attractions Reloaded* (Amsterdam: Amsterdam University Press, 2006), 289–352.

14. Mervyn Cooke, *A History of Film Music* (Cambridge: Cambridge University Press, 2008), 123.

15. On Steiner, see Peter Wegele, *Max Steiner: Composing, "Casablanca," and the Golden Age of Film Music* (Lanham, MD: Rowman & Littlefield, 2014); and Steven C. Smith, *Music by Max Steiner: The Epic Life of Hollywood's Most Influential Composer* (New York: Oxford University Press, 2020).

16. Another noteworthy instance is *Mr. Robinson Crusoe* (A. Edward Sutherland, 1932), in which Alfred Newman's score covers virtually each of the film's seventy minutes, not just as a neutral wallpaper but also with moments of functional accompaniment.

17. T. Thomas, *Film Score*, 68.

18. Christopher Palmer, *The Composer in Hollywood* (London: Marion Boyars, 1990), 29.

19. Gorbman, *Unheard Melodies*, 65.

20. See Kathryn Kalinak, *Settling the Score: Music and the Classical Hollywood Film* (Madison: University of Wisconsin Press, 1992), xvi; Michel Chion, *Audio-Vision: Sound on Screen*, trans. and ed. Claudia Gorbman (New York: Columbia University Press, 1994), 49–50; and Gary Marmorstein, *Hollywood Rhapsody: Movie Music and Its Makers, 1900 to 1975* (New York: Schirmer Books, 1997), 71.

21. Gorbman, *Unheard Melodies*, 87.

22. Music departments are described in Karlin, *Listening to Movies*, 177–95. A typical organization chart can be found in Prendergast, *Film Music*, 37.

23. For further reading on the composers' biographies, see T. Thomas, *Film Score*; T. Thomas, *Music for the Movies*; Palmer, *Composer in Hollywood*; William Darby and Jack Du Bois, *American Film Music: Major Composers, Techniques, Trends, 1915–1990* (Jefferson, NC: McFarland, 1990); and Marmorstein, *Hollywood Rhapsody*.

24. Copland's most important scores were those for *Of Mice and Men* (Lewis Milestone, 1939); *The Heiress* (William Wyler, 1949); and *The Red Pony* (Lewis Milestone, 1949).

25. On Korngold, see Jessica Duchen, *Erich Wolfgang Korngold* (London: Phaidon, 1996); and Brendan G. Carroll, *The Last Prodigy: A Biography of Erich Wolfgang Korngold* (Cleckheaton: Amadeus, 1997).

26. T. Thomas, *Music for the Movies*, 124.

27. For an in-depth analysis, see Ben Winters, *Erich Wolfgang Korngold's "The Adventures of Robin Hood": A Film Score Guide* (Lanham, MD: Scarecrow, 2007).

28. Ina Rae Hark, "Introduction," in *American Cinema of the 1930s: Themes and Variations*, ed. Ina Rae Hark (New Brunswick, NJ: Rutgers University Press, 2007), 24.

29. William Luhr, *Film Noir* (Malden, MA: Wiley-Blackwell, 2012), 6.

30. See David Bordwell, *On the History of Film Style* (Cambridge, MA: Harvard University Press, 1997), 211–36.

31. On the motivic modularity in Herrmann's music, see Tom Schneller, "Easy to Cut: Modular Form in the Film Scores of Bernard Herrmann," *Journal of Film Music* 5, no. 1/2 (2012): 127–51.

32. R. Brown, *Overtones and Undertones*, 153.

33. Miceli, *Musica per film*, 229.

34. Miklós Rózsa, *A Double Life: The Autobiography of Miklós Rózsa, Composer in the Golden Years of Hollywood* (1982; repr., New York: Wynwood, 1989).

35. The theremin is an electrophone instrument devised by Lev Theremin in 1928. Electronic oscillators are contained in a wooden box to which are attached a horizontal loop antenna and a vertical upright antenna. The player controls the pitch (with the upright antenna) and the volume (via the loop antenna) by moving his hands around the antennas, thus modifying the electric fields. Outside Hollywood, the theremin had already been introduced in film music by Dmitri Shostakovich in *Odna* (*Alone*, Leonid Trauberg and Grigori Kozintsev, 1931). The Ondes martenot was invented in 1928 by Maurice Martenot; it is technically similar to the theremin but instead controlled through a keyboard, which makes intonation easier, and it has a sweeter, softer sound. The Novachord—presented at the New York World's Fair in 1939 by the Hammond Company and featured in the score to *Rebecca* (Alfred Hitchcock, 1940, music by Franz Waxman) as the eerie musical manifestation of the protagonist's dead wife—was also operated through a keyboard but, unlike the Ondes martenot, was a polyphonic instrument. On the early electrophones, see Mark Brend, *The Sound of Tomorrow: How Electronic Music Was Smuggled into the Mainstream* (New York: Bloomsbury, 2012).

36. Roger Hickman, *Miklós Rózsa's "Ben-Hur": A Film Score Guide* (Lanham, MD: Scarecrow, 2011), 39.

37. Prendergast, *Film Music*, 64.

38. Salt, *Film Style and Technology*, 245–48; John Belton, "Il colore: dall'eccezione alla regola," in *Storia del cinema mondiale*, vol. 5, *Teorie, strumenti, memorie*, ed. Gian Piero Brunetta (Turin: Einaudi, 2001), 801–28; Douglas Gomery, *Shared Pleasures: A History of Movie Presentation in the United States* (Madison: University of Wisconsin Press, 1992), 226, 239–41.

39. Thompson and Bordwell, *Film History*, 311.

40. For a survey of the principal connotations carried by jazz in Hollywood cinema, see Emile Wennekes and Emilio Audissino, eds., *Cinema Changes: Incorporations of Jazz in the Film Soundtrack* (Turnhout: Brepols, 2019), ix–xxiii. On jazz in cinema

more generally, see Scott Yanov, *Jazz on Film: The Complete Story of the Musicians and Music Onscreen* (San Francisco, CA: Backbeat Books, 2004).

41. The music sounded so sexually evocative when matched with the visuals that it had to be toned down to comply with the prescriptions of the Production Code. See Cooke, *History of Film Music,* 216.

42. Adorno and Eisler, *Composing for the Films,* 21–29.

43. Palmer, *Composer in Hollywood,* 224; Rózsa, *Double Life,* 192.

44. On "Indian music," see Timothy E. Scheurer, *Music and Mythmaking in Film: Genre and the Role of the Composer* (Jefferson, NC: McFarland, 2008), 157–58.

45. Gomery, *Shared Pleasures,* 83–88.

46. Cooke, *History of Film Music,* 185.

47. James Wierzbicki, *Film Music: A History* (New York: Routledge, 2009), 186.

48. Friedhofer quoted in Karlin, *Listening to Movies,* 75.

Chapter 2. The Style of Classical Hollywood Music

1. Adorno and Eisler, *Composing for the Films,* 21–22.

2. Friedhofer quoted in T. Thomas, *Film Score,* 2. See also T. Thomas, *Music for the Movies,* 44–45; and Cooke, *History of Film Music,* 69.

3. Palmer, *Composer in Hollywood,* 19–23.

4. Caryl Flinn, *Strains of Utopia: Gender, Nostalgia, and Hollywood Music* (Princeton, NJ: Princeton University Press, 1992), 70–90.

5. Flinn, *Strains of Utopia,* 51–69.

6. Scheurer, *Music and Mythmaking in Film,* 14–18.

7. Yann Merluzeau, "Hollywood Bowl Conductor John Mauceri," *Film Score Monthly,* August 1996, 9.

8. David Bordwell, "The Classical Hollywood Style, 1917–60," in *The Classical Hollywood Cinema: Film Style and Mode of Production to 1960,* ed. David Bordwell, Janet Staiger, and Kristin Thompson (New York: Columbia University Press, 1985), 3–84.

9. T. Thomas, *Film Score,* 72, 246; Adorno and Eisler, *Composing for the Films,* 90; George Burt, *The Art of Film Music* (Boston: Northeastern University Press, 1994), 5–6. The composer Hugo Friedhofer gives an explanation in terms of work at the subliminal level in T. Thomas, *Film Score,* 214.

10. Gorbman, *Unheard Melodies,* 55. An argument against Gorbman's theory is in Jeff Smith, "Unheard Melodies? A Critique of Psychoanalytic Theories of Film Music," in *Post-Theory: Reconstructing Film Studies,* ed. David Bordwell and Noël Carroll (Madison: University of Wisconsin Press, 1996), 230–47.

11. Anahid Kassabian, *Hearing Film: Tracking Identifications in Contemporary Hollywood Film Music* (New York/London: Routledge, 2001), 2.

12. Stephen Prince, "Psychoanalytic Film Theory and the Problem of the Missing Spectator," in *Post-Theory: Reconstructing Film Studies,* ed. David Bordwell and Noël Carroll (Madison: University of Wisconsin Press, 1996), 71–86; Bordwell, "A Case for Cognitivism."

13. Annabel J. Cohen, "Film Music: Perspectives from Cognitive Psychology," in *Music and Cinema,* ed. James Buhler, Caryl Flinn, and David Neumeyer (Hanover, NH: Wesleyan University Press, 2000), 366–74.

14. Leonard B. Meyer, *Emotion and Meaning in Music* (Chicago: University of Chicago Press, 1956), 63; John A. Sloboda, *The Musical Mind: The Cognitive Psychology of Music*, new ed. (Oxford: Oxford University Press, 1999), 20; L. Meyer, *Style and Music*, 201.

15. David Bordwell, *Narration in the Fiction Film* (Madison: University of Wisconsin Press, 1985), 35; Chris Vogler, *The Writer's Journey: Mythic Structures for Writers*, 3rd ed. (Studio City, CA: Michael Wiese Productions, 2007), xiv.

16. L. Meyer, *Style and Music*, 209, 322.

17. L. Meyer, *Style and Music*, 340–42.

18. L. Meyer, *Emotion and Meaning in Music*, 158–66.

19. Wierzbicki, *Film Music*, 129.

20. Sometimes the clash between traditional associations and contrasting visuals is deliberately sought, most notably by Kubrick—for instance, in *2001: A Space Odyssey* (1968), he accompanied the rotating space station with Johan Strauss II's waltz *The Blue Danube* (*An Der Schönen Blauen Donau*, 1866, op. 314).

21. Prendergast, *Film Music*, 233.

22. Although in art music, "theme and variations" is more properly defined as a form rather than as a technique, here theme and variations is seen as a technique that film music employs to cope with a particular narrative need from the film.

23. For an extended study of the leitmotiv's definition and history, the problems involved in its conceptualization, and its musical strategies and usage (including film music), see Bribitzer-Stull, *Understanding the Leitmotif*.

24. Bribitzer-Stull, *Understanding the Leitmotif*, xx, 10.

25. R. Brown, *Overtones and Undertones*, 97–118.

26. Altman, *Silent Film Sound*, 52, 105.

27. For a difference between "explicit sync points" and "implicit sync points," see Miceli, *Musica per film*, 636–38.

28. On cartoon music, see Daniel Goldmark, *Tunes for 'Toons: Music and the Hollywood Cartoon* (Berkeley: University of California Press, 2005).

29. For Max Steiner's words on Mickey-Mousing, see Myrl A. Schreibman, "Memories of Max: An Archival Interview with Max Steiner. Part 1," *Film Score Monthly*, January/February 2005, 26.

30. James Buhler, "Analytical and Interpretive Approaches to Film Music (II): Analyzing Interactions of Music and Film," in *Film Music: Critical Approaches*, ed. K. J. Donnelly (New York: Continuum, 2001), 45.

31. For a historical account and an examination of the functions of the Mickey-Mousing technique, see Emilio Audissino, "The Function of Mickey-Mousing: A Re-assessment," in *Sound & Image: Audiovisual Aesthetics and Practices*, ed. Andrew Knight-Hill (New York: Routledge, 2020), 145–60.

32. Cohen, "Film Music," 371. The point is also sustained by Kalinak, *Settling the Score*, 86.

33. The negative connotations of the term "wallpaper music" can arguably be an effect of Igor Stravinsky's comments: "The film could not get along without [music], just as I myself could not get along without having the empty spaces of my living-room walls covered with wall paper. But you would ask me, would you, to regard my

wall paper as I would regard painting, or apply aesthetic standards to it?" Stravinsky quoted in Cooke, *Hollywood Film Music Reader*, 111.

34. On Hollywood film orchestras, see Adorno and Eisler, *Composing for the Films*, 70–77; and Karlin, *Listening to Movies*, 183–86.

35. Wierzbicki, *Film Music*, 48–49.

36. "Bow instruments, for centuries the foundation of the orchestra, actually do *not* comply with the peculiar demands of the microphone." Kurt London, *Film Music: A Summary of the Characteristic Features of Its History, Aesthetics, Technique; and Possible Developments* (London: Faber and Faber, 1936), 167.

37. Altman, *Silent Film Sound*, 308.

38. On orchestral timbres and musical dramaturgy, see Gerard Blanchard, *Images de la musique de cinéma* (Paris: Edilio, 1984).

39. Ian Sapiro, *Scoring the Score: The Role of the Orchestrator in the Contemporary Film Industry* (New York: Routledge, 2016), 38, 46.

40. For a survey, see Ian Sapiro, "Craft, Art, or Process: The Question of Creativity in Orchestration for Screen," in *The Routledge Companion to Screen Music and Sound*, ed. Miguel Mera, Ronald Sadoff, and Ben Winters (New York: Routledge, 2017), 305–17.

41. Wierzbicki, *Film Music*, 171; the conference is summarized on pages 169–74. Some of the conference's papers were published in Enzo Masetti, ed., *La musica nel film* (Rome: Bianco e Nero, 1950); and S. G. Biamonte, ed., *Musica e film* (Rome: Edizioni dell'Ateneo, 1959).

42. Much of the debate is collected in Wierzbicki, Platte, and Roust, *Routledge Film Music Sourcebook*, 127–46, while Morton's response to the vitriolic attacks of the European colleagues, originally published in 1951, is reprinted as Lawrence Morton, "Composing, Orchestrating, and Criticizing," in *The Hollywood Film Music Reader*, ed. Mervyn Cooke (New York: Oxford University Press, 2010), 327–40.

43. See Mark Evans, *Soundtrack: The Music of the Movies* (New York: Da Capo, 1979), 252.

44. Paul Andrew MacLean, "What Orchestrators Do," *Film Score Monthly*, 21 September 1997, https://www.filmscoremonthly.com/daily/article.cfm?articleID=2299.

45. Ben Winters, "The Composer and the Studio: Korngold and Warner Bros," in *The Cambridge Companion to Film Music*, ed. Mervyn Cooke and Fiona Ford (New York: Cambridge University Press, 2016), 52.

46. Winters, "The Composer and the Studio," 51.

47. Hopkins quoted in Wierzbicki, Platte, and Roust, *Routledge Film Music Sourcebook*, 141.

48. Masetti, *La musica nel film*, 28. It would be a naive idealization to assume that the past greats never had to bother about deadlines: Rossini had to create *The Barber of Seville* (two and a half hours of music) in twenty-one days.

49. Cooke, *Hollywood Film Music Reader*, viii.

50. For further reading on orchestration in cinema, see Karlin and Wright, *On the Track*, 320–30; and Richard Davis, *Complete Guide to Film Scoring: The Art and Business of Writing Music for Movies and TV* (Boston: Berklee, 1999), 111–16, which compares a composer's sketch and the resultant full score.

51. Rózsa quoted in Russell Lack, *Twenty Four Frames Under: A Buried History of Film Music* (London: Quartet Books, 1999), 189.

52. Lawrence Morton quoted in Wierzbicki, Platte, and Roust, *Routledge Film Music Sourcebook*, 134.

53. Steiner quoted in Schreibman, "Memories of Max. Part 1," 27; Myrl A. Schreibman, "Memories of Max: An Archival Interview with Max Steiner. Part 2," *Film Score Monthly*, March/April 2005, 23.

54. Herrmann quoted in Steven C. Smith, *A Heart at Fire's Center: The Life and Music of Bernard Herrmann*, 2nd. ed. (Berkeley: University of California Press, 2002), 81.

55. Prendergast, *Film Music*, 85.

56. Prendergast, *Film Music*, 85.

57. T. Thomas, *Music for the Movies*, 212–13; David Raksin, "Life with Charlie," in *The Hollywood Film Music Reader*, edited by Mervyn Cooke (New York: Oxford University Press, 2010), 69–81.

58. Danny Elfman, *Serenada Schizophrana*, CD booklet, Sony Classical 82876 89780 2, 2006.

59. Gorbman, *Unheard Melodies*, 88.

60. Peter Larsen, *Film Music*, trans. John Irons (London: Reaktion Books, 2005), 89.

61. Cooke, *History of Film Music*, 86.

62. Karlin and Wright, *On the Track*, 157–58.

63. Kalinak, *Settling the Score*, 187.

64. Bordwell, Staiger, and Thompson, *Classical Hollywood Cinema*, 3.

65. A narrative film is made up of a series of events that form the *plot*: what we see in the film in its given order. The viewer is actively engaged in the reconstruction of the correct chronological and causal order of the narrative events presented in the film's plot, and that viewer inferentially fills in the gaps when some narrative information is omitted. The result is the mental reconstruction of the *story*, that is, the correct chronological and causal order of all the events concerning the film's narrative and comprising both those events presented in the plot and those implied by the viewer's inference. On plot/story (*syuzhet/fabula*), see Bordwell, *Narration in the Fiction Film*, 48–62.

66. Chion, *Audio-Vision*, 11, 122.

67. Audissino, *Film/Music Analysis*, 136–38.

68. This is further discussed in Audissino, *Film/Music Analysis*, 29–36.

Chapter 3. The Modern Hollywood Music Style

1. To stick to the "language/techniques/means/function" four-point definition of a film-music style, "modern style" is used instead of "pop scoring," a term used in Jeff Smith, *The Sound of Commerce: Marketing Popular Film Music* (New York: Columbia University Press, 1998), 4. A hypothetical atonal score (*language*) with neither leitmotiv nor Mickey-Mousing (*techniques*) but played by a symphony orchestra (*musical means*) cannot be called "classical," but it is not "pop" either. Therefore, the term "modern style" constitutes a more precise and flexible definition for my scope.

2. Bordwell, *Narration in the Fiction Film*, 206–9.

3. Lack, *Twenty Four Frames Under*, 283.

4. Bresson quoted in Roberto Calabretto, *Lo schermo sonoro: La musica per film* (Venice: Marsilio, 2010), 148n. On Antonioni's dislike of and uneasiness about film music, see Calabretto, *Lo schermo sonoro*, 170. All translations are mine unless otherwise indicated.

5. Rohmer quoted in Calabretto, *Lo schermo sonoro*, 155n.

6. Comuzio, *Colonna sonora*, 120.

7. Lack, *Twenty Four Frames Under*, 161.

8. Barry Keith Grant, ed., *American Cinema of the 1960s: Themes and Variations* (New Brunswick, NJ: Rutgers University Press, 2008), 11.

9. Gary R. Edgerton, *The Columbia History of American Television* (New York: Columbia University Press, 2007), 193–95.

10. Grant, *American Cinema of the 1960s*, 12. In the classical period, the average annual output was 400 films, while in the 1960s it plummeted to 150 films. See Christopher Wagstaff, "Quasi un'appendice: Alcune cifre sull'industria cinematografica statunitense," in *Storia del cinema mondiale*, vol. 2, *Gli Stati Uniti*, ed. Gian Piero Brunetta (Turin: Einaudi, 2000), 1758.

11. Thomas Elsaesser, "American Auteur Cinema: The Last—or First—Picture Show?," in *The Last Great American Picture Show: New Hollywood Cinema in the 1970s*, ed. Thomas Elsaesser, Alexander Horwath, and Noel King (Amsterdam: Amsterdam University Press, 2004), 37.

12. On the new generation of the 1960s, see Rick Worland, *Searching for New Frontiers: Hollywood Films in the 1960s* (Chichester: Wiley-Blackwell, 2018).

13. On European film music, see Miguel Mera and David Burnand, eds., *European Film Music* (London: Ashgate, 2006).

14. Oscar Levant calls the closed musical number "over-all" or "mood" approach, in contrast with Hollywood's more popular "catch-all" Mickey-Mousing approach. Oscar Levant, *A Smattering of Ignorance* (Garden City, NY: Garden City Publishing, 1942), 105–8.

15. Jerrold Levinson, "Film Music and Narrative Agency," in *Post-Theory: Reconstructing Film Studies*, ed. David Bordwell and Noël Carroll (Madison: University of Wisconsin Press, 1996), 277.

16. J. Smith, *Sound of Commerce*, 131–53; Charles Leinberger, *Ennio Morricone's "The Good, the Bad and the Ugly": A Film Score Guide* (Lanham, MD: Scarecrow, 2004).

17. Ennio Morricone, "Towards an Interior Music," in *Celluloid Symphonies: Texts and Contexts in Film Music History*, ed. Julie Hubbert (Berkeley: University of California Press, 2011), 334.

18. Morricone quoted in Stefano Sorice, "Ennio Morricone racconta . . . (parte terza)," *Colonne Sonore*, November/December 2005, 9.

19. Sergio Miceli, *La musica nel film: Arte e artigianato* (Fiesole: Discanto, 1982), 319.

20. Morricone quoted in Ermanno Comuzio, *Colonna sonora: Dialoghi, musiche rumori dietro lo schermo* (Milan: Il Formichiere, 1980), 161.

21. Leinberger, *Ennio Morricone's "The Good, the Bad and the Ugly,"* 18.

22. On jazz in films, see Cooke, *History of Film Music*, 222.

23. See Robert Sklar, *Movie-Made America: A Cultural History of American Movies* (New York: Vintage Books, 1994), 269–304; and Thompson and Bordwell, *Film History*, 472–93.

24. For a survey of the relationship between cinema and popular music, see Arthur Knight and Pamela Robertson Wojcik, eds., *Soundtrack Available: Essays on Film and Popular Music* (Durham, NC: Duke University Press, 2001).

25. Altman, *Silent Film Sound*, 190.

26. Cooke, *History of Film Music*, 25.

27. Wierzbicki, *Film Music*, 114.

28. On the early attempts to market symphonic film-music albums, see Kyle S. Barnett, "The Selznick Studio, 'Spellbound,' and the Marketing of Film Music," *Music, Sound, and the Moving Image* 4, no. 1 (Spring 2010): 77–98.

29. Laura Mulvey, "Visual Pleasure and Narrative Cinema," *Screen* 16, no. 3 (Autumn 1975): 6–18.

30. On the aesthetics and functions of pop songs in films, see Cooke, *History of Film Music*, 412–14. On "pop scores" in general, see J. Smith, *Sound of Commerce*, 5–23.

31. J. Smith, *Sound of Commerce*, 32.

32. Marmorstein, *Hollywood Rhapsody*, 387.

33. Grant, *American Cinema of the 1960s*, 12.

34. Worland, *Searching for New Frontiers*, 3. Hollywood's reorganization is detailed in Tino Balio, ed., *The American Film Industry*, rev. ed. (Madison: University of Wisconsin Press, 1985), 401–632.

35. J. Smith, *Sound of Commerce*, 146.

36. J. Smith, *Sound of Commerce*, 145.

37. For a musical analysis of *American Graffiti*, see J. Smith, *Sound of Commerce*, 172–85.

38. Miceli, *Musica per film*, 679.

39. For a musical analysis of *Goldfinger*, see J. Smith, *Sound of Commerce*, 100–130.

40. Larsen, *Film Music*, 155.

41. Prendergast, *Film Music*, 26: "The song was placed in the film in the hopes that it would 'make the charts' and make that much more money for the film." Marmorstein, *Hollywood Rhapsody*, 384: "Utterly incongruous to the action, the song was the equivalent of an early music video."

42. This type of unabashedly promotional sequence is brilliantly spoofed by David Zucker, Jim Abrahams, and Jerry Zucker, the ZAZ trio, in *The Naked Gun: From the Files of Police Squad!* (1988). We see a montage showing Lt. Frank Drebin and his new fiancée, Jane, involved in a series of clichéd romantic activities, accompanied by a merry song. At the end of the sequence, as in an MTV video, the song's title, authors, album name, and record company—"Herman's Hermits, 'I'm Into Something Good,' The Naked Gun Soundtrack, Wheelo Records Inc."—appear on-screen, hilariously baring the economic motivation of the presence of songs in such sequences.

43. On "compilation scores," see J. Smith, *Sound of Commerce*, 163–72.

44. John Caps, *Henry Mancini: Reinventing Film Music* (Urbana: University of Illinois Press, 2012), 1.

45. Caps, *Henry Mancini*, 1–2.

46. J. Smith, *Sound of Commerce*, 78.

47. Eddie Kalish, "Mancini Debunks Album Values," 1961, reprinted in *Celluloid Symphonies: Texts and Contexts in Film Music History*, ed. Julie Hubbert (Berkeley: University of California Press, 2011), 318.

48. Jack Sullivan, *Hitchcock's Music* (New Haven, CT: Yale University Press, 2006), 277.

49. Cooke, *History of Film Music*, 396.

50. Herrmann quoted in S. Smith, *A Heart at Fire's Center*, 273.

51. Herrmann quoted in Sullivan, *Hitchcock's Music*, 288.

52. Sullivan, *Hitchcock's Music*, 283.

53. Goldsmith quoted in Irwin Bazelon, *Knowing the Score: Notes on Film Music* (New York: Arco, 1975), 190.

54. David Raksin, "Whatever Became of Movie Music?," in *Celluloid Symphonies: Texts and Contexts in Film Music History*, ed. Julie Hubbert (Berkeley: University of California Press, 2011), 373–74.

55. Mancini quoted in T. Thomas, *Film Score*, 257.

56. For a historical overview of the period from a film-music perspective, see L. E. MacDonald, *The Invisible Art of Film Music* (New York: Ardsley House, 1998), 173–333.

57. Bribitzer-Stull, *Understanding the Leitmotif*, 272.

58. Jack Sullivan, "Conversations with John Williams," *Chronicle of Higher Education*, 12 January 2007.

Chapter 4. *Star Wars*

1. *The Star Wars* was the original working title. J. W. Rinzler, *The Making of Star Wars: The Definitive Story behind the Original Film* (London: Ebury, 2007), 8.

2. Lucas quoted in Les Keyser, *Hollywood in the Seventies* (New York: A. S. Barnes, 1981), 26.

3. Rinzler, *Making of Star Wars*, 14–15.

4. Rinzler, *Making of Star Wars*, 48.

5. Rinzler, *Making of Star Wars*, 18–19.

6. Rinzler, *Making of Star Wars*, 31, 37, 178.

7. Lippincott quoted in Rinzler, *Making of Star Wars*, 105.

8. Scheurer, *Music and Mythmaking in Film*, 48–79.

9. Jeff Bond, CD booklet of *Planet of the Apes*, Varése Sarabande VSD-5848, 1997.

10. James Wierzbicki, *Louis and Bebe Barron's "Forbidden Planet": A Film Score Guide* (Lanham, MD: Scarecrow, 2005).

11. Cooke, *History of Film Music*, 442.

12. Kubrick quoted in Cooke, *History of Film Music*, 422.

13. Rinzler, *Making of Star Wars*, 273; Michael Matessino, "A New Hope for Film Music," CD booklet of *Star Wars: A New Hope*, BMG 09026 68772 2, 1997, p. 7.

14. Some sources suggest that a compilation score was the initial idea. Matessino, "A New Hope for Film Music," 6; Michael Goodson, "Yes, There's Life after Fiedler," *Boston Sunday Herald*, 27 January 1980; Williams quoted in T. Thomas, *Film Score*, 334–35; Cooke, *History of Film Music*, 462; Chris Malone, "Recording the *Star Wars* Saga: A Musical Journey from Scoring Stage to DVD," 6, version 1.4, 2012, http://www.malonedigital.com/starwars.pdf; Rinzler, *Making of Star Wars*, 292. On the other hand, when interviewed by Leonard Maltin, Lucas said that he had always had the idea of having an original score. George Lucas, video interview with Leonard Maltin, *The Empire Strikes Back*, VHS, Fox, 1995. However, *2001* was an influential model and Lucas had

already used a compilation score for *American Graffiti*; in the liner notes for the 1977 album—*Star Wars* LP album, 20th Century Records 2T-541 (0898), 1977—Williams seems to imply that Lucas originally wanted repertoire music, and Lucas, being the album producer, accepted at that time Williams's statement as true. To add uncertainty, in a recent interview, Williams confirms the compilation story, while Lucas, through his representatives, denies ever considering a compilation score. Alex Ross, "The Force Is Still Strong with John Williams," *New Yorker*, 21 July 2020.

15. Lucas, video interview with Leonard Maltin.

16. Lucas quoted in Jon Burlingame, "Spielberg and Lucas on Williams: Directors Reminisce about Collaborating with Hollywood's Greatest Composer," Film Music Society, *FMS Feature*, 8 February 2012, http://www.filmmusicsociety.org/news_events/features/2012/020812.html.

17. Rinzler, *Making of Star Wars*, 59.

18. Lucas quoted in Burlingame, "Spielberg and Lucas on Williams."

19. Williams quoted in Richard Dyer, "John Williams: New Horizons, Familiar Galaxies," *Boston Globe*, 4 June 1997.

20. Rinzler, *Making of Star Wars*, 60; Matessino, "A New Hope for Film Music," 6. In an interview, Williams stated, "I don't like to read scripts. . . . Having said that I don't even remember if George Lucas offered me a script to read." Craig L. Byrd, "The *Star Wars* Interview: John Williams," *Film Score Monthly*, January/February 1997, 18.

21. Williams, liner notes for the *Star Wars* LP album.

22. Ross, "Listening to *Star Wars*."

23. It is customary in contemporary Hollywood that a film's first cut should be coupled with a temporary repertoire music track in order to help the editor and the director in obtaining the required rhythm and mood. Then, the temp-tracked film is shown to the composer, who can gather from the director's musical choices how much music is needed and what kind of approach and language are required.

24. Fredric Jameson, *Postmodernism, or, The Cultural Logic of Late Capitalism* (Durham, NC: Duke University Press, 1991), 19.

25. The postmodern framework and the concept of "pastiche" are duly mentioned here but they will not be adopted in this book. See chapter 7.

26. Williams quoted in T. Thomas, *Film Score*, 335.

27. Timothy E. Scheurer, "John Williams and Film Music since 1971," *Popular Music and Society* 21, no. 1 (1997): 63.

28. Williams quoted in Byrd, "*Star Wars* Interview," 18.

29. Hamill quoted in Tim Greiving, "Mark Hamill on John Williams and His 'Gobsmacking' Importance to *Star Wars*," *Projector and Orchestra*, 1 December 2017, accessed 1 May 2020, http://projectorandorchestra.com/mark-hamill-on-john-williams-importance-to-star-wars/.

30. *Village Voice* review quoted in Kalinak, *Settling the Score*, 198; Greg Oatis, "John Williams Strikes Back, Unfortunately," *Cinemafantastique*, Fall 1980, 8

31. Kenneth Terry, "John Williams Encounters the Pops," *Downbeat* 48 (March 1981): 20.

32. Williams quoted in Timothy Mangan, "Composer for the Stars," *Gramophone* (US interview), May 2006, A7.

33. Malone, "Recording the *Star Wars* Saga," 11.

34. Williams quoted in Byrd, "*Star Wars* Interview," 19.

35. Lennox Mackenzie (LSO violinist) quoted in Christopher Cooper, "*Star Wars* in Concert," *Star Wars Insider*, November 2018, 31. This is the version of the story also reported on the LSO official website. Jo Johnson, "Happy 40th Birthday *Star Wars!*," London Symphony Orchestra, 25 May 2017, https://lso.co.uk/whats-on/alwaysplay ing/read/653-happy-40th-birthday-star-wars.html-.

36. "John Williams—The Maestro's Finale—The Rise of Skywalker," behind the scenes featurette, Lucasfilm, YouTube, March 19, 2020, https://www.youtube.com/watch?v=-g2LNSUowHc. Maurice Murphy (1935–2010) held the position of LSO's principal trumpet until 2007, having debuted precisely with the recording of the first *Star Wars* film in 1977. Murphy's unmistakable sound was indelibly linked to such Williams scores of the 1977–83 period as *Superman: The Movie* and *Raiders of the Lost Ark*, not to mention all the subsequent installments of the *Star Wars* saga, which Murphy rendered with a heroic impetus, a crystal-clear sound even in the higher register, and an impeccable rhythm and intonation, never surpassed and seldom equaled.

37. Malone, "Recording the *Star Wars* Saga," 11.

38. Richard Dyer, "Making *Star Wars* Sing Again," *Boston Globe*, 28 March 1999, reprinted in *Film Score Monthly*, June 1999, 18–21; Williams quoted in Richard Dyer, "Q&A with John Williams: Pops' Conductor Talks about His New Beat," *Boston Globe*, 27 April 1980; "*Star Wars: The Rise of Skywalker*, Behind the Scenes Sound Bites. John Williams, composer," Lucasfilm, YouTube, December 13, 2019, https://www.youtube .com/watch?v=oZfdpggIX18.

39. Among the preeminent film projects were *Things to Come* (William Cameron Menzies, 1936, music by Arthur Bliss), *The Four Feathers* (Zoltan Korda, 1939, music by Miklós Rózsa), *Dangerous Moonlight* (Brian Desmond Hurst, 1941, music by Richard Addinsell, featuring the famous *Warsaw Concerto*), *49th Parallel* (Michael Powell, 1941, music by Ralph Vaughan Williams), *Henry V* (Laurence Olivier, 1944, music by William Walton), *The Man Who Knew Too Much* (Alfred Hitchcock, 1956, music by Bernard Herrmann), and *The Three Worlds of Gulliver* (Jack Sher, 1960, music by Bernard Herrmann). For a list, see "LSO and Film Music," accessed 2 April 2020, https://lso.co .uk/orchestra/history/lso-and-film-music.html.

40. Malone, "Recording the *Star Wars* Saga," 7. The score was orchestrated by Herbert W. Spencer, Angela Morley, Alexander Courage, Arthur Morton, Al Woodbury, and Williams himself.

41. Malone, "Recording the *Star Wars* Saga," 11. The fanfare was reproduced using Newman's own 1954 recording dubbed down from the soundtrack of *River of No Return* (Otto Preminger, 1954).

42. Williams quoted in Josephine Reed, "Transcript of Conversation with John Williams," National Endowment for the Arts, *Art Works* (podcast), 2009, https://www .arts.gov/audio/john-williams.

43. The discarded alternate version can be heard on the CD *Star Wars: A New Hope*, CD 1, track 13, BMG 09026 68772 2, 1997.

44. Larsen, *Film Music*, 168.

45. Williams quoted in Byrd, "*Star Wars* Interview," 20.

46. Ross, "Listening to *Star Wars*"; Alex Ross, "John Williams's Gift to Film," CD booklet of *Lights, Camera . . . Music! Six Decades of John Williams*, BSO Classics 1704, 2017.

47. Most notably, Joseph Campbell, *The Hero with a Thousand Faces*, 2nd ed. (Princeton, NJ: Princeton University Press, 1968). For an analysis of the mythopoeic function of the *Star Wars* score, see Buhler, "*Star Wars*, Music, and Myth."

48. Williams quoted in Byrd, "*Star Wars* Interview," 20.

49. Williams, program notes for his *Horn Concerto*, Chicago Symphony Orchestra, Symphony Center, Chicago, IL, 29 November 2003.

50. Ian Lace, "The Film Music of John Williams," Musicweb International, 1998, www.musicweb-international.com/film/lacejw.htm; Matt Wolf, "The Olympics Offers John Williams Another Heroic Challenge," *South Coast Today* (MA), 21 July 1996.

51. Norman Lebrecht, "John Williams—The Magpie Maestro," *La Scena Musicale*, 20 November 2002, www.scena.org/columns/lebrecht/021120-NL-williams.html.

52. Ross, "Listening to *Star Wars*."

53. Williams quoted in Terry, "John Williams Encounters the Pops."

54. Scheurer, "John Williams and Film Music since 1971," 67.

55. Midget, "As a Classical Music Critic."

56. Paula J. Massood, "Movies and a Nation in Transformation," in *American Cinema of the 1970s: Themes and Variations*, ed. Lester D. Friedman (New Brunswick, NJ: Rutgers University Press, 2007), 185.

57. Rinzler, *Making of Star Wars*, 336.

58. "Star Wars," accessed 2 April 2020, https://www.riaa.com/gold-platinum/?tab_active=default-award&ar=John+Williams&ti=Star+Wars+%28soundtrack%29#search_section; Larsen, *Film Music*, 172–73.

59. Rinzler, *Making of Star Wars*, 336. As of 1983, this bonus share reportedly yielded $300,000. David Wessel, "The Force Is with Him . . . 'Rich Is Hard to Define,'" *Boston Globe*, 5 July 1983.

60. "Grammy Rewind: 20th Annual Grammy Awards," 17 January 2012, http://www.grammy.com/grammys/news/grammy-rewind-20th-annual-grammy-awards.

61. Newman quoted in Richard Dyer, "John Williams Is New Pops Maestro: A Musician's Musician," *Boston Globe*, 11 January 1980.

62. Rinzler, *Making of Star Wars*, 313–14; Gianluca Sergi, "Tales of the Silent Blast: *Star Wars* and Sound," *Journal of Popular Film and Television* 26, no. 1 (1998): 12–22.

Chapter 5. The Sage of the *Star Wars* Music

1. See Frank Lehman, "The Themes of *Star Wars*: Catalogue and Commentary," in *John Williams: Music for Films, Television, and the Concert Stage*, ed. Emilio Audissino (Turnhout: Brepols, 2018), 153–90; Frank Lehman, "Complete Catalogue of the Musical Themes of *Star Wars*," accessed 28 August 2020, https://franklehman.com/starwars/.

2. Michael Matessino, "John Williams Strikes Back," CD booklet of *The Empire Strikes Back*, BMG Classics 09026 68773 2, 1997, p. 6.

3. Frank Lehman, *Hollywood Harmony: Musical Wonder and the Sound of Cinema* (New York: Oxford University Press, 2018), 101. On the use of the Tarnhelm progression in Darth Vader's theme, see also Joakim Tillman, "The Villain's March Topic in John

Williams's Film Music," in *John Williams: Music for Films, Television, and the Concert Stage*, ed. Emilio Audissino (Turnhout: Brepols, 2018), 230–35.

4. Matessino, "John Williams Strikes Back," 12.

5. Williams quoted in Fred LeBrun, "John Williams: Movies' Music Man," *Times Union* (Albany, NY), 24 August 1984.

6. Bribitzer-Stull, *Understanding the Leitmotif*, 293.

7. Transcript from *"Star Wars: Episode I—The Phantom Menace*: John Williams Interview," videotape, Sony Classical, 9 April 1999.

8. Williams quoted in Bob Thomas, "Williams Looks backward in Composing Score for New *Star Wars* Movie," *Nevada Daily Mail*, 12 May 1999.

9. Williams quoted in Richard Dyer, "An Enduring Love for Music, Movies," *Boston Globe*, 23 June 2002.

10. Bribitzer-Stull, *Understanding the Leitmotif*, 293.

11. On the differences in orchestration between the first and the second trilogy, see Nicholas Kmet, "Orchestration Transformation: Examining Differences in the Instrumental and Thematic Colour Palettes of the *Star Wars* Trilogies," in *John Williams: Music for Films, Television, and the Concert Stage*, ed. Emilio Audissino (Turnhout: Brepols, 2018), 209–28.

12. The saga has always had a strong penchant for the exploitation of tie-in products: "In 1992, before the franchise's proliferation of videogames, and before the second trilogy opened the floodgates for yet more merchandise sales, . . . *Star Wars* had amassed over $2.5 billion from merchandise alone." Jonathan Gray, *Show Sold Separately: Promos, Spoilers, and Other Media Paratexts* (New York: New York University Press, 2010), 177.

13. "John Williams—The Maestro's Finale—The Rise of Skywalker."

14. Williams quoted in Anonymous, "Back Again to a Galaxy," *International Musician*, 28 May 2015, 16.

15. Williams quoted in Tim Greiving, "John Williams on *The Force Awakens* and the Legacy of *Star Wars*," *Projector and Orchestra*, 5 January 2016, accessed 1 May 2020, http://projectorandorchestra.com/john-williams-on-the-force-awakens-and-the-legacy-of-star-wars/.

16. Williams quoted in Greiving, "John Williams on *The Force Awakens*."

17. Williams quoted in Greiving, "John Williams on *The Force Awakens*."

18. Frank Lehman, "How John Williams's *Star Wars* Score Pulls Us to the Dark Side," *Washington Post*, 13 December 2019.

19. Williams quoted in Greiving, "John Williams on *The Force Awakens*."

20. Williams quoted in Greiving, "John Williams on *The Force Awakens*."

21. Williams quoted in Jon Burlingame, "John Williams Is on Target to Set Yet Another Oscar Record," *Variety*, 10 January 2018.

22. Jennifer Walden, "Ren Klyce: Mixing the Score for *Star Wars: The Last Jedi*," *PostPerspective*, 26 February 2018, https://postperspective.com/ren-klyce-mixing-score-star-wars-last-jedi/.

23. Thomas Smith, "And the Grammy Goes to . . . *Star Wars*: Galaxy's Edge Symphonic Suite," Disney Parks blog, 28 January 2020, https://disneyparks.disney.go.com/blog/2020/01/and-the-grammy-goes-to-star-wars-galaxys-edge-symphonic-suite/.

24. Williams quoted in Tracy Smith, "John Williams on Spielberg, *Star Wars*, and the Power of Music," transcript of video interview, *Sunday Morning*, CBS News, 22 September 2019, https://www.cbsnews.com/news/extended-transcript-john-williams-on-steven-spielberg-star-wars-and-the-power-of-music/.

25. "John Williams—The Maestro's Finale—The Rise of Skywalker."

26. Jon Burlingame, "With *Rise of Skywalker*, Composer John Williams Puts His Coda on *Star Wars*," *Variety*, 18 December 2019.

27. Lucas quoted in Burlingame, "Spielberg and Lucas on Williams."

28. In the TV industry, a showrunner is the person who supervises the work of the diverse writers and directors to make sure that the single episodes coalesce into a unified congruous series along a predefined developmental trajectory.

29. There is even a petition to Disney on Change.org claiming that "Episode VIII was a travesty. It completely destroyed the legacy of Luke Skywalker and the Jedi" and demanding that it be deleted from the official canon and reshot. The petition collected 116,776 signatures before it closed. "Have Disney Strike Star Wars Episode VIII from the Official Canon," Change.org, accessed 30 September 2020, https://www.change.org/p/the-walt-disney-company-have-disney-strike-star-wars-episode-viii-from-the-official-canon.

30. Williams quoted in Reed, "Transcript of Conversation with John Williams."

31. Williams quoted in Burlingame, "With *Rise of Skywalker*, Composer John Williams Puts His Coda on *Star Wars*."

32. J. Smith, *Sound of Commerce*, 217.

33. "Star Wars Tops AFI's List of 25 Greatest Film Scores of All Time," 23 September 2005, https://www.afi.com/afis-100-years-of-film-scores.

34. Richard Dyer, "John Williams Bows In," *Boston Globe*, 11 January 1980.

35. "Commencement Citation," *Boston University Today*, 29 May 1985.

36. Cyrus Meher-Homji, "Zubin Mehta: The Los Angeles Years," *Eloquence Classics*, 29 October 2018, https://www.eloquenceclassics.com/zubin-mehta-the-los-angeles-years; Mark Swed, "Zubin Mehta's Heady Days as Los Angeles Philharmonic Music Director," *Los Angeles Times*, 8 December 2012. A video extract of the concert can be seen at "Star Wars Concert," Daniel Flannery.com, accessed 9 November 2020, https://dflannery.com/portfolio-item/star-wars-concert/. The program also included Gustav Holst's *The Planets* and Richard Strauss's *Thus Spoke Zarathustra*.

37. William Livingstone, "John Williams and the Boston Pops: An American Institution Enters a New Era," *Stereo Review* 45, no. 6 (December 1980): 76.

38. Wessel, "The Force Is with Him."

39. On these "multimedia concerts," see chapter 12.

40. Scheurer, "John Williams and Film Music since 1971," 64.

41. Randall D. Larson, *Musique Fantastique: A Survey of Film Music in the Fantastic Cinema* (London: Scarecrow, 1985), 293; K. J. Donnelly, "Introduction," in *Film Music: Critical Approaches*, ed. K. J. Donnelly (New York: Continuum, 2001), 13; Kalinak, *Settling the Score*, 188; Larsen, *Film Music*, 166, 173; Marmorstein, *Hollywood Rhapsody*, 401; Miceli, *Musica per film*, 49.

42. Byrd, "*Star Wars* Interview," 19.

43. Stephen Farber, "Mr. Pops," *Dial—WGBH Boston*, July 1983, 11.

44. Wierzbicki, *Film Music*, 216.

45. Wierzbicki, *Film Music*, 209–27.

46. Kalinak, *Settling the Score*, 187.

47. Richard Dyer, "Where Is John Williams Coming From?," *Boston Globe*, 29 June 1980.

48. Malone, "Recording the *Star Wars* Saga," 14.

49. Cooke, *History of Film Music*, 469.

Chapter 6. Williams's Early Years

1. For additional information on Raymond Scott, see the website maintained by Scott's heirs, calling themselves Reckless Night Music, http://www.raymondscott.net.

2. Williams's biography has been reconstructed from a number of interviews given by the composer. The data of the following pages have been retrieved from Richard Dyer, "John Williams: Bringing Hollywood Magic to the Boston Pops," *Ovation*, June 1983, 14; Michael J. Colburn, "John Williams Returns to Bands where He Began 50 Years Ago," *Instrumentalist*, June 2004, 13; Gail Jennes, "The Boston Pops Gets a Movie Composer Who Doesn't Chase Fire Engines as Its New Boss," *People Weekly*, 23 June 1980, 51; Dyer, "Where Is John Williams Coming From?"; John Williams video interview for the TV program *Personal Notes*, produced by Michael Kerr, BBC, 1988; David Thomas, "King of Themes," *Sunday Telegraph*, 13 July 1997, 49.

3. Tim Grieving, "John Williams' Early Life: How a NoHo Kid and UCLA Bruin Became the Movie Music Man," *Los Angeles Times*, 18 July 2018.

4. Grieving, "John Williams' Early Life."

5. Grieving, "John Williams' Early Life"; Williams quoted in Reed, "Transcript of Conversation with John Williams."

6. Castelnuovo Tedesco was an Italian émigré Jew who had fled the 1938 racial laws of his country to settle in Hollywood, where he worked as an orchestrator and composer. His most notable contribution was *And Then There Were None* (René Clair, 1945). He was also an in-demand teacher among prospective film composers; other famous pupils were Jerry Goldsmith and Henry Mancini.

7. Colburn, "John Williams Returns to Bands," 13.

8. Paul Galloway, "Airman Composes Way to Movie Career," *Beacon*, 27 August 1954.

9. Dyer, "Where Is John Williams Coming From?"

10. "Rosina Lhévinne," accessed 3 April 2020, http://www.naxos.com/person/Rosina_Lhevinne/2230.htm. See also the 2003 documentary *The Legacy of Rosina Lhevinne*, by Salome Ramras Arkatov, synopsis at www.arkatovproductions.com/lhevinne.htm.

11. Terry, "John Williams Encounters the Pops," 21.

12. Williams quoted in Reed, "Transcript of Conversation with John Williams."

13. Williams quoted in Reed, "Transcript of Conversation with John Williams."

14. Williams quoted in Clemency Burton-Hill, 'John Williams, the Music Master,' *Financial Times*, 17 August 2012.

15. Williams quoted in Colburn, "John Williams Return to Bands," 15. On the jazz side of Williams, see Ryan Patrick Jones, "'Catch as Catch Can': Jazz, John Williams,

& Popular Music Allusion," in *John Williams: Music for Films, Television, and the Concert Stage*, ed. Emilio Audissino (Turnhout: Brepols, 2018), 41–70.

16. Emilio Audissino, "The Multiform Identity of Jazz in Hollywood: An Assessment through the John Williams Case Study," in *Cinema Changes: Incorporations of Jazz in the Film Soundtrack*, ed. Emile Wennekes and Emilio Audissino (Turnhout: Brepols, 2018), 87.

17. Dyer, "Q&A with John Williams"; Williams quoted in Reed, "Transcript of Conversation with John Williams."

18. Williams quoted in Dyer, "Where Is John Williams Coming From?" On Williams's television work, see Paula Musegades, "John Williams: Television Composer," in *John Williams: Music for Films, Television, and the Concert Stage*, ed. Emilio Audissino (Turnhout: Brepols, 2018), 27–40.

19. Williams quoted in Derek Elley, "The Film Composer: 3. John Williams, Part 2," *Films and Filming* 24, no. 11 (August 1978): 32.

20. On the "package-unit system," see Bordwell, Staiger, and Thompson, *Classical Hollywood Cinema*, 330.

21. This pigeonholing was typical of Hollywood: Tiomkin, for example, was known as a "Western composer" and Rózsa as the "composer for historical epics."

22. Williams quoted in Dyer, "John Williams: Bringing Hollywood Magic to the Boston Pops," 14.

23. Private conversation with John Williams, Boston, MA, 21 May 2008.

24. On *Images*, see Irwin Bazelon, "Interview with John Williams," in *Knowing the Score: Notes on Film Music* (New York: Arco, 1975), 202–6. The score is discussed further in R. Brown, *Overtones and Undertones*, 178–79. Williams has indicated this score as one of his favorites. Ross, "The Force Is Still Strong with John Williams."

25. Williams quoted in Bazelon, *Knowing the Score*, 195.

26. Caps, *Henry Mancini*, 3.

27. *Experiment in Terror* (1962), though excellent both musically and cinematically, has been excluded to avoid having too many Blake Edwards films in the sample but also to opt for films made in the second half of the 1960s, when the modern style was more steadily established.

28. Sam Wasson, *A Splurch in the Kisser: The Movies of Blake Edwards* (Middletown, CT: Wesleyan University Press, 2009), 12.

29. One of Edwards's most Tati-esque films is *The Party*. Wasson, *A Splurch in the Kisser*, 131.

30. Caps, *Henry Mancini*, 77.

31. On comic action sounds, see Altman, *Silent Film Sound*, 52.

32. The composer's responsibility is confirmed by Blake Edwards himself in his video interview for *Evening at Pops*, WGBH-Boston Symphony Orchestra, episode 2804, taped on 24 May 2004, WGBH Archives, Boston, MA.

33. Hawks is one of the founders of the screwball comedy, while Edwards can be said to have updated the slapstick comedy with a touch of Tati's abstractness.

34. "Wait until Dark," music by Henry Mancini, lyrics by Jay Livingston and Ray Evans, sung by Sue Raney.

35. The tam-tam is a kind of large indefinite pitched "gong" used in symphony orchestras. If rubbed with a metal stick instead of being hit by a mallet, it produces a harsh chilling sound largely used for horror effects.

36. T. Thomas, *Music for the Movies*, 270. Mancini had already employed quarter-tone scales to create dizziness in *Wait until Dark*. Jeff Smith, "That Money Making 'Moon River' Sound: Thematic Organization and Orchestration in the Film Music of Henry Mancini," in *Music and Cinema*, ed. James Buhler, Caryl Flinn, and David Neumeyer (Hanover, NH: Wesleyan University Press, 2000), 257–58.

37. Williams quoted in Bazelon, *Knowing the Score*, 200–201.

38. Very fast scales in which the individual tones are fused into a single ascending/descending-pitched sound, the glissando is typical of the harp, the strings, the slide trombones (in this case it is called *portamento*), and of any of those instruments that can bend the pitch of the notes.

39. While hitting the drumhead, the timpanist uses a pedal to change the tuning, thus obtaining an ascending or descending effect.

40. Williams quoted in Elley, "The Film Composer: 3. John Williams, Part 2," 30.

41. Ray Bennett, "John Williams, Composer," *Hollywood Reporter*, 8 March 2000.

Chapter 7. *Jaws*

1. Geoff King, *New Hollywood Cinema: An Introduction* (London: I.B. Tauris, 2002), 1.

2. Murray Smith, "Theses on the Philosophy of Hollywood History," in *Contemporary Hollywood Cinema*, ed. Steve Neale and Murray Smith (London: Routledge, 1998), 6–9.

3. King, *New Hollywood Cinema*, 3–5; Elizabeth Cowie, "Classical Hollywood Cinema and Classical Narrative," in *Contemporary Hollywood Cinema*, ed. Steve Neale and Murray Smith (London: Routledge, 1998), 178–90.

4. Justin Wyatt, *High Concept: Movies and Marketing in Hollywood* (Austin: University of Texas Press, 1994); Thomas Schatz, "The New Hollywood," in *Film Theory Goes to the Movies: Cultural Analysis of Contemporary Film*, ed. Jim Collins, Hilary Radner, and Ava Preacher Collins (London: Routledge, 1993), 8–36.

5. "Continuity theories" can be found in Bordwell, Staiger, and Thompson, *Classical Hollywood Cinema*, 367–77; and are also at the basis of Kristin Thompson, *Storytelling in the New Hollywood: Understanding Classical Narrative Cinema* (Cambridge, MA: Harvard University Press, 1999); and David Bordwell, *The Way Hollywood Tells It: Story and Style in Modern Movies* (Berkeley: University of California Press, 2006).

6. Bordwell, *Way Hollywood Tells It*, 63.

7. J. D. Connor, *The Studios after the Studios: Neoclassical Hollywood (1970–2010)* (Stanford: Stanford University Press, 2015).

8. Laurent Jullier, *L'écran post-moderne: Un cinéma de l'allusion et du feu d'artifice* (Paris: L'Harmattan, 1997), trans. by Carla Capetta as *Il cinema postmoderno* (Turin: Kaplan, 2006), 17–35.

9. "Grand narratives" or "metanarratives" (*métarécits*) are those overarching explanations of the culture, society, and philosophy of a given period, for example, Enlightenment for the eighteenth century, which postmodern thinkers reject. Jean-François Lyotard, *La condition postmoderne: rapport sur le savoir* (Paris: Éditions de Minuit, 1979),

7. Postmodernism posits that grand narratives are no longer able to explain the contemporary world—yet postmodernism offers a view to explain contemporary world that is itself quite similar to a grand narrative, problematically enough.

10. On this criticism, see Bordwell, *Way Hollywood Tells It*, 9; and Thompson, *Storytelling in the New Hollywood*, 8–9.

11. Jullier, *Il cinema postmoderno*, 53.

12. King, *New Hollywood Cinema*, 74.

13. Bordwell, *Narration in the Fiction Film*, 157–62.

14. One of the principal models was Campbell's comparative mythology work *The Hero with a Thousand Faces*.

15. An in-depth analysis of the classical narration of *Back to the Future* can be found in Thompson, *Storytelling in the New Hollywood*, 77–102.

16. Jullier, *Il cinema postmoderno*, 12; King, *New Hollywood Cinema*, 139. On the definitions and contexts of "postmodern," see John Hill, "Film and Postmodernism," in *The Oxford Guide to Film Studies*, ed. John Hill and Pamela Church Gibson (Oxford: Oxford University Press, 1998), 96–105, which gives a summary of such canonical texts as Lyotard, *La condition postmoderne*; Jameson, *Postmodernism*; and Jean Baudrillard, *Simulacres et Simulation* (Paris: Éditions Galilée, 1981).

17. For the same reason, the term "pastiche" will be avoided here. Defined by *Merriam-Webster* as "a literary, artistic, musical, or architectural work that imitates the style of previous work," the term is typically used in musicology to indicate those works that revive and update past styles. For example, Sergei Prokofiev's Symphony no. 1 in D Major ("Classical") is a pastiche after Haydn. Although it might have been appropriate in *this* sense within this book, the term is a problematic one as it has come to be closely associated with postmodernism and given an ideological connotation: "Pastiche is, like parody, the imitation of a peculiar or unique, idiosyncratic style, the wearing of a linguistic mask, speech in a dead language. But it is a neutral practice of such mimicry, without any of parody's ulterior motives, amputated of the satiric impulse, devoid of laughter. . . . [It is] the cannibalization of all the styles of the past, the play of random stylistic allusion." Jameson, *Postmodernism*, 17–18. For a discussion, see Margaret A. Rose, "Post-Modern Pastiche," *British Journal of Aesthetics* 31, no. 1 (January 1991): 26–38. Although more recent studies—such as Ingeborg Hoesterey, *Pastiche: Cultural Memory in Art, Film, Literature* (Bloomington: Indiana University Press, 2001); and Richard Dyer, *Pastiche* (New York: Routledge, 2006)—have given broader and more dynamic definitions, "pastiche" still sounds too connected to postmodernism to be used here.

18. Respectively in J. Smith, *Sound of Commerce*, 136; Ermanno Comuzio, *Musicisti per lo schermo: Dizionario ragionato dei compositori cinematografici* (Rome: Ente dello Spettacolo, 2004), 2:1051; and Cristina Catherine Losada, "Between Modernism and Postmodernism: Strands of Continuity in Collage Compositions by Rochberg, Berio, and Zimmermann," *Music Theory Spectrum* 31, no. 1 (April 2009): 57–100.

19. Williams is defined as "neoclassical" also in Flinn, *Strains of Utopia*, 152; and K. J. Donnelly, "The Classical Film Score Forever? 'Batman,' 'Batman Returns,' and Postclassical Film Music," in *Contemporary Hollywood Cinema*, ed. Steve Neale and Murray Smith (London: Routledge, 1998), 151.

20. King, *New Hollywood Cinema*, 106.

21. Connor, *The Studios after the Studios*, 14,

22. Williams quoted in Yann Merluzeau, "An Interview with John Williams," *Soundtrack!*, September 1993, 7.

23. The adapted concert pieces are the eight-minute *Cowboys Overture* and the twenty-minute suite for narrator and orchestra *The Reivers: An Old Man Reminisces*.

24. Richard Dyer, "Sounds of Spielberg," *Boston Globe*, 24 February 1998. *Duel* (1971) was produced for television and later expanded and reedited for theatrical release. Therefore, Spielberg's first feature film made expressly for the theaters was *The Sugarland Express*.

25. Steven Spielberg, "Steven Spielberg & John Williams Talk Music," video interview, 1982, YouTube, October 2, 2013, www.youtube.com/watch?v=uw4Ngb5F3Hk.

26. Glenn Man, "1975: Movies and Conflicting Ideologies," in *American Cinema of the 1970s: Themes and Variations*, ed. Lester D. Friedman (New Brunswick, NJ: Rutgers University Press, 2007), 154.

27. The success of *Jaws* led to the institution and exploitation of a minor trend, which could be called "zoological disaster movies." Examples are *Piranha* (Joe Dante, 1978), in which genetically modified piranhas invade a lake near a crowded summer camp; and *The Swarm* (Irwin Allen, 1978), in which swarms of vicious killer bees invade the United States.

28. Cynthia Lucia, Roy Grundmann, and Art Simon, "Setting the Stage: American Film History, 1976–1990," in *American Film History: Selected Readings, 1960 to the Present*, ed. Cynthia Lucia, Roy Grundmann, and Art Simon (Malden, MA: Wiley-Blackwell, 2016), 151. A "high concept" film is based on "a striking, easily reducible narrative which also offers a high degree of marketability." Wyatt, *High Concept*, 18.

29. Man, "1975" 149.

30. Thomas Schatz, "Seismic Shifts in the American Film Industry," in *American Film History Selected Readings, 1960 to the Present*, ed. Cynthia Lucia, Roy Grundmann, and Art Simon (Malden, MA: Wiley-Blackwell, 2016), 177.

31. Man, "1975," 149.

32. Linda Ruth Williams and Michael Hammond, eds., *Contemporary American Cinema* (Maidenhead: Open University Press, 2006), 117.

33. See Carl Gottlieb, *The Jaws Log* (New York: Newmarket, 2005); and the documentary *Jaws: The Inside Story*, A&E Television, distributed by Go Entertainment Ltd., 2009, DVD.

34. Gottlieb, *Jaws Log*, 89.

35. See *Jaws: The Inside Story*.

36. Gottlieb, *Jaws Log*, 198.

37. Ian Freer, *The Complete Spielberg* (London: Virgin, 2001), 50.

38. The analysis was made on the PAL-system DVD *Jaws: 30th Anniversary*, Universal, 2005. The running time on 35 mm film is 124 minutes.

39. K. J. Donnelly, *The Spectre of Sound: Music in Film and Television* (London: BFI, 2005), 93.

40. Levinson, "Film Music and Narrative Agency," 261.

41. Miguel Mera, "Materializing Film Music," in *The Cambridge Companion to Film Music*, ed. Mervyn Cooke and Fiona Ford (Cambridge: Cambridge University Press, 2016), 172; Giorgio Biancorosso, "The Shark in the Music," *Music Analysis* 29 (2010): 320.

42. See *Jaws: The Inside Story*.

43. Spielberg quoted in Laurent Bouzereau, "Jaws," CD booklet of *Jaws: The Collector's Edition Soundtrack*, Decca 467 045-2, 2000, p. 8.

44. Williams quoted in Jon Burlingame, "John Williams Recalls *Jaws*," Film Music Society, 14 August 2012, http://www.filmmusicsociety.org/news_events/features/2012/081412.html.

45. Williams quoted in Bouzereau, "Jaws," 8.

46. Williams quoted in Derek Taylor, *The Making of "Raiders of the Lost Ark"* (New York: Ballantine, 1981), 166.

47. Williams quoted in Bouzereau, "Jaws," 7.

48. Williams quoted in Rebecca Keegan, "John Williams and Steven Spielberg Mark 40 Years of Collaboration," *Los Angeles Times*, 8 January 2012.

49. Keegan, "John Williams and Steven Spielberg."

50. On film music resembling heartbeats, see Ben Winters, "Corporeality, Musical Heartbeats, and Cinematic Emotion," *Music, Sound and the Moving Image* 2, no. 1 (Spring 2008): 3–25.

51. Williams quoted in Bouzereau, "Jaws," 8–10.

52. Bribitzer-Stull, *Understanding the Leitmotif*, 281.

53. Spielberg quoted in Bouzereau, "Jaws," 7.

54. Williams quoted in Bouzereau, "Jaws," 8.

55. Williams quoted in Burlingame, "John Williams Recalls *Jaws*."

56. Williams quoted in Bouzereau, "Jaws," 10–11.

57. The fugue is a revered art-music form that can be traced back to the early Baroque period. It is one of the most rigorous compositional patterns, having two or more independent melodic lines (voices) interwoven contrapuntally. A *fugato* is a musical piece that employs the techniques of the fugue, without developing the fugue's entire formal structure.

58. Williams had previously received one Oscar for his arrangements and musical direction of *Fiddler on the Roof* (Norman Jewison, 1971).

59. Tom Shales of the *Washington Post* quoted in Wierzbicki, *Film Music*, 204.

60. *Jaws 2: Original Motion Picture Soundtrack*, MCA Records 3045, 1978, reissued on CD, Varèse Sarabande VSD-5328, 1990.

61. Williams quoted in Bennett, "John Williams, Composer."

62. Mark Richards, "The Use of Variation in John Williams's Film Music Themes," in *John Williams: Music for Films, Television, and the Concert Stage*, ed. Emilio Audissino (Turnhout: Brepols, 2018), 139.

Chapter 8. Williams's Neoclassicism

1. Andrea Briganti, Giulia Farina, Andrea Lanza, eds., *Enciclopedia della musica* (Milano: Garzanti, 1996), 593. For an in-depth definition, see Scott Messing, *Neoclassicism in Music: From the Genesis of the Concept through the Schoenberg–Stravinsky Polemic* (Ann Arbor, MI: UMI Research Press), 1988.

2. Guido Salvetti, *La nascita del Novecento*, 2nd ed. (Turin: EDT, 1991), 97–99. See also Maureen A. Carr, *After the Rite: Stravinsky's Path to Neoclassicism (1914–1919)* (New York: Oxford University Press, 2014).

3. Salvetti, *La nascita del Novecento*, 99.

4. Miceli, *Musica per film*, 248–49.

5. Hermann Danuser, "Rewriting the Past: Classicisms of the Inter-war Period," in *The Cambridge History of Twentieth-Century Music*, ed. Nicholas Cook and Anthony Pople (Cambridge: Cambridge University Press, 2004), 264.

6. Williams quoted in Thanos Fourgiotis, "John Williams Interview," *Cinema Magazine*, April 1992, https://www.douban.com/group/topic/1029421/.

7. Williams quoted in Bob Keefer, "Running Up the Score: John Williams Brings His Cinematic Compositions to Eugene," *Register-Guard* (OR), 20 September 2012.

8. Newman quoted in Dyer, "John Williams Is New Pops Maestro."

9. Miceli, *Musica per film*, 616–18 (translation mine).

10. Williams's idiom is analyzed in harmonic terms in Jérôme Rossi, "Le dynamisme harmonique dans l'ecriture filmique de John Williams: Harmonie fonctionnelle versus harmonie non fonctionnelle," in *John Williams: Un alchimiste musical à Hollywood*, ed. Alexandre Tylski (Paris: L'Harmattan, 2011), 113–40.

11. "Broadly speaking, functionalism in music may be defined as the implications which one musical event . . . has for some other musical event either on its own hierarchic level or some other." Leonard B. Meyer, *Music, the Arts, and Ideas. Patterns and Predictions in Twentieth-Century Culture* (Chicago: University of Chicago Press, 1967), 278.

12. Cooke, *History of Film Music*, 129.

13. Mervyn Cooke, "A New Symphonism for a New Hollywood: The Musical Language of John Williams's Film Scores," in *John Williams: Music for Films, Television, and the Concert Stage*, ed. Emilio Audissino (Turnhout: Brepols, 2018), 17.

14. Richards, "The Use of Variation," 119.

15. Ian Sapiro, "Star Scores: Orchestration and the Sound of John Williams's Film Music," in *John Williams: Music for Films, Television, and the Concert Stage*, ed. Emilio Audissino (Turnhout: Brepols, 2018), 203.

16. Frank Lehman, "Film Music and Neo-Riemannian Theory," *Oxford Handbooks Online*, August 2014, http://www.oxfordhandbooks.com.

17. Tom Schneller, "Modal Interchange and Semantic Resonance in Themes by John Williams," *Journal of Film Music* 6, no. 1 (2013): 51–52.

18. Frank Lehman, "Reading Tonality through Film: Transformational Hermeneutics and the Music of Hollywood" (PhD diss., Harvard University, 2012), 31.

19. Schneller, "Modal Interchange and Semantic Resonance," 68.

20. A comparison is in Irena Paulus, "Williams versus Wagner, or an Attempt at Linking Musical Epics," *International Review of the Aesthetics and Sociology of Music* 31, no. 2 (December 2000): 153–84. The use of leitmotiv has been compared in Bribitzer-Stull, *Understanding the Leitmotif*.

21. Williams quoted in Keefer, "Running Up the Score."

22. Williams quoted in Ross, "The Force Is Still Strong with John Williams."

23. Williams quoted in Sullivan, "Spielberg–Williams," 185.

24. Williams quoted in Lace, "The Film Music of John Williams."

25. Williams quoted in Sullivan, "Spielberg–Williams," 185.

26. For more details on Williams's use of the orchestra, see Sapiro, "Star Scores."

27. For a syntactical examination, see Zacharopoulos, "Musical Syntax."

28. Williams quoted in Andy Seiler, "Williams Adds Musical Magic to *Harry Potter*," *USA Today*, 13 November 2001.

29. Williams quoted in Anonymous, "Dialogue: John Williams," *Hollywood Reporter*, 10 January 2006.

30. See Richards, "The Use of Variation."

31. Zachary Woolfe, "A Summer Blockbuster, Far from the Multiplex," *New York Times*, 19 August 2012.

32. The "Emperor" theme is reprised in *Star Wars: Episode III—Revenge of the Sith* and then in *Star Wars: Episode IX—The Rise of Skywalker.*

33. Lehman, "How John Williams's *Star Wars* Score Pulls Us to the Dark Side."

34. The sequence under analysis starts at 4:10 and stops at 9:34 (running 5:24) and includes fifty-four explicit sync points, not counting the starting and closing sync points. The analysis was made on the DVD included in the box set *The Adventures of Indiana Jones*, Paramount, 2003.

35. Williams quoted in Reed, "Transcript of Conversation with John Williams."

36. Bribitzer-Stull, *Understanding the Leitmotif*, 101–2.

37. Williams, radio interview by Francine Stock, *The Film Programme*, BBC Radio 4, 14 April 2006.

38. Tom Schneller, "Sweet Fulfillment: Allusion and Teleological Genesis in John Williams's *Close Encounters of the Third Kind*," *Musical Quarterly* 97, no. 1 (Spring 2014): 131.

39. On the gratification effect given by the recognition of familiar melodies, following the "law of return" of the Gestalt theory, see L. Meyer, *Emotion and Meaning in Music*, 151–52; and the "pleasure of recognition" in L. Meyer, *Style and Music*, 210n185.

40. Williams quoted in Byrd, "*Star Wars* Interview," 19.

41. Sullivan, "Spielberg–Williams," 191.

42. Bordwell, *Way Hollywood Tells It*, 63.

43. A number of parallels are also pointed out in Kalinak, *Settling the Score*, 190–92.

44. Williams quoted in Derek Elley, "The Film Composer: 3. John Williams, Part 1," *Films and Filming* 24, no. 10 (July 1978): 23.

45. Steiner quoted in Schreibman, "Memories of Max. Part 2," 25.

46. Williams quoted in Wynn Delacoma, "Williams: From Celluloid to CSO," *Chicago Sun-Times*, 28 November 2003.

47. On Leone and Morricone, see Miceli, *Musica per film*, 641.

48. Williams quoted in Anonymous, "Dialogue."

49. Williams quoted in James C. McKinley Jr., "John Williams Lets His Muses Carry Him Along," *New York Times*, 19 August 2011.

50. Williams quoted in McNab, "They Shoot, He Scores."

51. Steiner quoted in Buhler, "Analytical and Interpretive Approaches," 45.

52. Bernie Dobroski and Claire Greene, "Pass the Popcorn: An Interview with John Williams," *Instrumentalist*, July 1984, 6.

53. Williams quoted in T. Thomas, *Film Score*, 334.

54. Williams quoted in McKinley, "John Williams Lets His Muses Carry Him Along."

55. Williams quoted in Burton-Hill, "John Williams, the Music Master."

56. Dobroski and Greene, "Pass the Popcorn," 6.

57. On Korngold's dislike for technical aids, see T. Thomas, *Music for the Movies*, 171–72.

58. Williams quoted in Anonymous, "Dialogue."

59. Williams quoted in Sullivan, "Spielberg–Williams," 193.

60. Williams quoted in Juliet Simon, "A Conversation with John Williams," BMI, 22 December 2015, https://www.bmi.com/special/john_williams.

61. Walden, "Ren Klyce: Mixing the Score for *Star Wars: The Last Jedi*."

62. See the 1995 documentary *Film Music Masters: Jerry Goldsmith*, directed by Fred Karlin.

63. Williams quoted in Burton-Hill, "John Williams, the Music Master."

64. Williams quoted in D. Thomas, "King of Themes," 50.

65. On Williams's concert music, see Wennekes, "No Sharks, No Stars."

66. On Newman and Waxman, see Palmer, *Composer in Hollywood*, 69–70, 95; on Herrmann, see S. Smith, *A Heart at Fire's Center*, 81–82, 135–36, 155–56, 187–88, 209–10, 217–18, 262–63, 336–37.

67. Williams quoted in Elley, "The Film Composer: 3. John Williams, Part 2," 32.

68. Steiner quoted in Schreibman, "Memories of Max. Part 2," 27.

69. Williams quoted in Stearns, "2 Emmys, 4 Oscars, 15 Grammys . . . ," 22.

70. When planning to perform suites from the film music repertoire, usually one has to contact the composer or the publisher in order to rent the score and orchestral parts. When the original material is not available, one has to resort to more or less faithful arrangements and transcriptions. As for Williams, more than forty orchestral sets (conductor's score plus orchestral parts) are easily available for purchase in the version that Williams himself conducts in concerts (see John Williams Signature Edition series, published by Hal Leonard).

71. Sullivan, "Spielberg–Williams," 186.

72. David Thomas, "Point Blank: The Total Film Interview; John Williams," *Total Film*, September 1997, 77.

73. For example, in the score for *The Three Worlds of Gulliver* (Jack Sher, 1960), Herrmann's use of closed forms like minuets and marches made it possible to compile a rich concert suite from the film score. *Bernard Herrmann Great Film Music*, National Philharmonic Orchestra conducted by Bernard Herrmann (1974–75), CD, Decca-London 443 899-2, 1996.

74. The "action scherzo," arguably Williams's most recurrent form for concert adaptations, is examined in Frank Lehman, "Film-as-Concert Music and the Formal Implications of 'Cinematic Listening,'" *Music Analysis* 37 (2018): 14–46.

75. Similarly, Korngold's music for the Sherwood ambush sequence in *The Adventures of Robin Hood* (Michael Curtiz and William Keighley, 1938) was transformed with minor modifications into the concert march "Robin Hood and His Merry Men." Compare the forest ambush sequence on the DVD *The Adventures of Robin Hood*, Warner Bros., 2003—in which it is possible to listen to the isolated music track—with the

second movement of the concert suite on the CD *The Film Music of Erich Wolfgang Korngold*, BBC Philharmonic conducted by Rumon Gamba, Chandos CHAN 10336, 2005.

76. The suite is described in Richard Dyer, "John Williams Casts Spell for 'Potter' Score," *Boston Globe*, 11 November 2001, and is published by Hal Leonard in the John Williams Signature Edition series.

77. Compare the concert piece *The Adventures on Earth* ("John Williams Signature Edition," Hal Leonard, 04490009) with the track titled "Adventure on Earth" on the original CD album of *E.T.* (MCA Records MCLD 19021, 1982).

78. Miceli, *Musica per film*, 249–50.

79. Other notable soloists in Williams's scores are the percussionist Stomu Yamash'ta in *Images* (Robert Altman, 1972), the harmonica virtuoso Toots Thielemans in *The Sugarland Express* (Steven Spielberg, 1974) and *Cinderella Liberty* (Mark Rydell, 1973), the trumpet player Tim Morrison in *Born on the Fourth of July* (Oliver Stone, 1989) and *JFK* (Oliver Stone, 1991), the Irish group the Chieftains in *Far and Away* (Ron Howard, 1992), the guitarist Christopher Parkening in *Stepmom* (Chris Columbus, 1998), the saxophonist Dan Higgins in *Catch Me If You Can* (Steven Spielberg, 2002), and both Itzhak Perlman and Yo-Yo Ma in *Memoirs of a Geisha* (Rob Marshall, 2005).

80. A significant example of the difference between an album created according to criteria of listening experience and one created with the aim of following "philologically" the music order in the film is the comparison between the *Star Wars: Episode I— The Phantom Menace* CD album (Sony Classical SK 61816, 1999), duration 74 minutes, and the two-disc special edition containing the full music track (Sony Classical SK2 89460, 2000), duration 124 minutes. In the latter CD, music fragmentation is evident.

81. John Williams, "John Williams on *Star Wars*," liner notes of *Star Wars*, LP album, 20th Century Records 2T-541 (0898), 1977.

82. Another example is the collector's edition double CD of *The Fury* (Brian De Palma, 1978): disc 2 contains the original album rerecorded with the London Symphony Orchestra (9 tracks, duration 40 minutes), while disc 1 contains the original music track (23 tracks, duration 55 minutes) recorded with a freelance US orchestra. The comparison between these two discs and the different duration of the pieces is a case study of this process of combining different cues, arranging the forms, and reorganizing their order from the original film score to the album release. "Main Title" lasts 2:08 on the music track and 3:08 on the album; "For Gillian" lasts 1:48 on the music track and 2:37 on the album; "Vision on the Stairs" lasts 1:48 on the music track and 4:03 on the album.

83. Lack, *Twenty Four Frames Under*, 329–30.

84. William Booth, "Shark Attack?! John Williams Liked the Sound of That," *Washington Post*, 5 December 2004.

85. Williams quoted in Elley, "The Film Composer: 3. John Williams, Part 1," 24. Williams and Spencer can be seen at work in the documentary *Star Wars: Music by John Williams*, by David Buckton, BBC, 1980, which is an excellent report on Williams's modus operandi.

86. On Korngold's orchestrators, see Duchen, *Erich Wolfgang Korngold*, 164–65.

87. Dobroski and Greene, "Pass the Popcorn," 6.

88. Williams quoted in Elley, "The Film Composer: 3. John Williams, Part 1," 24.

89. Hollenbeck quoted in Fernando Gonzalez, "Orchestrating *Indiana Jones*," *Boston Globe*, 18 June 1989. Herbert Spencer's account on the completeness of Williams's sketches can be found in Karlin, *Listening to Movies*, 37.

90. Elley, "The Film Composer: 3. John Williams, Part 1," 24.

91. Kalinak, *Settling the Score*, 191.

92. Williams quoted in "Back Again to a Galaxy . . . ," 16–17. Mark Graham at Jo-Ann Kane Music Service is the person supervising this process. See Sapiro, "Star Scores," 192–93.

Chapter 9. *Raiders of the Lost Ark* Background

1. Franco La Polla and Maria Teresa Cavina, eds., *Spielberg su Spielberg* (Turin: Lindau, 1995), 63–65; D. Taylor, *Making of "Raiders of the Lost Ark,"* 12; Ian Freer, *The Complete Spielberg* (London: Virgin, 2001), 96.

2. D. Taylor, *Making of "Raiders of the Lost Ark,"* 13.

3. Moreover, the Bond character has been played by a number of actors during the past fifty years, thus giving Bond a sort of ageless look and atemporal existence; he belongs to the 1960s as well as to the 1990s and 2000s. Dr. Jones, conversely, is rooted in a defined historical context and, in the films, has always been played by Harrison Ford; across the series, we can clearly see the character aging along with the actor (indeed, the fourth installment is set in the late 1950s, not in the 1930s, so as to be congruent with Ford's age). Thanks to Jeff Smith for pointing this out.

4. Spielberg quoted in D. Taylor, *Making of "Raiders of the Lost Ark,"* 13.

5. D. Taylor, *Making of "Raiders of the Lost Ark,"* 13.

6. D. Taylor, *Making of "Raiders of the Lost Ark,"* 1–2.

7. Lucas quoted in D. Taylor, *Making of "Raiders of the Lost Ark,"* 14.

8. Spielberg quoted in D. Taylor, *Making of "Raiders of the Lost Ark,"* 105.

9. Freer, *Complete Spielberg*, 99.

10. Kasdan quoted in "Indiana Jones and the Ultimate Tribute," *Empire*, October 2006, 74.

11. Ford quoted in Philip Taylor, *Steven Spielberg: The Man, His Movies, and Their Meaning*, 3rd ed. (London: B. T. Batsford, 1999), 107.

12. Freer, *Complete Spielberg*, 97; Omar Calabrese, *Neo-Baroque: A Sign of the Times* (Princeton, NJ: Princeton University Press, 1992), 173; P. Taylor, *Steven Spielberg*, 104.

13. Spielberg quoted in P. Taylor, *Steven Spielberg*, 105.

14. Warren Buckland, "A Close Encounter with *Raiders of the Lost Ark*: Notes on Narrative Aspects of the New Hollywood Blockbuster," in *Contemporary Hollywood Cinema*, ed. Steve Neale and Murray Smith (London: Routledge, 1998), 170.

15. Buckland, "Close Encounter," 171–72.

16. Robert McKee, *Story: Substance, Structure, Style, and the Principles of Screenwriting* (London: Methuen, 1998), 238–43.

17. Bordwell, *Narration in the Fiction Film*, 158.

18. On "symptomatic meaning," see David Bordwell, *Making Meaning: Inference and Rhetoric in the Interpretation of Cinema* (Cambridge, MA: Harvard University Press,

1989), 9. An interpretative analysis of the film can be found in Nigel Morris, *The Cinema of Steven Spielberg: Empire of Light* (London: Wallflower, 2007), 78–80.

19. Andrew Britton, "Blissing Out: The Politics of Reaganite Entertainment," in *Britton on Film: The Complete Film Criticism of Andrew Britton*, ed. Barry Keith Grant (Detroit, MI: Wayne State University Press, 2009), 97–154; Susan Jeffords, *Hard Bodies: Hollywood Masculinity in the Reagan Era* (New Brunswick, NJ: Rutgers University Press, 1993). On cinema in the Reagan era, see Sklar, *Movie-Made America*, 339–56.

20. Robin Wood, *Hollywood from Vietnam to Reagan . . . and Beyond*, rev. and exp. ed. (New York: Columbia University Press, 2003), 151.

21. On stereotypes, see Richard Dyer, "The Role of Stereotypes," in *Media Studies: A Reader*, ed. Sue Thornham, Caroline Bassett, and Paul Marris (Edinburgh: Edinburgh University Press, 2009), 206–12. On ideological representation, see John Cones, *Patterns of Bias in Hollywood Movies* (New York: Algora, 2012); and Michael Richardson, *Otherness in Hollywood Cinema* (New York: Continuum, 2010). One, and the most blatant, of the ideological positions that can be detected in the film is "Orientalism"—a series of generalized and stereotyped traits created from an Eurocentric perspective to separate Western culture from and define it vis-à-vis Eastern culture(s)—as analyzed by Edward Said in *Orientalism* (1978; repr., London: Penguin Books, 2003). The score, for example, resorts to a number of "Orientalist" clichés traditionally employed by Western music, like ethnic timbres, pentatonic scales for Eastern characters, and chromatic scales for Middle Eastern ones.

22. Wood, *Hollywood from Vietnam to Reagan . . . and Beyond*, 187.

23. See Peter Glick and Susan T. Fiske, "Sexism and Other 'Isms': Independence, Status, and the Ambivalent Content of Stereotypes," in *Sexism and Stereotypes in Modern Society: The Gender Science of Janet Taylor Spence*, ed. W. B. Swann Jr., J. H. Langlois, and L. A. Gilbert (Washington, DC: American Psychological Association, 1999), 193–221. On gender representation in film music, see Rebecca Fülöp, "Heroes, Dames, and Damsels in Distress: Constructing Gender Types in Classical Hollywood Film Music" (PhD diss., University of Michigan, 2012).

24. Williams quoted in Richard Dyer, "Williams Poised for Pops," *Boston Globe*, 26 April 1981.

25. Williams quoted in "Indiana Jones and the Ultimate Tribute," 81.

26. *The Music of Indiana Jones*, video documentary by Laurent Bouzereau, Lucasfilm, 2003, included in *The Adventures of Indiana Jones*, DVD box set, Paramount Home Video, 2003.

27. *Raiders March*, full orchestral score, "John Williams Signature Edition," Hal Leonard, 04490015.

28. Williams quoted in Lukas Kendall, "Raiders of the Los Ark: An Analysis by Lukas Kendall," CD booklet, *Raiders of the Lost Ark*, DCC Compact Classic-Silva Screen Raiders 001, 1995.

29. Williams quoted in Elley, "The Film Composer: 3. John Williams, Part 1," 23.

30. Williams quoted in M. R. Montgomery, "John Williams' Quiet Side," *Boston Globe*, 18 March 1981.

31. Williams quoted in Colburn, "John Williams Returns to Bands," 16.

32. See chapter 4 for the mythological nature of *Star Wars* and the archetypal heroic journey underlying the narrative. Luke Skywalker is just one of the many incarnations of the hero archetype, as is the leitmotiv, which can certainly be associated with Luke, but above all it comes to represent the film and the archetypes represented in it.

33. Williams quoted in "Indiana Jones and the Ultimate Tribute," 82.

34. Since access to the original score is not allowed, for the musical analysis of the main themes I have resorted either to transcriptions by ear ("The Ark's Motif" here, and "The Wrath of God Motif" in chapter 10) or to the concert versions published by Hal Leonard in the composer-approved series "John Williams Signature Edition."

35. See chapter 7 in this book for its appearance in *Jaws* (Steven Spielberg, 1975). The tritone is famously featured in the trombones motif at the beginning of Modest Mussorgsky's fantasy for orchestra, *A Night on the Bald Mountain*, which musically describes a witches' Sabbath.

Chapter 10. Raiders of the Lost Ark Analysis

1. The film analysis of *Raiders of the Lost Ark* is based on the PAL-system DVD (Paramount Home Video, 2003). I have also referred to the CDs from the film's original music track (*Raiders of the Lost Ark*, DCC Compact Classic-Silva Screen Raiders 001, 1995; and *Raiders of the Lost Ark*, Concord Records CRE-31002-02, 2008) to better identify the orchestration details in those passages in the film in which the dialogue and sound effects may mask the music.

2. On the characteristics of open-title sequences in classical Hollywood cinema, see Bordwell, Staiger, and Thompson, *Classical Hollywood Cinema*, 25–29.

3. Lucas quoted in "Indiana Jones and the Ultimate Tribute," 74.

4. At the time *Raiders* was released, Lucas had already planned at least another two chapters. See D. Taylor, *Making of "Raiders of the Lost Ark,"* 14.

5. On the "principle of saturation" and the psychological effects caused by ostinatos and music with prolonged tonal uncertainty, see L. Meyer, *Emotion and Meaning in Music*, 135–38.

6. On the reasons why the minor mode typically sounds either tragic or sad, see L. Meyer, *Emotion and Meaning in Music*, 222–28. On the connotative mechanisms of music, see L. Meyer, *Emotion and Meaning in Music*, 258–72. On the "metaphoric mimicry," see L. Meyer, *Style and Music*, 128–31.

7. For example, low-pitched trombones minor chords are used in Gottfried Huppertz's music for the kidnapping of Maria in the catacombs in *Metropolis* (Fritz Lang, 1927). This cliché had also been regularly used by Max Steiner since *The Most Dangerous Game* (Irving Pichel and Ernest B. Schoedsack, 1932). Once again, its antecedents can be found in theater music and opera, in the "ombra" or "shadow music," a suspense musical topic that dates at least back to Carl Maria von Weber's "Wolf's Glen Scene" in *Der Freischütz* (1821). See Michael Saffle, *The Music of Franz Liszt: Stylistic Development and Cultural Synthesis* (New York: Routledge, 2018), 50–51.

8. Tone clusters are groups of contiguous notes played simultaneously and therefore sounding highly dissonant and perceived as "fastidiously" grating.

9. On the psychological mechanisms of suspense in music, see L. Meyer, *Emotion and Meaning in Music*, 163–66.

10. This use of the *crescendo* or the stinger followed by a dramatic musical silence is typical of Steiner and can be found, for example, in *The Informer* (John Ford, 1935).

11. Williams quoted in Kendall, "Raiders of the Los Ark."

12. 1 Kings 19:12 (New American Standard Bible).

13. The song is "I Am the Monarch of the Sea" from the operetta *H.M.S. Pinafore* (1878), by Arthur Sullivan and W. S. Gilbert.

14. As in the previous example, in which the alleged torture instrument is transformed into a harmless clothes hanger, the music contributes to build a "mountain that has brought forth a mouse."

15. The "show-off modulation" (C major to D-flat major) can be spotted between measures 7 and 8 in figure 6.

16. Fragments of the main theme are presented in gradually longer configurations throughout the film, until the theme is finally stated in its full form in a topical scene requiring an emotional punch from the music.

17. The Mark Tree is a series of suspended small tubular bells arranged in a line from the shortest (highest pitch) to the longest (lowest pitch). When the bells are rubbed with a stick, they produce an ascending or descending silvery sound. A similarly sounding instrument is the bell tree.

18. Genesis 19:17.

19. Genesis 19:15–26. Marion, unlike Lot's wife, who turned into a pillar of salt, did not open her eyes.

20. Williams quoted in "Indiana Jones and the Ultimate Tribute," 82.

21. With the ancient natural horns, as well as with the hunting horn, it is possible (unlike the modern valved French horn) to produce only those tones that are within the harmonic series of the instrument.

22. Exodus 19:16, 18–19 (Complete Jewish Bible). Most English versions wrongly translate "shofar" as "trumpet" instead of "horn."

23. "Indiana Jones and the Ultimate Tribute," 82.

24. For a pioneering reading of Hollywood patriarchy, see Mulvey, "Visual Pleasure and Narrative Cinema."

25. The suite is built with "Indy 1," followed by "Indy 2," then "Marion's Theme" (love theme), and finally again "Indy 1," closing the end credits and the film with a powerful orchestral chord.

26. Freer, *Complete Spielberg*, 106.

27. Williams quoted in D. Taylor, *Making of "Raiders of the Lost Ark,"* 167–68.

28. Lebrecht, "John Williams."

29. Freer, *Complete Spielberg*, 101.

Chapter 11. Dark Neoclassicism

1. Noël Carroll, *The Philosophy of Horror: Or, Paradoxes of the Heart* (New York: Routledge, 1990). Carroll's is not the one and only theory of horror, but I find it useful to distinguish a horror from a thriller, for one. A horror film is one that elicits both *fear* and *disgust* and that features some kind of monster endowed with some kind of

supernatural power; such monster is the principal source of disgust. For this reason, I consider *Jaws* (Steven Spielberg, 1975) not a horror but a thriller with disaster-movie narrative dynamics. The shark in *Jaws* is surely monsterlike for its dimension and intelligence but it is not *properly* a monster (it has no supernatural status). I have already employed Carroll's theory and discussed it in Emilio Audissino, "A Matter of Form, Style, and Monsters: A Comparative Analysis of *Reazione a catena* and *Friday the 13th*," *L'avventura: International Journal of Italian Cinema and Media Landscapes* 6, no. 1 (January–June 2020): 3–22.

2. The literature is vast. The following are only the texts consulted for the preparation of this chapter: Barbara Brodman and James E. Doan, *The Universal Vampire: Origins and Evolution of a Legend* (Madison, NJ: Fairleigh Dickinson University Press, 2013); Leonard Wolf, ed., *Blood Thirsty: 100 Years of Vampire Fiction* (New York: Oxford University Press, 1997); Carol A. Senf, *The Vampire in Nineteenth-Century English Literature* (Madison: University of Wisconsin Press, 1988); Matthew Beresford, *From Demons to Dracula: The Creation of the Modern Vampire Myth* (London: Reaktion Books, 2008); Erik Butler, *Metamorphoses of the Vampire in Literature and Film: Cultural Transformations in Europe, 1732–1933* (Rochester, NY: Camden House, 2010); Ken Gelder, *Reading the Vampire* (New York: Routledge, 1994); William Hughes, *Bram Stoker's Dracula* (New York: Continuum, 2009); John S. Bak, ed., *Post/modern Dracula: From Victorian Themes to Postmodern Praxis* (Newcastle: Cambridge Scholars, 2007); Peter Day, *Vampires: Myth and Metaphors of Enduring Evil* (New York: Rodopi, 2006); Clive Leatherdale, *Dracula: The Novel and the Legend; A Study of Bram Stoker's Gothic Masterpiece* (Wellingborough: Aquarian, 1985); Raymond T. McNally and Radu Florescu, *In Search of Dracula: The History of Dracula and Vampires*, 2nd ed. (Boston: Houghton Mifflin, 1994). An excellent synthesis is Roger Luckhurst, ed., *The Cambridge Companion to Dracula* (New York: Cambridge University Press, 2018).

3. Jeffrey Weinstock, *The Vampire Film: Undead Cinema* (New York: Wallflower, 2012); Stacey Abbott, *Celluloid Vampires: Life after Death in the Modern World* (Austin: University of Texas Press, 2007); David J. Skal, *Hollywood Gothic: The Tangled Web of Dracula from Novel to Stage to Screen* (New York: W. W. Norton, 1990); Stephen Prince, ed., *The Horror Film* (New Brunswick, NJ: Rutgers University Press, 2004); Bruce F. Kawin, *Horror and the Horror Film* (New York: Anthem Press, 2012); Peter Hutchings, *The Horror Film* (London: Pearson, 2004); Harry M. Benshoff, ed., *A Companion to the Horror Film* (Malden, MA: Wiley-Blackwell, 2014).

4. Weinstock, *Vampire Film*, 7–8. See also Heike Bauer, "*Dracula* and Sexology," in *The Cambridge Companion to Dracula*, ed. Roger Luckhurst (New York: Cambridge University Press, 2018), 76–84; Kelly Hurley, *The Gothic Body: Sexuality, Materialism, and Degeneration at the Fin de Siècle* (New York: Cambridge University Press, 1996); and Patrick R. O'Malley, *Catholicism, Sexual Deviance, and Victorian Gothic Culture* (New York: Cambridge University Press, 2006).

5. Judith Halberstam, *Skin Shows: Gothic Horror and the Technology of Monsters* (Durham, NC: Duke University Press, 1995), 21.

6. Carol A. Senf, "'Dracula': Stoker's Response to the New Woman," *Victorian Studies* 26, no. 1 (Autumn 1982): 33–49; Charles E. Prescott and Grace A. Giorgio,

"Vampiric Affinities: Mina Harker and the Paradox of Femininity in Bram Stoker's *Dracula*," *Victorian Literature and Culture* 33 (2005): 487–515.

7. Sigmund Freud, *The Uncanny*, trans. David McLintock (1919; repr., London: Penguin Books, 2003). See also Roger Luckhurst, "Dracula and Psychology," in *The Cambridge Companion to Dracula*, ed. Roger Luckhurst (New York: Cambridge University Press, 2018), 66–75.

8. Anne Williams, *Art of Darkness: A Poetics of Gothic* (Chicago: University of Chicago Press, 1995), 78.

9. Edmund Burke, *A Philosophical Enquiry into the Origin of Our Ideas of the Sublime and Beautiful* (1757; repr., New York: P. F. Collier & Son, 1914), 20.

10. A. Williams, *Art of Darkness*, 76.

11. Johann Georg Sulzer quoted in L. Meyer, *Style and Music*, 203–4.

12. A. Williams, *Art of Darkness*, 77.

13. Agnes Murgoci, "The Vampire in Roumania," in *The Vampire: A Casebook*, ed. Alan Dundes (Madison: University of Wisconsin Press, 1998), 28.

14. James Deaville, "The Beauty of Horror: Kilar, Coppola, and Dracula," in *Music in the Horror Film: Listening to Fear*, ed. Neil Lerner (New York: Routledge, 2010), 187.

15. See Catherine Wynne, "*Dracula* on Stage," in *The Cambridge Companion to Dracula*, ed. Roger Luckhurst (New York: Cambridge University Press, 2018), 165–78.

16. The director's initial plan of shooting on black-and-white film—rejected by the producers but somewhat brought back in the desaturated 1991 "Director's Cut"—seems to confirm the direct homage to the antecedent. Brian Holcomb, "John Badham's 'Dracula,' the Rock Star," PopMatters.com, 15 January 2020, https://www.popmatters.com/john-badham-dracula-2644157427.html.

17. Stacey Abbott, "*Dracula* on Film and TV from 1960 to the Present," in *The Cambridge Companion to Dracula*, ed. Roger Luckhurst (New York: Cambridge University Press, 2018), 202.

18. Bram Stoker, *Dracula* (1897; repr., Cambridge: Cambridge University Press, 2013), 19.

19. Wynne, "*Dracula* on Stage," 172.

20. The film grossed the unimpressive figure of $20,158,970. "Dracula," Box Office Mojo, accessed 9 July 2020, https://www.boxofficemojo.com/title/tt0079073/?ref_=bo_se_r_7.

21. Roger Ebert, "*Dracula*," *Chicago Sun-Times*, 20 July 1979, available at https://www.rogerebert.com/reviews/dracula.

22. A. Williams, *Art of Darkness*, 165; Burke, *Philosophical Enquiry*, 38–39.

23. Although the exteriors were shot in Cornwall, the story is set in Whitby, North Yorkshire.

24. In an "unexplained and open ending . . . , the poet leaves the question of what we should think unaddressed" and "gently chides readers away from the gratifications of plot and suspense and instead exhorts them to the active role of making their own meaning." Michael Gamer, "Gothic Fictions and Romantic Writing in Britain," in *The Cambridge Companion to Gothic Fiction*, ed. Jerrold E. Hogle (New York: Cambridge University Press, 2002), 96.

25. Janet Maslin, "Screen: Langella's Seductive 'Dracula' Adapted from Stage," *New York Times*, 13 July 1979.

26. Williams in *The Revamping of Dracula*, documentary by Laurent Bouzereau, Universal Studios Home Video, 2004.

27. "The Bride of Corinth" recounts how a young maiden returns from the grave to carnally rejoin her betrothed. The two had been separated after the girl's mother had converted to Christianity and forced the daughter, instead of marrying her pagan fiancé, to join a nunnery, where she died of heartbreak.

28. Badham in *The Revamping of Dracula*.

29. On Bernard, see David Huckvale, *James Bernard, Composer to Count Dracula: A Critical Biography* (Jefferson, NC: McFarland, 2006).

30. Scheurer, *Music and Mythmaking in Film*, 185.

31. Isabella van Elferen, *Gothic Music: The Sounds of the Uncanny* (Cardiff: University of Wales Press, 2012), 48.

32. Scheurer, *Music and Mythmaking in Film*, 177.

33. Philip Hayward, "Introduction: Scoring the Edge," in *Terror Tracks: Music, Sound and Horror Cinema*, ed. Philip Hayward (London: Equinox, 2009), 2.

34. Hayward, "Introduction," 10.

35. Michael Hannan, "Sound and Music in Hammer's Vampire Films," in *Terror Tracks: Music, Sound and Horror Cinema*, ed. Philip Hayward (London: Equinox, 2009), 71.

36. L. Meyer, *Style and Music*, 203.

37. Van Elferen, *Gothic Music*, 10, 3, 11–12, 17, 18. On the Gothic in general, see A. Williams, *Art of Darkness*; Hogle, *The Cambridge Companion to Gothic Fiction*; and David Punter, ed., *A New Companion to the Gothic* (Malden, MA: Wiley-Blackwell, 2012).

38. A. Williams, *Art of Darkness*, 79.

39. Van Elferen, *Gothic Music*, 9, 4.

40. Julie Brown, "*Carnival of Souls* and the Organs of Horror," in *Music in the Horror Film: Listening to Fear*, ed. Neil Lerner (New York: Routledge, 2010), 5.

41. For an analysis of the score to *Close Encounters of the Third Kind*, see Audissino, *Film/Music Analysis*, 191–222.

42. William H. Rosar, "Music for the Monsters: Universal Pictures Horror Film Scores of the Thirties," *Quarterly Journal of the Library of Congress* 40, no. 4 (Fall 1983): 418.

43. The principal difference that distinguishes the minor from the major mode is the third degree of the scale: in the major mode, there is a major-third interval between the first and the third degree (C to E, in C major), while in the minor mode there is a minor-third interval (C to E-flat, in C minor).

44. L. Meyer, *Style and Music*, 272, 295.

45. Meyer differentiates between the primary parameters of music (syntactical) and the secondary parameters of music (statistical). Primary parameters are chordal progressions, syntactic relations between tones, etcetera, that is, those structural parameters responsible for the formal construction of the piece. These are predominant in the music of the classical period (e.g., Haydn and Mozart). Secondary parameters are affective and expressive more that structural, for example dynamics, tempo and agogics, register, timbre, and so on. L. Meyer, *Style and Music*, 14–16.

46. L. Meyer, *Style and Music*, 204. Quality versus quantity is not to be intended as a pejorative—meaning that Mahler's is not quality music. Instead, the quality of musical syntax is of lesser interest than the quantity of musical expressiveness, of the orchestra's size, of the scale of the musical structures, and so forth.

47. L. Meyer, *Style and Music*, 259.

48. L. Meyer, *Style and Music*, 204.

49. Jean-Marie Lecomte, "Postmodern Verbal Discourse in Coppola's Bram Stoker's *Dracula*," in *Post/modern Dracula: From Victorian Themes to Postmodern Praxis*, ed. John S. Bak (Newcastle: Cambridge Scholars, 2007), 113.

50. Lecomte, "Postmodern Verbal Discourse," 114.

51. Abatement is another recurrent trait that in Romantic music typically follows the apotheosis. L. Meyer *Style and Music*, 267–68.

52. Badham in *The Revamping of Dracula*.

53. Williams quoted in Mike Matessino, "Nocturne: John Williams and Dracula," liner notes to the CD *Dracula*, The Deluxe Edition, Varèse Sarabande, VCL 1018 1118, 2018, 30.

54. Alison Peirse, "*Dracula* on Film 1931–1959," in *The Cambridge Companion to Dracula*, ed. Roger Luckhurst (New York: Cambridge University Press, 2018), 182–83.

55. On the use of *Swan Lake* in *Murder in the Rue Morgue*, see Rosar, "Music for the Monsters," 399.

56. Rosar, "Music for the Monsters," 393–94.

57. For reasons of space, it is not feasible to include all the transcriptions, but the full Tchaikovsky score is available online: *Swan Lake*, Act II, esp. pp. 223–24, accessed 16 July 2020, http://ks4.imslp.net/files/imglnks/usimg/b/b1/IMSLP535915-PMLP09904-Tchaikovsky-Op20.FSJ.pdf.

58. Williams quoted in Matessino, "Nocturne," 30–33, emphasis added.

59. Deaville, "Beauty of Horror," 188.

60. Rosar, "Music for the Monsters," 418.

61. Larson, *Musique Fantastique*, 300.

Chapter 12. Reviving the Hollywood Music Classics beyond the Films

1. The Pops also reconvenes in December, for a series of holiday-themed concerts, first launched in 1974. *Boston Pops: The Story of America's Orchestra* (Boston: Boston Symphony Orchestra, 2000), 24–25.

2. Fiedler quoted in *Boston Pops*, 37.

3. Produced by Boston's WGBH Television (William Cosel, producer) and by the Boston Symphony, the series was broadcast nationwide by the Public Broadcasting Service (PBS), always ranking in the top positions of the network's viewing reports. On the history of *Evening at Pops*, see Ron Bachman, "Behind the Scenes at Evening at Pops," *Nine*, June 1989, 34–46; and "Evening at Pops: Putting on the Show," in *Boston Pops*, 44–47.

4. *Boston Pops*, 13.

5. Richard Dyer, "Williams Is Candidate for Fiedler's Job," *Boston Globe*, 6 January 1980.

6. Tim Smith, "Film Composer John Williams to Make Baltimore Conducting Première," *Baltimore Sun*, 1 June 2013,

7. Goodson, "Yes, There's Life after Fiedler."

8. Lockhart quoted in Emilio Audissino and Frank Lehman, "John Williams Seen from the Podium: An Interview with Maestro Keith Lockhart," in *John Williams: Music for Films, Television, and the Concert Stage*, ed. Emilio Audissino (Turnhout: Brepols, 2018), 407.

9. When André Previn was given the conductorship of the Houston Symphony in 1967 and then the London Symphony in 1968, his Hollywood output had become a minor facet of his musicianship; also, he stopped composing for films after starting his conducting career.

10. Previn quoted in Dyer, "John Williams Is New Pops Maestro."

11. Brown quoted in Margo Miller, "'A Wonderful Choice,'" *Boston Globe*, 11 January 1980.

12. Michael Knight, "John Williams Opens Season with Pops," *New York Times*, 30 April 1980.

13. Whitelaw quoted in Knight, "John Williams Opens Season with Pops."

14. Williams quoted in Dyer, "John Williams Bows In."

15. *Boston Pops*, 36.

16. "Theme and Dance from Star Wars" was released for the first time on the CD *The Arthur Fiedler Legacy: From Fabulous Broadway to Hollywood's Reel Thing*, Deutsche Grammophon 477 6124, 2007, with the deceptive title "Star Wars: Main Title" but without any mention of the arrangers' names (Richard Hayman and Newton Wayland), thus passing it off as the original version.

17. Concert program, 21 June 1981, Boston Symphony Orchestra Archives, Symphony Hall, Boston, MA.

18. Beverly Ford and John Impemba, "John Williams Quits Boston Pops," *Boston Herald*, 14 June 1984.

19. Constance Gorfinkle, "Williams Miffed by Hiss from Pops Orchestra?," *Patriot Ledger*, 14 June 1984. A later source reports that the target of the hisses was *Salute to Fred Astaire* (arranged by Sid Ramin). See Peter Catalano, "John Williams to Leave Boston Pops," *Los Angeles Times*, 21 December 1991. Williams has never confirmed either of the versions. Larry Katz, "Dr. Hollywood & Mr. Pops," *Boston Herald Magazine*, 28 April 1985.

20. Margo Miller, "Williams to Resign as Pops Conductor," *Boston Globe*, 14 June 1984.

21. Williams quoted in Peter Goodman, "A Great Little Visiting Band," *New York Newsday*, 11 June 1986.

22. Richard Dyer, "The Williams Years: Knowing What Counts," in concert program of the "Opening Night at Pops: A Gala Celebration for John Williams," 12 May 1993, p. 35, Boston Symphony Orchestra Archives, Symphony Hall, Boston, MA.

23. Constance Gorfinkle, "Why John Williams Changed His Mind," *Patriot Ledger*, 8 August 1984.

24. In exchange, players not willing to play during the Pops season agreed to have the share covering the period ($7,650) deducted from the annual stipend ($45,000). Gorfinkle, "Why John Williams Changed His Mind."

25. Williams quoted in Katz, "Dr. Hollywood & Mr. Pops."

26. Richard Dyer, "Pops' Williams to Retire in '93," *Boston Globe*, 20 December 1991.

27. Richard Dyer, "Pops Star: The Legacy of John Williams," *Boston Globe*, 12 December 1993.

28. Richard Dyer, "Williams to Stay on as Pops Adviser," *Boston Globe*, 4 February 1994.

29. For a discussion of film music as concert music, see Frank Lehman, "Film-as-Concert Music and the Formal Implications of 'Cinematic Listening,'" *Music Analysis* 37 (2018): 7–46.

30. An analysis of John Williams's multimedia concert formats (the "multimedia scene/sequence" vis-à-vis the "multimedia concert piece") can be found in Emilio Audissino, "Film Music and Multimedia: An Immersive Experience and a Throwback to the Past," in *Jahrbuch Immersiver Medien 2014: Sounds, Music & Soundscapes*, ed. Patrick Rupert-Kruse (Marburg: Schüren Verlag, 2014), 46–56.

31. A description of Williams's mastery in conducting live to film is given in "Angela Morley in Private Interview, 1999," YouTube, April 12, 2020, 36:10, https://www.youtube.com/watch?v=A3Xb9XDDeA0.

32. On the technicalities of live-accompanied films, see Audissino and Lehman, "John Williams Seen from the Podium," 402–7; Marina Muhlfriedel, "Live Movie Concerts: Experiencing Classic Films with Composer and Conductor David Newman," Harman, 22 August 2016, http://pro.harman.com/insights/harman-pro/live-movie-concerts-experiencing-classic-films-with-composer-and-conductor-david-newman; and Grace Lichtenstein, "Film Concerts Go Mainstream," Bachtrack, 2 May 2017, https://bachtrack.com/screenings-with-live-orchestra-film-game-music-month-may-2017.

33. On "cine-concerts," see Brooke McCorkle Okazaki, "Liveness, Music, Media: The Case of the Cine-Concert," *Music and the Moving Image* 13, no. 2 (Summer 2020): 3–24. Oddly enough, McCorkle Okazaki traces the historical precedents of today's cine-concerts without ever mentioning the foundational experiments of John Williams and the Boston Pops Orchestra.

34. Jon Burlingame, "Live Movie Concerts: A Cash Cow for Orchestras," *Variety*, 29 April 2015.

35. For one example, Gustav Holst's *The Planets*, op. 32 (1916) was featured in the concert "MIT Giant Leaps," celebrating the fortieth anniversary of the moon landing, with space footage projected on the screen and astronaut Buzz Aldrin as a narrator. Concert program, Boston Pops, 11 June 2009, Boston Symphony Orchestra Archives, Symphony Hall, Boston, MA.

36. David Patrick Stearns, "Music That's Light on the Baton: USA Orchestras Enjoy a Pops Explosion," *USA Today*, 26 April 1985.

37. *Pops in Space* soon became the best seller of the Philips Classics catalog at the time. Theodore W. Libbey Jr., "Disks Attest to the Versatile Talents of John Williams," *New York Times*, 27 February 1983.

38. See Saul Pincus and Mike Petersen, "Remaking Star Wars," *Film Score Monthly*, September/October 2005, 40–44.

39. David Patrick Stearns, "Hollywood Conductor Taps Studio Talent," *USA Today*, 31 July 1991.

40. The first occurrence is in *The Soundtrack Club* [*Film Score Monthly*], November 1991, 3.

41. Conducted by Richard Kaufman, *Film Score Monthly*, May 1996, 4.

42. Jeff Bond, "Stamps of Approval," *Film Score Monthly*, November 1999, 24–27.

43. Concerts listing in *Film Score Monthly*, March 2004, 8.

44. In the 2005–6 season (besides Williams on 25, 26, and 29 November), there was "Symphonic Hollywood," conducted by Richard Kaufman and featuring selections from *Psycho, Vertigo, Forrest Gump,* and *Nuovo Cinema Paradiso* (31 March). In the 2007–8 season, Joel McNeely conducted a Bernard Herrmann / Alfred Hitchcock concert (4 April). Concert programs, Chicago Symphony Orchestra Archives, Symphony Center, Chicago, IL.

45. *Violin Concerto No. 1 / Carmen Fantasie / Havanaise / Introduction & Rondo Capriccioso,* Zubin Mehta, Israel Philharmonic Orchestra, Maxim Vengerov, CD album, Teldec Classics 9031-73266-2, 1992.

46. Concerts listings in *Film Score Monthly*, October/December 1996, 2.

47. The LSO's American tour was from 3 to 20 September 2004. *Film Score Monthly*, June 2004, 8.

48. Jon Burlingame, "Leonard Rosenman Turns 80: Pioneering Composer to be Honored in Rome," *FMS Feature . . . ,* 7 September 2004, http://www.filmmusicsociety.org/news_events/features/2004/090704.html.

49. The Herrmann pieces featured were the overture from *The Man Who Knew Too Much,* a suite from *Marnie,* and the prelude from *North by Northwest.* Kyle Renick, "The Halls Are Alive," *Film Score Monthly*, May 1998, 13.

50. Concerts listings in *Film Score Monthly*, October/November 1998, 8.

51. Concerts listings in *Film Score Monthly*, March 2000, 8.

52. For more examples of Williams's music programmed in European concerts, see Sebastian Stoppe, "John Williams's Film Music in the Concert Halls," in *John Williams: Music for Films, Television, and the Concert Stage,* ed. Emilio Audissino (Turnhout: Brepols, 2018), 95–117.

53. Proms archive, accessed 27 July 2020, https://www.bbc.co.uk/proms/events/by/date/.

54. Lockhart quoted in Audissino and Lehman, "John Williams Seen from the Podium," 402–3.

55. James Miller, "Keeping Time with John: Inside the Tanglewood Film Music Seminar," *Film Score Monthly*, October/November 1998, 20–21; Richard Dyer, "Composers Learn Film Music from the Master," *Boston Globe*, 20 August 1998.

56. Phil Lehman, "When Capitals Collide: Maestros Slatkin and Williams Join Forces for a Series of Film Music Festivities," *Film Score Monthly*, February 2003, 12, 13, 47.

57. David Patrick Stearns, "Phila. Orchestra Celebrates 'Star Wars,' Classical Composer John Williams," *Philadelphia Enquirer*, 26 April 2016.

58. Dudamel quoted in Clemency Burton-Hill, "Gustavo Dudamel: 'I Thought John Williams Was Joking when He Asked Me to Conduct His Star Wars Music,'" *Telegraph*, 11 January 2016.

59. Lockhart quoted in Audissino and Lehman, "John Williams Seen from the Podium," 398–99.

60. "Classical Music in 2019," Bachtrack, https://bachtrack.com/files/158143-EN-Classical%20music%20statistics%202019.pdf.

61. "Princess of Asturias Award for the Arts," 5 June 2020, https://www.fpa.es/en/princess-of-asturias-awards/laureates/2020-ennio-morricone-and-john-williams.html?texto=acta&especifica=0.

62. Christoph Irrgeher, "John Williams: Sternstunden der Filmmusik," *Wiener Zeitung,* 20 January 2020, https://www.wienerzeitung.at/nachrichten/kultur/klassik/2046653-John-Williams-Sternstunden-der-Filmmusik.html.

63. "RPS Gold Medal," Royal Philharmonic Society, accessed 19 November 2020, https://royalphilharmonicsociety.org.uk/awards/gold-medal.

64. "Gold Medal Recipients since 1870," Royal Philharmonic Society, accessed 19 November 2020, https://royalphilharmonicsociety.org.uk/awards/gold-medal/gold-medal-recipients-since-1870.

65. "John Williams," Royal Philharmonic Society, accessed 19 November 2020, https://royalphilharmonicsociety.org.uk/awards/gold-medal/john-williams.

66. Dyer, "Pops Star."

Closing Remarks on Neoclassicism and Today's Hollywood Music

1. J. Smith, *Sound of Commerce,* 7.

2. James Lastra, *Sound Technology and the American Cinema: Perception, Representation, Modernity* (New York: Columbia University Press, 2000), 180–215. For a concise survey, see David Cooper, "'Pictures That Talk and Sing': Sound History and Technology," in *The Cambridge Companion to Film Music,* ed. Mervyn Cooke and Fiona Ford (New York: Cambridge University Press, 2016), 29–50.

3. Jay Beck, *Designing Sound: Audiovisual Aesthetics in 1970s American Cinema* (New Brunswick, NJ: Rutgers University Press, 2016).

4. Sergi, "Tales of the Silent Blast."

5. K. J. Donnelly, *Occult Aesthetics: Synchronization in Sound Film* (New York: Oxford University Press, 2014), 129.

6. Liz Greene and Danijela Kulezic-Wilson, eds., *The Palgrave Handbook of Sound Design and Music in Screen Media: Integrated Soundtracks* (London: Palgrave Macmillan, 2016), 2.

7. Jullier, *L'écran post-moderne,* 37.

8. The meaning of the term "music" is not uncontroversial. See Matt Sakakeeny, "Music," in *Keywords in Sound,* ed. David Novak and Matt Sakakeeny (Durham, NC: Duke University Press, 2015), 112–24. Today the tendency is, as explained by Danijela Kulezic-Wilson, a "non-departmentalized approach": "The first question one might reasonably ask when discussing the blurred line between sound design and music is: isn't music part of sound design already? The answer, however, depends on which school of thought one might belong to." Danijela Kulezic-Wilson, "Sound Design and Its Interactions with Music: Changing Historical Perspectives," in *The Routledge Companion to Screen Music and Sound,* ed. Miguel Mera, Ronald Sadoff, and Ben Winters (New York: Routledge, 2017), 128–29. Given the object of this book—film music composed according to the norms and grammar of the Western musical canon—my school of thought is "departmentalized" and I have treated music as conceptually separate

from sounds. The analysis of an element requires, first, that such element be separated from the others.

9. Miklós Rózsa quoted in Roger Manvell and John Huntley, *The Technique of Film Music*, 2nd ed. (New York: Hastings House, 1975), 230.

10. Elfman quoted in Lukas Kendall, "Danny Elfman. Part 2," *Film Score Monthly*, December 1995, 11.

11. Chion, *Audio-Vision*, 73. Two recent practice-oriented books are David Sonnenschein, *Sound Design: The Expressive Power of Music, Voice and Sound Effects in Cinema* (Studio City CA, Michael Wiese Productions, 2001); and, more technical and detailed, Andy Farnell, *Designing Sound* (Cambridge, MA: MIT Press, 2010).

12. Michael Hsu, "Movie Dialogue Too Quiet? Tips for Better Clarity," *Wall Street Journal*, 24 July 2015; Leo Barraclough, "Christopher Nolan's Use of Sound on 'Tenet' Infuriates Some, Inspires Others," *Variety*, 2 September 2020.

13. Wierzbicki, *Film Music*, 209–27.

14. Danijela Kulezic-Wilson, "Sound Design iIs the New Score," *Music, Sound, and the Moving Image* 2, no. 2 (2008): 127–31; Danijela Kulezic-Wilson, *Sound Design Is the New Score: Theory, Aesthetics, and Erotics of the Integrated Soundtrack* (New York: Oxford University Press, 2019).

15. The year 2000 is also chosen as a landmark in James Buhler and David Neumeyer, *Hearing the Movies: Music and Sound in Film History*, 2nd ed. (New York: Oxford University Press, 2015): chapter 13, "Music and Film Sound since 2000"; and chapter 14, "Music and Film Form since 2000."

16. Joakim Tillman, "Topoi and Intertextuality: Narrative Function in Hans Zimmer's and Lisa Gerrard's Music to *Gladiator*," in *Music in Epic Film: Listening to Spectacle*, ed. Stephen C. Meyer (New York: Routledge, 2016), 59–85; Frank Lehman, "Manufacturing the Epic Score: Hans Zimmer and the Sounds of Significance," in *Music in Epic Film: Listening to Spectacle*, ed. Stephen C. Meyer (New York: Routledge, 2016), 27–55.

17. Lehman, "Manufacturing the Epic Score," 27.

18. Lehman, "Manufacturing the Epic Score," 32.

19. Casey, "An Interview with Todd Haberman."

20. See, for example, Lisa Coulthard, "Dirty Sound: Haptic Noise in New Extremism," in *The Oxford Handbook of Sound and Image in Digital Media*, ed. Carol Vernallis, Amy Herzog and John Richardson (New York: Oxford University Press, 2013), 115–26; Kiri Miller, "Virtual and Visceral Experience in Music-Oriented Video Games," in *Oxford Handbook of Sound and Image in Digital Media*, 517–33; Martine Huvenne, "Intertwining Music and Sound in Film," in *Palgrave Handbook of Sound Design and Music in Screen Media*, 123–38.

21. Lehman, "Manufacturing the Epic Score," 33.

22. Buhler and Neumeyer, *Hearing the Movies*, 467.

23. Lehman, "Manufacturing the Epic Score," 33.

24. Karlin, *Listening to Movies*, 200–201; Jeff Bond, "Horner Revealed," *Film Score Monthly*, February 2004, 20.

25. Mark Kerins, "The Modern Entertainment Marketplace, 2000–Present," in *Sound: Dialogue, Music, and Effects*, ed. Kathryn Kalinak (New Brunswick, NJ: Rutgers University Press, 2015), 142. In his keynote speech at the 2014 Music and the Moving

Image Conference in New York, composer/orchestrator Patrick Russ made it very clear that a knowledge of MIDI and computer technology is a must for today's film composers. Patrick Russ, "The Changing Face of Orchestration for the Moving Image" (keynote presentation, Music and the Moving Image IX Conference, 30 May 2014, NYU Steinhardt, New York). On the contemporary film-music business, see Jeremy Borum, *Guerrilla Film Scoring: Practical Advice from Hollywood Composers* (Lanham, MD: Rowman & Littlefield, 2015), esp. ix–xix.

26. Bernard Herrmann had already opted for a similarly modular approach, preferring short motifs and colorism instead of full-fledged melodies. R. Brown, *Overtones and Undertones*, 153–55. On Herrmann's "module technique," see also William H. Rosar, "Bernard Herrmann: The Beethoven of Film Music?," *Journal of Film Music* 1, nos. 2–3 (2003): 136–37; and Schneller, "Easy to Cut."

27. Kerins, "Modern Entertainment Marketplace," 142.

28. Frank Lehman, "Trailers, Tonality, and the Force of Nostalgia," *Musicology Now* (blog), 4 November 2015, http://www.musicologynow.org/2015/11/trailers-tonality -and-force-of-nostalgia.html.

29. Jeff Bond, "The Fall of Troy," *Film Score Monthly*, April/May 2004, 18.

30. Bond, "Horner Revealed," 16–20.

31. See news listings in *Film Score Monthly*, August 1996, 2.

32. Ben Burtt reports the data in *Within a Minute: The Making of "Episode III,"* documentary by Tippy Bushkin, Lucasfilm, 2005.

33. Williams, videotaped lecture, 11 January 2006, Archives of the Thornton School of Music, University of Southern California–Los Angeles.

34. Wannberg in Bushkin, *Within a Minute: The Making of "Episode III."*

35. In the "customer reviews" section of Amazon regarding the 2004 DVD box set, the negative comments number nearly eight hundred. See "Star Wars Trilogy," accessed 3 April 2020, http://www.amazon.com/Trilogy-Empire-Strikes-Return-Wide screen/product-reviews/B00003CXCT/ref=pr_all_summary_cm_cr_acr_txt?ie=UT F8&showViewpoints=1.

36. Alexandra DuPont, "The Star Wars Trilogy," DVD Journal, 2004, http://www .dvdjournal.com/reviews/s/starwarstrilogy.shtml; Bill Hunt, "The Star Wars Trilogy," Digital Bits, 9 September 2004, http://www.thedigitalbits.com/site_archive/reviews 3/starwarstrilogy.html; update to the original review by the Digital Bits, reported widely, including "Star Wars DVD Audio Issues," Audio Review, 22 September 2004, http://forums.audioreview.com/favorite-films/star-wars-dvd-audio-issues-7032.html.

37. *Star Wars: Episode IV—A New Hope*, limited-edition double DVD, 20th Century Home Entertainment.

38. John Jurgensen, "The Last Movie Maestro," *Wall Street Journal*, 16 December 2011; Bruno Coulais, "Ce qui reste d'enfance en nous . . . ," quoted in Tylski, *John Williams*, 171.

39. Powell quoted in Rob leDonne, "With John Williams Stepping Aside, *Solo* Looks to Create a 'Modern' Musical Score for *Star Wars*," *Billboard*, 25 May 2018, https:// www.billboard.com/articles/news/8457839/star-wars-solo-music; Powell quoted in Jon Burlingame, "Solo Composer John Powell Reveals His Process for Tackling a *Star Wars* Movie," *Variety*, 24 May 2018.

40. Williams quoted in Didier C. Deutsch, Liner notes for *John Williams: Film Works*, CD, MCA 32877, 1997.

41. Williams adapted thirty-minute concert suites from each film of the classic trilogy and a fifteen-minute concert suite from *Star Wars: Episode I* but no concert suite at all from either *Episode II* or *Episode III*, which is a confirmation of the less-melodic nature of the latter two.

42. Williams quoted in Dyer, "Making *Star Wars* Sing Again."

43. Williams quoted in Ross, "The Force Is Still Strong with John Williams."

44. Anonymous, "Back Again to a Galaxy," 16–17.

45. Jon Burlingame, "Film Score Icons Williams, Morricone and Horner Loom Large in Oscar Race," *Variety*, 9 December 2015.

46. Williams quoted in Simon, "A Conversation with John Williams."

47. Burlingame, "With *Rise of Skywalker*"; Walden, "Ren Klyce."

48. Williams quoted in Greiving, "John Williams on *The Force Awakens* and the Legacy of *Star Wars*."

49. Williams quoted in Tracy Smith, "John Williams on Spielberg, *Star Wars*, and the Power of Music."

50. "Star-Geigerin Anne-Sophie Mutter im Interview," Nordbuzz, 29 May 2020, https://www.nordbuzz.de/people/star-geigerin-anne-sophie-mutter-spricht-interview-ueber-ihre-corona-infektion-13771243.html.

51. Seemingly, Williams's idiom has had a deeper influence on some video-game scores, for example, on Jeremy Soule's works. Thanks to Kevin Donnelly for bringing this to my attention.

52. Ned Lannamann, "America's Composer: John Williams; The Generous Professor," *Portland Mercury*, 23 April 2014.

53. Burlingame, "John Williams Is on Target to Set Yet Another Oscar Record."

54. Powell quoted in Burlingame, "Solo Composer John Powell Reveals His Process for Tackling a *Star Wars* Movie."

Appendix I.

1. Williams quoted in Jon Burlingame, "Master Class: Williams Earns Himself a Spot in Pantheon of Composers," *Variety*, 29 November 2005. Music critic Richard Dyer praised the resulting cross-cultural blend of the score: "Williams' music is transparent, evocative, and subtle, and much of it is colored by authentic Japanese timbres, musical gestures, and instruments. . . . Of course, like everything connected with this venture, beginning with the novel written by an American in Brookline, the score is a Westernized assimilation of and commentary on traditional Japanese music. But it's worth remembering that bridging the gap between Japanese and Western music was a goal of some Japanese musicians even as early as the period of the story (before World War II), and Williams' score to *Memoirs of a Geisha* is more than Hollywood music with a few touches of local color (just as Puccini's *Madama Butterfly* is more than an Italian opera with a few touches of Asian atmosphere)." Richard Dyer, "John Williams Scores Again: 2005 Produces Two More Oscar Nominations," *Boston Globe*, 5 February 2006.

2. Williams quoted in Anonymous, "Dialogue."

3. Williams quoted in Burlingame, "Master Class." For an analysis of the use of music in *Munich*, see David Ireland, "'Today I'm Hearing with New Ears': John Williams's Use of Audiovisual Incongruence to Convey Character Perspective in *Munich* and Spielberg's Historical Films," in *John Williams: Music for Films, Television, and the Concert Stage*, ed. Emilio Audissino (Turnhout: Brepols, 2018), 309–26.

4. Williams quoted in Ireland, "'Today I'm Hearing with New Ears.'"

5. The only breaks were *The Color Purple* (1985), which producer Quincy Jones composed the music for; *Bridge of Spies* (2015), which Williams had to turn down because of health issues, and was scored by Thomas Newman; and *Ready Player One* (2018), which was assigned to Alan Silvestri because of conflicting schedules.

6. Spielberg quoted in Burlingame, "Spielberg and Lucas on Williams."

7. Steven Spielberg, speech given at "John Williams 80th Birthday Gala," Tanglewood Festival, Lenox, MA, 18 August 2012.

8. Williams quoted in Stearns, "2 Emmys, 4 Oscars, 15 Grammys," 22.

9. Williams quoted in Tracy Smith, "John Williams on Spielberg"

10. Spielberg quoted in Keegan, "John Williams and Steven Spielberg."

11. Williams quoted in Reed, "Transcript of Conversation with John Williams."

12. For an analysis of the use of music in the film, see Audissino, *Film/Music Analysis*, 191–205.

13. Williams quoted in Elley, "The Film Composer: 3. John Williams, Part 1," 23.

14. Williams quoted in Mike Matessino, "There Will Be No Bombs Dropped Here!!!," CD booklet, *1941*, La-La Land Records LLLCD 1179, 2011, 7–8.

15. "Sing, Sing, Sing," music and lyrics by Louis Prima, was popularized and most famously covered by Benny Goodman.

16. Williams seems to have a particular fondness for the score for *The Quiet Man*: besides *1941*, the score is also referenced in *E.T. the Extraterrestrial* and *Far and Away*. Williams has acknowledged this: "The music for the film was composed by Victor Young, . . . who underscored the setting and the action by adapting music from Irish folk tunes. For much of the movie, he used a famous piece called The Rakes of Mallow. . . . He uses it in a lot of different ways throughout the film. I can remember several wonderful fight scenes between Wayne and Victor McLaglen, and the music is used to bring out the comedic element in these moments. In other scenes between O'Hara and Wayne, he uses the same folk tune in a very passionate and romantic way, such as the first time Wayne sees O'Hara across a field and wonders if what he sees is real. It's very inspiring music . . . and, along with the music that Bernard Herrmann composed for Hitchcock's *Vertigo*, it's one of the first scores that turned me on to the idea of writing music for the movies." Williams quoted in Derren Gilhooley, "Filmmakers on Film: John Williams," *The Telegraph*, 1 June 2002.

17. The girl is again played by Susan Backlinie, who portrayed Chrissie the blonde night swimmer, the first victim of the shark in *Jaws*.

18. Williams quoted in Marian Zailian, "John Williams: Master of Movie Scores," *San Francisco Examiner-Chronicle*, 18 July 1982.

19. Williams has provided the music to a number of flying scenes, which are a recurring and significant element in Spielberg's cinema. See Emilio Audissino, "Bicycles,

Airplanes and Peter Pans: Flying Scenes in Steven Spielberg's Films," *CINEJ Cinema Journal* 3, no. 2 (2014): 103–19.

20. For an analysis of how the score creates a "love network" in *E.T. the Extraterrestrial*, see Audissino, *Film/Music Analysis*, 205–14. The general sound design of *E.T.* is analyzed in Chloé Huvet, "John Williams and Sound Design: Shaping the Audiovisual World of *E.T.: The Extra-Terrestrial*," in Audissino, *John Williams: Music for Films, Television, and the Concert Stage*, ed. Emilio Audissino (Turnhout: Brepols, 2018), 293–308.

21. Williams in Laurent Bouzereau, *The Making of "E.T. the Extra-Terrestrial,"* documentary, MCA Home Video, 1996.

22. Williams in Bouzereau, *The Making of "E.T. the Extra-Terrestrial."*

23. Williams quoted in Laurent Bouzereau, "John Williams Interview," CD booklet of *E.T. the Extraterrestrial*, expanded edition, MCA MCAD-11494, 1996, 4.

24. Williams quoted in Jon Burlingame, "*E.T.* Turns 30: Williams' Score Soars on New Blu-Ray Release," Film Music Society, 10 October 2012, http://www.filmmusic society.org/news_events/features/2012/101012.html.

25. The choral piece was recorded at Boston's Symphony Hall: "Pops conductor John Williams received a call earlier this week from Steven Spielberg, who's directing the film 'Indiana Jones and the Temple of Doom' . . . in England and needed at once five minutes of music. . . . Williams called the work 'Sanskrit Sacrifice.' Yesterday afternoon 10 members of the Pops percussion and tympani section and 30 members of the Tanglewood Chorus gathered on stage for the recording, and a courier waited in the wings to rush the tape to Logan [airport] and a flight to London. Spielberg said it was essential that he receive this bit of music posthaste because he needed it to film the sequence. The movie director had hired a London Sanskrit scholar to write the chant and the Sanskrit lyrics were flown to Boston. . . . Williams got in touch with Joe Galeoto, a teacher at Berklee College of Music, who has an extensive collection of African musical instruments. The Pops members drummed away on such instruments as an African log drum, a *prempensua*, *bolia* and *dondos*, all drums; and a *jyle*, a sort of xylophone." George McKinnon, "Williams Answers Spielberg's Call for Music," *Boston Globe*, 13 May 1983.

26. On Jones providing the score for *The Color Purple*, see Merluzeau, "An Interview with John Williams," 9.

27. Freer, *Complete Spielberg*, 199.

28. Williams quoted in Richard Dyer, "John Williams: Making Movie-Music History: *Schindler* Composer Is Up for Fifth Oscar," *Boston Globe*, 20 March 1994.

29. Williams in "Anne-Sophie Mutter in Conversation with John Williams," video interview (Bernhard Fleischer, 2019), available in the box set *Across the Stars: Deluxe Edition*, Deutsche Grammophon 483 7459, 2019.

30. Williams quoted in Sullivan, "Conversations with John Williams."

31. Williams quoted in Dyer, "John Williams: Making Movie-Music History."

32. John Williams, introductory note to *Dry Your Tears, Afrika*, full orchestral score, John Williams Signature Edition series, Hal Leonard 044900085, no date.

33. Steven Spielberg, liner notes, *Saving Private Ryan*, CD album, DreamWorks Records DRD 50046, 1998.

34. According to Williams, in *The Music of "A.I.,"* documentary by Laurent Bou-zereau, DreamWorks Home Entertainment, 2002.

35. For a musical analysis, see Stefan Swanson, "Happily Never After: Williams's Musical Exploration of the 'Controversial' Ending to *A.I.: Artificial Intelligence*," in *John Williams: Music for Films, Television, and the Concert Stage*, ed. Emilio Audissino (Turn-hout: Brepols, 2018), 375–96.

36. Williams quoted in Dyer, "An Enduring Love for Music, Movies."

37. Williams quoted in Colburn, "John Williams Returns to Bands," 15.

38. Williams in *In Flight Service: The Music of "The Terminal,"* documentary by Laurent Bouzereau, DreamWorks Home Entertainment, 2004, included on the DVD *The Terminal*, DreamWorks Home Entertainment, 2004.

39. See "Spiegel Interview with Tom Cruise and Steven Spielberg," *Der Spiegel*, 27 April 2005, www.spiegel.de/international/spiegel/0,1518,353577,00.html; and J. Tirella, "Steven Spielberg's 9/11 Obsession," *Today*, 28 December 2005, http://www.today .com/id/10549050/ns/today-today_entertainment/t/steven-spielbergs-obsession/.

40. Williams in *Scoring "War of the Worlds,"* documentary by Laurent Bouzereau, DreamWorks Home Entertainment, 2005.

41. For a musical analysis of *War of the Worlds*, see Irena Paulus, "John Williams and the Musical Avant-garde: The Score for *War of the Worlds*," in *John Williams: Music for Films, Television, and the Concert Stage*, ed. Emilio Audissino (Turnhout: Brepols, 2018), 327–42.

42. Tellingly, the concert version of the first theme mentioned here is titled "Swashbuckler: The Adventures of Mutt" (first movement of the suite *The Adventures of Indiana Jones*, full orchestral score, John Williams Signature Edition series, Hal Leonard, 04490826).

43. Jon Burlingame, "Spielberg & Williams: Inseparable Tandem," *Variety*, 14 November 2012.

44. "Battle Cry of Freedom" was composed in 1862 by George Frederick Root.

45. Williams in "The BFG Interview," video, 2016, https://www.traileraddict.com/ the-bfg/interview-john-williams.

46. Spielberg quoted in Christina Radish, "Steven Spielberg on 'The BFG,' Self-Censoring on Historical Dramas, 'Ready Player One,' and More," *Collider*, 28 June 2016, https://collider.com/steven-spielberg-the-bfg-ready-player-one-interview/.

47. Spielberg quoted in Radish, "Steven Spielberg."

48. Brandon Katz, "Steven Spielberg on How He Made 'The Post' in Just Seven Months," *The Observer*, 4 January 2018.

49. Spielberg quoted in Jonathan Freeland, "Steven Spielberg: 'The Urgency to Make The Post Was Because of Trump's Administration,'" *The Guardian*, 19 January 2018.

50. Burlingame, "John Williams Is on Target."

51. Williams quoted in Burlingame, "John Williams Is on Target."

52. Williams quoted in Bennett, "John Williams, Composer."

53. Williams quoted in Elley, "The Film Composer: 3. John Williams, Part 1," 24.

54. Donner quoted in Gregg Kilday, "Steven Spielberg and Fellow Directors Reveal the Stories behind John Williams' Iconic Scores," *Hollywood Reporter*, 9 June 2016.

55. Williams quoted in Richard Dyer, "You'll Be Hearing from Him," *Boston Globe*, 31 August 1989.

56. Williams quoted in Merluzeau, "An Interview with John Williams," 5.

57. Columbus quoted in Kilday, "Steven Spielberg and Fellow Directors."

58. Williams quoted in Merluzeau, "An Interview with John Williams," 6.

59. Williams quoted in Bennett, "John Williams, Composer." For a musical analysis, see Laura Anderson, "Sounding an Irish Childhood: John Williams's Score for *Angela's Ashes*," in *John Williams: Music for Films, Television, and the Concert Stage*, ed. Emilio Audissino (Turnhout: Brepols, 2018), 277–92.

60. Williams quoted in Seiler, "Williams Adds Musical Magic to *Harry Potter*."

61. On Williams's *Harry Potter* triptych, see Jamie Lynn Webster, "Musical Dramaturgy and Stylistic Changes in John Williams's *Harry Potter* Trilogy," in *John Williams: Music for Films, Television, and the Concert Stage*, ed. Emilio Audissino (Turnhout: Brepols, 2018), 253–75.

62. Williams quoted in Baby A. Gil, "The Role of Music according to John Williams," *Philippine Star*, 14 February 2014, https://www.philstar.com/entertainment/2014/02/14/1290144/role-music-according-john-williams.

63. The piano-solo suite from *The Book Thief* can be listened to on the CD *John Williams: Themes and Transcriptions for Piano*, Simone Pedroni (pianist), Varèse Sarabande 302 067 478 8, 2017.

Bibliography

Abbott, Stacey. *Celluloid Vampires: Life after Death in the Modern World*. Austin: University of Texas Press, 2007.

———. "*Dracula* on Film and TV from 1960 to the Present." In *The Cambridge Companion to Dracula*, edited by Roger Luckhurst, 192–206. New York: Cambridge University Press, 2018.

Adorno, Theodor W., and Hanns Eisler. *Composing for the Films*. 1947. Reprint, London: Continuum, 2007.

Anderson, Laura. "Sounding an Irish Childhood: John Williams's Score for *Angela's Ashes*." In *John Williams: Music for Films, Television, and the Concert Stage*, edited by Emilio Audissino, 277–92. Turnhout: Brepols, 2018.

Aschieri, Roberto. *Over the Moon: La música de John Williams para el cine*. Santiago de Chile: Universidad Diego Portales, 1999.

Audissino, Emilio. "'Behold the Newest Technological Sensation! With Music!' The Use of Music in the Silent Cinema." In *Music and the Second Industrial Revolution*, edited by Massimiliano Sala, 429–47. Turnhout: Brepols, 2019.

———. "Bicycles, Airplanes and Peter Pans: Flying Scenes in Steven Spielberg's Films." *CINEJ Cinema Journal* 3, no. 2 (2014): 103–19.

———. *Film/Music Analysis: A Film Studies Approach*. Basingstoke: Palgrave Macmillan, 2017.

———. "Film Music and Multimedia: An Immersive Experience and a Throwback to the Past." In *Jahrbuch Immersiver Medien 2014: Sounds, Music & Soundscapes*, edited by Patrick Rupert-Kruse, 46–56. Marburg: Schüren Verlag, 2014.

———. "The Function of Mickey-Mousing: A Re-assessment." In *Sound & Image: Audiovisual Aesthetics and Practices*, edited by Andrew Knight-Hill, 145–60. New York: Routledge, 2020.

———. "John Williams and Contemporary Film Music." In *Contemporary Film Music: Investigating Cinema Narratives and Composition*, edited by Lindsay Coleman and Joakim Tillman, 221–36. Basingstoke: Palgrave Macmillan, 2017.

———, ed. *John Williams: Music for Films, Television, and the Concert Stage*. Turnhout: Brepols, 2018.

————. "A Matter of Form, Style, and Monsters: A Comparative Analysis of *Reazione a catena* and *Friday the 13th*." *L'avventura: International Journal of Italian Cinema and Media Landscapes* 6, no. 1 (January–June 2020): 3–22.

————. "The Multiform Identity of Jazz in Hollywood: An Assessment through the John Williams Case Study." In *Cinema Changes: Incorporations of Jazz in the Film Soundtrack*, edited by Emile Wennekes and Emilio Audissino, 85–98. Turnhout: Brepols, 2019.

————. "Overruling a Romantic Prejudice: Forms and Formats of Film Music in Concert Programs." In *Film in Concert, Film Scores and Their Relation to Classical Concert Music*, edited by Sebastian Stoppe, 25–43. Glücksstadt: VWH Verlag, 2014.

Audissino, Emilio, and Frank Lehman. "John Williams Seen from the Podium: An Interview with Maestro Keith Lockhart." In *John Williams: Music for Films, Television, and the Concert Stage*, edited by Emilio Audissino, 397–408. Turnhout: Brepols, 2018.

Altman, Rick. *Silent Film Sound*. New York: Columbia University Press, 2004.

Bachman, Ron. "Behind the Scene at Evening at Pops." *Nine*, June 1989, 34–35.

"Back Again to a Galaxy." *International Musician*, 28 May 2015, 16–17.

Bak, John S., ed. Post/modern Dracula: From Victorian Themes to Postmodern Praxis. Newcastle: Cambridge Scholars, 2007.

Balio, Tino, ed. *The American Film Industry*. Rev. ed. Madison: University of Wisconsin Press, 1985.

Barnett, Kyle S. "The Selznick Studio, 'Spellbound,' and the Marketing of Film Music." *Music, Sound, and the Moving Image* 4, no. 1 (Spring 2010): 77–98.

Barraclough, Leo. "Christopher Nolan's Use of Sound on 'Tenet' Infuriates Some, Inspires Others." *Variety*, 2 September 2020.

Baudrillard, Jean. *Simulacres et Simulation*. Paris: Éditions Galilée, 1981.

Bauer, Heike. "*Dracula* and Sexology." In *The Cambridge Companion to Dracula*, edited by Roger Luckhurst, 76–84. New York: Cambridge University Press, 2018.

Bazelon, Irwin. *Knowing the Score: Notes on Film Music*. New York: Arco, 1975.

Beck, Jay. *Designing Sound: Audiovisual Aesthetics in 1970s American Cinema*. New Brunswick, NJ: Rutgers University Press, 2016.

Belton, John. "Il colore: dall'eccezione alla regola." In *Storia del cinema mondiale*, vol. 5, *Teorie, strumenti, memorie*, edited by Gian Piero Brunetta, 801–28. Turin: Einaudi, 2001.

Bennett, Ray. "John Williams, Composer." *Hollywood Reporter*, 8 March 2000.

Benshoff, Harry M., ed. *A Companion to the Horror Film*. Malden, MA: Wiley-Blackwell, 2014.

Beresford, Matthew. *From Demons to Dracula: The Creation of the Modern Vampire Myth*. London: Reaktion Books, 2008.

Bernheimer, Martin. "Pop! John Williams on Philharmonic Podium." *Los Angeles Times*, 12 November 1983.

Biamonte, S. G., ed. *Musica e film*. Rome: Edizioni dell'Ateneo, 1959.

Biancorosso, Giorgio. "The Shark in the Music." *Music Analysis* 29 (2010): 306–33.

Blanchard, Gerard. *Images de la musique de cinéma*. Paris: Edilio, 1984.

Bond, Jeff. CD booklet of *Planet of the Apes*. Varése Sarabande VSD-5848, 1997.

———. "The Fall of Troy." *Film Score Monthly*, April/May 2004, 18–22.

———. "Ilium Revealed." *Film Score Monthly*, February 2004, 16–20.

———. "Stamps of Approval." *Film Score Monthly*, November 1999, 24–27.

Booth, William. "Shark Attack?! John Williams Liked the Sound of That." *Washington Post*, 5 December 2004.

Bordwell, David. "A Case for Cognitivism." *Iris* 9 (Spring 1989): 11–40.

———. "The Classical Hollywood Style, 1917–60." In *The Classical Hollywood Cinema: Film Style and Mode of Production to 1960*, edited by David Bordwell, Janet Staiger, and Kristin Thompson, 3–84. New York: Columbia University Press, 1985.

———. *Making Meaning: Inference and Rhetoric in the Interpretation of Cinema*. Cambridge, MA: Harvard University Press, 1989.

———. *Narration in the Fiction Film*. Madison: University of Wisconsin Press, 1985.

———. *On the History of Film Style*. Cambridge, MA: Harvard University Press, 1997.

———. *The Way Hollywood Tells It: Story and Style in Modern Movies*. Berkeley: University of California Press, 2006.

Bordwell, David, Janet Staiger, and Kristin Thompson. *The Classical Hollywood Cinema: Film Style and Mode of Production to 1960*. New York: Columbia University Press, 1985.

Borum, Jeremy. *Guerrilla Film Scoring: Practical Advice from Hollywood Composers*. Lanham, MD: Rowman & Littlefield, 2015.

Boston Pops: The Story of America's Orchestra. Boston: Boston Symphony Orchestra, 2000.

Bouzereau, Laurent. "Jaws." CD booklet of *Jaws: The Collector's Edition Soundtrack*. Decca 467 045-2, 2000.

———. "John Williams Interview." CD booklet of *E.T. the Extraterrestrial*, expanded edition. MCA MCAD-11494, 1996.

Brend, Mark. *The Sound of Tomorrow: How Electronic Music Was Smuggled into the Mainstream*. New York: Bloomsbury, 2012.

Bribitzer-Stull, Matthew. *Understanding the Leitmotif: From Wagner to Hollywood Film Music*. New York: Cambridge University Press, 2015.

Briganti, Andrea, Giulia Farina, Andrea Lanza, eds. *Enciclopedia della musica*. Milan: Garzanti, 1996.

Britton, Andrew. "Blissing Out: The Politics of Reaganite Entertainment." In *Britton on Film: The Complete Film Criticism of Andrew Britton*, edited by Barry Keith Grant, 97–154. Detroit, MI: Wayne State University Press, 2009.

Brodman, Barbara and James E. Doan. *The Universal Vampire: Origins and Evolution of a Legend*. Madison, NJ: Fairleigh Dickinson University Press, 2013.

Brown, Julie. "*Carnival of Souls* and the Organs of Horror." In *Music in the Horror Film: Listening to Fear*, edited by Neil Lerner, 1–20. New York: Routledge, 2010.

Brown, Royal S. *Overtones and Undertones: Reading Film Music*. Berkeley: University of California Press, 1994.

Buckland, Warren. "A Close Encounter with *Raiders of the Lost Ark*: Notes on Narrative Aspects of the New Hollywood Blockbuster." In *Contemporary Hollywood Cinema*, edited by Steve Neale and Murray Smith, 166–77. London: Routledge, 1998.

Buhler, James. "Analytical and Interpretive Approaches to Film Music (II): Analyzing Interactions of Music and Film." In *Film Music: Critical Approaches*, edited by K. J. Donnelly, 39–61. New York: Continuum, 2001.

———. *"Star Wars*, Music, and Myth." In *Music and Cinema*, edited by James Buhler, Caryl Flinn, and David Neumeyer, 33–57. Hanover, NH: Wesleyan University Press, 2000.

Buhler, James, and David Neumeyer. *Hearing the Movies: Music and Sound in Film History.* 2nd ed. New York: Oxford University Press, 2015.

Burke, Edmund. *A Philosophical Enquiry into the Origin of Our Ideas of the Sublime and Beautiful.* 1757. Reprint, New York: P. F. Collier & Son, 1914.

Burlingame, Jon. "A Career of Epic Proportion." *Los Angeles Times*, 3 February 2002.

———. "E.T. Turns 30: Williams' Score Soars on New Blu-Ray Release." *FMS Feature* . . . , 10 October 2012. http://www.filmmusicsociety.org/news_events/features/2012/101012.html.

———. "Film Score Icons Williams, Morricone and Horner Loom Large in Oscar Race." *Variety*, 9 December 2015.

———. "John Williams Is on Target to Set Yet Another Oscar Record." *Variety*, 10 January 2018.

———. "John Williams Recalls *Jaws*." Film Music Society, 14 August 2012. http://www.filmmusicsociety.org/news_events/features/2012/081412.html.

———. "Leonard Rosenman Turns 80: Pioneering Composer to be Honored in Rome." *FMS Feature* . . . , 7 September 2004. http://www.filmmusicsociety.org/news_events/features/2004/090704.html.

———. "Live Movie Concerts a Cash Cow for Orchestras." *Variety*, 29 April 2015.

———. "Master Class: Williams Earns Himself a Spot in Pantheon of Composers." *Variety*, 29 November 2005.

———. "Solo Composer John Powell Reveals His Process for Tackling a *Star Wars* Movie." *Variety*, 24 May 2018.

———. "Spielberg and Lucas on Williams: Directors Reminisce about Collaborating with Hollywood's Greatest Composer." *Film Music Society*, 8 February 2012. www.filmmusicsociety.org/news_events/features/2012/020812.html.

———. "Spielberg & Williams: Inseparable Tandem." *Variety*, 14 November 2012.

———. "With *Rise of Skywalker*, Composer John Williams Puts His Coda on *Star Wars*." *Variety*, 18 December 2019.

Burt, George. *The Art of Film Music.* Boston: Northeastern University Press, 1994.

Burton-Hill, Clemency. "Gustavo Dudamel: 'I Thought John Williams Was Joking when He Asked Me to Conduct His Star Wars Music.'" *Telegraph*, 11 January 2016.

———. "John Williams, the Music Master." *Financial Times*, 17 August 2012.

Butler, Erik. *Metamorphoses of the Vampire in Literature and Film: Cultural Transformations in Europe, 1732–1933.* Rochester, NY: Camden House, 2010.

Byrd, Craig L. "The *Star Wars* Interview: John Williams." *Film Score Monthly*, January/February 1997, 18–21.

Calabrese, Omar. *Neo-Baroque: A Sign of the Times.* Princeton, NJ: Princeton University Press, 1992.

Calabretto, Roberto. *Lo schermo sonoro: La musica per film.* Venice: Marsilio, 2010.

Campbell, Joseph. *The Hero with a Thousand Faces.* 2nd. ed. Princeton, NJ: Princeton University Press, 1968.

Caps, John. *Henry Mancini: Reinventing Film Music.* Urbana: University of Illinois Press, 2012.

Carr, Maureen A. *After the Rite: Stravinsky's Path to Neoclassicism (1914–1925).* New York: Oxford University Press, 2014.

Carroll, Brendan G. *The Last Prodigy: A Biography of Erich Wolfgang Korngold.* Portland, OR: Amadeus, 1997.

Carroll, Noël. *The Philosophy of Horror: Or, Paradoxes of the Heart.* New York: Routledge, 1990.

Casey, Kieron. "An Interview with Todd Haberman." *The Totality* (blog), September 2016, http://www.wondrouskennel.com/2016/09/todd-haberman-interview-hans-zimmer-remote-control.html.

Catalano, Peter. "John Williams to Leave Boston Pops." *Los Angeles Times*, 21 December 1991.

Chion, Michel. *Audio-Vision: Sound on Screen.* Translated and edited by Claudia Gorbman. New York: Columbia University Press, 1994. Originally published as *L'audio-vision: Son et image au cinéma* (Paris: Nathan, 1990).

Cohen, Annabel J. "Film Music: Perspectives from Cognitive Psychology." In *Music and Cinema*, edited by James Buhler, Caryl Flinn, and David Neumeyer, 360–77. Hanover, NH: Wesleyan University Press, 2000.

Colburn, Michael J. "John Williams Returns to Bands where He Began 50 Years Ago." *Instrumentalist*, June 2004, 11–16.

"Commencement Citation." *Boston University Today*, 29 May 1985.

Comuzio, Ermanno. *Colonna sonora: Dialoghi, musiche, rumori dietro lo schermo.* Milan: Il Formichiere, 1980.

———. *Musicisti per lo schermo: Dizionario ragionato dei compositori cinematografici.* 2 vols. Rome: Ente dello Spettacolo, 2004.

Cones, John. *Patterns of Bias in Hollywood Movies.* New York: Algora, 2012.

Connor, J. D. *The Studios after the Studios: Neoclassical Hollywood (1970–2010).* Stanford: Stanford University Press, 2015.

Cooke, Mervyn. *A History of Film Music.* Cambridge: Cambridge University Press, 2008.

———, ed. *The Hollywood Film Music Reader.* New York: Oxford University Press, 2010.

———. "A New Symphonism for a New Hollywood: The Musical Language of John Williams's Film Scores." In *John Williams: Music for Films, Television, and the Concert Stage*, edited by Emilio Audissino, 3–26. Turnhout: Brepols, 2018.

Cooper, Christopher. "*Star Wars* in Concert." *Star Wars Insider*, November 2018, 26–33.

Cooper, David. "'Pictures That Talk and Sing': Sound History and Technology." In *The Cambridge Companion to Film Music*, edited by Mervyn Cooke and Fiona Ford, 29–50. New York: Cambridge University Press, 2016.

Coulthard, Lisa. "Dirty Sound: Haptic Noise in New Extremism." In *The Oxford Handbook of Sound and Image in Digital Media*, edited by Carol Vernallis, Amy Herzog, and John Richardson, 115–26. New York: Oxford University Press, 2013.

Cowie, Elizabeth. "Classical Hollywood Cinema and Classical Narrative." In *Contemporary Hollywood Cinema*, edited by Steve Neale and Murray Smith, 178–90. London: Routledge, 1998.

Dahlhaus, Carl. *The Idea of Absolute Music.* Translated by Roger Lustig. Chicago: University of Chicago Press, 1991. Originally published as *Die Idee der absoluten Musik* (Kassel: Bärenreiter-Verlag, 1978).

Delacoma, Wynn. "Williams: From Celluloid to CSO." *Chicago Sun-Times,* 28 November 2003.

Danuser, Hermann. "Rewriting the Past: Classicisms of the Inter-war Period." In *The Cambridge History of Twentieth-Century Music,* edited by Nicholas Cook and Anthony Pople, 260–85. Cambridge: Cambridge University Press, 2004.

Darby, William, and Jack Du Bois. *American Film Music: Major Composers, Techniques, Trends, 1915–1990.* Jefferson, NC: McFarland, 1990.

Davis, Richard. *Complete Guide to Film Scoring.* Boston: Berklee, 1999.

Day, Peter. *Vampires: Myth and Metaphors of Enduring Evil.* New York: Rodopi, 2006.

Deaville, James. "The Beauty of Horror: Kilar, Coppola, and Dracula." In *Music in the Horror Film: Listening to Fear,* edited by Neil Lerner, 187–205. New York: Routledge, 2010.

Deutsch, Didier C. Liner notes for *John Williams: Film Works,* CD album. MCA 32877, 1995.

"Dialogue: John Williams." *Hollywood Reporter,* 10 January 2006.

Dobroski, Bernie, and Claire Greene. "Pass the Popcorn: An Interview with John Williams." *Instrumentalist,* July 1984, 6–9.

Donnelly, K. J. "The Classical Film Score Forever? 'Batman,' 'Batman Returns,' and Post-Classical Film Music." In *Contemporary Hollywood Cinema,* edited by Steve Neale and Murray Smith, 143–55. London: Routledge, 1998.

———, ed. *Film Music: Critical Approaches.* New York: Continuum, 2001.

———. *Occult Aesthetics: Synchronization in Sound Film.* New York: Oxford University Press, 2014.

———. *The Spectre of Sound: Music in Film and Television.* London: BFI, 2005.

Duchen, Jessica. *Erich Wolfgang Korngold.* London: Phaidon, 1996.

Dyer, Richard. *Pastiche.* New York: Routledge, 2006.

———. "The Role of Stereotypes." In *Media Studies: A Reader,* edited by Sue Thornham, Caroline Bassett, and Paul Marris, 206–12. Edinburgh: Edinburgh University Press, 2009.

Dyer, Richard (*Boston Globe*). "Composers Learn Film Music from the Master." *Boston Globe,* 20 August 1998.

———. "An Enduring Love for Music, Movies." *Boston Globe,* 23 June 2002.

———. "John Williams Bows In." *Boston Globe,* 11 January 1980.

———. "John Williams: Bringing Hollywood Magic to the Boston Pops." *Ovation,* June 1983, 12–15.

———. "John Williams Casts Spell for 'Potter' Score." *Boston Globe,* 11 November 2001.

———. "John Williams Is New Pops Maestro: A Musician's Musician." *Boston Globe,* 11 January 1980.

———. "John Williams: Making Movie-Music History; *Schindler* Composer Is Up for Fifth Oscar." *Boston Globe,* 20 March 1994.

———. "John Williams: New Horizons, Familiar Galaxies." *Boston Globe,* 4 June 1997.

———. "John Williams Scores Again: 2005 Produces Two More Oscar Nominations." *Boston Globe*, 5 February 2006.

———. "Making *Star Wars* Sing Again." *Boston Globe*, 28 March 1999. Reprinted in *Film Score Monthly*, June 1999, 18–19.

———. "Pops Star: The Legacy of John Williams." *Boston Globe*, 12 December 1993.

———. "Pops' Williams to Retire in '93." *Boston Globe*, 20 December 1991.

———. "Q&A with John Williams: Pops Conductor Talks about His New Beat." *Boston Globe*, 27 April 1980.

———. "Sounds of Spielberg." *Boston Globe*, 24 February 1998.

———. "Where Is John Williams Coming From?" *Boston Globe*, 29 June 1980.

———. "Williams Is Candidate for Fiedler's Job." *Boston Globe*, 6 January 1980.

———. "Williams Poised for Pops." *Boston Globe*, 26 April 1981.

———. "Williams to Stay on as Pops Adviser." *Boston Globe*, 4 February 1994.

———. "You'll Be Hearing from Him." *Boston Globe*, 31 August 1989.

Ebert, Roger. "Dracula." *Chicago Sun-Times*, 20 July 1979. https://www.rogerebert.com/reviews/dracula.

Edgerton, Gary R. *The Columbia History of American Television*. New York: Columbia University Press, 2007.

Elley, Derek. "The Film Composer: 3. John Williams, Part 1." *Films and Filming* 24, no. 10 (July 1978): 20–24.

———. "The Film Composer: 3. John Williams, Part 2." *Films and Filming* 24, no. 11 (August 1978): 30–33.

Elsaesser, Thomas. "American Auteur Cinema: The Last—or First—Picture Show?" In *The Last Great American Picture Show: New Hollywood Cinema in the 1970s*, edited by Thomas Elsaesser, Alexander Horwath, and Noel King, 37–71. Amsterdam: Amsterdam University Press, 2004.

Evans, Mark. *Soundtrack: The Music of the Movies*. New York: Da Capo, 1979.

Farber, Stephen. "Mr. Pops." *Dial—WGBH Boston*, July 1983, 9–12.

Farnell, Andy. *Designing Sound*. Cambridge, MA: MIT Press, 2010.

Flinn, Caryl. *Strains of Utopia: Gender, Nostalgia, and Hollywood Film Music*. Princeton, NJ: Princeton University Press, 1992.

Ford, Beverly, and John Impemba. "John Williams Quits Boston Pops." *Boston Herald*, 14 June 1984.

Fourgiotis, Thanos. "John Williams Interview." *Cinema Magazine*, April 1992. https://www.douban.com/group/topic/1029421/.

Freeland, Jonathan. "Steven Spielberg: 'The Urgency to Make The Post Was Because of Trump's Administration.'" *The Guardian*, 19 January 2018.

Freer, Ian. *The Complete Spielberg*. London: Virgin, 2001.

Freud, Sigmund. *The Uncanny*. Translated by David McLintock. 1919. Reprint, London: Penguin Books, 2003.

Fülöp, Rebecca. "Heroes, Dames, and Damsels in Distress: Constructing Gender Types in Classical Hollywood Film Music." PhD diss., University of Michigan, 2012.

Galloway, Paul. "Airman Composes Way to Movie Career." *Beacon*, 27 August 1954.

Gamer, Michael. "Gothic Fictions and Romantic Writing in Britain." In *The Cambridge Companion to Gothic Fiction*, edited by Jerrold E. Hogle, 85–104. New York: Cambridge University Press, 2002.

Gelder, Ken. *Reading the Vampire.* New York: Routledge, 1994.

Genette, Gérard. *Figures III.* Paris: Seuil, 1972.

Gil, Baby A. "The Role of Music according to John Williams." *Philippine Star,* 14 February 2014. https://www.philstar.com/entertainment/2014/02/14/1290144/role -music-according-john-williams.

Gilhooley, Derren. "Filmmakers on Film: John Williams." *The Telegraph,* 1 June 2002.

Glick, Peter and Susan T. Fiske. "Sexism and Other 'Isms': Independence, Status, and the Ambivalent Content of Stereotypes." In *Sexism and Stereotypes in Modern Society: The Gender Science of Janet Taylor Spence,* edited by W. B. Swann Jr., J. H. Langlois, and L. A. Gilbert, 193–221. Washington, DC: American Psychological Association, 1999.

Gomery, Douglas. *Shared Pleasures: A History of Movie Presentation in the United States.* Madison: University of Wisconsin Press, 1992.

Goldmark, Daniel. *Tunes for 'Toons: Music and the Hollywood Cartoon.* Berkeley: University of California Press, 2005.

Gonzalez, Fernando. "Orchestrating *Indiana Jones.*" *Boston Globe,* 18 June 1989.

Goodman, Peter. "A Great Little Visiting Band." *New York Newsday,* 11 June 1986.

Goodson, Michael. "Yes, There's Life after Fiedler." *Boston Sunday Herald,* 27 January 1980.

Gorbman, Claudia. *Unheard Melodies: Narrative Film Music.* London: BFI, 1987.

Gorfinkle, Constance. "Why John Williams Changed His Mind." *Patriot Ledger,* 8 August 1984.

———. "Williams Miffed by Hiss from Pops Orchestra?" *Patriot Ledger,* 14 June 1984.

Gottlieb, Carl. *The Jaws Log.* New York: Newmarket, 2005.

Grant, Barry Keith, ed. *American Cinema of the 1960s: Themes and Variations.* New Brunswick, NJ: Rutgers University Press, 2008.

Gray, Jonathan. *Show Sold Separately: Promos, Spoilers, and Other Media Paratexts.* New York: New York University Press, 2010.

Greene, Liz, and Danijela Kulezic-Wilson, eds. *The Palgrave Handbook of Sound Design and Music in Screen Media: Integrated Soundtracks.* London: Palgrave Macmillan, 2016.

Greiving, Tim. "John Williams' Early Life: How a NoHo Kid and UCLA Bruin Became the Movie Music Man." *Los Angeles Times,* 18 July 2018.

———. "John Williams on *The Force Awakens* and the Legacy of *Star Wars.*" *Projector and Orchestra,* 5 January 2016. Accessed 1 May 2020. http://projectorandorchestra .com/john-williams-on-the-force-awakens-and-the-legacy-of-star-wars/.

———. "Mark Hamill on John Williams and His 'Gobsmacking' Importance to *Star Wars.*" *Projector and Orchestra,* 1 December 2017. Accessed 1 May 2020. http://projec torandorchestra.com/mark-hamill-on-john-williams-importance-to-star-wars/.

Gunning, Tom. "The Cinema of Attraction: Early Film, Its Spectator, and the Avant-garde." *Wide Angle* 8, no. 3 (1986): 63–70.

Halberstam, Judith. *Skin Shows: Gothic Horror and the Technology of Monsters.* Durham, NC: Duke University Press, 1995.

Hannan, Michael. "Sound and Music in Hammer's Vampire Films." In *Terror Tracks: Music, Sound and Horror Cinema,* edited by Philip Hayward, 1–13. London: Equinox, 2009.

Hark, Ina Rae, ed. *American Cinema of the 1930s: Themes and Variations.* New Brunswick, NJ: Rutgers University Press, 2007.

Hayward, Philip. Introduction." In *Terror Tracks: Music, Sound and Horror Cinema,* edited by Philip Hayward, 1–13. London: Equinox, 2009.

Hickman, Roger. *Miklós Rózsa's "Ben-Hur": A Film Score Guide.* Lanham, MD: Scarecrow, 2011.

Hill, John. "Film and Postmodernism." In *The Oxford Guide to Film Studies,* edited by John Hill and Pamela Church Gibson, 96–105. Oxford: Oxford University Press, 1998.

Hoesterey, Ingeborg. *Pastiche: Cultural Memory in Art, Film, Literature.* Bloomington: Indiana University Press, 2001.

Hogle, Jerrold E., ed. *The Cambridge Companion to Gothic Fiction.* New York: Cambridge University Press, 2002.

Holcomb, Brian. "John Badham's 'Dracula,' the Rock Star." PopMatters.com, 15 January 2020. https://www.popmatters.com/john-badham-dracula-2644157427.html.

Hsu, Michael. "Movie Dialogue Too Quiet? Tips for Better Clarity." *Wall Street Journal,* 24 July 2015.

Huckvale, David. *James Bernard, Composer to Count Dracula: A Critical Biography.* Jefferson, NC: McFarland, 2006.

Hughes, William. *Bram Stoker's Dracula.* New York: Continuum, 2009.

Hurley, Kelly. *The Gothic Body: Sexuality, Materialism, and Degeneration at the Fin de Siècle.* New York: Cambridge University Press, 1996.

Hutchings, Peter. *The Horror Film.* London: Pearson, 2004.

Huvenne, Martine. "Intertwining Music and Sound in Film." In *The Palgrave Handbook of Sound Design and Music in Screen Media: Integrated Soundtracks,* edited by Liz Greene and Danijela Kulezic-Wilson, 123–38. London: Palgrave Macmillan, 2016.

Huvet, Chloé. *"D'Un nouvel espoir* (1977) à *La Revanche des Sith* (2005): Écriture musicale et traitement de la partition au sein du complexe audio-visuel dans la saga *Star Wars."* PhD diss., Université Rennes 2/Université de Montréal, 2018.

———. "John Williams and Sound Design: Shaping the Audiovisual World of *E.T.: The Extra-Terrestrial.*" In *John Williams: Music for Films, Television, and the Concert Stage,* edited by Emilio Audissino, 293–308. Turnhout: Brepols, 2018.

"Indiana Jones and the Ultimate Tribute." *Empire,* October 2006, 69–101.

Kalinak, Kathryn. *Settling the Score: Music and the Classical Hollywood Film.* Madison: University of Wisconsin Press, 1992.

Kassabian, Anahid. *Hearing Film: Tracking Identifications in Contemporary Hollywood Film Music.* New York: Routledge, 2001.

Ireland, David. "'Today I'm Hearing with New Ears': John Williams's Use of Audiovisual Incongruence to Convey Character Perspective in *Munich* and Spielberg's Historical Films." In *John Williams: Music for Films, Television, and the Concert Stage,* edited by Emilio Audissino, 309–26. Turnhout: Brepols, 2018.

Irrgeher, Christoph. "John Williams: Sternstunden der Filmmusik." *Wiener Zeitung,* 20 January 2020. https://www.wienerzeitung.at/nachrichten/kultur/klassik/2046653-John-Williams-Sternstunden-der-Filmmusik.html.

Kalish, Eddie. "Mancini Debunks Album Values." 1961. Reprint in *Celluloid Sympho-nies: Texts and Contexts in Film Music History*, edited by Julie Hubbert, 318–20. Berke-ley: University of California Press, 2011.

Karlin, Fred. *Listening to Movies: The Film Lover's Guide to Film Music*. Belmont, CA: Schirmer, 1994.

Karlin, Fred, and Rayburn Wright. *On the Track: A Guide to Contemporary Film Scoring*. 2nd ed. New York: Routledge, 2004.

Jameson, Fredric. *Postmodernism, or, The Cultural Logic of Late Capitalism*. Durham, NC: Duke University Press, 1991.

Jeffords, Susan. *Hard Bodies: Hollywood Masculinity in the Reagan Era*. New Brunswick, NJ: Rutgers University Press, 1993.

Jennes, Gail. "The Boston Pops Gets a Movie Composer Who Doesn't Chase Fire Engines as Its New Boss." *People Weekly*, 23 June 1980, 47–52.

Johnson, Jo. "Happy 40th Birthday *Star Wars!*" London Symphony Orchestra, 25 May 2017. https://lso.co.uk/whats-on/alwaysplaying/read/653-happy-40th-birthday-star -wars.html.

Jones, Ryan Patrick. "'Catch as Catch Can': Jazz, John Williams, & Popular Music Allusion." In *John Williams: Music for Films, Television, and the Concert Stage*, edited by Emilio Audissino, 41–70. Turnhout: Brepols, 2018.

Jurgensen, John. "The Last Movie Maestro." *Wall Street Journal*, 16 December 2011.

Jullier, Laurent. *L'écran post-moderne: Un cinéma de l'allusion e du feu d'artifice*. Paris: L'Harmattan, 1997. Translated by Carla Capetta as *Il cinema postmoderno* (Turin: Kaplan, 2006).

Katz, Brandon. "Steven Spielberg on How He Made 'The Post' in Just Seven Months." *The Observer*, 4 January 2018.

Katz, Larry. "Dr. Hollywood & Mr. Pops." *Boston Herald Magazine*, 28 April 1985.

Kawin, Bruce F. *Horror and the Horror Film*. New York: Anthem Press, 2012.

Keefer, Bob. "Running Up the Score: John Williams Brings His Cinematic Composi-tions to Eugene." *Register-Guard* (OR), 20 September 2012.

Keegan, Rebecca. "John Williams and Steven Spielberg Mark 40 Years of Collabora-tion." *Los Angeles Times*, 8 January 2012.

Kendall, Lukas. "Danny Elfman. Part 2." *Film Score Monthly*, December 1995, 11–14.

———. "Raiders of the Los Ark. An Analysis by Lukas Kendall." CD booklet. *Raiders of the Lost Ark*. DCC Compact Classic-Silva Screen Raiders 001, 1995.

Kerins, Mark. "The Modern Entertainment Marketplace, 2000–Present." In *Sound: Dialogue, Music, and Effects*, edited by Kathryn Kalinak, 133–56. New Brunswick, NJ: Rutgers University Press, 2015.

Keyser, Les. *Hollywood in the Seventies*. New York: A. S. Barnes, 1981.

Kilday, Gregg. "Steven Spielberg and Fellow Directors Reveal the Stories behind John Williams' Iconic Scores." *Hollywood Reporter*, 9 June 2016.

King, Geoff. *New Hollywood Cinema: An Introduction*. London: I.B. Tauris, 2002.

Kmet, Nicholas. "Orchestration Transformation: Examining Differences in the Instru-mental and Thematic Colour Palettes of the Star Wars Trilogies." In *John Williams: Music for Films, Television, and the Concert Stage*, edited by Emilio Audissino, 209–28. Turnhout: Brepols, 2018.

Knight, Arthur, and Pamela Robertson Wojcik, eds. *Soundtrack Available: Essays on Film and Popular Music*. Durham, NC: Duke University Press, 2001.

Knight, Michael. "John Williams Opens Season with Pops." *New York Times*, 30 April 1980.

Krakauer, Siegfried. *Theory of Film: The Redemption of Physical Reality*. New York: Oxford University Press, 1960.

Kulezic-Wilson, Danijela. "Sound Design and Its Interactions with Music: Changing Historical Perspectives." In *The Routledge Companion to Screen Music and Sound*, edited by Miguel Mera, Ronald Sadoff, and Ben Winters, 128–29. New York: Routledge, 2017.

———. "Sound Design Is the New Score." *Music, Sound, and the Moving Image* 2, no. 2 (2008): 127–131.

———. *Sound Design Is the New Score: Theory, Aesthetics, and Erotics of the Integrated Soundtrack*. New York: Oxford University Press, 2019.

Lace, Ian. "The Film Music of John Williams." Musicweb International, 1998. www.musicweb-international.com/film/lacejw.htm.

Lack, Russell. *Twenty Four Frames Under: A Buried History of Film Music*. London: Quartet Books, 1999.

Lannamann, Ned. "America's Composer: John Williams; The Generous Professor." *Portland Mercury*, 23 April 2014.

La Polla, Franco, and Maria Teresa Cavina, eds. *Spielberg su Spielberg*. Turin: Lindau, 1995.

Larsen, Peter. *Film Music*. Translated by John Irons. London: Reaktion Books, 2005.

Larson, Randall D. *Musique Fantastique: A Survey of Film Music in the Fantastic Cinema*. London: Scarecrow, 1985.

Lastra, James. *Sound Technology and the American Cinema: Perception, Representation, Modernity*. New York: Columbia University Press, 2000.

Leatherdale, Clive. *Dracula: The Novel and the Legend; A Study of Bram Stoker's Gothic Masterpiece*. Wellingborough: Aquarian, 1985.

Lebrecht, Norman. "John Williams—The Magpie Maestro." *La Scena Musicale*, 20 November 2002. www.scena.org/columns/lebrecht/021120-NL-williams.html.

LeBrun, Fred. "John Williams: Movies' Music Man." *Times Union* (Albany, NY), 24 August 1984.

Lecomte, Jean-Marie. "Postmodern Verbal Discourse in Coppola's Bram Stoker's *Dracula*." In *Post/modern Dracula: From Victorian Themes to Postmodern Praxis*, edited by John S. Bak, 107–22. Newcastle: Cambridge Scholars, 2007.

leDonne, Rob. "With John Williams Stepping Aside, *Solo* Looks to Create a 'Modern' Musical Score for *Star Wars*." *Billboard*, 25 May 2018. https://www.billboard.com/articles/news/8457839/star-wars-solo-music.

Lehman, Frank. "Film-as-Concert Music and the Formal Implications of 'Cinematic Listening.'" *Music Analysis* 37 (2018): 7–46.

———. "Film Music and Neo-Riemannian Theory." *Oxford Handbooks Online*, August 2014. http://www.oxfordhandbooks.com.

———. *Hollywood Harmony: Musical Wonder and the Sound of Cinema*. New York: Oxford University Press, 2018.

———. "How John Williams's *Star Wars* Score Pulls Us to the Dark Side." *Washington Post*, 13 December 2019.

———. "Manufacturing the Epic Score: Hans Zimmer and the Sounds of Significance." In *Music in Epic Film: Listening to Spectacle*, edited by Stephen C. Meyer, 27–55. New York: Routledge, 2016.

———. "Reading Tonality through Film: Transformational Hermeneutics and the Music of Hollywood." PhD diss., Harvard University, 2012.

———. "Scoring the President: Myth and Politics in John Williams's *JFK* and *Nixon*." *Journal of the Society for American Music* 9, no. 4 (2015): 409–44.

———. "The Themes of *Star Wars*: Catalogue and Commentary." In *John Williams: Music for Films, Television, and the Concert Stage*, edited by Emilio Audissino, 153–90. Turnhout: Brepols, 2018.

———. "Trailers, Tonality, and the Force of Nostalgia." *Musicology Now* (blog), 4 November 2015. http://www.musicologynow.org/2015/11/trailers-tonality-and-force -of-nostalgia.html.

Lehman, Phil. "When Capitals Collide: Maestros Slatkin and Williams Join Forces for a Series of Film Music Festivities." *Film Score Monthly*, February 2003, 12–13.

Leinberger, Charles. *Ennio Morricone's "The Good, the Bad and the Ugly": A Film Score Guide*. Lanham, MD: Scarecrow, 2004.

Lerner, Neil. "Nostalgia, Masculinist Discourse and Authoritarianism in John Williams' Scores for *Star Wars* and *Close Encounters of the Third Kind*." In *Off the Planet: Music, Sound and Science Fiction Cinema*, edited by Philip Hayward, 96–108. Eastleigh, UK: John Libbey, 2004.

Levant, Oscar. *A Smattering of Ignorance*. Garden City, NY: Garden City Publishing, 1942.

Levinson, Jerrold. "Film Music and Narrative Agency." In *Post-Theory: Reconstructing Film Studies*, edited by David Bordwell and Noël Carroll, 248–82. Madison: University of Wisconsin Press, 1996.

Libbey, Theodore W., Jr. "Disks Attest to the Versatile Talents of John Williams." *New York Times*, 27 February 1983.

Lichtenstein, Grace. "Film Concerts Go Mainstream." Bachtrack, 2 May 2017. https:// bachtrack.com/screenings-with-live-orchestra-film-game-music-month-may-2017.

Livingstone, William. "John Williams and the Boston Pops: An American Institution Enters a New Era." *Stereo Review* 45, no. 6 (December 1980): 74–77.

London, Justin. "Leitmotifs and Musical Reference in the Classical Film Score." In *Music and Cinema*, edited by James Buhler, Caryl Flinn, and David Neumeyer, 85–96. Hanover, NH: Wesleyan University Press, 2000.

London, Kurt. *Film Music: A Summary of the Characteristic Features of Its History, Aesthetics, Technique; and Possible Developments*. London: Faber and Faber, 1936.

Losada, Cristina Catherine. "Between Modernism and Postmodernism: Strands of Continuity in Collage Compositions by Rochberg, Berio, and Zimmermann." *Music Theory Spectrum* 31, no. 1 (April 2009): 57–100.

Lucia, Cynthia, Roy Grundmann, and Art Simon. "Setting the Stage: American Film History, 1976–1990." In *American Film History: Selected Readings, 1960 to the Present*, edited by Cynthia Lucia, Roy Grundmann, and Art Simon, 151–74. Malden, MA: Wiley Blackwell, 2016.

Luckhurst, Roger, ed. *The Cambridge Companion to Dracula*. New York: Cambridge University Press, 2018.

———. "Dracula and Psychology." In *The Cambridge Companion to Dracula*, edited by Roger Luckhurst, 66–75. New York: Cambridge University Press, 2018.

Luhr, William. *Film Noir*. Malden, MA: Wiley-Blackwell, 2012.

Lyotard, Jean-François. *La condition postmoderne: rapport sur le savoir*. Paris: Minuit, 1979.

MacDonald, Laurence E. *The Invisible Art of Film Music: A Comprehensive History*. New York: Ardsley House, 1998.

MacLean, Paul Andrew. "What Orchestrators Do." *Film Score Monthly*, 21 September 1997. https://www.filmscoremonthly.com/daily/article.cfm?articleID=2299.

Malone, Chris. "Recording the *Star Wars* Saga: A Musical Journey from Scoring Stage to DVD." Version 1.4, 2012. http://www.malonedigital.com/starwars.pdf.

Man, Glenn. "1975: Movies and Conflicting Ideologies." In *American Cinema of the 1970s: Themes and Variations*, edited by Lester D. Friedman, 135–56. New Brunswick, NJ: Rutgers University Press, 2007.

Mangan, Timothy. "Composer for the Stars." *Gramophone* (US interview), May 2006, A3–A7.

Manvell, Roger, and John Huntley. *The Technique of Film Music*. 2nd ed. New York: Hastings House, 1975.

Marmorstein, Gary. *Hollywood Rhapsody: Movie Music and Its Makers, 1900 to 1975*. New York: Schirmer Books, 1997.

Masetti, Enzo, ed. *La musica nel film*. Rome: Bianco e Nero, 1950.

Maslin, Janet. "Screen: Langella's Seductive 'Dracula' Adapted from Stage." *New York Times*, 13 July 1979.

Massood, Paula J. "Movies and a Nation in Transformation." In *American Cinema of the 1970s: Themes and Variations*, edited by Lester D. Friedman, 182–204. New Brunswick, NJ: Rutgers University Press, 2007.

Matessino, Michael. "John Williams Strikes Back." CD booklet, *The Empire Strikes Back*. BMG Classics 09026 68773 2, 1997.

———. "A New Hope for Film Music." CD booklet, *Star Wars: A New Hope*. BMG 09026 68772 2, 1997.

———. "Nocturne: John Williams and Dracula." CD booklet, *Dracula*, The Deluxe Edition. Varèse Sarabande, VCL 1018 1118, 2018.

———. "There Will Be No Bombs Dropped Here!!!" CD booklet, *1941*, La-La Land Records LLLCD 1179, 2011.

McCorkle Okazaki, Brooke. "Liveness, Music, Media: The Case of the Cine-Concert." *Music and the Moving Image* 13, no. 2 (Summer 2020): 3–24.

McKee, Robert. *Story: Substance, Structure, Style, and the Principles of Screenwriting*. London: Methuen, 1998.

McKinley, James, Jr. "John Williams Lets His Muses Carry Him Along." *New York Times*, 19 August 2011.

McKinnon, George. "Williams Answers Spielberg's Call for Music." *Boston Globe*, 13 May 1983.

McNab, Geoffrey. "They Shoot, He Scores." *The Times* (London), 25 September 2001.

McNally, Raymond T. and Radu Florescu. *In Search of Dracula: The History of Dracula and Vampires*. 2nd ed. Boston: Houghton Mifflin, 1994.

Meher-Homji, Cyrus. "Zubin Mehta: The Los Angeles Years." *Eloquence Classics*, 29 October 2018. https://www.eloquenceclassics.com/zubin-mehta-the-los-angeles -years.

Mera, Miguel. "Materializing Film Music." In *The Cambridge Companion to Film Music*, edited by Mervyn Cooke and Fiona Ford, 157–72. New York: Cambridge University Press, 2016.

Mera, Miguel, and David Burnand, eds. *European Film Music*. London: Ashgate, 2006.

Merluzeau, Yann. "Hollywood Bowl Conductor John Mauceri." *Film Score Monthly*, August 1996, 8–10.

———. "An Interview with John Williams." *Soundtrack!*, September 1993, 4–9.

Messing, Scott. *Neoclassicism in Music: From the Genesis of the Concept through the Schoenberg–Stravinsky Polemic*. Ann Arbor, MI: UMI Research Press, 1988.

Meyer, Leonard B. *Emotion and Meaning in Music*. Chicago: University of Chicago Press, 1956.

———. *Music, the Arts, and Ideas: Patterns and Predictions in Twentieth-Century Culture*. Chicago: University of Chicago Press, 1967.

———. *Style and Music: Theory, History, and Ideology*. Chicago: University of Chicago Press, 1996.

Miceli, Sergio. *Musica per film: Storia, Estetica, Analisi, Tipologie*. Lucca: LIM, 2009.

Midget, Anne. "As a Classical Music Critic, I Used to Think the *Star Wars* Score Was beneath Me. I Was Wrong." *Washington Post*, 18 January 2019.

Miller, James. "Keeping Time with John: Inside the Tanglewood Film Music Seminar." *Film Score Monthly*, October/November 1998, 20–21.

Miller, Kiri. "Virtual and Visceral Experience in Music-Oriented Video Games." In *The Oxford Handbook of Sound and Image in Digital Media*, edited by Carol Vernallis, Amy Herzog, and John Richardson, 517–33. New York: Oxford University Press, 2013.

Miller, Margo. "Williams to Resign as Pops Conductor." *Boston Globe*, 14 June 1984.

———. "A Wonderful Choice." *Boston Globe*, 11 January 1980.

Montgomery, M. R. "John Williams' Quiet Side." *Boston Globe*, 18 March 1981.

Moormann, Peter. *Spielberg-Variationen: Die Filmmusik von John Williams*. Baden-Baden: Nomos, 2010.

Morricone, Ennio. "Towards an Interior Music." In *Celluloid Symphonies: Texts and Contexts in Film Music History*, edited by Julie Hubbert, 334–36. Berkeley: University of California Press, 2011.

Morris, Nigel. *The Cinema of Steven Spielberg: Empire of Light*. London: Wallflower, 2007.

Morton, Lawrence. "Composing, Orchestrating, and Criticizing." In *The Hollywood Film Music Reader*, edited by Mervyn Cooke, 327–40. New York: Oxford University Press, 2010.

Moss, Stephen. "The Force Is with Him." *The Guardian* (London), 4 February 2002.

Muhlfriedel, Marina. "Live Movie Concerts: Experiencing Classic Films with Composer and Conductor David Newman." Harman, 22 August 2016, http://pro.har man.com/insights/harman-pro/live-movie-concerts-experiencing-classic-films-with -composer-and-conductor-david-newman.

Mulvey, Laura. "Visual Pleasure and Narrative Cinema." *Screen* 16, no. 3 (Autumn 1975): 6–18.

Murgoci, Agnes. "The Vampire in Roumania." In *The Vampire: A Casebook*, edited by Alan Dundes, 12–34. Madison: University of Wisconsin Press, 1998.

Musegades, Paula. "John Williams: Television Composer." In *John Williams: Music for Films, Television, and the Concert Stage*, edited by Emilio Audissino, 27–40. Turnhout: Brepols, 2018.

Neumeyer, David. "Introduction." In *Music and Cinema*, edited by James Buhler, Caryl Flinn, and David Neumeyer, 33–57. Hanover, NH: Wesleyan University Press, 2000.

Oatis, Greg. "John Williams Strikes Back, Unfortunately." *Cinemafantastique*, Fall 1980, 8.

O'Malley, Patrick R. *Catholicism, Sexual Deviance, and Victorian Gothic Culture.* New York: Cambridge University Press, 2006.

Orosz, Jeremy. "John Williams: Paraphraser or Plagiarist?" *Journal of Musicological Research* 34, no. 4 (2015): 299–319.

Palmer, Christopher. *The Composer in Hollywood.* London: Marion Boyars, 1900.

Pasles, Chris. "John Williams Brings Bland Offerings to the Art Center." *Los Angeles Times*, 4 April 1988.

Paulin, Scott D. "Richard Wagner and the Fantasy of Cinematic Unity: The Idea of the Gesamtkunstwerk in the History and Theory of Film Music." In *Music and Cinema*, edited by James Buhler, Caryl Flinn, and David Neumeyer, 58–84. Hanover, NH: Wesleyan University Press, 2000.

Paulus, Irena. "John Williams and the Musical Avant-Garde: The Score for *War of the Worlds*." In *John Williams: Music for Films, Television, and the Concert Stage*, edited by Emilio Audissino, 327–42. Turnhout: Brepols, 2018.

———. "Williams versus Wagner, or an Attempt at Linking Musical Epics." *International Review of the Aesthetics and Sociology of Music* 31, no. 2 (December 2000): 153–84.

Peirse, Alison. "*Dracula* on Film 1931–1959." In *The Cambridge Companion to Dracula*, edited by Roger Luckhurst, 179–91. New York: Cambridge University Press, 2018.

"People." *Time* magazine, 5 December 1977. http://content.time.com/time/magazine/ article/0,9171,915779,00.html.

Pincus, Saul and Mike Petersen. "Remaking Star Wars." *Film Score Monthly*, September/October 2005, 40–44.

Ponick, T. L. "Movie Music Raised to Its Rightful Place by Composer." *Washington Times*, 3 December 2004.

Prendergast, Roy M. *Film Music: A Neglected Art; A Critical Study of Music in Films.* New York: W. W. Norton, 1977.

Prescott, Charles E., and Grace A. Giorgio. "Vampiric Affinities: Mina Harker and the Paradox of Femininity in Bram Stoker's *Dracula*." *Victorian Literature and Culture* 33 (2005): 487–515.

Prince, Stephen. "Psychoanalytic Film Theory and the Problem of the Missing Spectator." In *Post-Theory: Reconstructing Film Studies*, edited by David Bordwell and Noël Carroll, 71–86. Madison: University of Wisconsin Press, 1996.

———, ed. *The Horror Film*. New Brunswick, NJ: Rutgers University Press, 2004.

Punter, David, ed. *A New Companion to the Gothic*. Malden, MA: Wiley-Blackwell, 2012.

Radish, Christina. "Steven Spielberg on 'The BFG,' Self-Censoring on Historical Dramas, 'Ready Player One,' and More." Collider, 28 June 2016. https://collider.com/steven-spielberg-the-bfg-ready-player-one-interview/.

Raksin, David. "Life with Charlie." In *The Hollywood Film Music Reader*, edited by Mervyn Cook, 69–81. New York: Oxford University Press, 2010.

———. "Whatever Became of Movie Music?" In *Celluloid Symphonies: Texts and Contexts in Film Music History*, edited by Julie Hubbert, 372–78. Berkeley: University of California Press, 2011.

Reed, Josephine. "Transcript of Conversation with John Williams." National Endowment for the Arts, *Art Works* (podcast), 2009. http://arts.gov/audio/john-williams.

Renick, Kyle. "The Halls are Alive." *Film Score Monthly*, May 1998, 13.

Richards, Mark. "The Use of Variation in John Williams's Film Music Themes." In *John Williams: Music for Films, Television, and the Concert Stage*, edited by Emilio Audissino, 119–52. Turnhout: Brepols, 2018.

Richardson, Michael. *Otherness in Hollywood Cinema*. New York: Continuum, 2010.

Rinzler, J. W. *The Making of Star Wars: The Definitive Story behind the Original Film*. London: Ebury, 2007.

Rosar, William H. "Bernard Herrmann: The Beethoven of Film Music?" *Journal of Film Music* 1, nos. 2–3 (2003): 121–50.

———. "Music for the Monsters: Universal Pictures Horror Film Scores of the Thirties." *Quarterly Journal of the Library of Congress* 40, no. 4 (Fall 1983): 390–421.

Rose, Margaret A. "Post-Modern Pastiche." *British Journal of Aesthetics* 31, no. 1 (January 1991): 26–38.

Ross, Alex. "The Force Is Still Strong with John Williams." *New Yorker*, 21 July 2020.

———. "John Williams's Gift to Film." CD booklet of *Lights, Camera . . . Music! Six Decades of John Williams*. BSO Classics 1704, 2017.

———. "Listening to *Star Wars*." *New Yorker*, 1 January 2016.

Rossi, Jérôme. "Le dynamisme harmonique dans l'ecriture filmique de John Williams: Harmonie fonctionnelle versus harmonie non fonctionnelle." In *John Williams: Un alchimiste musical à Hollywood*, edited by Alexandre Tylski, 113–40. Paris: L'Harmattan, 2011.

Rózsa, Miklós. *A Double Life: The Autobiography of Miklós Rózsa, Composer in the Golden Years of Hollywood*. 1982. Reprint, New York: Wynwood, 1989.

Saffle, Michael. *The Music of Franz Liszt: Stylistic Development and Cultural Synthesis*. New York: Routledge, 2018.

Said, Edward. *Orientalism*. 1978. Reprint, London: Penguin Books, 2003.

Sakakeeny, Matt. "Music." In *Keywords in Sound*, edited by David Novak and Matt Sakakeeny, 112–24. Durham, NC: Duke University Press, 2015.

Salt, Barry. *Film Style and Technology: History and Analysis*. 2nd ed. London: Starword, 1992.

Salvetti, Guido. *La nascita del Novecento*. Turin: EDT, 1991.

Sapiro, Ian. "Craft, Art, or Process: The Question of Creativity in Orchestration for Screen." In *The Routledge Companion to Screen Music and Sound*, edited by Miguel Mera, Ronald Sadoff, and Ben Winters, 305–17. New York: Routledge, 2017.

———. *Scoring the Score: The Role of the Orchestrator in the Contemporary Film Industry*. New York: Routledge, 2016.

———. "Star Scores: Orchestration and the Sound of John Williams's Film Music." In *John Williams: Music for Films, Television, and the Concert Stage*, edited by Emilio Audissino, 191–208. Turnhout: Brepols, 2018.

Schatz, Thomas. "The New Hollywood." In *Film Theory Goes to the Movies: Cultural Analysis of Contemporary Film*, edited by Jim Collins, Hilary Radner, and Ava Preacher Collins, 8–36. London: Routledge, 1993.

———. "Seismic Shifts in the American Film Industry." In *American Film History: Selected Readings, 1960 to the Present*, edited by Cynthia Lucia, Roy Grundmann, and Art Simon, 175–89. Malden, MA: Wiley-Blackwell, 2016.

Scheurer, Timothy E. "John Williams and Film Music since 1971." *Popular Music and Society* 21, no. 1 (Spring 1997): 59–72.

———. *Music and Mythmaking in Film: Genre and the Role of the Composer*. Jefferson, NC: McFarland, 2008.

Schneller, Tom. "Easy to Cut: Modular Form in the Film Scores of Bernard Herrmann." *Journal of Film Music* 5, no. 1/2 (2012): 127–51.

———. "Modal Interchange and Semantic Resonance in Themes by John Williams." *Journal of Film Music* 6, no. 1 (2013): 49–74.

———. "Out of Darkness: John Williams's *Violin Concerto*." In *John Williams: Music for Films, Television, and the Concert Stage*, edited by Emilio Audissino, 343–74. Turnhout: Brepols, 2018.

———. 'Sweet Fulfillment: Allusion and Teleological Genesis in John Williams's *Close Encounters of the Third Kind*." *Musical Quarterly* 97, no. 1 (Spring 2014): 98–131.

Schreibman, Myrl A. "Memories of Max: An Archival Interview with Max Steiner. Part 1." *Film Score Monthly*, January/February 2005, 24–27.

———. "Memories of Max: An Archival Interview with Max Steiner. Part 2." *Film Score Monthly*, March/April 2005, 22–26.

Seiler, Andy. "Williams Adds Musical Magic to *Harry Potter*." *USA Today*, 13 November 2001.

Senf, Carol A. "'Dracula': Stoker's Response to the New Woman," *Victorian Studies* 26, no. 1 (Autumn 1982): 33–49.

———. *The Vampire in Nineteenth-Century English Literature*. Madison: University of Wisconsin Press, 1988.

Sergi, Gianluca. "Tales of the Silent Blast: *Star Wars* and Sound." *Journal of Popular Film and Television* 26, no. 1 (1998): 12–22.

Shone, Tom. "How to Score in the Movies." *Sunday Times* (London), 21 July 1998.

Simon, Juliet. "A Conversation with John Williams." BMI, 22 December 2015. https://www.bmi.com/special/john_williams.

Skal, David J. *Hollywood Gothic: The Tangled Web of Dracula from Novel to Stage to Screen*. New York: W. W. Norton, 1990.

Sklar, Robert. *Movie-Made America: A Cultural History of American Movies.* New York: Vintage Books, 1994.

Sloboda, John A. *The Musical Mind: The Cognitive Psychology of Music.* New ed. Oxford: Oxford University Press, 1999.

Slowik, Michael. *After the Silents: Hollywood Film Music in the Early Sound Era, 1926–1934.* New York: Columbia University Press, 2014.

Smith, Jeff. *The Sound of Commerce: Making Popular Film Music.* New York: Columbia University Press, 1998.

———. "'That Money Making 'Moon River' Sound: Thematic Organization and Orchestration in the Film Music of Henry Mancini." In *Music and Cinema*, edited by James Buhler, Caryl Flinn, and David Neumeyer, 247–71. Hanover, NH: Wesleyan University Press, 2000.

———. "Unheard Melodies? A Critique of Psychoanalytic Theories of Film Music." In *Post-Theory: Reconstructing Film Studies*, edited by David Bordwell and Noël Carroll, 230–47. Madison: University of Wisconsin Press, 1996.

Smith, Murray. "Theses on the Philosophy of Hollywood History." In *Contemporary Hollywood Cinema*, edited by Steve Neale and Murray Smith, 3–20. London: Routledge, 1998.

Smith, Steven C. *A Heart at Fire's Center: The Life and Music of Bernard Herrmann.* 2nd ed. Berkeley: University of California Press, 2002.

———. *Music by Max Steiner: The Epic Life of Hollywood's Most Influential Composer.* New York: Oxford University Press, 2020.

Smith, Thomas. "And the Grammy Goes to . . . *Star Wars*: Galaxy's Edge Symphonic Suite." Disney Parks blog, 28 January 2020. https://disneyparks.disney.go.com/blog/2020/01/and-the-grammy-goes-to-star-wars-galaxys-edge-symphonic-suite/.

Smith, Tim. "Film Composer John Williams to Make Baltimore Conducting Première." *Baltimore Sun*, 1 June 2013.

Smith, Tracy. "John Williams on Spielberg, *Star Wars*, and the Power of Music." Transcript of video interview, *Sunday Morning*, CBS News, 22 September 2019. https://www.cbsnews.com/news/extended-transcript-john-williams-on-steven-spielberg-star-wars-and-the-power-of-music/.

Sonnenschein, David. *Sound Design: The Expressive Power of Music, Voice and Sound Effects in Cinema.* Studio City CA, Michael Wiese Productions, 2001.

"Spiegel Interview with Tom Cruise and Steven Spielberg," *Der Spiegel*, 27 April 2005. www.spiegel.de/international/spiegel/0,1518,353577,00.html.

Spielberg, Steven. Liner notes. *Saving Private Ryan*. CD album. DreamWorks Records DRD 50046, 1998.

"Star-Geigerin Anne-Sophie Mutter im Interview." Nordbuzz, 29 May 2020. https://www.nordbuzz.de/people/star-geigerin-anne-sophie-mutter-spricht-interview-ueber-ihre-corona-infektion-13771243.html.

Stearns, David Patrick. "Hollywood Conductor Taps Studio Talent." *USA Today*, 31 July 1991.

———. "Music That's Light on the Baton: USA Orchestras Enjoy a Pops Explosion." *USA Today*, 26 April 1985.

————. "Phila. Orchestra Celebrates 'Star Wars,' Classical Composer John Williams." *Philadelphia Enquirer*, 26 April 2016.

———— "7 Emmys, 4 Oscars, 15 Grammys . . . but, Hey, Who's Counting? Not John Williams, Hollywood's Most Honored Composer." *Arts & Entertainment*, February 1993, 21–22.

Stoker, Bram. *Dracula*. 1897. Reprint, Cambridge: Cambridge University Press, 2013.

Stoppe, Sebastian. "John Williams's Film Music in the Concert Halls." In *John Williams: Music for Films, Television, and the Concert Stage*, edited by Emilio Audissino, 95–117. Turnhout: Brepols, 2018.

Strauven, Wanda, ed. *Cinema of Attractions Reloaded*. Amsterdam: Amsterdam University Press, 2006.

Sullivan, Jack. "Conversations with John Williams." *Chronicle of Higher Education*, 12 January 2007.

————. *Hitchcock's Music*. New Haven, CT: Yale University Press, 2006.

————. "Spielberg–Williams: Symphonic Cinema." In *A Companion to Steven Spielberg*, edited by Nigel Morris, 175–94. Malden, MA: Wiley-Blackwell, 2017.

Swanson, Stefan. "Happily Never After: Williams's Musical Exploration of the 'Controversial' Ending to *A.I.: Artificial Intelligence*." In *John Williams: Music for Films, Television, and the Concert Stage*, edited by Emilio Audissino, 375–95. Turnhout: Brepols, 2018.

Swed, Mark. "Zubin Mehta's Heady Days as Los Angeles Philharmonic Music Director." *Los Angeles Times*, 8 December 2012.

Taylor, Derek. *The Making of "Raiders of the Lost Ark."* New York: Ballantine, 1981.

Taylor, Philip. *Steven Spielberg: The Man, His Movies, and Their Meaning*. 3rd ed. London: B. T. Batsford, 1999.

Terry, Kenneth. "John Williams Encounters the Pops." *Downbeat* 48 (March 1981): 20–22.

Thomas, Bob. "Williams Looks backward in Composing Score for New *Star Wars* Movie." *Nevada Daily Mail*, 12 May 1999.

Thomas, David. "King of Themes." *Sunday Telegraph*, 13 July 1997, 48–50.

————. "Point Blank: The Total Film Interview; John Williams." *Total Film*, September 1997, 74–79.

Thomas, Tony. *Film Score: The Art and Craft of Movie Music*. Burbank, CA: Riverwood, 1991.

————. *Music for the Movies*. 2nd ed. Los Angeles: Silman-James, 1997.

Thompson, Kristin. *Breaking the Glass Armor: Neoformalist Film Analysis*. Princeton, NJ: Princeton University Press, 1988.

————. *Eisenstein's "Ivan the Terrible": A Neoformalist Analysis*. Princeton, NJ: Princeton University Press, 1981.

————. *Storytelling in the New Hollywood: Understanding Classical Narrative Technique*. Cambridge, MA: Harvard University Press, 1999.

Thompson, Kristin, and David Bordwell. *Film History: An Introduction*. 3rd ed. New York: McGraw-Hill, 2010.

Tillman, Joakim. "Topoi and Intertextuality: Narrative Function in Hans Zimmer's and Lisa Gerrard's Music to *Gladiator*." In *Music in Epic Film: Listening to Spectacle*, edited by Stephen C. Meyer, 59–85. New York: Routledge, 2016.

———. "The Villain's March Topic in John Williams's Film Music." In *John Williams: Music for Films, Television, and the Concert Stage*, edited by Emilio Audissino, 229–52. Turnhout: Brepols, 2018.

Tirella, J. "Steven Spielberg's 9/11 Obsession." Today, 28 December 2005. http://www.today.com/id/10549050/ns/today-today_entertainment/t/steven-spielbergs-obsession/.

Tylski, Alexandre, ed. *John Williams: Un alchimiste musical à Hollywood*. Paris: L'Harmattan, 2011.

Valverde Amador, Andrés. *John Williams: Vida y obra*. Seville: Editorial Berenice, 2013.

van Elferen, Isabella. *Gothic Music: The Sounds of the Uncanny*. Cardiff: University of Wales Press, 2012.

Vernier, David. "Magnificent Modern Maestro." *Digital Audio*, March 1988.

Vogler, Chris. *The Writer's Journey: Mythic Structures for Writers*. 3rd ed. Studio City, CA: Michael Wiese Productions, 2007.

Wagstaff, Christopher. "Quasi un'appendice: Alcune cifre sull'industria cinematografica statunitense." In *Storia del cinema mondiale*, vol. 2, *Gli Stati Uniti*, edited by Gian Piero Brunetta, 1745–1772. Turin: Einaudi, 2000.

Walden, Jennifer. "Ren Klyce: Mixing the Score for *Star Wars: The Last Jedi*." *PostPerspective*, 26 February 2018. https://postperspective.com/ren-klyce-mixing-score-star-wars-last-jedi/.

Wasson, Sam. *A Splurch in the Kisser: The Movies of Blake Edwards*. Middletown, CT: Wesleyan University Press, 2009.

Webster, Jamie Lynn. "Musical Dramaturgy and Stylistic Changes in John Williams's *Harry Potter* Trilogy." In *John Williams: Music for Films, Television, and the Concert Stage*, edited by Emilio Audissino, 253–75. Turnhout: Brepols, 2018.

Wegele, Peter. *Max Steiner: Composing, "Casablanca," and the Golden Age of Film Music*. Lanham, MD: Rowman & Littlefield, 2014.

Weinstock, Jeffrey. *The Vampire Film: Undead Cinema*. New York: Wallflower, 2012.

Wennekes, Emile. "No Sharks, No Stars, Just Idiomatic Scoring and Sounding Engagement: John Williams as a 'Classical' Composer." In *John Williams: Music for Films, Television, and the Concert Stage*, edited by Emilio Audissino, 71–94. Turnhout: Brepols, 2018.

———. "'What's the Motive?,' She Asked: Tales from the Musical Pawnshop." In *Liber Plurium Vocum: Voor Rokus de Groot*, edited by Sander van Maas et al., 205–21. Amsterdam: University of Amsterdam, 2012.

Wennekes, Emile, and Emilio Audissino, eds. *Cinema Changes: Incorporations of Jazz in the Film Soundtrack*. Turnhout: Brepols, 2019.

Wessel, David. "The Force Is with Him . . . 'Rich Is Hard to Define.'" *Boston Globe*, 5 July 1983.

Wierzbicki, James. *Film Music: A History*. New York: Routledge, 2009.

———. Louis and Bebe Barron's "Forbidden Planet": A Film Score Guide. Lanham, MD: Scarecrow, 2005.

Wierzbicki, James, Nathan Platte, and Colin Roust, eds. *The Routledge Film Music Sourcebook*. New York: Routledge, 2012.

Williams, Anne. *Art of Darkness: A Poetics of Gothic.* Chicago: University of Chicago Press, 1995

Williams, John. Introductory note. *Dry Your Tears, Afrika.* Full orchestral score. John Williams Signature Edition series. Hal Leonard 044900085, no date.

———. "John Williams on *Star Wars.*" Liner notes of *Star Wars.* LP album, 20th Century Records 2T-541(0898), 1977.

Williams, Linda Ruth and Michael Hammond, eds. *Contemporary American Cinema.* Maidenhead: Open University Press, 2006.

Winters, Ben. "The Composer and the Studio: Korngold and Warner Bros." In *The Cambridge Companion to Film Music*, edited by Mervyn Cooke and Fiona Ford, 51–66. New York: Cambridge University Press, 2016.

———. "Corporeality, Musical Heartbeats, and Cinematic Emotion." *Music, Sound and the Moving Image* 2, no. 1 (Spring 2008): 3–25.

———. *Erich Wolfgang Korngold's "The Adventures of Robin Hood": A Film Score Guide.* Lanham, MD: Scarecrow, 2007.

———. "Musical Wallpaper? Towards an Appreciation of Non-narrating Music in Film." *Music, Sound, and the Moving Image* 6, no. 1 (Spring 2012): 41–54.

———. "The Non-Diegetic Fallacy: Film, Music, and Narrative Space." *Music and Letters* 91, no. 2 (2010): 224–44.

Wood, Robin. *Hollywood from Vietnam to Reagan . . . and Beyond.* Rev. and exp. ed. New York: Columbia University Press, 2003.

Wolf, Leonard, ed. *Blood Thirsty: 100 Years of Vampire Fiction.* New York: Oxford University Press, 1997.

Wolf, Matt. "The Olympics Offers John Williams Another Heroic Challenge." *South Coast Today* (MA), 21 July 1996.

Woolfe, Zachary. "A Summer Blockbuster, Far from the Multiplex." *New York Times*, 19 August 2012.

Worland, Rick. *Searching for New Frontiers: Hollywood Films in the 1960s.* Chichester: Wiley-Blackwell, 2018.

Wyatt, Justin. *High Concept: Movies and Marketing in Hollywood.* Austin: University of Texas Press, 1994.

Wynne, Catherine. "*Dracula* on Stage." In *The Cambridge Companion to Dracula*, edited by Roger Luckhurst, 165–78. New York: Cambridge University Press, 2018.

Yanov, Scott. *Jazz on Film: The Complete Story of the Musicians and Music Onscreen.* San Francisco, CA: Backbeat Books, 2004.

Zacharopoulos, Konstantinos. "Musical Syntax in John Williams's Film Music Themes." In *Contemporary Film Music: Investigating Cinema Narratives and Composition*, edited by Lindsay Coleman and Joakim Tillman, 237–62. London: Palgrave Macmillan, 2017.

Zailian, Marian. "John Williams: Master of Movie Scores." *San Francisco Examiner-Chronicle*, 18 July 1982.

Index

WISCONSIN FILM STUDIES

The Film Music of John Williams:
Reviving Hollywood's Classical Style, second edition
EMILIO AUDISSINO

The Foreign Film Renaissance on American Screens, 1946–1973
TINO BALIO

Marked Women: Prostitutes and Prostitution in the Cinema
RUSSELL CAMPBELL

Depth of Field: Stanley Kubrick, Film, and the Uses of History
Edited by GEOFFREY COCKS, JAMES DIEDRICK,
and GLENN PERUSEK

Tough as Nails: The Life and Films of Richard Brooks
DOUGLASS K. DANIEL

Dark Laughter: Spanish Film, Comedy, and the Nation
JUAN F. EGEA

Glenn Ford: A Life
PETER FORD

Luis Buñuel: The Red Years, 1929–1939
ROMÁN GUBERN and PAUL HAMMOND

Screen Nazis: Cinema, History, and Democracy
SABINE HAKE

A Cinema of Obsession: The Life and Work of Mai Zetterling
MARIAH LARSSON